# NORTH AFRICA
# AND THE
# MIDDLE EAST
# 1939–1942

*The Commanding Officers' Reports from
the Field and at Sea*

# NORTH AFRICA AND THE MIDDLE EAST 1939–1942

## Tobruk, Crete, Syria and East Africa

Introduced and compiled by
John Grehan and Martin Mace
with additional research by
Sara Mitchell

Pen & Sword
**MILITARY**

First published in Great Britain in 2015 by
**PEN & SWORD MILITARY**
An imprint of
Pen & Sword Books Ltd
47 Church Street
Barnsley
South Yorkshire
S70 2AS

ISBN 978-1-78346-217-9

Typeset by Concept, Huddersfield, West Yorkshire HD4 5JL.
Printed and bound in England by CPI Group (UK) Ltd, Croydon CR0 4YY.

Pen & Sword Books Ltd incorporates the imprints of Pen & Sword Archaeology, Atlas, Aviation, Battleground, Discovery, Family History,  History, Maritime, Military, Naval, Politics, Railways, Select, Social History, Transport, True Crime, and Claymore Press, Frontline Books, Leo Cooper, Praetorian Press, Remember When, Seaforth Publishing and Wharncliffe.

For a complete list of Pen & Sword titles please contact
PEN & SWORD BOOKS LIMITED
47 Church Street, Barnsley, South Yorkshire, S70 2AS, England
E-mail: enquiries@pen-and-sword.co.uk
Website: www.pen-and-sword.co.uk

# Contents

# List of Plates

Field Marshal Archibald Wavell, the Viceroy and Commander-in-Chief of the Indian Army is pictured with Field Marshal Sir Claude Auchinleck, and Field Marshal Bernard Montgomery, Chief of Imperial General Staff.

A unit of the Somaliland Camel Corps on patrol along the Somaliland-Abyssinian border in the summer of 1940.

A bomb bursting at Rutba Fort on 9 May 1941.

A Junkers Ju 90 military transporter – as used by *Sonderkommando Junck* during the German intervention in Iraq.

Habbaniya War Cemetery in Iraq contains 292 burials. A memorial within the cemetery commemorates an additional 106 soldiers and RAF Levies who died while serving in Iraq during the Second World War and were buried in remote and un-maintainable graves.

After the successful Battle of Palmyra (1 July 1941), Allied troops found this wreck of a Heinkel He 111, a relic of *Sonderkommando Junck*, on Palmyra airfield.

German *Fallschirmjäger* emplaning at the start of Operation *Merkur* (Mercury) – the code-name for the Axis invasion of Crete in 1941.

A German parachute drop underway over Crete, 20 May 1941.

A pair of gunners at one of the many British anti-aircraft positions surrounding Suda Bay, Crete, in May 1941.

Two British tank officers are pictured reading an Italian newspaper on 28 January 1941.

A British patrol is on the lookout for enemy movements over a valley in the Western Desert, on the Egyptian side of the Egypt-Libya border, in February of 1942.

A Junkers Ju 87 Stuka dive bomber attacking a British supply depot near Tobruk, Libya, during October 1941.

Two soldiers pictured at work producing a military newspaper or information sheet during the Siege of Tobruk.

Standing amongst the rubble, a soldier looks through holes made by Axis bombs into a church in Tobruk, 1941.

Disaster off Tobruk. A picture showing the Grimsby-class sloop HMS *Grimsby*, on the left, and the merchant ship SS *Helka*, on the right, sinking following the attack by Junkers Ju 87 Stukas.

The 3,359 GRT Dutch tanker MV *Adinda* pictured on fire in the harbour there during February 1941.

# Introduction

The Middle East Command was formed under General Sir Archibald Wavell in August 1939, having under its control the British and Commonwealth troops in Egypt, Palestine, Sudan, Cyprus, Kenya and, at the start of 1940, British Somaliland. At the outbreak of war the entire command, spread across all these countries, consisted of just twenty-one battalions of infantry with only sixty-four field guns. Reinforcements were received from as early as September 1939, and were continually added to, and these came predominantly from India, Australia and New Zealand, as well as Rhodesia, South Africa and even Malta, Mauritius and Poland. It was truly a multi-national force that had been assembled and was as prepared as could be when Italy declared war on France and Britain in June 1940 and the fighting in the Middle East began.

What Wavell's mixed force faced were 215,000 Italian troops in Libya and over 200,000 in Italian East Africa. Though considerably outnumbered, Wavell immediately went onto the offensive, sending raids into Libya. Nevertheless, the Italians gradually built up their strength on the Libya-Egyptian frontier and launched an assault across the border. This assault was beaten off at the cost of just 150 men; the Italians suffering around 3,500 casualties.

These operations are described in Wavell's first despatch as are those of General Platt in the Sudan. In this despatch Wavell refers to operations in British Somaliland which are covered in our volume on that theatre of war.

His second despatch deals exclusively with operations in the Western Desert. This saw his so-called Army of the Nile defeat the Italians at the Battle of Sidi Barrani and capture of the small port of Bardia and then of the more important port of Tobruk. Wavell followed this up with the almost total destruction of the enemy forces. During the two months from 7 December to 7 February 1940, Wavell's men had advanced 500 miles. They had beaten and destroyed an Italian army of four Corps comprising nine divisions and part of a tenth, and had captured an astonishing 130,000 prisoners, 400 tanks and 1,290 guns, as well as vast quantities of other war material. In these operations Wavell never employed a larger force than two divisions, of which one was armoured.

Wavell's third despatch deals with the British support for Greece and the defence and withdrawal from Crete. Despite Wavell's well-known objection at having been forced to halt his offensive against the Italians in order to send troops to Greece, he later concedes that 'The losses inflicted on the enemy in Crete undoubtedly saved the general position in the Middle East by destroying the greater part of the enemy's air-borne troops and a very large number of his aircraft.'

During the period covered in this, his final despatch from the Middle East, Wavell's Middle East Command was involved in six major operations – in Greece, Cyrenaica (Libya), Crete, Iraq, Syria, and in Italian East Africa. As Wavell points out the theatres of these operations were several hundreds of miles apart and in some instances well over a thousand miles.

Because he had halted his offensive in Libya to send troops to Greece, the Italians, having been joined by Rommel and the *Afrika Korps*, had pushed the Western Desert Force back to the Egyptian border, leaving the key port of Tobruk surrounded and besieged by the Axis forces. This disappointed Churchill who decided to replace Wavell with General Claude Auchinleck who had previously held India Command.

Wavell had actually performed well and this was acknowledged by Auchinleck: 'In no sense do I wish to infer [*sic*] that I found an unsatisfactory situation on my arrival – far from it. Not only was I greatly impressed by the solid foundations laid by my predecessor, but I was also able the better to appreciate the vastness of the problems with which he had been confronted and the greatness of his achievements, in a command in which some 40 different languages are spoken by the British and Allied Forces.' In reality the two men simply swapped jobs as Wavell was appointed to Auchinleck's previous Indian Command.

One of the first problems that Auchinleck had to deal with was the conclusion of the operation to occupy Lebanon and Syria by the combined Anglo-Free French forces. De Gaulle wanted complete control over the former French Protectorate but, in view of the Free French's limited military capacity this was impractical. Fortunately, after discussions with de Gaulle in Cairo, it was agreed that the Free French would take over the civil administration but that all Free French military forces would come under Middle East Command.

The next issue Auchinleck had to resolve was the situation in Iraq where anti-British sentiment was growing. It was decided that it was necessary to expel the Germans in that country and oust the nationalists that were opposed to Britain. This was accomplished along with Soviet troops entering Iraq from the north.

Auchinleck's main area of concern was, of course, with the Axis forces under Rommel and the siege of Tobruk. How Auchinleck intended to deal with the Germans and Italians was spelt out in a document issued to his corps commanders entitled 'Policy covering the defence of the Western Desert.' This is reproduced as an appendix to the despatch. Auchinleck optimistically saw that the Axis forces could be held and that as more tanks were delivered to him he could move onto the offensive. In this respect, it was the relief of the garrison at Tobruk that was his principal objective. Those operations against the Axis forces in Libya form part of Auchinlek's second despatch.

He believed that by the end of October, 1941, the land forces under his Command were strong enough and sufficiently well-equipped to warrant making an attack. However, he lacked the aerial support to make this possible which necessitated drawing together practically all the available air forces under his command, thus leaving Syria, Palestine and Cyprus unprotected. To help understand the situation in which he was placed, Auchinlek provides the Order of Battle for his entire command.

Auchinlek aimed to occupy the whole of Libya, firstly by trapping and destroying the Axis forces in Eastern Cyrenaica. This having been achieved he would then attempt to drive what remained of the enemy forces out of Tripolitania. The success of the second stage depended on how well he was able to overcome the difficulty of supplying his forces over such great distances.

The initial plan was to destroy the German armoured divisions which Auchinlek rightly regarded as 'the backbone' of the enemy's army. To accomplish this, his three armoured brigades were concentrated together and given the task of seeking out and destroying Rommel's armour. The panzers had dominated the desert fighting but now the tables would be turned.

Almost nothing went as expected and the British armour was practically wiped out. This Auchinlek attributes, in no small measure, to the artillery. 'Whenever our tanks attempted to take the enemy in the rear,' he wrote, 'they were confronted by formidable 88 millimetre guns to which we possessed no counterpart.' The Italian tanks also proved to be better than expected.

Nevertheless, the Germans had themselves received 'a hammering' and their strength had been considerably reduced by the British attacks both on land and from the air. 'It became therefore a question of maintaining the momentum of our attack,' Auchinlek wrote, 'and I was determined that it should be maintained.'

It was as the Eighth Army was grinding inexorably forwards that Japan entered the war. As this meant that Wavell's Indian Command would have its hands full dealing with this new enemy, Middle East Command had to take over responsibility for Iraq and Persia. It also meant that reinforcements originally destined for Egypt were diverted to India. Auchinlek was also asked to send some of his tanks and aircraft to the Far East.

Consequently Auchinlek consolidated his gains before further augmentation of his strength enabled him to resume his offensive. Auchinlek provides a detailed account of the operations in Libya. This despatch numbers more than 90,000 words – the length of a standard-size book.

*   *   *

The objective of this book is to reproduce those despatches as they first appeared to the general public some seventy years ago. They have not been modified or edited in any way and are therefore the original and unique words of the commanding officers as they saw things at the time. The only change is the manner in which the footnotes are presented, in that they are shown at the end of each despatch rather than at the bottom of the relevant page as they appear in the original despatch. Any grammatical or spelling errors have been left uncorrected (for instance Auchinlek spells Benghazi as Bengasi which is the old Italian spelling) to retain the authenticity of the documents. Where words are no longer legible, due to the passage of time, this has been indicated in the text.

# Abbreviations

| | |
|---|---|
| A/C | Aircraft |
| A/S | Anti-Submarine |
| A/T | Anti-Tank |
| AA | Anti-Aircraft |
| ADC | *Aide-de-Camp* |
| AFC | Air Force Cross |
| AFV | Armoured Fighting Vehicle |
| AIF | Australian Imperial Force |
| AMES | Air Ministry Experimental Station |
| AOC-in-C | Air Officer Commanding-in-Chief |
| Armd Div | Armoured Division |
| ATK | Anti-Tank |
| Bde | Brigade |
| Bde GP | Brigade Group |
| BGGS | Brigadier-General General Staff |
| BGRA | Brigadier-General Royal Artillery |
| BGS | Brigadier, General Staff |
| BM | Brigade Major |
| Bn | Battalion |
| Bty | Battery |
| B.T.E. | British Troops in Egypt |
| C. in C. | Commander-in-Chief |
| CB | Companion of The Most Honourable Order of the Bath |
| CBE | Commander of the Order of the British Empire |
| CD unit | Civil Defence unit |
| CIE | Companion of The Most Eminent Order of the Indian Empire |
| CIGS | Chief of the Imperial General Staff |
| CMG | Companion of The Most Distinguished Order of Saint Michael and Saint George |
| CSI | Companion of the Order of the Star of India |
| Div | Division |
| DME | Director of Medical Services |
| DOS | Director of Ordnance Services |
| DQMG | Deputy Quartermaster General |
| DSO | Distinguished Service Order |

| | |
|---|---|
| DST | Director of Supply and Transport |
| E Boats | *See S-Boot* |
| EDES | National Republican Greek League |
| ELAS | Greek People's Liberation Army |
| FDL | Forward Defended Locality |
| GCB | Knight Grand Cross of The Most Honourable Order of the Bath |
| GCIE | Knight Grand Commander of The Most Eminent Order of the Indian Empire |
| GCSI | Knight Grand Commander of The Most Exalted Order of the Star of India |
| GCVO | Knight Grand Cross of The Royal Victorian Order |
| Gds | Guards |
| GHQ | General Headquarters |
| GOC | General Officer Commanding |
| GOC in C | General Officer Commanding-in-Chief |
| GSOI | General Staff Officer I |
| HM | His Majesty |
| HQ | Head Quarters |
| Hrs | Hours |
| Ind | Indian |
| KCB | Knight Commander of the Most Honourable Order of the Bath |
| KCIE | Knight Commander of The Most Eminent Order of the Indian Empire |
| KCMG | Knight Commander of The Most Distinguished Order of Saint Michael and Saint George |
| KCSI | Knight Commander of The Most Exalted Order of the Star of India |
| KCVO | Knight Commander of The Royal Victorian Order |
| KRRC | *King's Royal Rifle Corps* |
| KT | Knight Companion of The Most Ancient and Most Noble Order of the Thistle |
| L of C | Line(s) of Communication |
| LCT | Landing Craft (Tank) |
| Lieut | Lieutenant |
| LST | Landing Ship Tank |
| Lt-Gen | Lieutenant Colonel |
| Maj-Gen | Major General |
| MC | Military Cross |
| ME | Middle East |
| MEF | Middle East Forces |
| MESB | Middle East Supply Board |
| MG | Machine-Gun |

| | |
|---|---|
| MMG | Medium Machine-Gun |
| MNBDO | Mobile Naval Base Defence Organisation |
| MOV & TN | Movements and Transport |
| MT, M/T | Motor Transport |
| NCO | Non Commissioned Officer |
| NZ | New Zealand |
| OBE | Most Excellent *Order of the British Empire* |
| OETA | Occupied Enemy Territory Administration |
| para | parachute/paratrooper |
| pdr | pounder |
| RA | Royal Artillery |
| RAF | Royal Air Force |
| RAOC | Royal Army Ordnance Corps |
| RASC | Royal Army Service Corps |
| Regts | Regiments |
| RHA | Royal Horse Artillery |
| RM | Royal Marine |
| RTR | Royal Tank Regiment |
| *S-Boot* | *Schnellboot* (meaning 'fast boat') |
| SA | South Africa(n) |
| SAAF | South African Air Force |
| Sqn | Squadron |
| TK | Tank |
| VC | Victoria Cross |
| W/T | Wireless Telegraphy/Wireless Telephony |
| WDF | Western Desert Force(s) |

# 1

# GENERAL WAVELL'S DESPATCH ON OPERATIONS AUGUST 1939 TO NOVEMBER 1940

*The War Office, May 1946*
OPERATIONS IN THE MIDDLE EAST
FROM AUGUST, 1939 TO NOVEMBER, 1940.
*The following Despatch was submitted to the Secretary of State for War on 10th December, 1940, by GENERAL SIR ARCHIBALD P. WAVELL, K.C.B., C.M.G., M.C., Commander-in-Chief, in the Middle East.*

1. This despatch covers the period from the formation of the Middle East Command in August, 1939, to the middle of November, 1940, when the war with Italy had lasted approximately 5 months.

2. The Middle East Command, with a staff of five officers, was formed at the beginning of August, 1939, as a planning staff for the Middle East. Its original Charter is given as Appendix A. General Headquarters Middle East now comprises over 225 graded staff officers, exclusive of attached officers and non-graded officers.

*September, 1939, to April, 1940.*
3. On the outbreak of war with Germany on 3rd September, 1939, the Middle East Command assumed operational control over the troops in Egypt, Palestine, Sudan and Cyprus. It was responsible for military plans in British Somaliland, but did not assume full operational control of this theatre till 13th January, 1940. The garrison of these countries at the outbreak of war consisted of the following:-

A. Egypt.
  (i) 7th Armoured Division –
    Two Armoured Brigades (each of two regts. only).
    One Armoured Car Regiment.
    One Motor Battalion,
  (ii) 4th Indian Division –
    One Regiment of Artillery.
    One Infantry Brigade.
  (iii) R.A. Group –
    7th Medium Regiment.
    3rd Regiment R.H.A. (A.T.).

    4th Regiment R.H.A.
    31st Field Regiment R.A.
  (iv) Eight British Infantry Battalions.
B. Palestine.
  (i) 8th Division –
    Two Brigades – each of three British Battalions.
    No artillery.
  (ii) Two British Cavalry Regiments.
  (iii) Four additional British Battalions (less one Company of one Battalion in Cyprus).
C. Sudan.
  (i) Three British Battalions.
  (ii) Sudan Defence Force consisting of 20 Companies in all, of which the greater part were employed on internal security over the vast area of the Sudan.
D. Cyprus.
One Company British Battalion.
E. British Somaliland.
H.Q. and three Companies of Camel Corps.

The fighting forces in the Middle East thus included no complete formation of any kind. There were in all twenty-one battalions of infantry, but only 64 field guns. There were only 48 A/T guns and 8 A.A. guns.

4. The Egyptian Army comprised:

One Light Tank Regiment,
One Light Car Regiment,
One Horsed Cavalry Regiment,
One 2-pdr. Anti-Tank Battery,
Two Fortress Anti-Tank Batteries,
Two Anti-Aircraft Regiments,
One Light Anti-Aircraft Regiment,
Two Searchlight Regiments,
Four Heavy Coast Defence Batteries,
Nine Regular Battalions,
Nine Reserve Battalions,
Two Machine Gun Battalions,
Eight Light Car Squadrons (Frontier Force),

and was in many respects much better equipped than most of the British forces. But Egypt did not declare war on Germany and the amount of support to be counted on from the Egyptian Army was problematical.

5. Since Italy did not enter the war with her ally Germany, the Middle East was not immediately engaged in operations. During the first months of the war I was concerned largely with establishing relations with the neighbouring French

Commanders in Syria, in North Africa and in French Somaliland, and later with the military authorities in Turkey after that country signed the Treaty of Alliance on 19th October, 1939. I also visited Aden, Iraq, the Sudan and British Somaliland.

The winter of 1939/1940 was mainly occupied with three-cornered discussions between the French in Syria, the Turks and ourselves on the means of implementing the military clauses of the Treaty with Turkey. Conferences took place at Ankara in October, 1939, in Cairo in February, 1940, at Aleppo in March, and at Beirut and Haifa in May. A plan was drawn up for assistance to the Turks in Thrace if attacked by Germany. This plan was, however, conditional on Italy remaining neutral.

6. In December I paid a short visit to England to discuss the problems of the Middle East with the C.I.G.S. General Weygand from Syria was in Paris at the same time and an inter-allied conference on Middle East problems was held in Paris.

7. A conference was also held in March with the Chief of the General Staff India and other representatives on a plan for the landing of a force at Basra in case of necessity.

8. Preparations against the eventuality of Italy's joining in the war were impeded by the desire of His Majesty's Government to do nothing which might impair the existing relations with that country. I was not even permitted to set up a proper Intelligence service in Italian territory, or to get in touch with patriot chiefs in Abyssinia.

9. During this time the responsibilities of the Middle East Command were growing rapidly. It soon became obvious that operational control could not be exercised without at least some control over administration, and the Command gradually began to assume a considerable measure of administrative responsibility. Complete administrative responsibility was assumed in June, 1940. The Command also had to watch closely the political situation in Egypt, Palestine, Iraq and the neighbouring countries, and the work of the Middle East Intelligence Centre was considerably enlarged. It was also necessary to form a number of Training Establishments.

10. The only reinforcements received in the Middle East between September, 1939, and March, 1940, were:

5th Indian Infantry Brigade, which arrived in Egypt on 4th October, 1939;
2nd Battalion Durham Light Infantry, which arrived in Egypt from China on 31st January, 1940;
1st Cavalry Division (Horsed), which completed arrival in Palestine on 24th March, 1940. It was incomplete in training and equipment.
16th Australian Infantry Brigade and a portion of divisional troops of 6th Australian Division, who arrived in Palestine in the middle of February.

4th New Zealand Infantry Brigade with some divisional troops of the New Zealand Division arrived in Egypt at the same time.

These Dominion contingents were magnificent material, but were only partially trained and equipped.

The Secretary of State for War, Mr. Anthony Eden, paid a special visit to Egypt to greet the arrival of these contingents.

11. On 3rd February, 1940, the East African Command, which had previously been directly under the War Office, was placed under Middle East for operational control, though administration remained under the War Office.

In March I visited the East African Command and then went on to South Africa and Southern Rhodesia for discussions with the Governments and Military Authorities of those countries. The Union Government decided to send a Brigade and an Air Force contingent to Kenya. These actually reached Kenya during June. Their quality was extremely high, and they are proving themselves excellent troops.

12. At the end of April a valuable reinforcement of 24 officers and 666 men had been received from Southern Rhodesia. These were posted to various arms and units in which they formed, as far as possible, separate sub-units. The quality of the personnel was high and a considerable number have since received commissions. Southern Rhodesia had already, in September, 1939, sent a number of officers and N.C.Os. to reinforce the Camel Corps in British Somaliland. These were of great value.

13. Other British Colonies are also represented in the Middle East. Malta has supplied an efficient A.A. battery which forms part of the defences of Alexandria, and many Maltese are serving in the R.A.S.C. and technical units.

Cyprus has made a very considerable military effort. A Cyprus Regiment has been formed which includes an infantry battalion, Pioneer companies and Pack Transport companies. Some of these, which served with distinction in France, have now returned to the Middle East. A number of Cypriots have also enlisted as drivers in the R.A.S.C. and are doing good service.

Mauritius has sent a valuable draft of 100 tradesmen for the R.A.O.C. The British Mandated Territory of Palestine has also contributed a large number of men, both Arabs and Jews, for service with the British forces, either as combatant companies or in various Services. A Palestinian Pioneer Company served in France, where its work earned high praise, and has now returned to the Middle East.

### *May to June*, 1940

14. Meanwhile our relations with Italy were deteriorating, and during May, as a result of the success of the German attack on France, it became obvious that Italy was likely to enter the war. On 10th June Italy declared war.

The military situation at the time of the entry of Italy into the war was as follows:

There were estimated to be over 215,000 Italian troops in Libya and over 200,000 in Italian East Africa. Egypt, Sudan, Kenya, and British Somaliland, which had frontiers with these countries, became at once liable to attack. Their garrisons at the time of Italy's entry into the war were as follows:-

Egypt.

(*a*) 7th Armoured Division – comprising:

   4th Armoured Brigade, of two regiments, only partly equipped.

   7th Armoured Brigade, of two regiments, only partly equipped.

   Support Group (two Battalions).

   3rd R.H.A. (Anti-tank regiment), and

   4th R.H.A.

(*b*) 4th Indian Division – comprising:

   Two Regiments of Artillery.

   Two mixed Infantry Brigades (5th and 11th).

(*c*) Part of New Zealand Division – comprising:

   One Cavalry Regiment (less one squadron).

   One Field Regiment New Zealand Artillery.

   Three Infantry Battalions.

   One Machine Gun Battalion (incomplete in training and equipment).

(*d*) Fourteen British Infantry Battalions.

   7th Medium Regiment R.A.

   31st Field Regiment R.A.

      Total about 36,000.

Sudan (with 1,000 miles of frontier with Italian East Africa).

   Three British Battalions and

   Sudan Defence Force.

      Total about 9,000.

Kenya (with over 700 miles of frontier with Italian East Africa).

   Two East African Brigades.

   Two Light Batteries.

      Total about 8,500.

(Two Brigades from West Africa had been ordered to Kenya and arrived during July.)

British Somaliland.

   H.Q. and five Companies Somaliland Camel Corps.

   One King's African Rifles Battalion.

      Total about 1,475.

Palestine, Aden Protectorate and Cyprus were also liable to attack. Their garrisons were:

Palestine.

   1st Cavalry Division (incomplete in training and equipment).

Two British Cavalry Regiments.
One Brigade of three British Infantry Battalions.
Two British Battalions.
6th Australian Division – comprising:
Two Brigades.
Two Artillery Regiments.
Divisional Recce Unit (incomplete in training and equipment).
   Total about 27,500.
Aden.
  Two Indian Battalions.
    Total about 2,500.
Cyprus.
  One British Battalion.
    Total about 800.

15. Very little equipment had been sent to the Middle East and no single unit or formation was fully equipped. There was a dangerous lack of A.A. guns, A.Tk. guns and other artillery.

16. The enemy also had a very considerable numerical advantage in the air. This was countered by the superior technical qualities of our machines and by the higher training and morale of the pilots of the R.A.F. and S.A.A.F., who quickly established an ascendancy over the Italians which they have maintained ever since.

17. The shortest route by which the Middle East could be reinforced, through the Mediterranean, now became too precarious; over 7,000 badly needed reinforcements which were ready for despatch in May, and of whom some were actually waiting at Marseilles, were held up and did not reach the Middle East till the end of August. It was even uncertain whether the long sea route via the Cape might not also be rendered unsafe by the action of the enemy air forces and naval forces in Italian East Africa operating in the narrow waters of the Red Sea. Alternative routes via Basra, Baghdad, Haifa and via Mombasa and the Nile Valley were reconnoitred. Up to date, however, convoys have used the Red Sea route without loss, in spite of enemy attacks.

18. The position on the Western Frontier of Egypt was that our foremost defended positions were at Mersa Matruh, over 200 miles west of Alexandria and about 120 miles from the Egyptian frontier with Libya. There was a railway and road as far as Matruh and a good metalled road from Matruh to Sidi Barrani, about 50 miles from the frontier. Between Sidi Barrani and the frontier there was no good road. The small harbour of Sollum on the frontier offered no facilities for the supply of a force and had no water supply. It was therefore impossible to maintain any large number of troops on the frontier, even had they been available, and our policy had always been to allow the enemy to advance on our defences at Matruh before meeting him in any force.

It was decided, however, to place a small covering force on the frontier; and I ordered that this force should, as soon as possible after the outbreak of war, attack the Italian frontier posts.

19. In the Sudan it was obviously impossible, with the very small force available, to cover the long and vulnerable frontier, but I directed that small mobile forces should occupy the principal places on the frontier until attacked by superior forces. Although these small forces could obviously not resist any attack which the greatly superior Italian forces could make, I considered it desirable that they should fight a delaying action against the enemy rather than abandon the frontier posts without any fighting at all, as had been the previous policy.

The small mobile forces of the Sudan Defence Force made several most successful raids on the Italian frontier posts in the earlier days of the war, and when finally attacked at Kassala on 4th July and at Gallabat on 6th July by greatly superior Italian forces fought successful delaying actions and inflicted heavy loss on the enemy, who did not follow up his success in spite of the great disparity in numbers.

20. In Kenya a similar policy of holding the frontier posts for as long as possible was followed. The principal engagement took place at Moyale, where a company of the King's African Rifles held the small fort on the British side of the frontier for several weeks against an Italian force which amounted to about a brigade. It was not until a second Italian brigade was brought up that it was decided to withdraw the Company, which was successfully done on 15th July, although the enemy had by this time practically surrounded the post.

21. Enemy propaganda exaggerated these small successes, obtained by sheer force of numbers, so loudly that they succeeded in causing them to be accepted in some quarters as British defeats.

22. Such preparations as possible had been made with a view to assisting the patriot leaders in Abyssinia on the outbreak of war with Italy. For the reasons stated in paragraph 8 above, our preparations had been considerably hampered, but a number of arms had been collected and a Mission had been formed to get in touch with the patriots as soon as possible. The Emperor, His Majesty Haile Selassie, arrived in the Sudan, with the object of providing a focus for the rising. Arrangements were made for him to be accommodated at Khartoum until it should be possible for him to enter Abyssinia.

23. Meanwhile, on 17th June, the French Government had asked for armistice terms, which they accepted on 22nd June. It was at first hoped that the French Colonies and Over-sea territories would continue the struggle; but General Nogues in North Africa, after a little hesitation, decided to obey the orders to capitulate, and his example was followed shortly afterwards by General Mittelhauser in Syria, who only a few days earlier had declared to me at Beirut his

unalterable determination to continue the straggle. General Legentilhomme at Jibuti held out for nearly a month longer.

The collapse of the French in North Africa meant that the Italians could employ the whole weight of their large ground and air forces in Libya against the Western frontier of Egypt. The defection of Syria meant that Palestine no longer had a secure and friendly northern flank and that the French force of three divisions which had constituted the general reserve of the Middle East for assistance to Turkey or Greece, or for the defence of Egypt if required, could no longer be counted on.

A certain number of officers and men from Syria, including the greater part of a Colonial battalion which had, at the request of the French, been stationed at Cyprus, joined the British forces and were formed into a mobile battalion which is now engaged on the Western Frontier of Egypt. A Polish force of some 4,000 men, which had been formed and was under training by the French in Syria, came to Palestine and joined the British Forces.

A note on the foreign contingents which have joined the Forces in the Middle East is given in Appendix B.

24. Thus before the end of July it became obvious that unless reinforcements in men and material were sent to the Middle East forthwith, there was grave danger of our being unable to withstand the enemy's attacks. I received orders to visit England to discuss the situation with the military authorities and the War Cabinet. As a result of the discussions reinforcements were despatched to the Middle East. The greater part of the forces available who were sufficiently equipped and trained were moved to the Western Desert. This included a New Zealand Brigade Group and later an Australian Brigade Group.

*Italian Attack on Somaliland*

25. Meanwhile in French Somaliland General Legentilhomme had found himself unable, in spite of his gallant efforts, to induce the Colony to continue to fight. The Italians were thus enabled to concentrate the whole weight of their very numerous forces in the East of Italian East Africa against British Somaliland, which they invaded early in August. The operations, which resulted in the temporary loss of British Somaliland, have already been described in a despatch dated 12th September, 1940.

*Operations on Western Frontier of Egypt. June–November, 1940.*

26. The force sent to the Western frontier of Egypt was the 7th Armoured Division less one armoured brigade. Actually the troops to proceed to the frontier were the 7th Hussars, a light tank regiment of the 4th Armoured Brigade; the 11th Hussars, armoured car regiment; the 1st King's Royal Rifle Corps and 2nd Rifle Brigade, motor battalions; and two regiments of Royal Horse Artillery, one of which was an anti-tank regiment with 37 mm. Bofors guns for which only a limited supply of ammunition was available. The 6th Royal Tank Regiment, the second regiment of the 4th Armoured Brigade, was kept in divisional reserve.

The 4th Armoured Brigade had no third regiment, and all its units were much below establishment.

27. Just east of the Egyptian frontier an escarpment several hundred feet high runs from Sollum south-eastwards for about 30 miles, and is passable to mechanised vehicles only at a few places. At Sollum itself the road up the escarpment is steep with a number of hairpin bends. South and west of the escarpment the ground is generally easily passable by all types of mechanised vehicles. Between the escarpment and the sea the going is more difficult and movement is generally confined to certain tracks.

Our force on the frontier was operating at a distance of 120 miles from the railhead at Matruh which made the administrative problem an extremely difficult one and limited the number of troops that could be employed.

28. On the night of 11/12th June the 11th Hussars crossed the frontier and captured a detachment of two Italian officers and 59 other ranks. On 14th June the enemy's two frontier forts at Capuzzo and Maddalena were attacked and captured by the 7th Hussars, 11th Hussars and a company of the King's Royal Rifle Corps, about 220 prisoners being captured.

29. On 16th June a most successful action was fought by the 7th Hussars and 11th Hussars supported by a troop of "J" Battery R.H.A. nine miles north of Sidi Omar. Twelve enemy tanks were destroyed, and a considerable number of the enemy killed and about 160 prisoners taken. Three guns and a number of lorries were also captured or destroyed. On the same day a troop of the 11th Hussars intercepted a convoy on the Tobruk – Bardia road, destroyed 30 lorries and captured a number of prisoners, including a general officer.

Several other successful patrol actions were fought during the next few weeks. An operation to capture the Jerabub Oasis was planned for the beginning of July, but abandoned owing to great heat. Meanwhile large enemy forces, amounting to at least two divisions, had advanced towards the frontier. An enemy brigade reoccupied the ruins of Fort Capuzzo, which had been destroyed, and advanced towards Sollum, but was repulsed. The enemy's position at Fort Capuzzo was made extremely uncomfortable for him. His force was continually shelled by our artillery, and transport bringing up supplies from Bardia was constantly attacked or shelled, with the result that the enemy undoubtedly suffered extremely heavy casualties both in men and in vehicles.

By the middle of July the enemy had two divisions, and elements of two more, on the Egyptian frontier; but our small force continued to dominate the situation and to inflict considerable casualties.

30. During the remainder of July operations continued on the same lines. The enemy continued to suffer heavy casualties but gradually moved forward his camps and established a force of at least four divisions within easy reach of the Egyptian frontier. During this period the 8th Hussars relieved the 7th Hussars, who went back for a rest, and H.Q. of the 7th Armoured Brigade relieved H.Q.

4th Armoured Brigade. All vehicles were beginning to show considerable signs of wear, and replacement was difficult owing to the distance from railhead and the almost entire absence of spares in Egypt for the armoured fighting vehicles. For this reason about the end of July, I gave instructions that track vehicles should be withdrawn from the frontier for overhaul and refit, as I was afraid that otherwise when the enemy advanced our armoured fighting vehicles would be very largely out of action. Of 306 tanks on the War Establishment 200 were normally available with units, the remainder being under repair in workshops. There was no reserve of tanks to meet war wastage.

31. After the withdrawal of the Armoured Brigade the frontier was held by a force under the command of the Support Group of the Armoured Division, consisting of the 3rd Coldstream Guards from the Matruh garrison, the 1st K.R.R.C., 2nd Rifle Brigade, 11th Hussars, one squadron 1st Royal Tank Regiment and two batteries of Royal Horse Artillery (one of anti-tank guns, one of 18–25 pdrs.). A section of the 7th Medium Regiment was also brought forward to harass the enemy. This small force was distributed over a front of some 60 miles from Sollum to Fort Maddalena. The troops continued the same policy of active patrolling, but the enemy's numbers were now very much increased, his artillery was numerous and active and the opportunities for effective action were fewer. Nevertheless this small force continued to inflict heavy casualties on the enemy with practically no loss to itself, and to hold in check a force of four or five divisions for a further six weeks. A skilful use was made of dummy tanks to deceive the enemy.

32. By 10th September it became obvious that an enemy advance across the frontier was imminent. All preparations had already been made for the withdrawal of our frontier force and the first stage of this was now put into execution. On 13th September the enemy advance began, a large force being deployed under heavy artillery preparation against the escarpment above Sollum, which had for some time past been held only by a platoon and had by now been evacuated. At the same time another enemy column advanced on the Halfaya Pass down the escarpment towards Sollum. Both these columns were engaged by our artillery, which inflicted considerable losses on them.

It had been uncertain whether the enemy would make his main advance along the coast road, or would attempt a wide movement south of the escarpment. There is some reason to believe that the latter may have been the enemy's original intention, but in the event his advance was made on a narrow front along the coast road with two divisions in the front line and two in support, and one more and a Mobile Force (Maletti Group) in close reserve. He was supported by a numerous artillery and by about 200 light and medium tanks.

The part of our covering force which was north of the escarpment and on which this attack fell consisted of the 3rd Coldstream Guards, one battery 3rd Royal Horse Artillery and one section of the 7th Medium Regiment. It was subsequently supported by a detachment of the 1st K.R.R.C. and a company of the French battalion.* The remainder of our covering force was south of the escarpment to provide against an enemy movement from that flank. The 1st Royal Tank Regiment, which was south of the escarpment, was moved to the northern flank when the direction of the enemy advance became evident, but for various reasons arrived too late to take any part in the actions during the withdrawal.

33. For four days, from 13th September to 16th September, our small force withdrew along the coast road from Sollum to the east of Sidi Barrani. The enemy reached Sidi Barrani, which is merely a collection of a few houses and a landing ground, on 16th September and there halted. Although the enemy had large numbers of medium and light tanks with his forward troops and the leading infantry was in M.T., his advance was slow and unenterprising. He made little attempt to use his immensely superior numbers or his mobility to outflank and overwhelm our small force. His artillery was boldly used, even in front of the leading infantry, but their fire, though reasonably accurate, was ineffective. His tanks were mainly used for the protection of the infantry columns, and only on one occasion, on 16th September, was any attempt made to use them to outflank our troops; and even on this occasion their timidity and hesitation lost them an opportunity.

34. The withdrawal of our small force was effected with admirable skill, and there is no doubt whatever that very serious losses were inflicted on the enemy, both by the artillery, which was boldly and effectively handled, and, whenever opportunity offered, by machine gun and small arms fire. Our own losses were under 50 men and a small number of vehicles.

The greatest possible credit is due to Brigadier W.H.E. Gott, M.C., commanding the Support Group, and to Lieut.-Colonel J.C. Campbell, M.C., commanding the Artillery, for the cool and efficient way in which this withdrawal was carried out, also to the troops for their endurance and tactical skill.

Since their advance to Sidi Barrani the enemy has remained practically stationary for the last two months. Small mobile columns formed from the 7th Armoured Division have continually engaged and harassed the enemy in the same manner as on the frontier and with similar success. The enemy has, in the same way as on the frontier, placed his troops in a number of defended camps with all round perimeters, from Maktila on the coast, 10 to 15 miles east of Sidi Barrani, to Sofafi on the escarpment southwest of Sidi Barrani. He is undoubtedly suffering considerable administrative difficulties and it is at present uncertain whether he will continue his advance.

35. I wish to draw special attention to the work of the small covering force on the Western Frontier of Egypt during the period from the outbreak of war with Italy in June to the middle of September, when the Italian advance halted at Sidi Barrani. For over three months in hard and difficult climatic conditions this force

---

* *See* Appendix B.

not only held in check an Italian force many times its superior in numbers, but established a definite ascendency over it, penetrating well into enemy territory, taking the offensive whenever the least opportunity offered, and inflicting very heavy losses at trifling cost to itself. The published Italian casualties in Libya for the period were approximately 3,500, while our total casualties were just over 150. Over 700 prisoners were taken, and a considerable number of guns, tanks and lorries were captured or destroyed. Major-General M. O'Moore Creagh, M.C., Commander of the 7th Armoured Division, directed these operations with admirable skill and initiative, and was ably seconded by his brigade and regimental commanders. Of the units which took part, the 11th Hussars, the Armoured Car Regiment, was continuously in the front line, and usually behind that of the enemy, during the whole period; its tireless and daring search for information and constant harassing of the enemy showed a spirit and efficiency worthy of the best traditions of this fine regiment. The light tank regiments, first the 7th Hussars, later relieved by the 8th Hussars, showed a similar eagerness to take opportunities and skill to make the most of them, while the 1st and 6th Royal Tank Regiments backed up the light tank regiments most efficiently when required. The batteries of the R.H.A. were handled with great dash and most effectively; they unquestionably made themselves feared by the enemy and inflicted heavy losses on them. The engineer work of the Force was effectively carried out by 2nd Cheshire Field Squadron, which had been borrowed from the 1st Cavalry Division. Finally, the infantry battalions in or attached to the Support Group, the 3rd Coldstream Guards, 1st Battalion K.R.R.C. and the 2nd Battalion Rifle Brigade, provided a solid backing of fire power when required, were readily mobile, and gained a complete mastery of the debateable area between themselves and the enemy by active night patrolling.

*Operations in the Sudan. October–November*, 1940.

36. Soon after the arrival of Indian reinforcements in the Sudan I instructed Major-General W. Platt, C.B., D.S.O., to make plans for minor offensive operations as soon as he could do so, and indicated the recapture of the frontier post of Gallabat as a suitable objective. A plan was accordingly prepared by Major-General L.M. Heath, C.B., C.I.E., D.S.O., M.C., commanding the 5th Indian Division, for an operation against the Italian troops in the Gallabat – Metemma area, to be carried out by the 10th Indian Brigade and a squadron of the 6th Royal Tank Regiment, which had been sent to the Sudan early in September when an enemy advance from the Kassala area with armoured fighting vehicles appeared possible.

37. The two frontier posts of Gallabat and Metemma, the former in the Sudan and the latter in Italian East Africa, face one another across a *khor* (ravine) in a valley about two miles wide. Both posts are on forward slopes and have behind them higher features. Gallabat had, as already related in para. 19, been occupied by the Italians since July. The Italian troops in the Gallabat – Metemma area consisted, at the time that the attack was planned, of five Colonial Battalions

with a battery, a machine-gun battalion, an anti-tank platoon, and a number of irregulars, totalling about 5,300 men.

38. The operation was originally intended to take place on 8th November, but at the end of October information was received of a large convoy from Gondar approaching the Metemma area. Air action was taken to delay the march of this column but was only partially successful. It was therefore decided to advance the date of the attack to 6th November in the hope of forestalling the arrival of the reinforcements.

39. The operation, although it resulted in our retaking Gallabat and inflicting very heavy losses on the enemy, was not as successful as had been hoped owing to certain factors which could not be foreseen.

The first of these was the breakdown, mainly from mechanical causes, of all the tanks except one light tank during the capture of Gallabat. The chief causes of the breakdown were damage to the tracks by the rough ground, or by enemy mines. The second factor was a temporary loss of command of the air due to six of our fighter aircraft being shot down in a combat with the enemy.

40. Gallabat was captured early on 6th November by the 3rd Garhwal Rifles and the squadron of the Royal Tank Regiment with few casualties, one enemy colonial battalion being practically destroyed. The further advance on Metemma had, however, to be postponed owing to the breakdown of the tanks. The enemy positions at Metemma were very heavily wired and defended by a large number of machine guns, and without tank support it was considered inadvisable to attempt their capture. The further advance was therefore postponed till the afternoon when it was hoped that some of the tanks would be repaired.

41. During the morning, however, the enemy gained control of the air and developed an extremely heavy bombing attack on our forward troops, the Garhwal Rifles who had captured Gallabat and the 1st Essex Regiment who were in process of relieving them. There was little cover and the ground was too rocky to dig shelter trenches. Both battalions suffered heavy casualties and their morale was temporarily affected. Also the workshop lorry of the Tank squadron was destroyed by a bomb and three fitters were wounded, which greatly hampered the task of repairing the tanks.

42. The Brigade Commander therefore decided that he must cancel the attack on Metemma, and that in view of the enemy's continued command of the air and the target offered by Gallabat it would be necessary to withdraw the somewhat shaken troops from that area.

A withdrawal was therefore made to the high ground west of Gallabat on the evening of 7th November.

43. Gallabat has since been reoccupied as an outpost position, the main position being established on the high ground to the west of it. The enemy fort at Metemma has been practically destroyed and rendered untenable by artillery fire

and he has also withdrawn his troops to the high ground to the east. Minor actions still continue between the main positions.

44. I should like to call special attention to the behaviour of the personnel of "B" Squadron of the 6th Royal Tank Regiment in this action. The attack on Gallabat was made with great dash and the way in which the men of the squadron stuck to their task of trying to get their tanks which were broken down into action again under extremely heavy bombing was admirable.

45. Our losses on 6th and 7th November in killed, wounded and missing were 86 British and 88 Indian, of which only about 20 were incurred in the original attack and most of the remainder were due to air bombing. The action showed again how necessary protection against air attack is for all forward troops. Owing to the general shortage of anti-aircraft guns in the Middle East, none were available for the support of the 10th Brigade, and after our fighter aircraft had been put out of action the enemy bombers were unopposed.

46. It is known that casualties of well over 600 were inflicted on the enemy. Two guns and much material were captured in Gallabat Fort.

47. During the month of October and the first half of November our mobile troops in the Kassala sector fought many successful patrol actions and inflicted heavy losses on the enemy at small cost to themselves. The largest of these small engagements was in the area north of Kassala, in which over 300 of the enemy were taken prisoner.

### Occupation of Crete – November, 1940.
48. On 28th October, Italy made an unprovoked attack on Greece. To enable more effective control of the Aegean to be exercised by the Navy, it was decided to establish a naval base at Suda Bay at the north-western end of Crete. With the full approval of the Greek Government, the British forces in the Middle East assumed responsibility for the defence of Crete. The 1st battalion York and Lancaster Regiment, some A.A. artillery and a Field Company were despatched on 31st October to Suda Bay. On 17th November another battalion, 2nd The Black Watch, was sent.

### Visit of Secretary of State.
49. At the end of October the Secretary of State for War, Mr. Anthony Eden, paid a visit to the Middle East, in the course of which he went to the Western Desert, Palestine, Trans-Jordan, and the Sudan, and saw many of the troops. His visit was of the greatest value for the discussion of future plans and was a source of much encouragement to the troops. At Khartoum he met General Smuts who had flown up from South Africa to visit the East African front.

### Summary.
50. From the above brief account of events it can be seen that the Middle East Command has passed through three stages during the period of some 15 months

under review. The first period, from the outbreak of war with Germany till Italy entered the war in June, 1940, was one of comparative inactivity. Plans in the Middle East were directed mainly towards the support of Turkey against a German advance in S.E. Europe. Italy was assumed to be neutral and if she did enter the war could be neutralised by the French forces. Little equipment of any kind was received during this period and the reinforcements sent (1st Cavalry Division and the Australian and New Zealand contingents) were not equipped for modern war and were only partially trained.

Therefore the second stage, after the entry of Italy into the war and the collapse of France, was one of considerable danger, during which the frontiers of Egypt, the Sudan, Kenya, and British Somaliland were threatened by vastly superior forces, and the communications between the United Kingdom and the Middle East were long and doubtful. That the Italians failed to take advantage of their opportunities was due firstly to our Air Force, who in spite of inferior numbers everywhere took and kept the initiative; and to the stout action of the small covering forces in Egypt, Sudan and East Africa; and finally to the enemy's lack of preparation or desire for hard fighting. We thus escaped these dangerous months with the loss only of British Somaliland – where our small garrison of a few battalions was driven to withdraw, after a short but gallant resistance, by an Italian force of seven brigade groups – and a few unimportant frontier posts in the Sudan and Kenya. During this period all available equipment and troops were being retained in the United Kingdom against the threat of invasion; and it was not until the second half of September that reinforcements in men and material began to reach the Middle East in any quantity

The third stage has now begun, when the defence of our positions in the Middle East is reasonably assured and offensive operations are being planned and undertaken.

51. The Middle East Command has to keep in close touch with the political situation in the countries included in the Command, particularly in Egypt, Palestine and Iraq. The work of the Middle East Intelligence Centre, under the able direction of Colonel W.J. Cawthorn, has been of the greatest value in this respect. The situation in Egypt has often been difficult, since it is the main base of operations for the Middle East, yet the country is not at war, and has still large numbers of enemy subjects at large. Close touch with the Embassy is maintained by weekly meetings of the Ambassador and the Commander-in-Chief, while the Embassy staff, the staff of Headquarters British Troops in Egypt, and my staff are in daily consultation on matters of common interest. There has been no serious difference of opinion on any matter of importance.

*Co-operation of other Services.*

52. I desire to acknowledge the indebtedness of the Middle East Command to the work of the Royal Navy in the Mediterranean, the Red Sea and the Indian Ocean. The Commander-in-Chief, Mediterranean Fleet, Admiral Sir Andrew B.

Cunningham, K.C.B., D.S.O., has always afforded the Army the closest support both in planning and in actual operations.

The work of H.M. ships in the East Indies Command under Vice-Admiral R. Leatham, C.B., in bringing the convoys for the Middle East across the Indian Ocean and through the Red Sea without the loss of a ship has earned the gratitude and admiration of the large numbers from all parts of the Empire who have thus appreciated the power and efficiency of the Royal Navy. I have already spoken of the work of the Royal Navy in the operations in Somaliland in the despatch dealing with that campaign.

53. It would be difficult to speak too highly of the work of the Royal Air Force in the Middle East and of their support of the Army to the limit of their capacity. Both the original A.O.C.-in-C., Air Chief Marshal Sir William Mitchell, K.C.B., C.B.E., D.S.O., M.C., A.F.C., and his successor, Air Chief Marshal Sir Arthur Longmore, K.C.B., D.S.O., have co-operated wholeheartedly in combining the operations of the Army and the Air Force to the best advantage; and the relations between the two Services, at G.H.Q. and in the various Commands, have been always close and cordial.

It has become more obvious with every phase of the war in the Middle East both that the development and reinforcement of the R.A.F. must keep pace with the growth of the ground forces, which it has not done up to date, and that co-operation between the ground and air forces in all stages of any operation need the closest study.

54. Co-operation in planning between the three Services is maintained by the Joint Planning Staff, whose work has been uniformly excellent. They have never failed to produce an agreed solution of any problem put to them.

55. I desire to express my gratitude to the Commander-in-Chief in India, General Sir Robert Cassels, G.C.B., C.S.I., D.S.O., and to the Army in India for the manner in which requests for assistance in units, officers or material have invariably been met to the limit of India's capacity. The Indian troops sent to the Middle East are well maintaining their high reputation in the camp and in the field.

56. The co-operation of the Egyptian Army in the defence of Egypt has been hampered by the lack of a definite policy by the Egyptian Government, who have never quite decided the point at which resistance to the enemy by the Egyptian Army should begin. For some time Egyptian units formed part of the garrison of Matruh, and an Egyptian A.A. unit did excellent work in defending Matruh against air attack though frequently subjected to heavy bombing.

At present part of the Egyptian Frontier Force is defending the Siwa Oasis, and an Egyptian Mobile Force, under Prince Ismail Daoud, is in readiness to support the garrison of Siwa. Egyptian A.A. and C.D. units are assisting in the defence of the Fleet Base at Alexandria; the Egyptian Army provides a force for the defence of Wadi Haifa against possible enemy raids, and guards vulnerable points in the Delta.

*Appreciation of Services.*

57. I should like to call particular attention to the services of Lieutenant-General Sir H.M. Wilson, K.C.B., D.S.O., G.O.C.-in-C. British Troops in Egypt. He has had a very onerous task in providing for the defence of Egypt with inadequate resources, in fitting for war the troops sent to his Command, in organising the expansion of the base in Egypt, in securing the co-operation of the Egyptian Army, and in dealing with many difficult and delicate problems in the relations between the forces in Egypt and the Egyptian Government and people. His sound knowledge and imperturbable common sense have enabled him to deal effectively with all these problems and he has obtained the confidence and liking of the Egyptians with whom he has had to work. It is largely due to his direction that the small British force in the Western Desert has so effectively delayed and checked the Italian advance.

58. Major-General W. Platt, C.B., D.S.O., has commanded the troops in the Sudan throughout the period with marked efficiency. He kept his head during the dangerous period when the Sudan was exposed to the attack of greatly superior Italian forces and used his slender resources to the best effect to meet the danger. With the arrival of reinforcements he has initiated offensive action against the enemy whenever possible, though still inferior in numbers.

59. Lieutenant-Generals M.G.H. Barker, K.C.B., D.S.O., G.J. Giffard, C.B., D.S.O., and P. Neame, V.C., C.B., D.S.O., have in succession held the command in Palestine. I consider that all three have shown ability and tact in dealing with the military and political problems of the country.

60. Major-General D.P. Dickinson, D.S.O., O.B.E., M.C., did most valuable work in the early part of the war in organising our war effort in East Africa under difficult conditions.

61. I have been fortunate in my staff and desire to place on record my appreciation of their work, their willingness and their efficiency. In particular, I owe a deep debt of thanks to Major-General A.F. Smith, D.S.O., M.C., Deputy Chief of the General Staff, who has been the chief General Staff Officer of the Middle East Command since its beginning. He has shown himself an admirable staff officer in every way, and his personality and unfailing cheerfulness has made its influence felt throughout the staff and has impressed the many foreign officers with whom he has had to deal. Major-General B.O. Hutchison, C.B.E., Deputy Quarter-Master General, joined Middle East in October, 1939, as principal administrative officer and has directed the expansion of its administrative responsibilities ever since. His capacity for hard work, organizing ability and foresight have been most marked. He is an outstanding administrative staff officer.

APPENDIX A.
*Army Council Instructions to the General Officer Commanding-in-Chief
in the Middle East.*

1. You are appointed General Officer Commanding-in-chief in the Middle East.

2. The area over which your command extends *in peace* comprises:-
Egypt.
The Sudan.
Palestine and Trans-Jordan.
Cyprus.

3. In these areas you will exercise general control over all British land forces in matters of high policy in peace and will, in particular, be responsible for the review and co-ordination of war plans for reinforcements in emergency, including, the distribution of available land forces and material between these areas.

4. In addition you will be responsible for the preparation of all war plans, in co-operation with the local military or air force commanders, for the employment of land forces in British Somaliland, Aden, Iraq, and the shores of the Persian Gulf.

5. In carrying out these tasks you will where appropriate consult and co-operate with the Naval Commander-in-Chief, Mediterranean, the Naval Commander-in-Chief, East Indies Station, the Commander-in-Chief in India, the Inspector General, African Colonial Forces, and the Air Officer Commanding-in-Chief in the Middle East.

6. You will maintain close touch with His Majesty's Ambassador in Egypt; His Majesty's Ambassador in Iraq; the Governor General in the Sudan; the High Commissioner for Palestine and Trans-Jordan; the Governors of Cyprus, Aden and British Somaliland; and the Political Resident in the Persian Gulf.

7. The policy of His Majesty's Government with regard to the Egyptian Forces is that they shall be developed into efficient modern forces capable of co-operating with the British forces in the defence of Egypt. You will maintain close touch with His Majesty's Ambassador in Egypt, the Head of the British Military Misson, and the Egyptian General Staff in all matters of high policy affecting the development and employment in war of the Egyptian Army, with due regard to the existing responsibilities of the General Officer Commanding-in-chief, Egypt in such matters as local defence, cooperation between British and Egyptian troops, and training. You will delegate to the General Officer Commanding-in-chief, The British Troops in Egypt, such matters as are, in your opinion, best arranged by him direct with the appropriate Egyptian authorities and, subject to the agreement of the Egyptian Government at the time, command of the Egyptian Army in war.

The agreement of the Egyptian Government to place the Egyptian Army under the command of the General Officer Commanding-in-chief in Egypt will be obtained by His Majesty's Ambassador through whose intermediation all requests to the Egyptian Government will be made.

8. You should bear in mind that His Majesty's Ambassador must retain in all circumstances his existing position *vis-à-vis* the Egyptian Government. This does not exclude direct communication between the General Officer Commanding-in-chief, British Troops in Egypt, and the Egyptian authorities on routine matters agreed by His Majesty's Ambassador.

The same considerations will apply as regards your relations with His Majesty's Diplomatic Representatives in the other countries included in the area over which your command will extend in war. In the case of Iraq, this will not preclude direct communication with the Inspector General of the Iraq Army on such matters as may be agreed by His Majesty's Ambassador to Iraq.

9. You will visit all areas which are included in war in your Command (vide paragraph 14 below) to study local situations and inform yourself of local problems.

10. Subject to the direction of the Chiefs of Staff, and of the War Office in respect of the land forces, you are responsible, in conjunction with the Naval Commander-in-Chief, Mediterranean, the Naval Commander-in-Chief, East Indies Station, and the Air Officer Commanding-in-chief, Middle East, for co-ordinating the British war plans with the war plans of Allies of His Majesty's Government in the Near and Middle East and North Africa.

This will involve at present co-ordination with the French military authorities in North Africa, Syria and French Somaliland; the Turkish General Staff; and possibly ultimately the Greek and Roumanian General Staffs.

You will arrange to exchange visits with these authorities as may be required.

11. To assist you in these tasks you will be provided with a staff for your own use. Of this Staff, the Senior General Staff Officer will also be a member of the Joint Planning Staff for the Middle East, which will include the Chief Staff Officers of the Commander-in-Chief, Mediterranean, and the Air Officer Commanding- in-chief, Middle East. The Joint Planning Staff will be responsible for the inter-service co-operation of all war plans as may be directed by the Commanders concerned, namely, the Commander-in-Chief, Mediterranean, the Commander-in-Chief, East Indies, the Air Officer Commanding-in-Chief, Middle East and yourself.

12. Your requirements as regards intelligence will be provided by the Middle East Intelligence Centre, which is being established in Cairo.

13. Your headquarters will be located at Cairo.

14. Should war break out the area of your Command will be extended to include all military forces in British Somaliland, Aden, Iraq and the shores of the Persian Gulf, with the exception of those which are normally under the control of the Royal Air Force.

15. Your tasks *in war* are to co-ordinate (in consultation with the Air Officer Commanding-in-Chief, Middle East, for matters affecting Iraq and Aden) the action of the land forces in the areas under your command and the distribution of available resources between them. You will be guided by the policy for the conduct of operations which will be communicated to you from time to time.

You will co-ordinate the operations of the forces under your command with the operations of the various allied forces in the areas mentioned in paragraph 10.

For this purpose you will work in direct cooperation with allied military commanders concerned.

By Command of the Army Council.
*H.J. Creedy.*

The War Office,
24th July, 1939.

## APPENDIX "B."
### *Co-operation of Allies.*

On 28th June, 1940, General Mittelhauser, the Commander-in-Chief of the French Forces in the Middle East, decided to accept the German terms. In consequence a number of French sub-units and individual French soldiers immediately made their way into Palestine to join the British forces. In addition, the Polish Carpathian Brigade which had been serving with the French in Syria, and a large party of Czechs who had been awaiting onward passage to France, decided to continue the struggle. These formed the nucleus of the various Allied Contingents in the Middle East, details of which are given below:

(a) *French.*
After a short stay in Palestine, it was decided to bring the French contingent to Moascar. There they have been reorganised into:
   (i) A motorised infantry battalion,
   (ii) A squadron of Spahis.
   (iii) A training depot.
One Company of the Infantry Battalion was put under the command of 7th Armoured Division on 8th September, 1940, and has taken its part in operations in the Western Desert. The remainder of the battalion was sent to Daba on 23rd October, 1940, for further training before joining the first Company.

The Spahis were sent to the Sudan a week later, and it is hoped that they will shortly be engaged in active operations on the Abyssinian frontier.

In Cairo there is a very active French National Committee under the presidency of Baron de Benoist. The Chief of the Cabinet Militaire is Commandant des Essars, who has very ably carried out the responsible duties of General de Gaulle's military representative in the Middle East. He has recently been appointed Chief of Staff to General Catroux, the new Delegate General of Free France in the Middle East. Commandant des Essars is in close touch with the situation in Greece (where there is a strong French Committee), in Syria and in French Equatorial Africa.

(b) *Polish.*
The Polish Brigade was originally stationed at Latrun in Palestine, but early in October it was moved to Egypt to take up a defensive position on the Western outskirts of Alexandria. A reserve Depot was left at Latrun and here new arrivals from the Balkans are equipped and trained before joining the Brigade.

The flow of recruits from the Balkans fluctuates with the political situation; according to a recent estimate by the Military Attaché at Ankara, the maximum rate we can expect at present is 100 per week. The Brigade is still over 1,000 under strength in other ranks, but has a surplus of officers. It has now been decided (at General Kopanski's suggestion) to form these surplus officers into an Officers' Legion for garrison duties in Alexandria. It has also been decided that the Brigade should ultimately be organised on a British W.E. – as and when equipment becomes available.

(c) *Czechoslovak.*
The Czechoslovak contingent is stationed at Gedera in Palestine; it consists of an Infantry Battalion (on British W.E.), a training depot and a small contingent headquarters. At present there are some 35 surplus officers, but the contingent is nearly 600 under strength in other ranks.

The chief source of supply for Czech volunteers is S.E. Europe. Owing to German pressure and to the fact that there are no Czech legations in the Balkan countries, the Military Attaché Ankara considers that the maximum flow from the Balkans and Russia will not exceed 100 per month. There are at present over 600 potential Czech volunteers in Russia; but owing to financial difficulties few have as yet arrived.

General Gak, the Chief of the Czechoslovak Military Mission in the Middle East, arrived in August, and he and his staff are responsible for co-ordinating the recruiting of Czech volunteers from Egypt, Palestine, Iran and the Balkans.

(d) *Spanish.*
There is no separate Spanish contingent. Spanish volunteers, who are ex-members of the French Foreign Legion, are accepted for training at the Free French Depot. When a party of twenty-five has been collected, they are drafted into a Commando after formal enlistment and attestation into the British Army. There are at present some fifty Spanish volunteers serving with 50 (ME) Commando.

(e) *Belgians.*
Owing to the comparatively small size of the Belgian communities in Egypt and elsewhere in the Middle East, and to the fact that many men were already serving with the Belgian Army prior to the French collapse, it was not possible to form a separate Belgian contingent. Individuals with special qualifications, however, have been accepted for service in the British Army – notably as officers in the

British Arab Force. Recently a small party of Belgian volunteers left to join the Belgian forces in the U.K. It was decided, for the present, not to accept offers of service from Belgian units or individuals in the Congo, as they could best help the common cause by maintaining the situation in Central Africa.

(f) *Greeks.*

Negotiations are now in progress with the Greek authorities for the raising and training of units of the Greek Army in Egypt. It is proposed to form as soon as possible technical units initially for service with the British Army. In addition, it is proposed to organise a training depot with a view to the ultimate formation of a Greek Brigade Group, when more equipment is available. The Greek Government is prepared to send a liaison mission of 15 officers and 20 cadets to assist in training. Colonel Oeconnomopoulos has already arrived as Chief Liaison Officer.

# 2

# GENERAL WAVELL'S DESPATCH ON OPERATIONS 7 DECEMBER 1940 TO 7 FEBRUARY 1941

*The following despatch was submitted to the Secretary of State for War on 21st June, 1941, by General Sir Archibald P. Wavell, G.C.B., C.M.G., M.C., Commander-in-Chief in the Middle East.*

PART I. – FIRST PHASE – BATTLE OF SIBI BARRANI –
DECEMBER 7 TO 13, 1940.

1. *Introductory.*

1. In a former despatch I gave a summary of events in the Middle East Command down to the 15th November, 1940. The present despatch will deal with events in one part of the Middle East only, the Western frontier of Egypt and Cyrenaica, from the 7th December, 1940, when the counter-offensive against the Italian army began, down to the 7th February, the date on which Benghazi surrendered.

2. In the previous despatch the advance of the Italians to Sidi Barrani was described. In accordance with our pre-arranged policy, little opposition had been offered to the enemy's advance, and it was not proposed to oppose him in strength until he reached our prepared defences at Mersa Matruh. It was not, however, intended that the defence should be a passive one. On the 21st September I had issued orders for a counter-stroke to be prepared against the enemy, so soon as he became engaged with the defences of Matruh. I found that General Wilson, Commander of British Troops in Egypt, and General O'Connor, Commanding the Western Desert Force, had already made the preliminary arrangements for such a counter-stroke. During the next month, as our defences and our forces grew in strength, so the plan for the counter-stroke was developed; and a scheme was eventually prepared for striking at the enemy as he approached Matruh. This plan was studied in detail by the commanders and troops concerned, and all possible arrangements made to put it into effect, if the enemy advanced against Matruh in the manner that we judged most probable.

2. *Preparation of Plan of Attack.*

3. About the middle of October, when the enemy had been stationary for a month and there seemed no immediate probability of his further advance, I began to consider the possibility of an early offensive action in spite of our numerical inferiority. The enemy's defensive arrangements seemed to me to be thoroughly

faulty. He was spread over a wide front in a series of fortified camps which were not mutually supporting and were separated by wide distances. His defences seemed to lack depth.

On the 20th October I issued a personal note to General Wilson instructing him to consider the possibility of an attack on the enemy forward camps. The plan I directed him to consider was an attack at both ends of the enemy's line, by the 7th Armoured Division reinforced with some mobile infantry battalions against the enemy's right flank on the escarpment near Sofafi, and by the 4th Indian Division, reinforced, if possible, by one additional brigade, against the camps immediately east of Sidi Barrani, near the coast. If the initial attacks were successful, I proposed that the Armoured Division should exploit its success northwards towards the coast and the 4th Indian Division westwards. I stated that the operations would be dependent on all the troops being made mobile and being able to move 30 to 40 miles in a night, so as to cover in two successive nights the distance between our front and the enemy's and to attack on the morning following the second night march. I suggested that it would probably only be possible to stage an operation lasting four or five days, since that appeared to be the limit for which supply arrangements could be made.

4. Meanwhile, General Wilson and General O'Connor had also been considering plans for an offensive. After discussion with them, it was agreed that there were objections to an attack on the Sofafi group of camps owing to their comparative strength and to the greater distance from our starting base at which they lay. It was decided to make the attack against the enemy's centre, leaving his flanks, on the coast and at Sofafi, to be contained by small forces. I directed that detailed plans and preparations should be put in hand at once.

At this time Mr. Eden, the Secretary of State for War, visited Egypt and was made aware of the plans, to which he gave approval and promised his full support. It was largely this support which enabled us to obtain the air reinforcement on which the success of the plan greatly depended.

The provisional date originally selected was in the last week of November. It soon, however, became obvious that the preparations for the attack, especially the provision of additional transport and the re-equipment of the artillery with 25-pdrs., would not be completed in time. Further, the invasion of Greece by Italy at the end of October brought a demand for support from Greece, and instructions from the War Cabinet to send certain troops from the Middle East to occupy Crete and to assist Greece. It looked at one time as if this might cause the postponement or abandonment of the plan, since it very seriously weakened the air support available and also removed from the Western Desert some anti-aircraft guns, engineers, transport and other troops which it had been intended to employ in the operation. Owing to the intervention of the Secretary of State, reinforcements of aircraft were promised, and it was decided to stage the operation if the air situation made it at all possible. The date was postponed till about the end of the first week in December.

5. In order to maintain secrecy, as few persons as possible were made aware of the plan. Its details were worked out by Generals O'Connor, Creagh (commanding 7th Armoured Division), and Beresford-Peirse (commanding 4th Indian Division). General Wilson and myself visited the Western Desert at frequent intervals and discussed the progress of the plan and the additional troops required in the Western Desert. Practically nothing whatever was put on paper, and not more than a dozen senior commanders and staff officers knew of the plan until shortly before its execution.

6. On the 25th and 26th November a training exercise was held near Matruh, which was, in fact, a rehearsal of the proposed operation. Entrenched camps were marked out on the ground to represent the enemy camps to be attacked, though this was of course known only to the few who were aware of the forthcoming operation. To the troops it was represented as a training exercise in attack on enemy camps, and it was intimated that a further exercise would be held at a date early in December. As a result of this exercise it was possible to make several improvements in the plan of attack, and General Wilson issued a paper laying down certain methods, which were used in the actual attack and proved to be sound.

7. Co-operation with the Royal Navy was arranged through a naval liaison officer attached to General O'Connor's headquarters, and the air plan was drawn up by Wing Commander Collishaw, commanding the Air Force in the Western Desert. Needless to say, both Royal Navy and Royal Air Force co-operated most wholeheartedly, both in the plans for attack and in maintaining complete secrecy.

### 3. *Enemy's Position and Strength.*

8. The Italian force East of the Egyptian frontier was believed to consist of 6 or 7 divisions (of which two or three were Libyan divisions, two were Blackshirt divisions and two Metropolitan divisions) and an armoured group. The total strength was believed to be about 80,000 (63,000 Italian, 17,000 Libyan), with 250 guns and 120 tanks.

9. These forces were distributed in a series of fortified camps, from the sea East of Sidi Barrani to the escarpment about Sofafi, a distance of about 50 miles, in echelon from the left flank. The camps were usually circular, with an anti-tank obstacle round them and defences consisting for the most part of stone sangars. There was a gap of over 20 miles between the enemy's right flank at Sofafi and the next camp at Nibeiwa. It was through this gap that General O'Connor intended to pass the attacking force. Arrangements were made during the planning stage to prevent the enemy establishing a camp to close this gap.

To the North of Nibeiwa lay the Tummar group of camps, occupied by the 2nd Libyan Division, and to the North-East of these lay the enemy's most advanced camp near the sea coast at Maktila, occupied by the 1st Libyan Division. There were further fortifications round Sidi Barrani, but there did not otherwise seem to be any organised second line of defence.

### 4. *Plan of Attack.*

10. The troops taking part in the attack were:-

| | |
|---|---|
| 7th Armoured Division | General Creagh. |
| 4th Indian Division | General Beresford-Peirse |
| 16th Infantry Brigade | (Brigadier Lomax, attached to the 4th Indian Division.) |
| 7th Battalion R.T.R. | (Infantry tanks.) |
| Matruh Garrison Force | (Brigadier Selby – a brigade group made up from the Matruh Garrison.) |

Total force consisted of approximately 31,000 men, 120 guns, 275 tanks, of which more than half were light tanks, 50 were infantry tanks and remainder cruisers, and 60 armoured cars.

11. In view of the limited amount of transport available it was necessary to form dumps of ammunition, water and petrol in the desert between our lines at Matruh and those of the enemy. This was successfully accomplished, apparently without attracting the enemy's notice. Several days' supplies for the whole force were actually stored some 20 to 30 miles in advance of our fortified lines, covered only by our advanced patrols.

12. The general plan of attack was as follows:-

The Support Group of the 7th Armoured Division was to observe the group of enemy camps round Sofafi and prevent the enemy from these camps intervening in the battle. The remainder of the Armoured Division and the 4th Indian Division were to pass through the gap between the Sofafi camps and Nibeiwa camp. A brigade of the 4th Indian Division with the 7th Battalion R.T.R. (Infantry tanks) was then to attack Nibeiwa camp from the West, while the Armoured Division covered the attack and prevented any intervention from the enemy to the North.

After the capture of Nibeiwa camp, another brigade of the 4th Indian Division, again supported by 7th R.T.R., was to attack the Tummar groups of camps from the West. It was intended that their capture should conclude the first day's operation. Meanwhile, the Matruh Garrison force was to observe and contain the enemy camp at Maktila.

If the attacks on Nibeiwa and Tummar were successful, it was intended to attack and capture Sidi Barrani on the following day, and thereafter exploit success as far Westward as possible.

13. Although our forces were numerically inferior to those of the enemy, their morale, training and equipment was believed to be sufficiently high to compensate for this. The enemy had so far shown little enterprise or power of manoeuvre.

The plan involved a preliminary movement of some 70 miles for the majority of the troops over open desert. This was to be covered in two marches on successive nights (the whole force being mechanised or motorised), the attack taking place on the early morning following the second night march. It would thus be necessary for the whole force to spend one day in the open desert, within about 30 miles of the enemy, and it was feared that, if the enemy observed this movement, heavy air attacks would be made by his numerically superior air force. This risk, however, had to be taken, and it was hoped to counter it by concealment and dispersion and by the protection of our fighter aircraft and anti-aircraft guns. In fact, the enemy made no attack whatever.

### 5. *The Battle of Sidi Barrani.*

14. Operations began on the night of the 7th/8th December, during which the whole force moved forward over the desert. The movement was made without difficulty, owing to good training and discipline, and the troops reached their appointed positions up to time.

During the 8th December the force remained in the desert, expecting attack by the enemy air force which never took place. Next night the force moved forward again and took up its positions for the next days attack. This movement also was made without a hitch.

15. The attack on Nibeiwa was begun at 0700 hours on the 9th December by 11th Indian Infantry Brigade (Brigadier Savory – consisting of 2nd Cameron Highlanders, I/6th Rajputana Rifles and 4/7th Rajput Regiment) and the 7th battalion R.T.R. The enemy force holding this camp was believed to consist of some 3,000 men with a considerable number of guns and tanks, under General Maletti. During a short bombardment the 7th R.T.R. moved forward and entered the perimeter at 0735 hours. They soon destroyed the enemy tanks and then met an extremely hot fire from artillery and weapons of all descriptions. This the heavy armour of the Infantry tanks resisted, to the surprise and demoralisation of the enemy. The leading infantry battalion, 2nd Cameron Highlanders, advanced in M.T. behind the tanks to within 700 yards of the perimeter, where they debussed and entered the camp. By 0830 hours the camp was completely in our hands. General Maletti was killed.

16. At 0830 hours the Commander of the 4th Indian Division ordered the 5th Indian Infantry Brigade (Brigadier Lloyd – consisting of 1st Royal Fusiliers, 3/1st Punjab Regiment and 4/6th Rajputana Rifles) to move to the West of the Tummar camps in readiness for an attack on them. The 16th British Infantry Brigade (Brigadier Lomax – consisting of 2nd Queens, 2nd Leicesters and 1st Argyll & Sutherland Highlanders) was moved up to a position just west of Nibeiwa. The artillery and 7th R.T.R., having refilled at Nibeiwa, also moved into position for the attacks on Tummar camps. The third brigade of the Indian Division, the 7th Brigade, was held in reserve. It took charge of prisoners and protected the line of communications, but took no part in the actual fighting.

At 1330 hours the artillery concentration on the Tummar camps began and at 1350 hours the 7th R.T.R., now reduced to 22 tanks, entered Tummar West from the North. The leading infantry, 1st Royal Fusiliers, followed in lorries

20 minutes after the tanks, and debussed within 500 yards of the camp. Events inside the camp followed much the same sequence as at Nibeiwa, except that there were few enemy tanks in this camp. After the occupation of Tummar West the Commander 4th Indian Division ordered an attack to be launched against Tummar East. Just as the advance began with the 7th R.T.R. leading, followed by one battalion, 4/6th Rajputana Rifles, an enemy counter-attack was met but quickly repulsed. By dark the greater part of Tummar East was in our hands.

17. At 1615 hours, in view of the successful progress of operations, the Commander of the 4th Indian Division ordered the 16th Infantry Brigade to push forward as far as possible before darkness towards Sidi Barrani. Two regiments of artillery were to join the brigade during the night, while the 7th R.T.R. were to refit as far as possible and be ready for operations next day.

18. Meanwhile 7th Armoured Division had successfully fulfilled its rôle of protecting the left flank of the 4th Indian Division and cutting the Sidi Barrani – Buq Buq road. By 1000 hours 4th Armoured Brigade, moving West of the enemy camps, had got astride the Sidi Barrani – Buq Buq road. The 7th Armoured Brigade remained in reserve. During this advance the 4th Armoured Brigade captured a number of prisoners and vehicles and inflicted considerable losses on the enemy.

19. At dawn on the 10th December the 16th Infantry Brigade advanced in lorries towards Sidi Barrani with the object of getting astride the roads leading Westwards and cutting off the Italian forces. The 11th Indian Infantry Brigade was moved up from Nibeiwa to near the Tummar camps, while the 5th Indian Infantry Brigade completed the occupation of Tummar East.

At about 0730 hours the right battalion of the 16th Brigade; 2nd Battalion Leicester Regiment, engaged a defended Italian camp and captured it, after a short fight, with about 2,000 prisoners of the 4th Blackshirt Division. Meanwhile the remainder of the 16th Infantry Brigade continued their advance in a violent dust storm. They suffered some casualties from enemy fire but continued to push on, and were assisted by the arrival of some 10 tanks of the 7th R.T.R. which over-ran some enemy guns. The 11th Indian Infantry Brigade moved up on the right flank of the 16th Brigade.

20. At about 1330 hours the Commander of the 4th Indian Division was at 16th Infantry Brigade Headquarters and ordered an attack on Sidi Barrani, placing part of 11th Indian Infantry Brigade under Brigadier Lomax. This attack was launched at 1615 hours by the 2nd Queen's on the right and 2nd Cameron Highlanders, on the left, supported by artillery fire, some tanks of the 7th R.T.R., and by an attack, by 2nd R.T.R. (cruiser tanks) North of the Sidi Barrani – Buq Buq road. The attack was completely successful, and Sidi Barrani was in our hands when darkness fell, many prisoners and guns being captured.

21. The force organised from Matruh Garrison had advanced towards Maktila camp and established itself two miles East of Maktila by the evening of the

8th December. This force was a composite one, in which the 3rd Battalion Coldstream Guards was the only complete unit. Detachments of Royal Artillery, 7th Hussars (light tanks), 1st Durham Light Infantry, 1st South Staffords, machine gunners from 1st Royal Northumberland Fusiliers and 1st Cheshires, as well as a number of dummy tanks, made up the balance. It remained in observation of Maktila camp until the afternoon of the 9th December, when, learning that Nibeiwa had been captured, Brigadier Selby gave orders to move forward and endeavour to prevent the withdrawal Westwards of the 1st Libyan Division. Owing to the comparative weakness of the force and difficult going, it was unable to prevent the withdrawal of the enemy towards Sidi Barrani, but pursued them with all possible speed on the 10th December. The situation at nightfall on the 10th December was that Sidi Barrani had been captured and the 2nd Libyan and 4th Blackshirt Divisions destroyed. East of Barrani, however, the 1st Libyan Division from Maktila was still of some fighting value, and an enemy camp at Point 90 had not been attacked and remained intact.

22. On the evening of the 10th December General O'Connor issued instructions to the Armoured Division to send a force early the following day to prevent any enemy withdrawal from the Sofafi area; to send another force to Buq Buq to deal with any enemy in that direction; and in the event of further retreat to pursue the enemy towards Halfaya, Sidi Omar and Sollum.

### 6. *Exploitation after Sidi Barrani.*

23. I had always intended if possible to send the 4th Indian Division to reinforce the Sudan during the winter 1940/41, in order to enable our forces in the Sudan to recapture Kassala and to take the offensive against the enemy. I had proposed to relieve them in the Western Desert by the 6th Australian Division as soon as this was ready and equipped. For several reasons, the principal of which was the availability of shipping, I had to decide while the battle of Sidi Barrani was still in progress whether or not to carry out this relief. There was an opportunity to do so after the operations of the 11th December and the capture of Sidi Barrani, since the supply organisation would only permit of a very limited force being used for further pursuit of the enemy. I decided therefore to withdraw the 4th Indian Division and to replace it by the 6th Australian Division as soon as this could be brought forward. The 16th Infantry Brigade, which had been attached to the 4th Indian Division, remained in the forward area available for pursuit.

I should have liked also to employ the New Zealand Brigade Group which had been in the forward area for some time and was available, but the New Zealand Division itself was not complete, one brigade being in the United Kingdom, and I knew that it was the wish of the New Zealand Government that the division should be employed as a whole if possible.

24. From the 11th December onwards the operations consisted of a pursuit by 7th Armoured Division, followed up by 16th Infantry Brigade.

The 7th Armoured Division advanced at first in two main groups, the 7th Armoured Brigade North of the escarpment towards Sollum and the 4th Armoured Brigade South of the escarpment towards Halfaya, Sidi Omar and Capuzzo. On the afternoon of the 11th December 7th Armoured Brigade made contact with a long enemy column between Buq Buq and Sollum. It promptly attacked and by dusk had secured 14,000 prisoners, 68 guns and much other material. By the 15th December all enemy troops had been driven out of Egypt, and the 7th Armoured Division had concentrated South-West of Bardia. The 4th Armoured Brigade now cut the Bardia – Tobruk road while the Support Group engaged the Western and South-Western defences of Bardia. Meanwhile, the 16th Infantry Brigade moved up to the South-East face of the Bardia perimeter, to cover our use of Sollum harbour. The greater part of the Italian army remaining in Cyrenaica had withdrawn within the defences of Bardia, which was now isolated. It was decided to capture Bardia with the 6th Australian Division as soon as ready, while 7th Armoured Division protected their left flank and prevented any movement along the Bardia – Tobruk road.

25. This ended the first phase of the operation, which may be called the Battle of Sidi Barrani. It had resulted in the destruction of the greater part of five enemy divisions. Over 38,000 prisoners, 400 guns, some 50 tanks and much other war material had been captured. Our own casualties were only 133 killed, 387 wounded and 8 missing.

26. This outstanding success may be attributed to –

(a) Good co-operation between the three Services;
(b) Effect of surprise;
(c) Fine leadership and fighting qualities displayed by all personnel.

Our equipment, in particular the Infantry Tanks, Cruiser Tanks and 25-pounders, proved to be excellent.

PART II. – SECOND PHASE –
OPERATIONS FROM BARDIA TO TOBRUK –
DECEMBER 15, 1940, TO JANUARY 21, 1941.
*7. Bardia – Enemy Position and Strength.*

27. The enemy forces within the perimeter of Bardia comprised the greater part of four infantry divisions, together with guns and tanks. Some of these formations had taken part in the later stages of the fighting after the capture of Sidi Barrani.

28. The defences of Bardia, apart from coastal and anti-aircraft defences, consisted of a perimeter seventeen miles in extent, lying mainly on a level plain South-West of the escarpment. The perimeter itself consisted of concrete posts at intervals of some seven hundred yards, containing machine guns and antitank guns, each post being wired and having an anti-tank ditch. Five hundred yards behind the first line was a second but less elaborate line of support posts. Outside the whole ran a continuous anti-tank trench and wire obstacle. Only at the

Southern end of the perimeter was there an additional switch line, three to four thousands yards from the outer line.

### 8. *Plan of Attack on Bardia.*

29. The troops available for the attack were:-

7th Armoured Division: Major-General Creagh.
6th Australian Division: Major-General Mackay.
16th Infantry Brigade.
7th Battalion R.T.R.: Now reduced to 26 tanks.
1st Battalion Royal Northumberland Fusiliers: Machine-gun battalion.
Corps Artillery: Consisting of one field and one medium regiment.

Two squadrons of the Australian Divisional Cavalry Regiment had been diverted to observe Jarabub, to which a considerable enemy force had withdrawn. The rôle of 7th Armoured Division was to prevent the enemy reinforcing from or escaping to the North, and the assaulting troops therefore consisted of approximately 20,000 men, 122 guns and 26 tanks.

30. The diminished resources of infantry tanks necessitated a bold employment of infantry both in the assault and in the exploitation. This demanded a high expenditure of ammunition for their protection. The period of sixteen days between the arrival of the first infantry outside Bardia and the launching of the attack was occupied mainly in bringing up large additional supplies of ammunition from railhead at Mersa Matruh. The harbour of Sollum, which the enemy withdrawal behind the defences of Bardia had put at our disposal, was used for this purpose, and its possession greatly facilitated the task.

31. The following was the general plan:-

One infantry battalion, of the 16th Australian Brigade, closely followed by engineers, was to attack at dawn at a point due West of Bardia, where the anti-tank ditch and the wire nearly coincided. Covered by a heavy artillery concentration, the battalion was to seize and hold a bridge-head while the engineers filled in the anti-tank ditch at five separate points. This achieved, tanks and infantry were to enter the perimeter and sweep South-Eastwards on a wide front as far as the road Bardia – Capuzzo and the edge of the escarpment overlooking Bardia. Thereafter units of the 17th Australian Brigade were to break into the perimeter South of the original point of entry, and, driving still further to the South-East, contain the enemy forces manning the strongest positions at the Southern end. The attack would then be exploited East and North-East to Bardia.

While these operations were in progress demonstrations were to be made against parts of the perimeter remote from the real attack; on the North by 7th Armoured Division, and on the South by those units of 17th Australian Brigade not taking part in the attack. The area North of the road Bardia – Tobruk was to be subjected to heavy bombardment both from the sea and from the air.

### 9. *The Assault on Bardia.*

32. By the 27th December, the 16th and 17th Australian Brigades were in position opposite the defences, and on New Year's Day the 19th Australian Brigade also arrived. On the 3rd January, at 0530 hours, the attack began. The 2/1st Battalion Australian Infantry successfully established the bridge-head, and the engineers had completed their task within 50 minutes. 16th and 17th Australian Brigades (Brigadiers Allen and Savige) captured their objectives with small loss, in spite of a counter-attack by enemy tanks. At 1745 hours on 4th January tanks and infantry entered Bardia; and on the 5th the defenders of the South-Eastern sector surrendered. 45,000 prisoners and 462 guns, of which 216 were field guns, were taken – 117 light and 12 medium tanks were also captured.

### 10. *Tobruk. – Enemy Position and Strength.*

33. With the loss of Bardia, the Italian forces remaining in Cyrenaica were:-

(*a*) At Tobruk:-
> 61st Sirte Infantry Division.
> Headquarters and Corps troops of XXII Corps.
> Coast Defence and Anti-Aircraft units of Tobruk garrison.
> Remnants of the divisions from the forward areas.

(*b*) Further West –
> 60th Infantry Division.

(*c*) About Mechili –
> Nucleus of armoured formation under General Babini.

Even before Bardia fell I had decided that an attack on Tobruk was justified on both operational and administrative grounds. By the 6th January, 7th Armoured Division had cut the roads Tobruk – Derna and Tobruk – Mechili, and was in contact with the perimeter and with enemy troops East of Derna and Mechili, causing the enemy to abandon the aerodromes at Gazala, Tmimi and Bomba. By the 7th January, 19th Australian Infantry Brigade (Brigadier Robertson) was in position facing the Eastern defences, and the remainder of 6th Australian Division, with 7th R.T.R., was also moving Westwards.

34. The perimeter of Tobruk was 27 miles in length and resembled that of Bardia, except that the anti-tank ditch was at many points not deep enough to be effective. Anti-tank minefields were known to exist. The harbour and installations of Tobruk were well defended with coast defence and anti-aircraft guns.

### 11. *Plan of Attack on Tobruk.*

35. The following troops were available for the attack:-

7th Armoured Division.
6th Australian Division.
7th Battalion Royal Tank Regiment (consisting now of only 16 tanks).
1st Battalion Royal Northumberland Fusiliers (Machine-gun battalion).
1st Battalion Cheshire Regiment (Machine-gun battalion).

Corps Artillery, consisting of two field and one medium regiments, one additional medium battery.

36. As at Bardia, preparations were made to provide a heavy scale of artillery support. Between the 7th and the 19th January, ammunition was brought up and artillery positions prepared. Detailed and continuous reconnaissance of the forward defences and aggressive patrolling against the perimeter at points distant from that selected for the attack were carried out while preparations went forward.

37. The general plan was as follows. 16th Australian Infantry Brigade and infantry tanks were to penetrate the perimeter at a point on its Southern face where the anti-tank ditch was shallow, and where the minefields could be easily removed. The point chosen was midway between the roads Tobruk – Bardia and Tobruk – El Adem, whose junction lay 8,000 yards inside the perimeter at Sidi Mahmoud. Their task was to secure a line some 4,000 yards from the point of entry, which would involve the over-running of all the forward enemy battery positions in this sector. When this line had been secured, 19th Australian Infantry Brigade was to form up within the captured battery area and advance under a barrage to the junction of the two main roads, at Sidi Mahmoud. From this point, 19th Brigade would exploit South-West, West and North; while units of the 17th Brigade would assume control of the ground overlooking the declivities towards the sea. 16th Australian Infantry Brigade would then concentrate near the road Tobruk – El Adem. The infantry tanks were to be used solely to reduce the defensive and battery positions in the Southern sector of the perimeter.

The task of the artillery, which amounted to 146 guns and 20 howitzers, was:-

(*a*)  To provide a barrage and flank concentrations for the initial penetration by the leading battalion.

(*b*)  To neutralise hostile batteries on the entry of the infantry tanks.

(*c*)  To provide barrages for the protection of infantry in the later stages of the advance, and a concentration on the Sidi Mahmoud area.

In addition, a proportion of guns was to be engaged throughout on counter-battery rôles.

7th Armoured Division, as at Bardia, was to make demonstrations against the defences from the North and to prevent either reinforcement or escape.

### 12. *Assault on Tobruk.*

38. The attack was launched at 0530 hours on the 21st January, having been postponed for one day owing to severe sandstorms. 19th Australian Brigade followed the 16th through the gap at 0830 hours. The fire of our artillery was heavy and accurate, and the enemy opposition was not great. Both brigades were established on their objectives by twelve noon with small loss. Armoured carriers of the Divisional Cavalry Regiment reached a point on the edge of the escarpment 3,000 yards above Tobruk early in the afternoon, but were compelled to withdraw owing to accurate fire from the enemy coast defence and anti-aircraft guns

at Tobruk. Determined opposition was encountered about Palastrino, a point in the middle of the perimeter 9,000 yards South-West of Tobruk. Elsewhere successful exploitation carried the advance to the edge of the escarpment overlooking the town. And by nightfall the Western and South-Western portion of the perimeter, amounting to about one-third of the whole, was in our hands.

39. Early on the morning of the 22nd, the town was entered without resistance. During the night, fires and explosions had been seen and heard, and it was found that demolitions had been carried out in the harbour and on other installations and stores. Further West, the Free French companies of the Armoured Division had penetrated the perimeter near the sea. No further resistance was offered. The number of prisoners amounted to nearly 30,000, among whom were many specialists and a naval detachment of over 2,000. 236 guns of 75 mm. and over, 87 tanks and much motor transport were also taken, but many of these proved to have been damaged before capture.

40. Co-operation by Royal Air Force and Royal Naval units was excellent and invaluable. For three nights before the battle the Royal Air Force bombed Palastrino, Sidi Mahmoud, the harbour, the road leading up the escarpment out of Tobruk towards Sidi Mahmoud, and other key areas. These areas were also bombed from 0330 to 0600 hours on the first day of the battle, and thereafter at need. The Royal Navy bombarded Palastrino and the road leading out of Tobruk as well as two areas on the North-West of the perimeter near the road Tobruk – Derna on the nights 19th/20th and 20th/21st January. In the course of this bombardment from both air and sea the cruiser *San Giorgio* was sunk in the harbour.

## PART III. – FINAL PHASE – INTERCEPTION AND FINAL DESTRUCTION OF ENEMY NORTH OF AGEDABIA, JANUARY 22 TO FEBRUARY 7.

### 13. *Preparations for further Advance.*

41. The fall of Tobruk left the remainder of the Italian forces in Cyrenaica in two main detachments. The first comprised the 60th Division, less one Infantry Brigade Group, in position just East of Derna. The second, which consisted of a formation of about 160 tanks, and the remaining Brigade Group of the 60th Division, was in the area Mechili under the command of General Babini. The Northern force held the coast road to Benghazi, while the Southern lay across the track which led there direct across the desert, at the point where it is joined by the only tracks leading Southward through the Jebel Akhdar from the coast.

   The dispersal of the enemy in two forces, the strong grounds for belief that no reinforcements had yet reached Cyrenaica, the shortening of our lines of communication by the capture of Tobruk and its harbour, and the additional motor transport and fuel, taken at Tobruk and Bardia, offered the opportunity of a rapid advance on Benghazi and a decisive victory.

42. The enemy's position at Derna was a strong one, unless it were threatened by an advance from Mechili. The first plan considered was to contain him at Derna until the force at Mechili could be attacked and destroyed. The 19th Australian Infantry Brigade was moved forward in motor transport on the 22nd January immediately after the fall of Tobruk, to relieve patrols of 7th Armoured Division who were in contact East of Derna. The bulk of 7th Armoured Division started on the same day towards Mechili and gained contact with the enemy before that place by the evening of the 23rd January.

During the night the 26th–27th January the enemy force at Mechili withdrew North-Westwards towards Slonta, the Armoured Division and the Royal Air Force inflicting loss on him as he went. The flank of the enemy at Derna was thus exposed, and the desert route to Benghazi opened. But 7th Armoured Division was by now reduced to 50 cruiser tanks and 95 light tanks; and our supply situation in the forward area did not yet permit of an advance.

43. I discussed the situation with General O'Connor, and approved a plan for a rapid advance by the Armoured Division and an infantry brigade group South of the Jebel Akhdar by the desert route to cut the road South of Benghazi, while the remainder of the force pressed the enemy along the Northern route. The advance was to be made as soon as the supply situation permitted, which was estimated as the 12th February, by which date also a reinforcement of a fresh unit of cruiser tanks was expected.

44. The 6th Australian Division sent the 17th Australian Infantry Brigade to increase the pressure on Derna while the 16th Australian Infantry Brigade was to join 7th Armoured Division in the Mechili area as soon as depots of supplies were established in that area. 7th Armoured Division was to show activity to the North-West, but to do nothing to attract attention to the desert route South of Mechili.

### 14. *Interception and Destruction of Enemy.*

45. Early on the 30th January the enemy withdrew from his advanced positions East of Derna whilst still holding his ground on the Wadi Derna. By Monday the 3rd February air reconnaissance proved beyond doubt that the enemy had decided on further withdrawal. Large columns were moving Westward, tanks were being entrained at Barce and general cessation of hostile air activity indicated the abandoning of aerodromes South of Benghazi. It was therefore decided to move, at once across the desert without awaiting completion of force or of supply arrangements. H.Q., 13th Corps, accordingly directed 7th Armoured Division to move on Msus with all available resources, from where it could operate against either Soluch or Agedabia as required; 6th Australian Division was to press hard against the enemy's rearguard on the Northern route. The R.A.F. was ordered to bomb the railway terminals at Barce and Soluch and the junction at Benghazi, in order to interfere with the move of enemy tanks to what might become a decisive flank.

46. 7th Armoured Division moved from its position about Mechili at first light on the 4th February. The cruiser reinforcements had not arrived and the tank strength of this Division was now the equivalent of one Armoured Brigade. Difficulties were further increased by lack of reconnaissance of the ground between Mechili and Msus, which, for purposes of deception, had been previously forbidden. The first 50 miles was extremely rough going, which reduced the pace and took toll of vehicles; particularly light tanks. West of Bir-el-Gerrari the track improved and the advance was continued in moonlight. By daybreak on the 5th February the Division was just east of Msus, which had been occupied by our armoured cars.

From the administrative aspect the accelerated advance South-Westwards of 7th Armoured Division placed a severe strain on the maintenance organisation since the stocking up of new advanced depots near Mechili had only just begun. The Armoured Division moved with two days' rations, a sufficiency of ammunition and petrol, but the margin was very close.

47. Early on the 5th February Commander, 7th Armoured Division, sent forward two detachments. The Southern (consisting of 11th Hussars (less one squadron), one squadron K.D.G., one battery each 3rd and 4th R.H.A., one anti-tank battery and 2nd Rifle Brigade) was directed straight to the coast via Antelat with orders to cut the main road Benghazi – Tripoli North of Agedabia. Antelat was to be avoided if found to be occupied by the enemy. The 4th Armoured Brigade (7th Hussars and 2nd R.T.R.) was to follow this detachment as soon as possible. The Northern detachment (comprising 1st R.H.A. and 1st K.R.R.C.) was directed on Soluch, via Sceleidima.

At 1700 hours the same, day, situation 13th Corps was briefly as follows:-

(*a*) 6th Australian Division pressing hard on retreating enemy 60th Division along the coast between Derna and Barce.

(*b*) Northern detachment of 7th Armoured Division closing in on the main road West of Soluch, having overcome enemy resistance at Sceleidima.

(*c*) 4th Armoured Brigade approaching Beda Fomm.

(*d*) Southern detachment of 7th Armoured Division established since 1200 hours astride the two main routes South-West of Beda Fomm, with armoured car patrols, both to the North and South.

(*e*) Remainder 7th Armoured Division in area of Antelat.

(*f*) Advanced H.Q. 13th Corps moving to, or at, Msus.

On this same evening a retreating enemy column, strength approximately 5,000, mainly artillery, but with a considerable proportion of civilians, and a number of guns, met the Southern detachment block and, completely surprised, surrendered. Meanwhile to the North a further enemy column was surrounded and captured by 4th Armoured Brigade.

48. From an early hour on the 6th February the enemy main columns began to appear, and severe fighting occurred throughout the day as successive enemy

groups, including a large number of tanks, attempted unsuccessfully to break through the 4th Armoured Brigade, later reinforced by 7th Armoured Brigade (1st R.T.R.) as more and more enemy tanks continued to appear – 84 were put out of action during the day's fighting. By nightfall the situation was unchanged. The enemy's position was desperate, with a confused mass of vehicles almost 20 miles in length pinned to the roads between our Armoured Brigades in the South and the Northern detachment in the Soluch area, now beginning to turn South-West. Certain enemy groups had, however, managed to evade the 4th Armoured Brigade by moving through the sand dune area between the main road and the sea. One group in particular, consisting of tanks strongly supported by infantry, repeatedly attacked the Southern detachment, now reinforced by a third R.H.A. battery, during the night 6th/7th February and early morning 7th February. In all nine attacks were delivered against 2nd Rifle Brigade, and although on one occasion tanks penetrated to the Reserve Company areas, all were repulsed. These enemy attacks were pressed home with considerable vigour, but lacked co-ordination, 1st R.T.R. (7th Armoured Brigade) had been put under command of the Southern detachment early on the 7th February, but did not arrive in time to take part in this fight.

Shortly after dawn on the 7th February a final attempt was made by 30 enemy tanks to break through. When this, too, failed, General Berganzoli surrendered unconditionally.

49. Previously, on the 6th February, the Corps Commander had by wireless directed 6th Australian Division to send a detachment, made mobile from divisional resources, along the coast road to Ghemines, in order to complete the encirclement of the enemy. This detachment, comprising the equivalent of a Brigade Group, pressed on with great resolution and received the surrender of Benghazi, but did not reach Ghemines until about noon on the 7th February, by which time all fighting had ceased.

50. The surrender completed the destruction of the Italian Tenth Army, whose commander, General Tellera, was killed during the action. Enemy losses in this final phase were approximately 20,000 personnel, of whom the large majority were captured, 120 tanks and 190 guns.

### PART IV. – SUMMARY AND ACKNOWLEDGEMENTS.

51. During the two months from the 7th December to the 7th February, the Army of the Nile had advanced 500 miles. They had beaten and destroyed an Italian army of four Corps comprising nine divisions and part of a tenth, and had captured 130,000 prisoners, 400 tanks and 1,290 guns, besides vast quantities of other war material. In these operations we never employed a larger force than two divisions, of which one was armoured. Actually three divisions took part, since the 6th Australian Division relieved the 4th Indian Division after the Sidi Barrani battle. The 7th Armoured Division took part in the operations throughout, at the end of which it was practically reduced to a skeleton.

Our casualties were extremely light and amounted to 500 killed, 1,373 wounded, 55 missing only.

52. The outstanding success of these operations was very largely due to the most capable commanders of the formations engaged: Lieut.-General Sir Maitland Wilson, G.O.C.-in-C. Egypt; Lieut.-General R.N. O'Connor, commanding Western Desert Corps; Major-General M.O.M. Creagh, commanding 7th Armoured Division; Major-General N.M. Beresford-Peirse, commanding 4th Indian Division; and Major-General I.G. Mackay, commanding 6th Australian Division.

53. All combatant troops engaged displayed high fighting qualities and resolute skill in manoeuvre. The 7th Armoured Division, during three months' continuous fighting in the van of the battle, showed great tactical efficiency and powers of endurance; the untiring work of the technical personnel which enabled so many vehicles to be kept in action for so long a period was admirable.

Special mention must be made of one unit, the 11th Hussars. As the only armoured car regiment in the force it was continually in the Western Desert for a period of about nine months, from the entry of Italy into the war till the fall of Benghazi. During this period it always supplied the most advanced elements in close contact with the enemy. Seldom can a unit have had a more prolonged spell of work in the front line or performed it with greater skill and boldness.

7th Royal Tank Regiment, equipped with infantry tanks, assaulted five strongly defended positions (Nibeiwa, Tummar, Sidi Barrani, Bardia, Tobruk) in a little over one month, and advanced more than 200 miles during this period. The resolution shown in these assaults and the technical skill and hard work by which so many tanks were kept in action over so long a range deserve great credit.

The Royal Engineer units and Royal Corps of Signals did much hard and admirable work.

54. The work of the ancillary corps, Royal Army Service Corps, Royal Army Ordnance Corps, Royal Army Medical Corps, Pioneer Corps, deserves all praise. Conditions in the desert were difficult and onerous. Drivers of lorries or ambulances had to cover long distances over bad tracks, sometimes in dust storms; mechanics in the field and at the Base worked long hours on repair and maintenance; pioneers unloaded stores under air bombing or artillery fire.

55. The Army owes much to the Royal Navy, under Admiral Sir Andrew Cunningham, for its support through the operation, both in prearranged bombardments of enemy positions previous to the attacks on Sidi Barrani, Bardia and Tobruk, and in answering emergency calls during the actual attacks. The effect of these accurate bombardments on enemy morale alone was very considerable, and did much to simplify the task of the Army. Lastly, the maintenance problems in this quick-moving operation over a distance of 500 miles would have been insurmountable without the Navy's assistance in keeping open the sea supply lines and opening up of Sollum, Bardia and Tobruk, thereby shortening the

L. of C. and releasing Motor Transport for the vital task of stocking up successive Field Supply Depots.

56. During the operations the Royal Air Force, under the able direction of Air Chief Marshal Sir Arthur Longmore, obtained and maintained, in spite of inferior numbers, complete superiority over the Italian air force. They thereby contributed greatly to the successes won by enabling our ground forces to move freely, with little interference or loss from enemy air attack. They also provided accurate information of enemy movements, and on many occasions inflicted considerable loss on his forces. The Army owes a special debt to Air Commodore R. Collishaw, commanding air forces in the Western Desert, for his wholehearted co-operation and for the energy and optimism which were an inspiration to all.

# 3

# GENERAL WAVELL'S DESPATCH ON OPERATIONS FEBRUARY 1941 TO 15 JULY 1941

*The War Office, July 1916*
OPERATIONS IN THE MIDDLE EAST
FROM 7TH FEBRUARY, 1941 TO 15TH JULY, 1941
*The following Despatch was submitted to the Secretary of State for War on 5th September, 1941, by GENERAL SIR ARCHIBALD P. WAVELL, G.C.B., C.M.G., M.C., Commander-in-Chief, in the Middle East.*

OPERATIONS IN THE MIDDLE EAST.
7th FEBRUARY, 1941, TO 15th JULY, 1941.
*Situation after Capture of Benghazi.*

1. While the operations in the Western Desert and Cyrenaica, described in my despatch covering the period 7th December, 1940, to 7th February, 1941, were taking place, a campaign which was to prove of almost equal importance to the fortunes of the British Forces in the Middle East was being fought in Greece and Albania.

The unprovoked and treacherous attack of the Italians on Greece which had begun at the end of October, 1940, had been repulsed by a swift Greek counter-stroke, and the Italians had been driven back into Albania. During the winter, of 1940/41 the Greeks, in spite of appalling conditions of weather and in most difficult country, gradually forced the Italians back in Albania and had hopes of driving them out of Albania altogether. A small British air force with certain army units for its protection and service, had been in Greece since November.

2. At first the senior partner of the Axis had seemed to be disinterested in the Italian misfortunes in Albania as well as in Libya, but early in 1941 German troops were fully established in occupation of Rumania and it became clear that a further movement south-east was impending. The attitude of Bulgaria, obviously to be the next victim of German aggression, did not long remain doubtful, and it soon became fairly certain that her rulers did not intend to resist a German advance through Bulgaria, which might be directed either at Turkey or at Greece, our only two remaining allies in Europe who were likely to resist German aggression.

3. In the middle of January, while operations against Tobruk were still in progress, I had been ordered by the War Cabinet to visit Greece and to make an offer to the Greeks of armoured troops, field artillery, anti-tank artillery and anti-

aircraft guns to assist their forces in the defence of Salonika and Macedonia against possible German aggression. I was in Athens from 13th to 17th January and had a series of conferences with the Greek Premier, General Metaxas, and the Greek Commander-in-Chief, General Papagos. As a result, the offer of the British Government was declined, mainly on the grounds that the landing of further British forces in Greece was likely to provoke German aggression without being strong enough to check it. Had this offer been accepted, it is improbable that it would have been possible to continue the operations in Cyrenaica beyond Tobruk. After the refusal of assistance by the Greeks, an offer was made by the Prime Minister of assistance, especially by air forces, to Turkey, which was also declined on similar grounds.

4. Immediately after the fall of Benghazi on 7th February, I received a telegram from the Chiefs of Staff setting out a new policy for the forces in the Middle East. General Metaxas had died towards the end of January and the new Greek Government had sent a request on 8th February for information as to what help we could afford them in the event of a German attack. The War Cabinet accordingly directed that no operations were to be undertaken beyond the frontier of Cyrenaica, which should be held with the minimum possible force necessary to secure the flank of our Egyptian base, and that it was essential to be able to send the largest possible army and air forces from the Middle East to assist the Greeks against a German attack through Bulgaria. At the same time the operations against the Italian Dodecanese, which were in preparation, were to be pressed on and undertaken at the earliest possible moment.

5. The Chiefs of Staff's telegram stated that the Foreign Secretary, Mr. Eden, and the Chief of the Imperial General Staff, General Sir John Dill, were setting out by air for Cairo on 12th February to discuss our policy and strategy in the Middle East. They were delayed owing to bad weather in the Mediterranean and did not arrive in Cairo till late at night on 19th February, five valuable days being thus lost at a critical time. Shortly after their arrival, on 22nd February, British representatives, including Mr. Eden, General Sir John Dill, Air Chief Marshal Sir Arthur Longmore (Air Officer Commanding-in-Chief, Middle East) and myself flew to Greece and held a series of conversations that evening at Tatoi Palace near Athens.

*Military Position in Middle East at beginning of February.*
6. It is necessary at this stage to recapitulate the troops available in the Middle East Command and their state of readiness for battle.
    The following formations existed:-

| | |
|---|---|
| *In Western Desert* | 7th Armoured Division. |
| | 6th Australian Division. |
| *In Egypt* | 2nd Armoured Division. |
| | New Zealand Division. |

|                  | 6th British Division (in process of formation). |
|                  | Polish Brigade Group. |
| *In Palestine*   | 7th Australian Division. |
|                  | 9th Australian Division. |
| *In Eritrea*     | (Engaged in front of Keren). |
|                  | 4th Indian Division. |
|                  | 5th Indian Division. |
| *In East Africa* | 1st South African Division, |
|                  | 11th African Division, |
|                  | 12th African Division (about to begin operations against Kismayu). |

7. Of the above, the 7th Armoured Division had been fighting continuously for eight months and was mechanically incapable of further action; only a fraction of its tanks had succeeded, thanks to most skilful maintenance, in reaching Beda Fomm for the final engagement of the Cyrenaican campaign. It was obvious that the armoured vehicles of this division would require a complete overhaul and would be in workshops for many weeks to come. For all practical purposes the 7th Armoured Division had ceased to be available as a fighting formation.

The 2nd Armoured Division, which arrived from the United Kingdom on 1st January, 1941, consisted of two Cruiser regiments and two Light Tank regiments only, the other two regiments of the division having been sent out some months previously to bring up to strength the 7th Armoured Division which had always been short of two regiments of its establishment. These two regiments of the 2nd Armoured Division had formed part of the 7th Armoured Division throughout the Western Desert operation and shared with the rest of the 7th Armoured Division the same mechanical exhaustion.

Thus all the armoured troops available were the four regiments and Support Group of the 2nd Armoured Division, and from these I had to find armoured forces for both Cyrenaica and Greece. The Commander of the 2nd Armoured Division Major-General J.C. Tilly, on arrival in Egypt gave me a most alarming account of the mechanical state of his two Cruiser regiments, of which he said the tracks were practically worn out, while the engines had already done a considerable mileage. He had been informed that fresh tracks would be supplied him in the Middle East, which had been specially made in Australia. After some investigation these tracks were discovered but on trial proved to be practically useless; and the two Cruiser regiments continued with their old tracks, which it was hoped would give less trouble in the desert than they had at home.

8. Of the three Australian divisions, the 6th Australian Division had taken part in the Cyrenaican campaign from Bardia to Benghazi, was seasoned and fully equipped and had not suffered heavy casualties. The 7th Australian Division had had no training as a division and was still in process of equipment, while the 9th Australian Division had only recently arrived, was only partially trained and was very short of equipment.

The New Zealand Division was fully trained and equipped and available for operations, but the 6th British Division, which was being formed out of various British battalions in Egypt, had practically speaking no existence as a division and was without artillery and supporting arms; it was being trained for landing operations against the Italian Dodecanese. The Polish Brigade Group was available but was not fully equipped.

The 4th and 5th Indian Divisions were engaged in front of Keren; it was hoped, should Keren fall and the campaign in Eritrea be concluded, to withdraw one of these divisions to garrison Cyrenaica; meantime neither division could be reckoned as available.

Of the troops in East Africa, the South African Division had been provided by South Africa for the operations in East Africa only and had not been released for operations further north, while the two African divisions were not suitable in personnel, training or equipment for operations in North Africa or on the continent of Europe.

9. Thus the maximum force that could be made available for Greece was part of the 2nd Armoured Division, the New Zealand Division, two Australian Divisions (the 6th and 7th) and the Polish Brigade Group, and of these both the 7th Australian Division and the Polish Brigade Group were still incomplete in equipment. It was not considered that any smaller force than the above would be likely to affect the operations in Greece, but the despatch of this force involved removing from the Middle East practically the whole of the troops which were fully equipped and fit for operations.

10. At the time when the decision as to the maximum force which could be despatched to Greece had to be made, there seemed no serious risk to our position anywhere in North Africa. The Italian armies in Cyrenaica had been so completely defeated that any counter-attack by them could be ruled out for some time to come, practically the whole of their armoured fighting vehicles and nearly all the Italian artillery in North Africa had been captured or destroyed and the fighting value of the Italian troops remaining in Tripolitania could, for all practical purposes, be discounted.

Though unconfirmed reports had been received from time to time of the preparation of German troops for despatch to Libya and of their progress via Italy and Sicily, no definite information to justify our expecting the presence of German troops in Africa had been received up to the middle of February. Our intelligence from Italy was meagre in the extreme and usually unreliable; nor were sufficient long range aircraft available for more than a very occasional reconnaissance of shipping in Italian harbours or in Tripoli. From North Africa itself our intelligence reports were practically none, since no service of agents had been established there during the period before Italy came into the war nor was it possible now to establish one. We were thus working almost entirely in the dark as to the possibility of German formations being sent to Libya, and on the whole the balance of our information was against any such troops having been sent or being on their way to Libya. Actually, the landing of a German Light Armoured Division at Tripoli had begun early in February.

I estimated that it would be at least two months after the landing of German forces at Tripoli before they could undertake a serious offensive against Cyrenaica, and that, therefore, there was not likely to be any serious threat to our positions there before May at the earliest. I accordingly considered that a garrison of one armoured brigade and one division would be sufficient to leave as a flank guard in Cyrenaica and that it would be safe to leave comparatively unequipped and untrained troops there so long as their training and equipment would be completed by May, by which time I hoped to have reinforcements available of at least one Indian Division from the Sudan.

I had intended originally that the division to be left in Cyrenaica should be the 6th Australian Division, and that the 7th Australian Division should be the first Australian division to proceed to Greece. This would mean that at least one fully equipped and seasoned division would be available for the defence of Cyrenaica for the first month or so, since it was calculated that the despatch of the total force to Greece would take 10 weeks to complete. General Blamey, commanding the Australian Forces, insisted, however, and as it proved rightly so, that the 7th Division was not sufficiently trained or equipped and that the 6th Division must be the first to proceed. This involved relieving the 6th Australian Division at once by the 9th Australian Division, which was only partially trained and equipped.

The armoured troops for the defence of Cyrenaica would have to be found by taking one brigade from the 2nd Armoured Division, leaving the other brigade available for despatch to Greece; both brigades would consist of one Cruiser regiment and one light tank regiment only. I decided to send part of the Support Group with each brigade and to send the Headquarters of the 2nd Armoured Division to Cyrenaica. General Tilly, soon after reaching Egypt, had died and Major-General Gambier-Parry was now in command of the division.

To increase the armoured troops in Cyrenaica, I decided to form a unit from captured Italian medium tanks.

### Conversations with Greek Government.
11. At the conversations held at Tatoi Palace on the evening of 22nd February, the Greek Commander-in-Chief, General Papagos, described his proposals for defence in the event of a German attack on Greece. It will be obvious that against a German attack through Bulgaria the long narrow strip of Macedonia and Western Thrace would be, in spite of the limited approaches through the mountain ranges to the north, extremely difficult to defend owing to the lack of depth. The Greeks had prepared a fortified line covering Macedonia which had considerable strength; but the greater part of the garrison had already been taken for operations in Albania, and the troops remaining, even with the proposed British reinforcements, would be insufficient to hold this long line. The same

objections applied to a somewhat shorter position approximately on the line of the Struma Valley covering Salonika. West of Salonika there was a much shorter and naturally strong defensive line along the line of hills west of the Vardar, following in part the line of the Aliakhmon river. This defensive position was called by General Papagos the "Aliakhmon Line." He stated that, if the Yugoslavs would act as allies, there was every advantage in holding a line covering Salonika since this was the only port through which munitions and supplies could be sent to Yugoslavia; in view, however, of the dubious attitude of the Yugoslavs it was impossible to rely on their cooperation; and he therefore proposed to withdraw the Greek troops in Macedonia and Eastern Thrace, except for covering detachments, to the Aliakhmon Line to prepare a defensive position there. He also indicated that it would probably be necessary to begin the withdrawal of the Greek forces in Albania to a shorter line and to use a part of them for the reinforcement of the Aliakhmon Line. He stated that it would require some twenty days to withdraw the troops in Macedonia and that he would then have a concentration of thirty-five battalions on the Aliakhmon line with one or two divisions in reserve. When joined by the British contingent, this would constitute a formidable defensive force in a very strong, natural position. The main danger to it lay in the exposure of the left-flank if German forces succeeded in advancing through Southern Yugoslavia and in entering Greece by the valley of the Cherna or Monastir Gap. It was considered, however, that the Yugoslavs, even if they would not beforehand make common cause with the Allies in resisting the Germans, would fight to deny them passage through Yugoslavia and that, if so, the mountainous nature of the country would make the German turning movement slow and difficult.

The proposals of General Papagos appeared to offer a reasonable prospect of establishing an effective defence against German aggression in the north-east of Greece. It was recognised that our chief dangers would come from our inferiority in the air, the uncertainty of the Yugoslav attitude and the dangers to our shipping in the narrow waters of the Aegean. It was considered, however, that the importance of bringing timely assistance to Greece was such that these risks were acceptable. The conference agreed to the proposals of General Papagos; and it was understood that he would at once begin the withdrawal of troops from Macedonia to the Aliakhmon line.

12. While active preparations were made for the despatch of the force to Greece, the Foreign Secretary and the Chief of the Imperial General Staff, accompanied by my Chief of the General Staff, proceeded to Turkey for discussions with the Turkish Government and General Staff. Though the Turks showed themselves still cordial to the alliance and approved our action in supporting Greece, they professed themselves unable, owing to lack of modern equipment, to take any action should the Germans enter Bulgaria, or to give assistance to the Greeks should the Germans attack them. While these conversations were still in progress the Germans, on 1st March, entered Bulgaria.

13. From Turkey the party proceeded direct on a further visit to Athens. On arrival there they found to their dismay that General Papagos had changed his attitude. He had not, apparently for political reasons, ordered the withdrawal of the troops in Macedonia to the Aliakhmon Line and he now declared this to be impossible in view of the German entry into Bulgaria, since the troops might be attacked while in process of withdrawal. He also stated that any withdrawal of reserves from Albania was impossible. He now proposed that the British contingent should land at Salonika and be sent forward to hold the advanced line in Macedonia which he had agreed at the previous conference was strategically unsound.

The British representatives were therefore faced with the situation that, instead of a strong and effective Greek force to hold the Aliakhmon Line, there would only be one weak division, and that there was every prospect of the Greek forces being defeated in detail. In these circumstances I was summoned to Athens and a series of long conferences took place between 2nd and 5th March, as a result of which it was decided that the Greek army should leave three divisions in Macedonia to defend the prepared positions on the frontier, but would concentrate on the Aliakhmon Line three divisions and seven independent battalions, to hold the line and prepare it for defence until the arrival of the British contingent, which would be disembarked mainly at the Piraeus, except for certain units and stores which would be landed at Volos. This was a very unsatisfactory arrangement in comparison with the original proposal but it was found impossible to persuade the Greeks to move back the troops in Macedonia, and the alternative of refusing to send aid to the Greeks altogether seemed politically impossible.

14. The despatch of the British force to Greece began on 5th March. The formations were to proceed in the following order:-

1st Armoured Brigade.
New Zealand Division.
6th Australian Division.
Polish Independent Brigade Group.
7th Australian Division.

It was estimated that the programme would be completed by 11th May.

### Concentration of British Forces in Greece

15. General Sir H.M. Wilson had been selected for command of the British forces in Greece, his place in Cyrenaica being taken by Lieut.-General P. Neame from Palestine. General Wilson arrived in Athens on 4th March, but owing to the insistence of the Greek Government on the avoidance of anything that might be held to provoke the Germans he was compelled for a month to remain incognito under the pseudonym of Mr. Watt. This restriction hampered him in supervising the occupation of the Aliakhmon position and in reconnoitring the ground over which operations might take place. Several representations to the Greek

Government, however, were met with a request that his incognito should be preserved, although it was quite obvious that the Germans were well informed both of his presence and of the landing of British troops. It was agreed with the Greek Government that General Wilson, when the time came, should be in command of all the troops, British and Greek, in the Aliakhmon position. This force was subsequently entitled "W" Force. The Greek portion of it was known as the Central Macedonian Army. Its original composition was the 12th Division from Macedonia (six battalions, one field battery, one or two mountain batteries and a group of seven 150 mm. guns); the 20th Division from Florina (six battalions, one or two field batteries and one or two mountain batteries); and the 19th Mechanized Division from Larissa, which had only recently been formed, had little training and was of slight value. The 19th Division was removed to another front on the arrival of the New Zealand Division. There were also seven battalions to be withdrawn from Western Thrace. This Greek force consisted of second line troops of doubtful fighting value, and was a very poor substitute for the original force of five good divisions promised by General Papagos.

16. The general situation in Greece at this time was that practically the whole of the Greek army was involved in Albania, where some 300,000 troops had been concentrated. The aim of the Greek army in Albania had been, ever since their successful counter-attack at the end of 1940, to reach the line Berat – Valona. Not only would this line enable them considerably to shorten their front, but it was estimated that if the port of Valona passed out of Italian hands, the Italians would be quite unable to support the large force they had assembled in northern Albania. The Greeks had made frequent representations to the British Government that British naval and air forces should combine to prevent the transport of reinforcements from Italy across the Adriatic to Albania. In the narrow waters of the Adriatic it was impossible to maintain a sufficient naval force, and our air resources were never sufficient to keep up a heavy scale of attack on the ports in Italy or Albania. Consequently the Italians were able to keep up a continual flow of reinforcements into Albania and to prevent the Greeks from attaining their main objective of Valona. As a result of the appalling conditions of their long winter campaign the Greek army had begun to deteriorate in morale and fighting value.

When the German menace developed it would obviously have been sound strategy for the Greeks to withdraw from Albania to a shorter front, so as to make available reserves for north-eastern Greece to meet the German attack. General Papagos, however, while recognising the theoretical soundness of this move, felt that a withdrawal would have a disastrous effect on the morale of the Greek army after its series of successes over the Italians. Further, the lack of mechanical transport and shortage even of pack animals, together with the very poor communications available, made it almost impossible to transfer any considerable portion of the Greek army from the Albanian front elsewhere without very long delays. A further consideration that influenced General Papagos in delaying any transfer of troops till too late was the hope that, the Yugoslavs might yet join the Allies, and by attacking the Italian forces in the rear compel the evacuation or surrender of the Italian army in Albania. This would have enabled a large proportion of the Greek army to be transferred to meet the Germans without loss of morale.

17. The undeveloped state of communications in Greece and the poor equipment of the Greek army must be borne in mind throughout in considering the operations in Greece. Greece is for the most part a country of high and difficult mountains with poor communications, where pack transport or ox wagons are the normal means of communication. There are few good roads and these are usually narrow where they pass through the mountains, making the use of mechanical transport extremely difficult. The Greek army was almost entirely unprovided with mechanical transport, except such as we had supplied, while our own troops on a mechanized basis and without pack transport often found extreme difficulty in working mechanical transport on the difficult, hilly roads or in the conditions of deep mud in the plains. The climate during March and April is severe in the hilly country, where snow falls were frequent, and there was much rain in the plains, rendering the poor roads even more difficult.

So far as was possible, the Greek troops with their pack transport held the hilly country, while the British forces were employed to cover the main roads by which alone their mechanical transport could operate.

18. The first flight of the British force disembarked at the Piraeus on 7th March, nearly a week after the Germans had entered Bulgaria. The first fighting troops to arrive were the 1st Armoured Brigade Group, under Brigadier H.V.S. Charrington. It consisted of:-

4th Hussars (Light Tanks).
3rd R.T.R. (Cruiser Tanks).
2 R.H.A. (25-pounders).
Northumberland Hussars (Anti-tank).
3rd. Cheshire Field Squadron, R.E.
Rangers (Motor Battalion).

It completed its concentration in the forward area about 21st March, and was given the task of operating east of the defensive position in order to cover the occupation of the position and the preparation of demolitions by the Royal Engineers.

The next to arrive was the New Zealand Division, under Major-General Freyberg, which was concentrated on the right of the position, in the Katerini area, by 2nd April. The 6th Australian Division, under Major-General Sir Ivan Mackay, was still in process of arrival when the Germans invaded Greece.

19. The attitude of the Yugoslav Government had, as already indicated, been most uncertain. Finally, towards the end of March, they signed an agreement with the Germans. This caused deep resentment to the greater part of the Yugoslav nation

and led to a *coup d'etat* on the 27th March in which the existing Government was overthrown and a new one formed, pledged to defend Yugoslavia against any German attack. The reaction of the Germans was practically immediate, and on 6th April German forces invaded both Greece and Yugoslavia.

Although repeated efforts had been made to get into touch with the Yugoslav authorities and to concert some plan of action in the event of Yugoslavia defending herself against a German attack, it had proved impossible to get the Yugoslavs to agree to any plan of combined action or even to a meeting. On 9th March the Yugoslav General Staff had sent an officer in mufti, under the name of Mr. Hope, to Athens for discussion, but he had had no power to commit the Yugoslav General Staff to any plans and did not even seem to be aware if any plan existed. Eventually, after the *coup d'etat*, the C.I.G.S., Sir John Dill, flew to Belgrade on 1st April, but was unable to obtain agreement to a combined plan of action. Two days later a meeting was arranged with considerable difficulty at Florina, at which General Papagos and General Wilson met General Jankovitch, the newly appointed Yugoslav Director of Military Operations and Intelligence. The discussions revealed that the Yugoslavs were completely unready, had no practical plan of action, had an entirely exaggerated idea of the strength of the British forces in Greece and had made no preparations to meet a German attack. The German attack took place two days later and no further touch was obtained with the Yugoslav army.

### German Counter Attack in Cyrenaica.

20. Before describing the campaign in Greece it will be convenient to turn to events in Cyrenaica. During March, while the concentration in Greece was proceeding, the situation in Cyrenaica gave me increasing cause for anxiety. Evidence accumulated of the presence of German armoured troops in Libya; but, as already explained, our intelligence reports from Italy and Libya were so scanty and so few aircraft were available for long-range reconnaissance that we remained very much in the dark as to the enemy's real strength or intentions. I still considered, from the evidence available, that an enemy attack was unlikely before the middle of April at the earliest, and I hoped that it might not take place before May, by which time I hoped to be able to strengthen considerably the force in Cyrenaica.

21. The position in Cyrenaica was rendered more difficult by the German air attacks on Benghazi. These began soon after our occupation and in the absence of any effective defence, since practically all available fighter aircraft and antiaircraft guns were required for Greece, made it hazardous to bring shipping into Benghazi. By the third week in February, the air attacks had become so heavy that it was agreed that the Navy should not risk any more shipping into Benghazi until an effective air defence could be provided. This meant that all supplies had to be brought from Tobruk, increasing the line of communications to the forward troops by more than 200 miles. This was most serious, since it meant that practically all the transport available had to be used in transporting supplies

and the mobility of the forward troops was greatly affected. In particular, the 2nd Armoured Division had to be supplied from dumps, instead of having its own transport. This fact later had a very serious effect on operations.

22. The shortage of transport was probably the most hampering factor on all operations in the Middle East during the first six months of 1941. I had been informed by the War Office that from January onwards a supply of some 3,000 vehicles a month would arrive in the Middle East from the United States; and I based my plans for the organisation of my troops and operations on the arrival of this transport. In fact, during the first four months, less than half of the amount promised arrived (2,341 in January, 2,094 in February, 725 in March, 705 in April). The consequent shortage hampered operations in Cyrenaica, in Crete, in Iraq, and in Syria. The force sent to Greece was made up to its full complement of transport at the expense of other theatres, and the whole of this transport, some 8,000 vehicles, was lost in the evacuation of Greece.

23. Our covering forces, towards the end of March, on the frontier of Cyrenaica, just east of Agheila, 150 miles south of Benghazi, consisted of the 2nd Armoured Division, less 1st Armoured Brigade Group in Greece. The division comprised an armoured car regiment, the 3rd Armoured Brigade and a portion of the Support Group. The armoured car regiment, the King's Dragoon Guards, were only newly converted from horsed cavalry to this role and had little experience of the desert. The 3rd Armoured Brigade consisted of the 3rd Hussars (light tanks), 5th Royal Tank Regiment (Cruisers), and 6th Royal Tank Regiment, armed with captured Italian tanks. Of the above, 3rd Hussars had had, at the end of March, only 29 light tanks in action out of their establishment of 52, and these were in a poor mechanical state; the 5th Royal Tank Regiment had only 23 cruisers available out of 52, and these had done a very considerable mileage and were in an even poorer mechanical state. 6th Royal Tank Regiment had, on 30th March, only one squadron available, while the second was formed two days later, the day after the enemy attack began. They had had little time to become accustomed to the Italian tanks. Headquarters 2nd Division had only arrived in the forward area in the third week in March and had not had time to settle down; the same applied to the Support Group, which consisted of the 1st Tower Hamlets, the 104th Royal Horse Artillery (25-pdrs.), 3rd Royal Horse Artillery (Anti-Tank Regiment), and one company Royal Northumberland Fusiliers (Machine-gun Regiment). The whole formation was unpractised and required at least another month to find its feet. I had hoped that this period would be available before the enemy attacked. I did not become aware of the dangerously poor mechanical state of the armoured troop till a few days before the enemy attack. The strongest position for defence on the Cyrenaican frontier was west of Agheila, where some salt marshes confined the approaches from the west. I had given orders that this position should be occupied, but owing to the transport shortage mentioned above, it was found impossible to carry out the maintenance of the force if it pushed forward this additional 40 miles.

24. My instructions to General Neame, commanding in Cyrenaica, were that, if attacked, he was to fight a delaying action between his forward position, east of Agheila and Benghazi. I told him that he should not hesitate to give up ground if necessary as far as Benghazi, and even to evacuate Benghazi if the situation demanded it, but to hold on to the high ground above Benghazi for as long as possible. The 9th Australian Division had only two brigades forward, the third having to remain back at Tobruk owing to shortage of transport. I instructed General Neame to conserve his armoured troops as much as possible, since I could not provide him with any armoured reinforcements before May and without armoured troops his whole position would be compromised. I still believed at this time that no enemy advance in strength was probable for another three or four weeks.

25. Before describing the enemy's counter attack, it may be mentioned that on 21st March the last Italian detachment left in Cyrenaica had been captured. This was the force occupying Jarabub Oasis, which had retreated there in the middle of December after the battle of Sidi Barrani. It originally comprised about 800 Italian and 1,200 native troops. Ever since then it had been merely observed by the divisional cavalry regiment (mechanised) of the 6th Australian Division. I had not the transport available to maintain a larger force at such a distance from the main line of communications and estimated that the exhaustion of its supplies would compel the surrender of the force. Although practically the whole of the native troops had surrendered, the Italian part of the garrison was still in its defences by the middle of March and was being supplied by air. Since the force observing Jarabub was required in Greece I determined to attack and capture the garrison. This was carried out by the 2nd/9th Australian Infantry battalion under Brigadier Wootten, and the Divisional Cavalry Regiment already in front of Jarabub. In face of a skilfully conducted attack the garrison surrendered, putting up a poor fight in spite of its strong defences.

26. On 31st March the enemy counter offensive against our troops in Cyrenaica began. The attacking force consisted of the 5th German Light Armoured Division and two Italian divisions (one armoured, one motorised). It was supported by a considerable air force, the enemy being numerically superior throughout the operations, although they did not make full use of this superiority, largely as a result of the initiative and aggressiveness of our R.A.F. During the first three days the 2nd Armoured Division withdrew slowly northwards, and by the evening of 2nd April was north of Agedabia. The enemy so far had not pressed his advance with much vigour. Our intention was that the armoured force should maintain a position from which they would be on the flank of any enemy advance by the main road to Benghazi and would also block any attempt to turn our positions in Cyrenaica by taking the desert route to Mechili. The Commander of the 2nd Armoured Division had originally intended to counter attack the enemy north of Agedabia if opportunity offered; but on being warned that no tank

reinforcements were available and that he should not attack unless a specially favourable opportunity offered, he decided to continue the withdrawal.

27. The 3rd April was the unfortunate day of these operations. It was intended to continue the gradual withdrawal east of and parallel to the Benghazi road, and the force was in process of taking up position about Sceleidima, when a report was received that a large enemy armoured force was approaching Msus, where the principal dump of petrol and supplies for the armoured division was. As a result of this report there was considerable confusion. The Support Group finally continued its retirement to Regima on the left flank of the 9th Australian Division, while the 3rd Armoured Brigade moved to Msus. On arrival there it found that the detachment guarding the dump had destroyed all the petrol on hearing that the enemy were approaching. From now onwards the movements of the 3rd Armoured Brigade were almost entirely dictated by the lack of petrol. Benghazi had been evacuated on 3rd April, after extensive demolitions. On the night of 3rd/4th April, General Neame decided, in view of the weakness of the 2nd Armoured Division, which had been reduced, more by mechanical breakdowns than by enemy action, to about a dozen Cruisers, 20 light tanks and 20 Italian tanks, to withdraw the whole force to the line of the Wadi Derna-Mechili. He ordered 9th Australian Division to withdraw to the Wadi Derna; and ordered 2nd Armoured Division to Mechili, where it would join the 3rd Indian Motor Brigade which had been moved from the Tobruk area to protect that place. The 3rd Indian Motor Brigade consisted of three motorised Indian cavalry regiments which had recently arrived in Middle East and had been sent to Cyrenaica to complete their training. The Brigade had no armoured vehicles, and I had warned General Neame of the danger of exposing it to attack by the enemy's armoured troops.

28. The 9th Australian Division, after repulsing an enemy tank attack at Regima, withdrew without particular incident and in good order. It was found impossible, in view of the development of events to the south, to maintain a position on the Wadi Derna, and the Division was finally withdrawn to Tobruk, where one of its brigades already was. It had established itself west of the Tobruk defences by 7th April.

29. The fate of the 2nd Armoured Division was very different. From 4th April onwards, owing to breakdown of communications and difficulties as regards petrol supply, Headquarters 2nd Armoured Division was never properly in touch with the whole of the force under its command. The enemy air force repeatedly attacked the Division and made a particular set at wireless vehicles and at petrol carrying transport, which still further increased the difficulties of communication and petrol supply. Headquarters 2nd Armoured Division finally reached Mechili on the evening of 6th. April. The intention was that 3rd Armoured Brigade should follow it to Mechili but owing to shortage of petrol the Brigade Commander appears to have decided to go to Derna. He, with his Brigade Headquarters and the greater part of the remains of the Brigade, were cut off in Derna

and captured. The King's Dragoon Guards (armoured cars) and the Support Group had also gone by Derna and the majority of them succeeded in making good their withdrawal to Tobruk. The Support Group fought a skilful and determined action on the eastern outskirts of Derna and checked a strong enemy force, putting out of action a number of tanks.

30. Thus on 7th April the force in Mechili consisted of the Headquarters 2nd Armoured Division (practically all unarmoured vehicles), 3rd Indian Motor Brigade and elements of certain other units, including part of the 1st Royal Horse Artillery. Enemy troops had arrived at Mechili on the afternoon of 6th April; they seem to have consisted of motorised infantry and artillery. The Indian Motor Brigade had no difficulty in holding them off and captured some prisoners. On 7th April the enemy made a series of small attacks on Mechili which were easily beaten off, a number of prisoners being captured. Demands from the enemy for surrender were treated with contempt. The whole force could have withdrawn on this day, but it was still hoped that the remains of the 3rd Armoured Brigade would join it, and it was not till evening that orders were received from Force Headquarters to withdraw to El Adem, south of Tobruk.

On 8th April an attempt was made to break out of Mechili at dawn. The enemy had by this time been reinforced by armoured troops, and our troops came under heavy artillery and machine gun fire. Certain parties which showed great determination and resource, managed to escape. In particular the detachment of the 1st Royal Horse Artillery with some Indian troops broke away to the south and eventually reached Sollum on 11th April. Another party of the 18th Indian Cavalry Regiment with some Australian Anti-Tank guns also got away. The remainder of the force, including practically the whole of the Headquarters of the Division, was captured.

31. There was a further misfortune to the force during the night of 6th/7th April. Lieut.-General Sir Richard O'Connor and Lieut.-Colonel Combe, 11th Hussars, had been sent up to Cyrenaica to assist General Neame during the withdrawal in view of their knowledge of this area and of desert operations. All three officers remained behind at Barce after Force Headquarters had gone back through Derna towards Tobruk. They were proceeding to rejoin their Headquarters when they were held up by an enemy mechanised patrol which had penetrated towards Derna and were all three taken prisoner.

32. The disaster to the 2nd Armoured Division can be attributed mainly to the poor mechanical state of its vehicles, nearly half of which were in workshops while the remainder were in no condition for a prolonged retreat; to the shortage of transport which tied the Division to a vulnerable system of dumps; to the change of plan consequent on the report on 3rd April of the enemy being at Msus; and finally to the breakdown of communications due to loss of wireless vehicles by enemy action and lack of opportunity for charging batteries. The loss of this armoured force created a dangerous situation since there were few armoured

vehicles left available for the defence of Egypt, and without an armoured force it was extremely difficult in the open desert to check the enemy advance.

33. I decided that it was essential to hold Tobruk, in order to secure the large reserves of supplies there and to prevent the enemy obtaining the use of the port and water supply for his further advance. The Italian defences, which had an outer perimeter of some 27 miles, were extremely extended for the force available. I ordered a brigade of the 7th Australian Division to be embarked and sent round to Tobruk to strengthen the defence. It arrived in Tobruk on 7th April. Some tanks which had been under repair in Tobruk were available for the defence and I reinforced this armoured detachment with some more tanks from Egypt.

A mobile force consisting of the remains of the Support Group of the 2nd Armoured Division, strengthened by certain other detachments, was left outside the defences of Tobruk about El Adem. This force was driven back to the Egyptian frontier about Sollum by 11th April and from this date Tobruk became invested.

### Operations in Greece, 6th April to 30th April.
34. The situation of the Imperial Forces on 6th April when the German attack opened was that the 1st Armoured Brigade Group and the New Zealand Division had arrived complete in the forward area and that the 6th Australian Division was in process of arrival. The 12th and 20th Greek Divisions were in the line but the so-called "mechanised" 19th Division had been moved across the River Axios and put under the command of the Eastern Macedonian Army, when the New Zealand Division took up its position.

35. The line held ran from the Aegean Sea east of Mount Olympus to Veria and Edessa and thence northwards to the Yugoslav frontier. Its length was approximately 100 miles, through high mountains in which there were four main passes – those on either side of Mount Olympus and those at Veria and Edessa. The railway ran between Mount Olympus and the coast, and roads through each of the other passes.

The New Zealand Division held the right of the line, including the two Olympus Passes; the 6th Australian Division was to assume the defence of the Veria Pass with one Brigade, the second being at Kozani, and the third in reserve. On the left of the Australians along the mountains was the 20th Greek Division; the 12th Greek Division, which was being relieved by the arrival of the Dominion troops, was also designed for a position in the mountains, for which its pack and ox-drawn transport was as suitable as our mechanical transport was unsuitable.

The position was naturally a strong one provided it was not turned through Yugoslavia. If the Germans succeeded in forcing a way through Yugoslavia the whole position could be outflanked from an easy valley which ran from Monastir down to Kozani. As early as 27th March General Wilson had begun to form a detachment at Amynteion to watch this gap, consisting of the 3rd Royal Tank Regiment, the 27th New Zealand Machine-gun Battalion, less two companies, and the 64th Medium Regiment, the whole under Brigadier Lee. On 8th April, three days after Germany invaded Yugoslavia and Greece, it became clear that Yugoslav resistance in the south had collapsed and that from Monastir southwards the road was open to the Germans. To meet this threat it was decided that no further relief in the Veria Pass should be undertaken by units of the 6th Australian Division, and that a force should be formed about Veve under Major-General Mackay, consisting of 19th Australian Infantry Brigade, less one battalion, with a Field Regiment and an Anti-Tank Regiment. Brigadier Lee's force was added to General Mackay's and later the remainder of the 1st Armoured Brigade, after blowing the demolition belts east of the main position, also joined his command. At the same time Major-General Freyberg was ordered to move one brigade group of the New Zealand Division to Servia as a pivot on which any subsequent withdrawal from the north could be based.

These moves were completed early on 10th April.

36. The line was now held as follows:-

On the right was the New Zealand Division, one brigade group of the 6th Australian Division, the bulk of the 12th Greek Division (whose relief had been interrupted by the diversion of General Mackay's command to Amynteion) and certain other troops. All troops in this sector, Greek and Dominion, were under the command of General Blamey.

The centre sector, under Greek command, included the 20th and part of the 12th Greek Division.

The left sector, about Amynteion, consisted of the troops described above under the command of General Mackay, who was directly under the command of General Wilson.

On 12th April the 6th Australian Division and the New Zealand Division, hitherto called the 1st Australian Corps, became known as the "Anzac Corps." The revival of this historic title was welcomed with pride by all in the corps.

37. The first contact was made with the enemy on 8th April, when detachments of the 1st Armoured Brigade encountered elements of the enemy on the line of the River Axios. On the evening of 10th April, General Mackay's force was attacked in the Amynteion area. This developed next day into the first serious engagement, which lasted for two days. Although the enemy attack was held and heavy casualties inflicted on him, it was obvious that the Olympus – Veria – Amynteion position could not be held for ever. The position was much too extended for the troops available; there had not been time to consolidate it properly; the left flank was protected only by a Greek cavalry division on an extremely wide front, and between this cavalry division and the Greek forces in Albania there was a large gap through which the enemy were likely to penetrate.

A new line was therefore decided on, that running from Mount Olympus along the line of the River Aliakhmon. This was a strong position provided that the Yugoslavs and the Greeks were able to close the roads by which the line could be turned. The withdrawal began on the night 11th/12th April and was completed by dawn on the 13th. But during its course it became obvious that the 12th and 20th Greek Divisions were disintegrating. They soon became thoroughly disorganized and only a few sub-units retained any fighting value. This was due in no way to lack of courage or fighting spirit, but to their lack of modern armament and their ox-drawn transport, which was too slow and unwieldy as soon as it became necessary to embark on a long move. The withdrawal of General Mackay's force from Amynteion had to be covered by the 1st Armoured Brigade, who carried out successful counter-attacks on enemy armoured fighting vehicles. During this withdrawal the brigade experienced considerable mechanical trouble, similar to that of the 3rd Armoured Brigade in Cyrenaica, and had to leave many of their tanks behind.

38. While the withdrawal was in progress the news reaching General Wilson was of such gravity that he already began to consider the necessity for further withdrawal. It was reported that the Yugoslav army in the south had capitulated and it became obvious that the Greek armies in Albania were incapable of withdrawing to take their place in the line west of General Wilson's force and in fact that very little reliance could be placed on the fighting ability of the Greek army. The difficulties that General Papagos had foreseen in any attempt to withdraw from Albania and its effect on Greek morale had been justified and were increased by the collapse of the Yugoslavs.

General Wilson therefore decided to continue the withdrawal to the Thermopylae Line, which could be held at least temporarily by the Imperial forces alone. At a meeting between General Wilson and General Papagos on 14th April General Papagos approved this decision and made for the first time a suggestion that the British forces should evacuate Greece to avoid further fighting and devastation of that country.

39. Meanwhile, under circumstances of great difficulty, the Anzac Corps had taken up its new line and on it had had its first experience of the intense aerial bombardment by the German Air Force against its positions and its lines of communication. No great enemy pressure was developed against its positions, although on the morning of 15th April, determined small-scale attacks were made in both the Servia and the Katerini Passes. An attack on the positions of the 4th New Zealand Brigade in the Servia Pass was repulsed with the loss to the enemy of 180 prisoners and at least several hundred killed and wounded. Our losses were negligible. The Greek troops, which had been under General Wilson, had reverted to Greek command on the occupation of the new position.

40. General Wilson was anxious for the safety of his left flank during this new withdrawal, the more so as the Germans were known to have broken through the Greek troops at Kleisoura. Consequently, a force had to be found to block the roads leading southwards from the Grevena and Matsova areas into the Larissa Plain. Actually, no threat came from this flank and the main danger to the with-

drawal arose from the speed with which the enemy followed it up from the north and from the heavy attack launched against a combined New Zealand and Australian force in the Peneios Gorge. This attack began late on 15th April and was pressed home by infantry and tanks, which proved to be the leading elements of one armoured and one mountain division. The 16th Australian Infantry Brigade which had been detailed to form a left flank guard on the Larissa-Kalabaka road was diverted, except for one battalion, to cover the western exit of the Peneios Gorge and to afford support to the 21st New Zealand Battalion, which was holding the gorge alone. The attack was made in such strength as to necessitate the transference of the weight of the defence from west to east. The defence of the gorge was carried out with such spirit that when at last on the evening of 18th April the Germans were masters of the gorge, the main body of the Anzac Corps had successfully withdrawn past its western exit. The 21st New Zealand Battalion had been overrun and the whole of the 2nd/2nd Australian Battalion had been forced off their line of withdrawal into the hills after a stubborn fight against greatly superior forces. This action, together with other minor ones, and the use of skilful demolitions, prevented the enemy's armoured and mechanized units from following up closely. During the first two vital days of the withdrawal, enemy air action had fortunately been prevented by mist and low clouds, but from Larissa onwards columns on the road suffered air attack without respite. Otherwise, thanks to the rear-guard actions described above, the withdrawal was successfully carried out under the orders of General Blamey almost without interference.

41. By the morning of 20th April, the withdrawal to the Thermopylae line was practically complete. This naturally strong position was occupied by the New Zealand Division on the right from the sea to the summit of the mountains, covering the coast road; while the 6th Australian Division occupied the Brailos position covering the main road to Thebes and Athens. The 1st Armoured Brigade, which by this time had lost the greater part of its tanks from mechanical failure, was in reserve and protected the right and rear of the Anzac Corps against a threat from Euboea. The weakness of the position lay in the fact that the disintegration of the Greek forces made possible a German penetration on the extreme left of the line about Delphi.

42. Meanwhile in anticipation of the possible necessity of the evacuation of Greece, a committee of the Joint Planning Staff had been formed in the Middle East and was sent to Athens on 17th April under Rear-Admiral Baillie Grohman. The general situation in Greece now betokened the near end of Greek resistance. The Greek forces on the left of the Imperial troops had already disintegrated and it was obvious that little more could be expected from the Greek armies in Albania. The Piraeus had been so heavily bombed that it was practically unusable as a port, so that to send further reinforcements or supplies to Greece had become a matter of extreme difficulty. I cancelled the sailing of the Polish Brigade and the 7th Australian Division and went to Athens myself on 19th April.

The Greek Prime Minister had committed suicide on 18th April. I saw General Wilson and General Blamey and had audience with His Majesty the King, who was now acting as head of his Government. It was decided, with the full approval of His Majesty the King and the Greek Government, that the evacuation of the British forces was essential. It was obviously impossible, in view of the overwhelming superiority of the German air force, to use the Piraeus or any other port for the re-embarkation of the force, which would have to take place from open beaches. I instructed General Wilson that the embarkation should take place on as wide a front as possible and that any troops who were cut off or were unable to embark on the beaches selected should not surrender but should make for the Peloponnesus, where there might be possibilities of evacuating them later.

43. General Wilson originally selected 28th April as the first night for embarkation, but the capitulation of the Greek army in the Epirus on 21st April made it necessary to advance the date, since it was now possible that a German force might reach Athens from the west before the Imperial forces could be re-embarked. It was accordingly decided to begin the embarkation on the night 24th–25th April and to endeavour to complete it in three nights. The time had afterwards to be extended.

44. The withdrawal from the Thermopylae position to the beaches was covered by a brigade group of the New Zealand Division, which inflicted severe casualties on the enemy and knocked out a considerable number of tanks on 26th April.

On 23rd April the remaining Hurricanes, about twelve in number, on which reliance had been placed to protect the convoys during the first part of their journey from Greece, were, owing to unavoidable lack of A.A. defences, all destroyed on the ground at Argos by enemy action. The embarkation programme was accordingly revised to enable a greater number of troops to be embarked in the Peloponnesus whence the journey to Crete would be shorter and less exposed to air attack. Fortunately, however, the plan remained elastic, and when the Corinth Canal was cut by enemy parachutists in the early morning of 26th April, it was possible again to change the plans and to embark the 4th New Zealand Brigade from a beach east of Athens, Porto Rafti, instead of from the Peloponnesus.

45. Thanks to the excellent arrangements by the Royal Navy, the air cover of some few Blenheim fighters and the good work of the Joint Planning Staff sent to Greece, the embarkations were carried out according to plan except in two places. At Nauplion on the night of 26th–27th April, some 1,700 personnel had to be left behind owing to one of the ships, which had been set on fire by enemy bombing, having blocked the channel, so that the destroyers could not get alongside the quay. Another merchant ship which conveyed troops from this place was bombed and set on fire soon after leaving Greece and two destroyers which picked up the survivors from the ship were both sunk by bombs within a few minutes of each

other. Some 700 troops are believed to have lost their lives. These were practically the only casualties during the voyage from Greece.

The second failure to embark personnel was at Kalamata, in the south of the Peloponnesus, on the night of 28th–29th April. The senior officer at this port had neglected to make proper arrangements for local protection or reconnaissance, and a German force entered the town and reached the quays just as embarkation was due to begin. By the efforts of a number of officers who got together small parties and organised counter attacks on their own, the enemy was driven out and 150 prisoners taken. But in the meantime the Royal Navy had been informed that the Germans were in the town and that the quays were mined, and no information appears ever to have reached them that the enemy had been driven out again. The Naval Commander, therefore, naturally decided not to risk his valuable forces by entering the harbour. The troops at Kalamata are believed to have numbered some 8,000, including 1,500 Yugoslavs. The greater part of the remainder were labour units and details, and comparatively few were fighting troops. Unfortunately, among them were the first reinforcements of the New Zealand Division.

46. The total number of troops sent to Greece was approximately 57,660; of these, close on 43,000 were safely re-embarked. All guns, transport and equipment other than personal were, however, lost. In view of the complete enemy air superiority, the re-embarkation of so many troops may be considered an extremely fine performance. It was due to the magnificent work of the Royal Navy, the good staff arrangements made by those concerned, and the discipline and endurance of the troops themselves. Of the troops re-embarked, about 27,000 were landed in Crete and the remainder taken back to Egypt. The reason for landing so many troops in Crete was to shorten the sea journey and to make possible quicker and more frequent journeys.

### Summary of Greek Operations.

47. As will be seen from the above account, the expedition to Greece was ill starred from the first. The change of plan by the Greek Commander-in-Chief after the first decision to despatch a force resulted in the position on which the Imperial forces were to concentrate being held by a very inadequate Greek force instead of the five organised divisions which General Papagos had promised. The uncertainties of the Yugoslav attitude seriously affected the plans both of ourselves and of the Greeks, while the complete collapse of their armies on the German invasion exposed the flank of what was otherwise an extremely strong position. The German attack took place while the Imperial force was still in process of concentration and before it had time to get properly settled down. That the Greek army which had fought so heroically against the Italians disintegrated so rapidly under the German attack is not surprising. They had already been strained to the uttermost and neither their organisation nor equipment were sufficiently up to date to enable them to face the German army. Finally the enemy bombing attacks on the Piraeus closed the only good port, deprived us of any

chance of removing any of our heavy equipment and made the re-embarkation of the personnel of the force an extremely hazardous operation. Thus, while the whole expedition was something in the nature of a gamble, the dice were loaded against it from the first. It was not really such a forlorn hope from the military point of view as it may seem from its results.

### Situation in Middle East after Greek Campaign.

48. The situation in the Middle East at the beginning of May was full of anxiety. I was threatened with having to undertake operations simultaneously in no fewer than five theatres with my resources in men and material very seriously depleted by the losses in Greece. There was an obvious possibility, which was soon confirmed, that the enemy would undertake operations against Crete; or he might reinforce his effort in the Western Desert, which though checked for the present still constituted a serious menace to Egypt; responsibility for dealing with the revolt in Iraq was handed over to Middle East from India in the first week in May; the Germans were making use of air bases in Syria which might constitute a very serious threat to the defence of the Canal and Egyptian ports as well as to Palestine; and finally there still remained the remnants of the Italian forces in Abyssinia to be cleared up if possible before the rainy season set in.

To deal with these many responsibilities my resources were completely inadequate. To equip the forces for Greece I had had to strip many units of weapons and transport and all equipment that could not be carried had been lost. Transport was still reaching Middle East in very limited quantities and was the chief obstacle to completing for war a number of units and formations. My armoured troops, except for the detachment in Tobruk, consisted only of one weak battalion of Cruiser tanks and one, also incomplete, of "I" tanks. The formations which had fought in Greece, the 6th Australian Division and the New Zealand Division, required rest, reorganisation and re-equipment, but were at present divided between Crete and Egypt. The 7th Australian Division was complete but had one brigade locked up in Tobruk. The 9th Australian Division was in the Tobruk defences. The 6th Division had never been completely formed. It had only two infantry brigades (22nd Guards and 16th) and one other battalion, the Buffs. The 14th Brigade, which should have completed it, had been transferred to Crete. Of these two brigades, the 22nd Guards Brigade had 50 per cent, of its transport, while the 16th Brigade and the Buffs had practically none. It had only one field regiment of artillery and only two field companies of Engineers. The Polish Brigade was not complete in transport. The 1st Cavalry Division in Palestine had been stripped of its artillery, Engineers, Signals and transport to provide for the needs of other formations; it could provide one motorised cavalry brigade by pooling the whole of the divisional motor transport. Of the unbrigaded infantry battalions, two were under orders to reinforce Malta, and the remainder were hard put to it to find the necessary guards and escorts for the prisoners of war (of whom there were still over 100,000 in Egypt) and other internal security duties in Egypt and Palestine. All these battalions were short of transport and were equipped for static duties only.

From the above, which included no single complete formation available, I had to provide for the defence of the western frontier of Egypt, the defence of Crete, the restoration of the situation in Iraq and for a possible commitment in Syria. The German attacks by air on the Canal which began in February caused a fresh commitment, since large numbers of observers were required to watch for mines dropped in the Canal. Eventually the Egyptian Army took over a large part of this duty, and thus gave most effective aid to the defence of the Canal. The 4th Indian Division was on its way from East Africa and the 1st South African Division would be available very shortly. But the move of both of these divisions depended on the provision of shipping, which was hard to come by.

49. The enemy advance in Cyrenaica had been checked on the frontier of Egypt and the active defence of the garrison of Tobruk constituted a menace to the enemy's line of communications, which was likely to prevent his further advance. He had made one determined attack on Tobruk on 1st May and had been severely repulsed with heavy losses in tanks and in men. But the garrison of Tobruk was small for the perimeter it had to defend and it was known that another German armoured division, which might include as many as 400 medium tanks, had been landed in Libya and was on its way to the forward area, where it was expected to appear early in May. If the enemy also reinforced his air forces in Libya and delivered a determined attack on the Tobruk defences and harbour, we might be hard put to it to maintain the Tobruk garrison.

50. The 6th Division, as already stated, had been preparing and training for an operation against the Italian Dodecanese. Since, however, the Navy had been unable to support any expedition against the Dodecanese while engaged in convoying our troops to Greece, it had been necessary to postpone the operation until the completion of the move to Greece. When the German counter-offensive against Cyrenaica took place, it was necessary to move the 6th Division from their training areas to man the defences of Mersa Matruh, to guard against a German break through to the Delta. The 7th Australian Division (less one brigade in Tobruk) had also to be used for the defence of the Western Desert, and the Polish Brigade to man the Delta defences. The one incomplete armoured brigade was also allotted to the western defence of Egypt.

Thus, practically the whole of the resources at my disposal had to be used to safeguard the Egyptian base against the threat from the west; the one mobile force which could be improvised in Palestine, the cavalry brigade group, was soon to be despatched to the rescue of Habbaniyeh in Iraq; and my only reserves in Egypt and Palestine were the New Zealand and Australian reinforcements.

51. There was on its way across the Mediterranean a convoy of ships containing some 200 tanks to re-equip the 7th Armoured Division and to counter the German armoured troops in the Western Desert. They were due to arrive in

Egypt on 12th May, and all preparations to equip these tanks with the necessary fittings for use in the desert, and to place them in action with the least possible delay were made. The great majority of these tanks, however, were "I" tanks, the limited range and slowness of which made them ill-suited for use against fast moving German tanks in the wide open spaces of the Western Desert.

The convoy duly reached Egypt on 12th May with the loss of one ship containing 57 tanks, which was sunk by a mine. The problem now was whether these tanks could be manned and put into action before the German reinforcements arrived in the forward area. It was originally hoped that it might be possible to get all the tanks unloaded, through the workshops and ready for action by about the end of May. This estimate was to prove optimistic.

### The Defence of Crete.

52. Meanwhile the arrangements for the defence of Crete were my particular preoccupation. Evidence accumulated fast of the German intentions. There was a large concentration of German aircraft in the south of Greece, and information of the presence of airborne troops and of preparations for an attack on Crete on a large scale by air and by sea.

My original intention after the evacuation of Greece had been to relieve the Australian and New Zealand troops which had been landed in Crete by the infantry of the 6th Division, so as to enable the 6th Australian Division and the New Zealand Division to be reorganized, in Palestine and Egypt respectively, as soon as possible. During the early part of May, however, the Royal Navy was fully engaged in the operations necessary for the passage of the convoy mentioned in para. 51 above through the Mediterranean, and was unable to provide the necessary escorts for any large shipping movements between Crete and Egypt. Later, it became obvious that there would be no time to effect reliefs before the German attack developed and that it would be necessary to meet that attack with the troops already in Crete and to defer any question of relief until the German attack had been repulsed. Further, the German attacks on shipping to Crete were so intensive as to make it difficult and dangerous for shipping to approach the island. I visited Crete on 30th April and placed Major-General Freyberg in command. I instructed him to organize the defence of the island with the troops available and with such additional resources as I was able to send him from Egypt.

53. British forces had been first sent to Crete on 1st November, 1940. The force sent was only the Headquarters of an infantry brigade, two battalions, 2nd Battalion The Black Watch and 1st York and Lancaster Regiment, and certain other details. There was then a Greek division in the island; there seemed no immediate threat to Crete, and the only requirement was to secure Suda Bay as a refuelling base for the navy. The defensive arrangements were all made with this end in view. There was at the time no prospect of the island becoming an air base, and the coast defences, anti-aircraft defences and infantry defences, were designed solely to protect the naval anchorage at Suda Bay.

Towards the end of November the whole of the Greek troops in the island were removed. One additional British battalion (1st Welch Regiment) was sent to Crete in February, and orders were issued to prepare a base for one division. Meanwhile an aerodrome was under construction at Maleme, west of Canea, and the landing ground at Heraklion in the east of the island was being improved. With the constant shortage of aircraft in the Middle East, however, it was never possible to station any aircraft permanently in the island. At the end of November a Commando was sent to the island, its object being to carry out raids on the adjacent Italian islands. Otherwise the garrison remained at three battalions until after the evacuation from Greece. During the operations in Greece, however, Suda Bay became of greater importance to the Navy and it was therefore decided to send the Mobile Naval Base Defence Organisation (M.N.B.D.O.), which had lately arrived in the Middle East, to improve the defence of Suda Bay.

54. In the light of after events, if we had been able to develop the defences of Crete more highly during the early period of occupation, we could have made the enemy's task in seizing it even more costly than it was. The value of the island was fully appreciated, but the constant shortage of troops and material in the Middle East was an effective obstacle to any large-scale defence measures, and any work would have been at the expense of other commitments in the Middle East, which at the time appeared more important. Engineer units and equipment were always short, and were more urgently required in Greece, in the Western Desert and elsewhere. It was already necessary severely to ration steel for reinforced concrete works in the Western Desert and on the northern frontier of Palestine; and shipping to Crete was always scarce. It has been suggested that local labour could have been employed, but practically all able-bodied men in the island were serving in the Greek forces in Albania, while to collect the inhabitants from the long and poorly developed island a considerable quantity of transport would have been required, and this, as already stated, was the chief difficulty in all theatres in the Middle East.

55. The total troops in Crete when the German attack took place was approximately 28,600. Of these the great majority were in need of rest and reorganisation after the operations in Greece. There was a shortage of equipment of all kinds, and a proportion of the personnel was unarmed. Improvised units were formed from these men and were equipped with such arms as were available. It was intended to evacuate from the island before the German attack all such personnel as could not usefully be employed in the defence; but owing to the shortage of shipping and escorts mentioned above it was only possible to remove a small proportion before the German attack. As an additional embarrassment, there were 16,000 Italian prisoners of war, captured by the Greeks, under guard on the island.

Every effort was made to send stores and material to increase the means of defence; nine infantry tanks, a number of captured Italian guns, a certain amount of transport, and other arms and equipment were shipped. A considerable proportion, however, was sunk on the voyage, as the enemy scale of attack on shipping rapidly increased in intensity. The materials sunk included about half the field guns and more than half the engineer stores required for constructing defences.

56. The island of Crete is about 160 miles long and about 40 miles wide. It is very mountainous and there is only one main road which runs the whole length of the north coast, on which are, all available harbours. The roads from north to south are few and poor. It is possible to find landing places in the south of the island, but there are usually no easy exits from them and no communications with the rest of the island. It had always been intended to develop landing places on the south of the island and roads from them to the north, in order to avoid the exposed passage round the north of the island; but there had never been, for the reasons given above, sufficient means to carry this out.

57. General Freyberg disposed his troops in four sectors as follows:-

(a) *Heraklion.*
Commander – Brigadier Chappell.
   Two British battalions.
   Three Greek battalions.
   300 Australian riflemen.
   250 Artillerymen armed as infantry.
(b) *Retimo.*
Commander – Brigadier Vasey.
   H.Q. 19th Australian Infantry Brigade.
   Four Australian battalions.
   Six Greek battalions.
(c) *Suda Bay.*
Commander – Maj.-Gen. Weston, R.M.
   16th and 17th Australian battalions, both improvised.
   Some 1,200 British riflemen, formed from various units.
   106th Regiment, R.H.A., armed as infantry.
   Two Greek battalions.
(d) *Maleme.*
Commander – Brigadier Puttick, N.Z. Div.
   4th New Zealand Brigade in area west of Canea.
   5th New Zealand Brigade in Maleme area.
   10th (Improvised) Infantry Brigade of composite battalions formed from various New Zealand personnel and two Greek battalions.
   One additional Greek battalion.

There were anti-aircraft defences round Suda Bay and at Maleme and Heraklion. The field artillery consisted of captured Italian guns intended for static defence only. Two infantry tanks had been provided for each of the aerodromes at Heraklion, Retimo and Maleme; and three additional "I" tanks were also sent to the island. The single means of land communication between the various sectors was the road which ran along the north coast of the island and was obviously likely to be the target of enemy air attack. The shortage of transport in any case prevented the possibility of large scale reinforcement from one part of the island to another. Each of the three main groups, at Heraklion, at Retimo, and in the Suda Bay – Maleme area, had to fight as a separate force. The general scheme of defence was the same at each, to prevent enemy landings on the aerodromes and landings, whether air-borne or seaborne, at the beaches.

58. The main enemy attack was preceded by air attacks, principally on Suda Bay and on shipping, which gradually increased in intensity. It soon became obvious that it would be impossible for our small force of fighter air-craft to maintain itself on the island and that it would merely be destroyed on the ground. It was accordingly decided to withdraw the few aeroplanes that remained, which was done on 19th May. There were thus none of our aircraft on the island during the attack, except two Hurricanes which reached Crete on 23rd May.

59. In a communication sent to me three days before the attack, General Freyberg reported that he had just returned from a final tour of the defences and felt greatly encouraged. He described the excellent morale of the troops and the strenuous efforts to render the island as strong as possible. He said in conclusion that while he did not wish to be over-confident, he felt that at least the defenders would give a good account of themselves, and trusted that with the aid of the Navy, Crete would be held. He did not anticipate, any more than anyone else, the overwhelming strength in which the German Air Force was to make the attack, nor how carefully and skilfully their plans had been laid nor the losses they were prepared to accept to attain their object.

60. The main enemy attack began soon after dawn on 20th May, with a heavy bombing attack on Maleme aerodrome. Under cover of the clouds of dust and smoke which resulted, and while the bombing was still in progress, between 50 and 100 gliders landed troops in a river bed west of the aerodrome, whence they attacked the aerodrome. About the same time large numbers of parachutists began to land near Maleme, south and south-west of Canea and on the Akrotiri Peninsula north of Suda Bay, where gliders also landed. The great majority of these parachutists were accounted for, but a certain number succeeded in establishing themselves at various points and caused some trouble. His Majesty the King of Greece had a narrow escape from a party of parachutists which landed near the house in which he was. He made his escape with difficulty, and then under the protection of a platoon of New Zealanders, crossed the mountains by narrow, tracks to the south coast, where he was taken off by a destroyer.

In the afternoon, similar attacks by parachutists were made against Heraklion and Retimo. At the former it is estimated that about 2,000 were landed, the great majority of whom had been killed or captured by the following morning. At Retimo, about 1,700 appear to have landed; the majority of these were also accounted for, but a party of about 100 succeeded in establishing themselves in buildings on the route between Retimo and Suda Bay, and thus cut off communications by land between Retimo and Force Headquarters during the remainder of the fighting. An effort to dislodge this party made several days later was unsuccessful. Altogether, it is estimated that over 7,000 men, armed and equipped with great forethought, were landed on this day from the air. They suffered extremely heavy casualties and only at Maleme aerodrome did they succeed in establishing any serious footing.

61. On 21st May, every effort was made to eject the enemy from Maleme aerodrome. The experience of the previous day had shown what tremendous support was afforded to the enemy by his air forces, which made movement by day almost impossible. A night attack was therefore made by the 20th New Zealand Battalion and the 28th Maori Battalion, who recaptured almost the whole of the ground lost, but were exposed at daylight to intensive bombing by the enemy air forces and compelled to withdraw.

During the 21st and 22nd May troop-carrying aircraft continued to land on and about Maleme aerodrome although under artillery fire. It is estimated that as many as 600 troop carriers landed on one day. Their losses must have been extremely heavy, but they were able to establish a sufficiently strong force to drive back our troops in the Maleme sector with the aid of intensive support from bombing and fighting aircraft, which made movement by day practically impossible.

During the nights 21st/22nd May and 22nd/23rd May the Royal Navy intercepted and sunk large numbers of small craft transporting enemy troops, but suffered considerable losses during daylight from enemy air attack.

62. On 24th May and 25th May the fighting continued with the same intensity. The enemy continued to land troops and to force back our line from the Maleme area towards Canea, which was heavily bombed and almost destroyed. General Freyberg now abolished the separate Maleme sector and put the New Zealand troops who had formerly occupied it under General Weston, Royal Marines, the commander of the M.N.B.D.O.

63. I had meanwhile been sending to the island such reinforcements as were available and could be transported. By this time no merchant ship had any chance of survival within 50 miles of the island, and the only means of sending reinforcements was by fast warship which could reach Suda Bay under cover of darkness, disembark their troops and get clear of the island before dawn. This limited both the number and type of troops that could be sent, even if such reinforcements had been available. It was, for instance, impossible to send any more guns by this method. As already stated in para. 48, the reinforcements available were in any case extremely limited, in all three battalions (2nd Battalion the Queen's, 2nd Battalion Argyll and Sutherland Highlanders, 1st Battalion Leicester Regiment) and two battalions of Layforce, a body of specially picked troops who had

been sent out from the United Kingdom for combined enterprises. Headquarters 16th Infantry Brigade and 2nd Queen's set out for the island, but the ship in which they were being transported was hit during the passage and had to return to Alexandria. Of the reinforcements sent, the Leicester's and Argyll and Sutherland Highlanders were landed at Tymbaki on the south of the island and the former regiment and part of the latter made their way overland to the Heraklion sector; the remainder of the reinforcing units were landed at Suda Bay.

64. 26th May proved the critical day. Our line west of Canea was broken and driven back on Suda Bay, so that a considerable portion of the base area fell into enemy hands Suda Bay became no longer tenable. All troops were much exhausted and the enemy air bombing was as intensive as ever. The enemy had by this time landed some 30,000 to 35,000 troops on the island. Early on the morning of 27th May General Freyberg decided that evacuation was inevitable, and reported to me accordingly. In view of the situation he described and the impossibility of sending further reinforcements, I gave orders for the withdrawal of our garrisons from Crete.

65. Meanwhile the troops at Heraklion had had considerable fighting but had never been seriously pressed. The enemy had, however, continued to land troops in a valley to the east, outside the range of our defences, and was gradually accumulating a large force there. The whole of the garrison, except those wounded who could not be moved, were evacuated by cruiser and destroyer on the night of 28th–29th May. At the moment of embarkation there were many indications that an attack was about to come in from the force which had been built up to the east, and which had been joined by tanks and additional troops landing from the sea near Matea.

66. It is impossible at present to relate the full story of events at Retimo. Headquarters, 19th Australian Brigade, had been summoned to Suda Bay area early in the battle and the command passed to Lieut.-Colonel I. Campbell. Communication by land had been blocked by the enemy detachment described above; the garrison had no cyphers and was unable to communicate except by W/T in clear. General Freyberg reported that he was unable to communicate to the defenders the decision to withdraw and asked that an aeroplane might be sent to drop orders on the garrison. The aeroplane never returned and it is now known that the orders were never received. The 2/1st and 2/11th Australian Battalions under Lieut.-Colonel Campbell held their position until 31st May, when, after gallant fighting, they were overwhelmed by greatly superior forces including tanks. Most of the garrison became prisoners; a few escaped to the hills and small parties reached Egypt some weeks later.

67. The remains of the troops from the Maleme – Canea – Suda Bay area withdrew south across the island to Sphakia. The withdrawal was covered in the early stages by Layforce, 5th New Zealand Brigade and 19th Australian Brigade, the two latter working as one force. 4th New Zealand Brigade, some light tanks of

3rd Hussars, some guns and a battalion of Royal Marines also covered the retreat, which, in spite of very great difficulties was carried out with much bravery and determination, under the direction of General Weston. This withdrawal by troops who had already endured six days of the sternest fighting imaginable was a magnificent performance. The only blot on the story of the defence of Crete was the indiscipline of a certain proportion of the disorganized and unarmed elements of the force whom it had not been possible to evacuate before the attack. When the withdrawal to the southern beaches began, they much hampered both the retirement and orderly embarkation. The road ends some miles short of the beach and thence there are only rough paths down to the beach. The climb from the beach to the high ground above, which was held by the rearguard troops, took a minimum of two hours.

68. The first evacuation from Sphakia took place during the nights of 28th–29th and 29th–30th May, when the wounded and non-fighting troops were mostly embarked. On 30th May the enemy made contact with the rearguard, but was repulsed and made little further effort to interfere with the re-embarkation.

The Navy had sustained heavy losses in ships during the passage to and from Crete, and it had been decided that the evacuation must end on the night of 31st May–1st June. The embarkation during the last two nights was carried out under conditions of considerable difficulty, rations and water were limited and the troops, scattered in various hiding places during the day to shelter from enemy air attack, were difficult to collect for embarkation. I ordered General Freyberg to return to Egypt on the night of 30th–31st May, and he and his staff were taken off by flying boat. General Weston remained in command and was taken off on the following night. It is regretted that a considerable number of troops had to be left behind, including an Australian battalion and the bulk of Layforce, who had all fought most skilfully and gallantly to the end.

Out of the total of 27,550 Imperial troops on the island at the beginning of the attack, 14,580 were evacuated (7,130 out of 14,000 British, 2,890 out of 6,450 Australians, 4,560 out of 7,100 New Zealanders). What proportion of the 13,000 casualties were killed and wounded cannot yet be determined.

69. The failure to hold Crete was due mainly to the overwhelming superiority of the enemy aircraft and the way in which it was handled in conjunction with ground troops. Officers who had fought through the last war and had been engaged in France during this war have expressed their opinion that the bombardment the troops underwent in Crete was severer and more continuous than anything they had ever experienced. The handicap under which the force laboured in regard to lack of equipment and the difficulties of reinforcing the island with either men or material have been explained, but it was the enemy air force which was the deciding factor. Even had the German attack been beaten off it is very doubtful whether the troops in Crete could have been maintained in face of the enemy air force, which made the approach of shipping to the island most hazardous.

The troops, including the Greeks on the island, fought magnificently under the most stern conditions, and deserve the very greatest credit for their efforts. General Freyberg and General Weston, and the subordinate commanders under them such as Brigadiers Puttick, Chappell, Hargest, Vasey and Colonel Campbell, set a fine example to their men and handled their troops with determination and skill.

The work of the Royal Navy in preventing the enemy attempts at invasion by sea and in evacuation of the troops in spite of extremely heavy losses in ships and in men was beyond all praise. To Admiral Sir Andrew Cunningham himself, who took the responsibility of ordering the evacuation to proceed in spite of the losses, the Army owes a deep debt of gratitude.

Although they were completely outmatched in numbers, the Royal Air Force never failed to do their utmost to support the Army. Though they were obliged to operate from distant places in Egypt, they attacked to the utmost of their ability and in spite of heavy and inevitable losses.

70. The defence of Crete, though unsuccessful, undoubtedly frustrated the enemy plan for future operations by destroying so large a portion of his air-borne troops. The total enemy losses were at least 12,000–15,000, of whom a very high proportion were killed. The defence saved in all probability Cyprus, Syria, Iraq and perhaps Tobruk. Thus our losses in Crete, though heavy, were very far from being in vain, and the gallant resistance of the force saved our position in the Middle East at a critical time. The fighting in Crete may prove a turning point of the war.

### Revolt in Iraq.

71. While our preparations for the defence of Crete and of the Western Desert were absorbing practically our whole attention and resources, a critical situation in Iraq suddenly made fresh demands on Middle East.

Our relations with the Iraq Government during the war had become increasingly unsatisfactory. By treaty Iraq was pledged to give us assistance in war and to permit the passage of British troops through Iraq. There was a British Military Mission with the Iraq Army and the Royal Air Force had stations at Habbaniyah, some 40 miles west of Baghdad, and at Shaibah, near Basra. For the protection of the R.A.F. establishments there were locally enlisted Iraq Levies.

All operational aircraft were removed from Iraq early in the war, and there remained only a few obsolete machines at Shaibah and a depôt and training school at Habbaniyah with training aircraft only.

72. Although the Iraq Government, after some pressure, broke off diplomatic relations with Germany, they did not declare war; and when Italy entered the war they did not even break off relations with the Italian Government and allowed the Italian Legation to remain in Baghdad, a hot bed of anti-British propaganda and espionage. As the military successes of the Axis powers increased, so did the unfriendly influence of Rashid Ali become more effective in controlling the

conduct of the Iraq Government. The Mufti of Jerusalem and other malcontents from Palestine, to whom Iraq had given asylum, formed a centre of anti-British intrigue. A force had been under preparation in India for use in Iraq should enemy forces reach that country, but the situation in Middle East after the Italians entered into the war and the Japanese threat to Malaya made it necessary to divert this force in other directions which were of more urgent importance.

73. Early in 1941 it was decided to take diplomatic action to try and improve relations with the Iraq Government and to this end Sir Kinahan Cornwallis was appointed ambassador. There was, however, considerable delay in his despatch to Iraq and he did not reach Baghdad till a few days before the revolt broke out.

74. Political crises and frequent changes of Government are an ordinary feature in Iraq. The beginning of the troubles was a change of Government which brought into power as Prime Minister Rashid Ali Ghailani, who was known to our Intelligence to be in the pay of the Axis. At first he professed himself as desirous of co-operating with His Majesty's Government, but his subservience to Axis direction became more and more manifest and he even contemplated re-establishing diplomatic relations with Germany. It was also clear that the real power behind him was four well-known pro-Axis generals in the Iraqi army who were popularly known as the Golden Square.

75. On 31st March, the Regent of Iraq, learning of a plot to arrest him, left Baghdad for Basra and shortly afterwards took refuge on a British warship. Later he flew to Transjordan with his most prominent supporters. The general position in Iraq became so threatening that about the middle of April His Majesty's Government decided to land a force at Basra in accordance with our treaty rights of passing troops through Iraq. A line of communications from Basra to Baghdad by rail and thence by road across the desert to Haifa, had been prepared early in the war as an alternative line of communications to the Middle East, should the Red Sea be rendered unsafe by enemy action; a large sum of money had been spent in improving the road across the desert from Haifa to Baghdad.

76. A brigade group was about to sail from India as reinforcement to Malaya; this brigade was diverted at short notice to the Persian Gulf and landed at Basra on 18th April.
    Control of the military situation in Iraq had been a responsibility of the Middle East since the beginning of the war, but the Commander-in-chief in India had lately raised the question whether, in the event of operations in Iraq, these should not be controlled from India. Since the great majority of troops in Iraq would in all probability be Indian and the line of communications through the Persian Gulf to Basra must be under Indian direction, I agreed that there would be considerable advantage in India assuming command, at all events of the Basra base and of operations in lower Iraq. Accordingly, on the landing of this force at Basra, responsibility for Iraq was handed over to the Commander-in-Chief in India.

77. The first effects of the landings of troops were favourable. But when Rashid Ali was informed that a second brigade would shortly be landed, he sought to refuse permission until the original brigade had moved out of Iraq. While the question was still under discussion Rashid Ali and the pro-Axis elements in Baghdad decided to take action against the Royal Air Force station at Habbaniyah, to which place the British women and children in Baghdad had been transferred on 29th April, in view of the obviously threatening attitude of certain elements in Baghdad.

78. The Air Force station at Habbaniyah lies on low ground near the River Euphrates, and is completely overlooked and commanded by high ground to the west between the station and Lake Habbaniyah. This ground is 150 ft. high and only some 1,000 yards from the station. The small force of levies at Habbaniyah was quite insufficient to occupy this high ground, on which the Iraqi mechanized force of approximately a brigade, with several batteries and a number of tanks and armoured cars, installed itself on 30th April. While the Ambassador at Baghdad was trying to secure the withdrawal of this Iraqi force by diplomatic means, its numbers were increased, till by the evening of 1st May, the total was about 11 battalions with some 50 guns, over 9,000 men in all. Their attitude became so threatening that the Air Officer Commanding Iraq, Air Vice-Marshal Smart, decided that it was essential to attack these troops without further warning. Accordingly, in the early morning of 2nd May, an improvised air force, made up mainly from the machines in the training school attacked the Iraqi forces. It was hoped that the effect of air bombing might shake the morale of the Iraqi troops and cause them to withdraw. The attacks did not, however, have the desired effect, the Iraqis finding good concealment in broken ground and maintaining their positions, although the ultimate result of this bombing must have contributed to their subsequent defeat and further air attacks on reserves prevented effective reinforcement.

79. The situation of the Royal Air Force in Habbaniyah was now critical. The defenders comprised only some 350 British infantry (flown up from Basra), R.A.F. Armoured Car Company of 18 cars, about 1,000 Royal Air Force personnel, and six companies of levies. They had no artillery and had to defend a perimeter of 7 miles, including the river frontage. The Iraqis on the high ground could command at close range with artillery and even with machine-guns the aero1drome from which machines had to take off and land and had they made a determined assault, it would hardly have been possible to withstand them. As it was they contented themselves with artillery fire, which did little damage. The Iraqi Air Force also began bombing attacks on Habbaniyah. Reinforcement or relief of the garrison presented considerable difficulty; it was flood season in Iraq, which made movement from Basra by rail, road or river towards Baghdad difficult, and Iraqi forces had occupied points on the Tigris and on the railway to prevent movement northwards from Basra. A British battalion (1st King's Own Royal Regiment) was sent by air from Basra to Habbaniyah to reinforce the garrison

and such aeroplanes as could be spared from Middle East were sent to Habbaniyah. These put the Iraqi Air Force out of action by 7th May, but meanwhile German air forces were being transported to Iraq, using landing grounds in Syria on the way, without interference and without protest from the Vichy French.

80. On 5th May, the War Cabinet transferred the responsibility for Iraq back from India to Middle East, and I was instructed to send a force across the desert to relieve Habbaniyah and occupy Baghdad. The only mobile force I could make available from Palestine was one cavalry brigade group. If this force was despatched to Iraq, there would be no possibility of providing a force for Syria should the need arise. The Chiefs of Staff accepted this conclusion and took the responsibility of ordering this force to be sent to Iraq. Accordingly, I made up a motorised column consisting of the 4th Cavalry Brigade, under Brigadier Kingstone (Household Cavalry Regiment, Wiltshire Yeomanry, Warwickshire Yeomanry), 60th Field Regiment, R.A., from Egypt and 1st Essex Regiment. The whole force was placed under the command of Major-General J.G.W. Clark, the Commander of the 1st Cavalry Division. The Arab Legion, a military police force enlisted in Transjordan from Bedouin Arabs, also accompanied the force and gave invaluable assistance.

There was extreme difficulty in raising sufficient transport for even this small force, and it was not until 10th May that it was possible for the force to advance across the Iraq frontier. Meanwhile, Iraqi forces had occupied the fort at Rutbah. The distance from Haifa to the Transjordan frontier is 284 miles, thence to Habbaniyah, 285 miles.

81. On 7th May, the garrison at Habbaniyah made a successful sortie and drove the Iraqi troops from the high ground overlooking the station, capturing some 400 prisoners, six guns and much equipment. The Iraqi forces retreated to Fallujah on the Euphrates.

On 18th May, Habforce, as Major-General Clark's column was termed, after recapturing Rutbah, where the Arab Legion greatly distinguished itself, reached Habbaniyah. It then began an advance on Baghdad by Fallujah, where, however, it was delayed for some days owing to the floods making the approaches to the river impassable for mechanical vehicles. After the road had been repaired with some difficulty, Fallujah was captured on 19th May. On 22nd May, an Iraqi force made a determined attack on Fallujah and succeeded temporarily in reoccupying the town. It was, however, driven out by a counter attack with considerable losses.

82. On 23rd May I flew to Basra to meet the Commander-in-Chief in India, General Sir Claude Auchinleck, to discuss further reinforcements and operations in Iraq. I instructed General Quinan, commanding the Indian forces, now that the situation at Basra was in hand, to push a force by the line of the railway from Shaibah towards Baghdad as rapidly as possible. It was decided that India would send reinforcements to complete a total of two divisions in Iraq.

83. After repulsing the Iraqi counter attack at Fallujah, General Clark's small force moved on Baghdad in two columns. After overcoming the delays due to floods and the enemy's destruction of communications, he arrived within a short distance of Baghdad on 30th May. His strength was 1,200 men with eight guns and a few armoured cars.

Although there was practically the whole of a division of the Iraqi army in Baghdad and a further force at Ramadi on the Euphrates, in rear of General Clark's force, Rashid Ali and his supporters had lost heart and fled; and the Mayor of Baghdad sent out a white flag and asked for terms for capitulation. After discussion with the Ambassador, who had been confined to the Embassy for the past four weeks, satisfactory terms were arranged. The Regent of Iraq and some of his ministers, who had escaped to Transjordan at the time of Rashid Ali's *coup d'etat*, returned to Baghdad on 1st June and formed a legitimate Government.

A small force of the Household Cavalry regiment and one battery with some armoured cars was at once sent on to Mosul to secure the landing ground there, which had been used by German air forces during the revolt. A Gurkha battalion was then flown up from Baghdad.

84. We may consider ourselves exceedingly fortunate to have liquidated what might have been a very serious commitment with such small forces and with little trouble. Rashid Ali and his adherents seem to have lost heart at the weakness of the support accorded to them by the Germans. The gallant defence of Habbaniyah and the bold advance of Habforce discouraged the Iraqi army, while the Germans in their turn were prevented from sending further reinforcements by the desperate resistance of our troops in Crete, and their crippling losses in men and aircraft. The majority of the Iraq population, especially the tribesmen outside the principal towns, did not give any active support to the revolutionary government but had the Germans sent sufficient forces to enable the Iraqi rebels to score a. success, the whole country might well have risen against us. The Iraqi army admitted to losses of 1,750, including 500 killed. Our own losses were slight.

*The Syrian Problem.*

85. Early in May, while Middle East was busily engaged with the problems of Crete, the Western Desert, and Iraq, a fresh commitment arose from the German infiltration into Syria. At the end of April the Chiefs of Staff pointed out the danger of the Germans establishing a footing in Syria and instructed me to be prepared to send a force into Syria if necessary to support any French resistance to the Germans. I replied that my information was to the effect that General Dentz, High Commissioner in Syria, was completely subservient to Vichy and was most unlikely to resist German penetration; and that the largest force I could make available in Palestine was one incomplete cavalry brigade group. I advised against an approach to Dentz, which had been suggested by the Chiefs of Staff, as I considered it would only result in our strength, or rather weakness, becoming known to the enemy.

At this time the question of the use of the Free French forces in Syria came to the front. Some battalions of the Free French had been sent to the Middle East early in 1941 and had been used in the Sudan in operations against Eritrea. After the capture of Massawa, General de Gaulle requested that all the Free French forces in the Middle East should be concentrated in Egypt to be formed into a division under General Legentilhomme. Some additional units were on their way to Egypt. I arranged for the formation of the division in Egypt, and later agreed to transfer the French troops to Palestine on General de Gaulle's representations that he would like them to be readily available for use in Syria if the French in Syria resisted German penetration. By about the middle of May the Free French forces in Palestine consisted of six battalions, a battery and a company of about 20 tanks. They were located near Qastima, to the south of Jaffa. They were incomplete in transport, and in some instances in weapons.

86. Early in May, as already related, I was instructed to send the only mobile force available in Palestine to Iraq. When this had departed, the whole of the troops in Palestine were practically immobile and a great proportion of the civil transport available had been hired to make up Habforce. Nevertheless I was still being urged to enter Syria to expel the Germans from it.

87. Late on the evening of 18th May General Catroux, the Free French Commissioner in Middle East, came to me and said he had certain information that the French in Syria were withdrawing the whole of their troops into the Lebanon and were handing over the remainder of Syria to the Germans. He declared that the road to Damascus was open and that it was urgently necessary to take advantage of the opportunity and to send a force into Syria immediately. He was most insistent that I should issue orders to this effect there and then. Previous experience had taught me to regard the information produced by the Free French from Syria with caution, and what General Catroux stated was not confirmed by intelligence I had received from other sources. Quite apart from this, as stated above, I had not the troops or the transport available to send a force into Syria. I therefore refused to take any immediate action but summoned a meeting for the following morning to consider the whole question. At this meeting there was general agreement as to the desirability of forestalling the Germans in Syria, but the only means available was by weakening the defence of Egypt in the Western Desert. In the meantime, I insisted on verification of the Free French information before acting on it.

88. I reported General Catroux's request to the Chiefs of Staff, who again urged me to take immediate action in Syria, and, if I was unable to provide a force, to allow the Free French to enter Syria alone. I pointed out that the Free French could not move without transport which I was unable to supply and that they were unwilling to move without the support of some British artillery. I gave my opinion that nothing smaller than a corps with an armoured division would be sufficient for the effective occupation of Syria, and that it would be most unwise

to attempt operations with a small, ill-equipped force, such as the Free French contingent.

On 21st May General Catroux, who had gone to Palestine to meet a French officer from Syria, cabled admitting that his information was entirely incorrect; that far from withdrawing into the Lebanon the French were moving troops south of Damascus and taking up positions to defend the routes to that city. He said that nothing but a large force could attempt the occupation of Syria. Meanwhile I had been receiving telegrams from General de Gaulle in West Africa, couched in imperative language, enquiring why the Free French troops were not already on the march to Damascus. This incident illustrates the difficulties there sometimes were in dealing with the Free French.

89. It was, however, apparent that I might have to take action in Syria in spite of my weakness. The dangers to the Suez Canal and our bases in Egypt if the enemy succeeded in establishing himself in Syria were obvious. Cyprus would be at his mercy, and a German occupation of Syria would practically complete the encirclement of Turkey and make it difficult for the Turks to continue to resist German demands.

I therefore decided that some risk to the defence of Egypt in the Western Desert must be accepted, and issued orders for the 7th Australian Division (less one brigade in Tobruk) to move to northern Palestine, and I sent to the northern frontier of Transjordan the 5th Indian Infantry Brigade of the 4th Division which had just arrived from the Sudan. I instructed General Wilson, G.O.C. Palestine, to make preparations for a possible advance into Syria. As usual, one of the principal difficulties was to find the necessary transport and signals for the force and the usual process of scraping from other units and formations had to be resorted to to produce any force at all.

90. On 25th May I reported to the War Office that I was preparing a plan for an advance into Syria with the 7th Australian Division less one brigade, the Free French troops, and certain units of the 1st Cavalry Division. This was a much smaller force than I considered necessary, also I disliked using the Free French since I knew that this would be likely to stiffen the resistance of the French in Syria, but I had no other troops I could make available. I was instructed by the Chiefs of Staff to advance into Syria as soon as the above force was reasonably prepared. I reported that 7th June was the earliest date by which the operation could start, actually it began on 8th June.

91. The general plan was to advance into Syria on a broad front. On the right the 5th Indian Brigade was to occupy Deraa and the line of the Yarmuk railway. The Free French force was then to pass through and advance on Damascus. On the left the 7th Australian Division was to advance in two columns, one by Merjayun, one by the coast road to Beirut. I realized that if the French resisted progress would be slow and that the force might not be strong enough to accomplish its object. The Vichy French were in greatly superior numbers and

had some 90 tanks, while no armoured vehicles could be spared from the Western Desert. The air support was bound to be comparatively weak, since the greater part of the air forces was required to support the attack which was being staged shortly afterwards in the Western Desert.

The Navy would support the advance with a squadron along the coast. Protection to this squadron from enemy air attack occupied the greater proportion of our fighter aircraft available.

92. The advance began early on 8th June and at first made fair progress. The French had obviously expected attack by a much larger force; but finding how weak we were, they soon took heart and their resistance stiffened. On the right the Free French had advanced to within about ten miles of Damascus by 12th June. On the left the Australian right column captured Merjayun, while on 9th June the left column after an extremely hard fight had crossed the river Litani on the coast. In this action a commando from Cyprus effected a landing on the coast and assisted in the Australian success, though at the cost of somewhat heavy casualties. The French now began a series of counterattacks. On the right they sent a column from Damascus which made a turning movement by the Jebel Druze and attacked our lines of communication between Deraa and Damascus. Further west another column attacked the 1st Royal Fusiliers at Kuneitra and captured the greater part of the battalion. Another column advanced on Merjayun and recaptured it, the Australian forces in this area having made a wide outflanking movement against the next French position and having thus left the main road open. On the coast also there was severe fighting. In all these counter-attacks the French used their medium tanks effectively. Although all these counter-attacks were driven back, their effect was to bring our advance almost to a standstill. I realized that I should have to send reinforcements. By the middle of June, by taking transport as it came off the ships and issuing it direct to units, I was able to make one brigade of the 6th Division and an artillery regiment mobile and placed them at General Wilson's disposal. Meanwhile a very fine effort by the 5th Indian Brigade under Brigadier Lloyd and by the Free French had resulted in the capture of Damascus by 21st June after some very bitter fighting, with heavy casualties on both sides.

93. Towards the end of June, I was able to make use of troops from Iraq to increase the pressure on Syria. Two brigades of General Quinan's force moved from Baghdad up the Euphrates by Abu Kemal and Deir Ez Zor towards Aleppo, while Habforce moved across the desert towards Palmyra and Homs. The Free French moved north from Damascus towards Homs, while the 6th Division, of which two brigades were now ready, moved northwest from Damascus towards Rayak. The 7th Australian Division which had advanced to Sidon prepared to assault the last remaining French position at Damour covering Beirut.

The 10th Indian Division (less one brigade) from Baghdad reached Deir Ez Zor without opposition other than air attack: Habforce had a hard fight before capturing Palmyra; and the 6th Division met strong resistance on the road to

Rayak; on 9th July the Australians assaulted and captured the French defences at Damour, with the assistance of bombardment from the sea by a naval squadron. Under pressure of these attacks the French asked for an armistice on 11th July. Terms were finally signed on 14th July, and Syria passed into Allied occupation.

94. The French in Syria put up an extremely stout fight on ground which was eminently favourable to the defence, and casualties on both sides were heavy. The feeling between the Vichy French and Free French was extremely bitter, and the French professional soldiers were also undoubtedly fighting with a view to preserving their professional honour.

General Wilson handled a difficult problem with his usual skill and imperturbability. General Lavarack commanded the 7th Australian Division, and later, the whole of the forces in Syria, most ably. The 7th Australian Division, most of whom were engaged for the first time, had a hard fight and acquitted themselves with great credit. A particular word of praise must be said for Brigadier Lloyd's 5th Indian Brigade, to whose determination and self-sacrifice the capture of Damascus is mainly due. The Free French fought stoutly in most unpleasant circumstances, their Commander, General Legentilhomme, carrying on in spite of a wound which broke his arm early in the operations.

We must be again considered fortunate in achieving our objective with forces which were really insufficient for their task. It was only skilful handling and determined fighting that brought about success.

### Operations in the Western Desert.

95. During May and the early part of June, while the operations already described in Crete, Iraq and Syria were in progress, preparations were being made to reform the 7th Armoured Division with the tanks sent from home and tanks which had been repaired in the workshops in Egypt, and to undertake operations against the enemy on the western frontier of Egypt with the object of driving him back and recovering Cyrenaica, at least as far as Tobruk.

On 1st May I had instructed Lieut.-General Sir Noel Beresford-Peirse, commanding in the Western Desert, to prepare an offensive operation as soon as our armoured strength permitted. It was hoped that it might be possible to re-equip the 7th Armoured Division before the end of May and to assume the offensive at the beginning of June. Meantime, however, the enemy was also being reinforced and was expected to bring forward an additional German armoured division by the middle of May. There was always the possibility that the enemy might forestall us and advance on the Delta before we were in a position to take the offensive ourselves. Defensive preparations in the Matruh area had therefore to be made at the same time.

96. In the middle of May, before the reinforcements from the United Kingdom could be unloaded, there seemed to be a fleeting opportunity of attacking the enemy forward troops on the Egyptian border near Sollum in favourable circumstances. Our intelligence seemed to show that the enemy strength in armoured

fighting vehicles in the forward area was small and that he was in difficulties with his supplies. I decided to make a limited attack with the small number of tanks I had available, about 30 Cruisers and 25 "I" tanks, in the hope of recovering Sollum and Capuzzo and thus securing a good jumping off place for an attack on a larger scale as soon as my reinforcements were available.

The attack was made on 15th May and was at first successful, Sollum and Capuzzo being captured and considerable losses inflicted on the enemy. Next day, however, the enemy succeeded in bringing up a large force of tanks from his reserve and we were compelled to retire. The enemy tanks showed a disinclination to engage closely, although in superior numbers, and we were able to withdraw with little loss.

97. The process of unloading the tanks from the United Kingdom and carrying out the necessary fittings and adjustments proved a longer and more difficult job than had been expected. In spite of every effort it was impossible to get all the tanks ready by the end of May. One of the ships had to be sent to Port Said for unloading since the cranes in Alexandria harbour were unable to lift the tanks from the hold. Many of the tanks required considerable overhaul, besides the fitting of sand filters and desert camouflage, and some of them were of a pattern which had not previously been in the Middle East. It was not until the first week in June that all the tanks were available, and then the state of training and readiness for battle of the 7th Armoured Division caused me considerable anxiety. The personnel of the Division had been without tanks since February, and so short had equipment been that there had not even been sufficient tanks or wireless sets available for them to continue their training while waiting to be re-equipped. Apart from normal wastage, detachments had been sent to Tobruk and to Crete, as well as to the Sudan. The units were, therefore, in no state to take over new equipment and immediately to be put into battle. Many light tank drivers and crews had to be put to man Cruisers or "I" tanks, the crews were as strange to one another as they were to their machines, and no high standard of driving, gunnery or maintenance could be looked for without at least a month's hard training. I was, however, being urged to attack with the least possible delay, and was myself anxious to forestall, if possible, the arrival of more German reinforcements.

10th June was the earliest possible date by which a sufficient force was available to take the offensive with any chance of success, but the Commander of the 7th Armoured Division, Major-General Sir Michael O'Moore Creagh, asked for at least five days to enable his crews to fire their guns and obtain some working knowledge of the new machines they were to take into action, as well as to allow staffs and commanders, many of whom were new since the Division had last been a formation, to settle down and become acquainted with each other. I therefore decided to attack on 15th June.

98. Meanwhile the enemy, on 27th May, had made a short advance in considerable strength and had driven my light covering forces back from the Halfaya Pass, which he occupied and began to prepare intensively for defence.

99. The length of my line of communications, 120 miles from Matruh to the Egyptian frontier across waterless desert, limited the size of the force it was possible to employ. In any event it was obvious that the battle would be decided mainly by the respective armoured forces, and I put into action the largest armoured force I could make available by this date. The 7th Armoured Division consisted of the 11th Hussars (Armoured Cars), the 7th Armoured Brigade of two Cruiser regiments and 4th Armoured Brigade of two "I" tank regiments, and a Support Group comprising two regiments of 25-pounders, one anti-tank regiment, one motorised infantry battalion and some light anti-aircraft artillery. Each armoured brigade was thus short of one regiment, but it would not have been possible to complete the brigades to their full complement of three regiments till the end of June or early in July. The pace and radius of action of the two armoured brigades was so widely different that it would obviously be extremely difficult to combine them. The Cruiser tanks had a speed of 15–20 miles an hour and a radius of action of 80–100 miles, whereas the "I" tanks had a radius of action of only 40 miles and a speed of no more than about 5 miles an hour in action.

100. The course of operations on or near the Egyptian frontier is largely conditioned by the escarpment which runs south-east from Sollum. It is steep and about 200 ft. high, impassable to tanks or vehicles for about 50 miles from Sollum except at Sollum itself and at Halfaya Pass. An advance along the coast therefore would have to find its way up one of these steep routes, while an advance south of the escarpment involved the exposure of the line of communications to a flanking attack from the south.

The plan drawn, up by Lieut.-General Sir Noel Beresford-Peirse, which I approved, was to advance in three columns. The right column, along the sea coast, consisted of the 11th Indian Infantry Brigade, Central India Horse, one field regiment and one field company; it was to advance to Sollum, assisting the centre column to capture Halfaya. The centre column, to move south of the escarpment, consisted of the 4th Armoured Brigade (two "I" tank battalions), two field regiments, one medium battery, one anti-tank regiment, and the 22nd Guards Brigade. It was to advance south of the escarpment, cross the frontier well to the south of Sollum, thus avoiding the enemy's prepared defences, and then turn north and capture Musaid, Bir Waer and Capuzzo. A detachment was to capture Halfaya. The left column, 7th Armoured Division less 4th Armoured Brigade was to advance further south of the escarpment to protect the left flank of the centre column and to attack the enemy tank forces wherever encountered. It was anticipated that the attack of the right and centre columns on the enemy defended areas, while the left column threatened the enemy's rear and supplies, would lead to reaction by the enemy armoured forces and bring on a tank battle either east of the frontier during the attack on Halfaya or west of the frontier after our capture of Capuzzo.

If the first stage of the attack was successful and the enemy forces on the frontier were defeated, it was intended to continue the advance to the Tobruk –

El Adem area, and to engage the enemy there in conjunction with a sortie in force by the Tobruk garrison.

101. It was estimated that there were in the forward area Bardia – Capuzzo – Sollum about 5,700 Germans with about 100 medium tanks and 50 armoured cars, 20 field guns and 70 anti-tank guns. The Italian forces in the same area were estimated at 7,500 with about 50 guns and 20 anti-tank guns. In the Tobruk – El Adem area there were over 11,000 Germans, with 120 medium and 70 light tanks, about 36 field guns and 80 anti-tank guns; there were about 16,000 Italians with 120 field guns, 32 anti-tank guns and a few tanks. Altogether, if he brought up his tanks from the Tobruk area, the enemy could concentrate 300 against our total of approximately 200.

102. The air forces available to support the attack consisted of six fighter squadrons, four medium bomber squadrons, and four squadrons (less detachments) of heavy night bombers. This force owing to other demands only became available just before the attack; in the week or ten days preceding the attack very little preparatory air action had been possible. Owing to the lack of equipment and some technical failures in the equipment available, photographic reconnaissance of the enemy positions before the battle had been scanty and disappointing. There was a great shortage of trained pilots for tactical reconnaissance.

103. During 15th and 16th June the attack progressed fairly satisfactorily. The 22nd Guards Brigade occupied Capuzzo and Bir Waer taking several hundred prisoners and some guns, and the Cruiser tanks of the 7th Armoured Division inflicted considerable casualties on the enemy tanks. The enemy, however, still held out at Halfaya and Sollum, one squadron of Cruiser tanks had lost practically all its vehicles in an attack west of Capuzzo by running on to a concealed enemy anti-tank gun position; and we had suffered considerable casualties in "I" tanks from enemy minefields and some enemy high velocity guns at Halfaya. On the evening of 16th June a strong force of enemy tanks attempted an outflanking movement to the south and was engaged by the 7th Armoured Brigade near Sidi Omar. Our Cruiser tanks inflicted casualties on the enemy but found themselves at the conclusion of the engagement heavily outnumbered and were compelled to withdraw.

104. The situation on the morning of 17th June was that the 22nd Guards Brigade was still in position at Capuzzo, Musaid and Bir Waer, with the 4th Armoured Brigade protecting its left flank. Enemy detachments still held out in Sollum and at Halfaya and strong enemy columns with a large number of armoured fighting vehicles were advancing south from Bardia and eastwards from southwest of Capuzzo. To the south the 7th Armoured Division had been forced back from Sidi Omar and was in the Sidi Suleiman area. An enemy column containing artillery and some 75 tanks had advanced east from Sidi Omar towards Halfaya and was threatening to cut off our troops in the forward area. The 7th Armoured Brigade had only some 20 Cruiser tanks remaining in action.

During the night of 16th/17th June General Creagh had asked General Messervy who was commanding the troops in the forward area, to release the 4th Armoured Brigade to attack southward against the enemy column from Sidi Omar while the 7th Armoured Brigade attacked northwards. Owing to mechanical breakdowns and the exhaustion of his crews Brigadier Gatehouse, commanding the 4th Armoured Brigade, was unable to move before daylight. As soon as he began to move southwards, a large enemy column of tanks advanced against the left flank and rear of the 22nd Guards Brigade, and General Messervy was compelled to request Brigadier Gatehouse to return and counter attack. The 4th Armoured Brigade drove back the enemy tanks, but incurred some losses. When it again attempted to move southwards to attack the enemy column from Sidi Omar, the enemy again advanced against the 22nd Guards Brigade, and General Messervy was compelled to inform General Creagh that he could not hold his position without the support of the 4th Armoured Brigade.

105. I had gone up to General Beresford-Peirse's Headquarters at Sidi Barrani on the afternoon of 16th June. On the morning of 17th June, hearing of the critical situation at the front, I flew to General Creagh's Headquarters. Before I reached General Creagh's Headquarters, General Messervy had ordered the withdrawal of the forward troops, as it appeared to him that unless he withdrew without delay the enemy column from Sidi Omar combined with the enemy column from the westward would completely surround him and close his line of retreat. The 7th Armoured Brigade had by this time, as already stated, only some 20 Cruiser tanks in action, while the 4th Armoured Brigade was reduced to less than 20 "I" tanks. Both air force and ground observation estimated the advancing enemy columns as containing at least 200 tanks supported by numerous artillery. In the circumstances I considered that General Messervy's decision to withdraw was justified and that any delay would have led to his force being cut off and in all probability the loss of the greater part of it without any corresponding gain. The withdrawal was carried out in good order, and the enemy tanks, which were heavily attacked by the bombers of the Royal Air Force, made only half hearted attempts to close with our forces.

106. Our losses in personnel in this three days' battle were just over 1,000, of whom approximately 150 were killed and 250 missing. Our losses in tanks were unfortunately heavy, 25 cruiser tanks and 70 "I" tanks were lost. The great majority of the cruiser tanks were lost by enemy action, but a considerable proportion of the "I" tank losses were due to mechanical breakdowns which could have been put right had time been available, but had to be left behind during the withdrawal, for lack of transporters to bring them back. It is estimated that 40–50 enemy tanks were destroyed by ground action and much mechanical transport, in addition to numbers destroyed by air action. The enemy personnel losses are not known but must have been heavy; 220 German and 350 Italian prisoners were taken, and a large number of enemy were buried.

107. The main cause of our failure was undoubtedly the difficulty in combining the action of cruiser and "I" tanks, the cramping effect on manoeuvre of having only two regiments in each armoured brigade and the lack of training in the 7th Armoured Division. Had tank crews had more practice with their weapons they would have destroyed a much larger number of enemy tanks; and had they all been more experienced in maintenance there would have been fewer tanks out of action through mechanical breakdown; so that instead of being so outnumbered at the end of the battle, we should have been in sufficient strength to have defeated the enemy.

The enemy manoeuvred his forces skilfully but showed little boldness or inclination to close and had undoubtedly a most healthy respect for the efficiency of the 2-pdr. and the shooting of our artillery. He was prepared for our attack and had anticipated the lines it would probably take, which were dictated by the lie of the ground. He succeeded in concentrating practically the whole of his tank forces in the forward area without our becoming aware of it.

108. After the action I withdrew the 7th Armoured Division to Matruh to refit and held the forward area as before by small columns of mobile infantry and artillery. The enemy made no attempt to exploit his success and had undoubtedly been severely handled. In fact, his attitude ever since has been entirely defensive both on the Egyptian frontier and outside Tobruk.

*Summary of Operations.*

109. In the six months covered by this despatch, from 7th February (date of the capture of Benghazi) to 14th July (date of the signing of the Convention with the French in Syria), Middle East was called upon to conduct no fewer than six major campaigns – in Greece, in Cyrenaica, in Crete, in Iraq, in Syria, and in Italian East Africa. During May, five of these were being conducted simultaneously, and there were never less than three on hand at one time. The theatres of these operations were several hundreds of miles apart, in some instances well over a thousand. Resources to meet the enemy strength were inadequate, both on the ground and in the air. In the circumstances, the fact that three of these campaigns, in Italian East Africa, in Iraq and in Syria, were brought to successful conclusions, and that the enemy counter offensive in Cyrenaica was firmly checked, may be considered to reflect credit on the troops and commanders concerned. In Greece and in Crete, the odds against our forces, especially in the air, were too heavy for successful defence; but in both theatres the great majority of the troops engaged were withdrawn, thanks to the skill and self-sacrifice of the Royal Navy, after having repulsed many enemy attacks and without having suffered tactical defeat. The losses inflicted on the enemy in Crete undoubtedly saved the general position in the Middle East by destroying the greater part of the enemy's airborne troops and a very large number of his aircraft.

110. Throughout these operations the morale of the troops remained high and they had always well justified confidence that with anything like material equality,

they were more than a match for any German troops. The defence of Crete and of Tobruk will rank among the finest achievements of the forces of the British Empire.

111. The operations in Italian East Africa are being described in a separate despatch.

### Co-operation of other Services.

112. The Army in the Middle East owes a deep debt of gratitude to the Royal Navy in the Mediterranean, and to Admiral Sir Andrew Cunningham in particular, not only for its magnificent work in twice embarking large forces from open beaches in circumstances of great difficulty and danger, but also for its day to day co-operation in protecting convoys, in carrying stores, in attacking enemy lines of communication and in assisting military operations by every possible means. In particular, the successful defence of Tobruk has only been possible by reason of the Navy's work in keeping the port open and the garrison supplied in spite of continual enemy air attack. The successful occupation of Syria also owed much to naval co-operation.

113. The Royal Air Force has suffered throughout the operations described from possibly an even greater paucity of adequate means than the Army. So far as their resources allowed they have given to the Army the most self-sacrificing support. The forms of Army co-operation known and practised before the war, such as artillery observation and close tactical reconnaissance, have for all practical purposes ceased, since the machines designed for these tasks can no longer be flown in the presence of the enemy, and the supply of pilots trained for army co-operation is almost exhausted. Means of photographic reconnaissance have also never been sufficient for army requirements. The technique of close support of the Army by the Air Force on the battlefield, such as the Germans have put into practice with such effect, has hardly yet begun to be studied in our forces and the necessary machines and technical equipment are lacking. Over the opposing air forces the Royal Air Force have shown throughout the period their usual superiority in skill and efficiency; and subject to their numbers, and the limitations mentioned above, have always co-operated most whole-heartedly with the operations of the army in the Middle East, on whose behalf I desire to express my grateful thanks to Air Chief Marshal Sir Arthur Longmore and to his successor Air Marshal A.W. Tedder.

### Appreciation of Services.

114. I should like to take this opportunity to bring to notice a small body of men, who have for a year past done inconspicuous but invaluable service, the Long Range Desert Group. It was formed under Major (now Colonel) R.A. Bagnold in July, 1940, to reconnoitre the great Libyan desert on the western borders of Egypt and the Sudan. Operating in small independent columns, the group has penetrated into nearly every part of desert Libya, an area comparable in size with that of India. Not only have the patrols brought back much information, but they

have attacked enemy forts, captured personnel, transport and grounded aircraft as far as 800 miles inside hostile territory. They have protected Egypt and the Sudan from any possibility of raids and have caused the enemy, in a lively apprehension of their activities, to tie up considerable forces in the defence of distant outposts. Their journeys across vast regions of unexplored desert have entailed the crossing of physical obstacles and the endurance of extreme summer temperatures, both of which would a year ago have been deemed impossible. Their exploits have been achieved only by careful organization, and a very high standard of enterprise, discipline, mechanical maintenance and desert navigation. The personnel of these patrols was originally drawn almost entirely from the New Zealand forces; later, officers and men of British units and from Southern Rhodesia joined the group. A special word of praise must be added for the R.A.O.C. fitters whose work contributed so much to the mechanical endurance of the vehicles in such unprecedented conditions.

115. As will be gathered from the facts related, the staff of the Middle East Command has had to work under continual severe pressure. I owe much to my two principal staff officers, Lieut.-General A.F. Smith and Major-General B.O. Hutchison, whose example of hard work and efficiency combined with cheerfulness and tact has inspired the whole staff. I wish here to express my deep appreciation of the work and spirit of all who have served me so loyally in G.H.Q., Middle East.

116. Lieut.-General Sir Thomas Blamey was appointed Deputy Commander-in-Chief in May, 1941. His sound advice and ready assistance did much to lighten the burden on my shoulders.

117. The Middle East Command owes a deep debt of gratitude to India. During the period of nearly two years while I was Commander-in-Chief, Middle East, Inever made any request on India for men or material that was not instantly met if it was within India's resources to do so. I desire to express my thanks to the Government of India, to General Sir Robert Cassels, Commander-in-Chief, India, and to his successor, General Sir Claude Auchinleck, who now succeeds me in the Middle East Command.

118. I should like to express my thanks to the large body of voluntary workers who by organising Service Men's clubs and in many other ways have done so much to improve the amenities for the men in the various theatres under my command.

# 4

# GENERAL AUCHINLECK'S DESPATCH ON OPERATIONS 5 JULY 1941 TO 31 OCTOBER 1941

*The War Office, August 1941*
OPERATIONS IN THE MIDDLE EAST,
5 JULY 1941 TO 31 OCTOBER 1941.
*The following despatch was submitted to the Secretary of State for War on the 8th March 1942 by GENERAL SIR CLAUDE J.E. AUCHINLECK, C.B., C.S.I., D.S.O., O.B.E., A.D.C., Commander-in-Chief the Middle East Forces.*

1. On taking over command of the Middle East Forces on the 5th July 1941 I found the general position incomparably better than it had been a year earlier on the collapse of France. This improvement was entirely due to the energy of my predecessor, General Sir Archibald Wavell, and to his vigour in seeking out the enemy wherever he was to be found. The defeat and capture of the Italian armies in East Africa had eliminated one serious threat to our bases and communications, and the winter offensive in Cyrenaica had resulted in the destruction of another large Italian Army. Although the fresh forces brought up by the enemy had succeeded in recapturing most of Cyrenaica, they were unable to proceed much further without first reducing Tobruk. Moreover our operation in June, though unsuccessful, had robbed their armoured forces of much of their offensive power. In the East, the overthrow of the rebel government had cleared the atmosphere in Iraq, while the operations in Syria, though as yet unfinished, would deny potential air and land bases in that country to the Axis.

Only in the North had recent events made our position more difficult. The enemy occupation of Greece and Crete increased the threat of aerial attacks on our bases and lines of communication, and, even more important, seriously restricted the movements of the Fleet in the Central Mediterranean. The enemy's hold on Cyrenaica greatly increased this restriction. The running of convoys with supplies and reinforcements to Malta from Egypt thus became more difficult. The German attack on Russia, however, had come at a very opportune moment for ourselves as it prevented the enemy from exploiting to the full his success in the Balkans and the Aegean.

Although there was thus no immediate threat to our base, there was every reason to believe that in time such a threat would materialise on either flank, and I found preparations to meet this well in hand.

2. General Wavell's campaigns in Libya, Eritrea, Abyssinia, Greece, Crete, Iraq and Syria had followed each other with such bewildering rapidity and had been undertaken with such inadequate forces and equipment that a considerable degree of disorganisation in the Army as a whole was inevitable. Brigades had perforce become separated from their divisions and units from their brigades, while some formations, especially those of the armoured forces, had practically ceased to exist. This entailed a comprehensive programme of reorganisation, improvization, re-equipment and training, which I found in progress on taking over.

In no sense do I wish to infer that I found an unsatisfactory situation on my arrival – far from it. Not only was I greatly impressed by the solid foundations laid by my predecessor, but I was also able the better to appreciate the vastness of the problems with which he had been confronted and the greatness of his achievements, in a command in which some 40 different languages are spoken by the British and Allied Forces.

3. I soon found that the work of the operations, planning and intelligence branches of the General Staff was good and thorough, and that a sound system existed for the administration of personnel, supplies, ordnance and medical arrangements.

Liaison between the Navy, Army and Air Force was excellent and it may here be of interest to give some details of interservice co-operation.

(a) On the highest level there is the Middle East War Council with the Minister of State in the chair. This body is mainly concerned with political matters affecting the Services and other problems of the Middle East.

(b) Then there is the Middle East Defence Committee which met for the first time on the 25th August. It consists of the Minister of State, who presides, and the three Commanders-in-Chief. It deals with major operations and plans.

(c) Next comes the Commanders-in-Chiefs' Committee which is also attended by senior Staff Officers and deals with all important operational and administrative questions. The above normally meet once a week.

(d) Daily liaison is maintained in General Headquarters by an Inter-Service Intelligence Staff Conference and an Inter-Service Operational Staff Conference and by individual officers of all three Services.

(e) The Inter-Service Air Defence Committee makes recommendations for the disposal of available anti-aircraft units and equipment, and has been of great value.

(f) Moreover I myself am in constant personal touch with the Commander-in-Chief Mediterranean and the Air Officer Commanding-in-Chief.

It will thus be seen that a firm foundation exists to ensure that the efforts of the Navy, Army and Royal Air Force are co-ordinated.

4. I readily subscribed to my predecessor's policy of concentrating on reorganisation and training, as an essential part of the preparations for driving the

enemy out of Libya and for meeting his eventual thrust in Asia. These were my chief preoccupations during the period under review. The paragraphs which follow are, therefore, chiefly concerned with local aspects of these preparations as they arose in the various areas of the Middle East.

## SYRIA AND PALESTINE.

5. The Syrian Campaign was drawing to a close when I assumed command. In the northeast the 10th Indian Division, which formed part of the forces under Lieutenant-General E.P. Quinan in Iraq and which the Commander-in-Chief, India, had placed at General Wavell's disposal, had advanced along the River Euphrates as far as Deir ez Zor and along the railway from Tel Kotchek towards Kameschle. In the West the enemy were resisting stubbornly along the line of the River Damour, on the southern slopes of the Lebanon and on the southern and western slopes of the Anti-Lebanon.

In the Euphrates Province the 10th Indian Division made steady progress in the face of heavy air attacks, and by the 8th July, with the capture of Raqqa and Kameschle, they were in control of the key points of the Province. On the line Hama – Homs – Anti-Lebanon the Vichy French were thinning out, until on the 10th July Homs was threatened by the 4th Cavalry Brigade who had cut the railway to the South and now stood before the town. The crossing of the River Damour by the 17th Australian Infantry Brigade on the 7th July, and the capture of the town itself by the 21st Australian Infantry Brigade on the 9th July removed the chief obstacle to our advance on Beirut from the South. The town was also threatened from the direction of Damascus by the 16th Infantry Brigade (6th Division), which on the 10th July attacked the enemy holding positions astride the road near Dimas.

Having lost control of the Northern Desert and the Euphrates Province, and being threatened with the imminent loss of Beirut General Dentz decided to ask for an armistice.

6. On the evening of the 11th July, I received a wireless message from General Dentz, proposing the suspension of hostilities six hours later, at midnight. General Dentz declared himself ready to engage in talks on the basis of a memorandum presented to him that morning by the United States Consul at Beirut on behalf of the British Government. But he made the reservation that he was empowered by the French Government to treat only with the British representatives to the exclusion of those of the Free French.

General Dentz's proposals were considered at once by the Middle East War Council, which also took into account the opinion of the American Consul at Beirut, that Dentz was entirely insincere and might be playing for time in the hope of a last minute rescue by the Germans. Accordingly his conditions were rejected and he was called on to send his plenipotentaries to the British outpost on the Beirut-Haifa Road at or before 0900 hrs. on the 12th July, under threat of resuming hostilities at that hour.

The Vichy French Representatives duly appeared and were conducted to Acre, where discussions began at once. We were represented by General Sir Henry Wilson, Air Commodore L.O. Brown and Captain J.A.V. Morse, Royal Navy, the Free French by General Catroux, and the Vichy French by General de Verdillac. At 2200 hrs. on the 12th July the Convention was initialled and was finally signed by General Wilson and General de Verdillac at Acre on the 14th July 1941.

7. The Commission of Control, set up in accordance with Article 21 to supervise the execution of the terms of the Convention, assembled formally for the first time on the 16th July at Ain Sofar in the Lebanon under the presidency of Major-General J.I. Chrystall.

The question of repatriation was difficult, as our desire to clear the country of Vichy French troops and civilians at the earliest possible moment conflicted with the Free French wish to retain them as long as possible, in the hope that after a prolonged period of propaganda a larger number of recruits would be obtained. Events proved the anticipations of the Free French to be over-optimistic, for of 37,736 personnel of the Troupes Français du Levant, who were offered the choice, only 5,668 declared in favour of Free France.

In all eight convoys, three hospital ships and one "gleaner" ship sailed for France between the 7th August and the 27th September 1941. The total number of persons repatriated, both civilian and military was 37,563. It speaks well for the work of the Embarkation Board that these convoys were cleared without any unfortunate incident. After the departure of these ships, nearly all personnel of the Troupes Français du Levant had been repatriated.

The return of British Prisoners of War who had been evacuated from Syria and the Lebanon placed the Troupes Français du Levant in an unfortunate position, particularly when it was established that a number of these prisoners had been sent out of Syria after the Convention had been initialled. The delay in obtaining the return of prisoners led to the detention in Palestine of General Dentz and twenty-nine of his most senior officers. They were released in due course as the British prisoners were returned to Syria.

The work of the Commission of Control and its twenty sub-committees deserves the highest praise. In the space of ten weeks they accomplished the task of arranging the orderly evacuation of an army 37,000 strong, of checking and handing over all its equipment and of transferring the public services from one administration to another, in conditions which the war had rendered chaotic.

8. The capitulation of the Vichy Forces and the occupation of Syria by the British and Free French made it necessary to take a number of decisions, political and military. General de Gaulle considered that the Armistice terms did not give the Free French enough facilities for rallying the Vichy troops, and did not fully safeguard the position of Free France. After discussions between the Minister of State and General de Gaulle in Cairo in the first week of July, agreements were reached under which the civil authority in Syria and the Lebanon was to rest in

the hands of the Free French provided that our military security was not jeopardised. General de Gaulle recognised the unity of command and placed the Free French Forces throughout the Middle East under the British Commander-in-Chief for operational purposes. He also recognised that in the British Military Zone the civil authority must carry out the requests of the military authority where the security of the armed forces was concerned.

Meanwhile the Free French took over the civil administration of Syria under General Catroux as Délégué Général de la France, the title of High Commissioner being dropped. Unfortunately the French were short of experienced personnel. On the civilian side out of about 1,200 Frenchmen in Syria (excluding religious orders and their dependents), about one-third rallied to the Free French, one-third were allowed to remain in Syria on sufferance without rallying, and one-third returned to France. No doubt a number of those who rallied did so as a matter of personal expediency. In any case, the lack of first-rate men with administrative ability was severely felt, and there were many complaints from the Syrians and Lebanese that former Vichy officials who were corrupt or discredited, were being retained in their old positions. The first weeks were also marked by a good deal of friction between the British and French, particularly in connection with the work of the Disarmament Commission. Mistakes were made on both sides but obstacles were gradually overcome. The Spears Mission, working under difficult conditions, established good relations with their Free French colleagues. A British Security Mission was appointed under Brigadier A.S. Mavrogordato and a joint Anglo-French propaganda plan was agreed upon.

9. Early in September economic difficulties led to a crisis. Stocks of essential commodities were short owing to the British blockade before the fall of the Vichy régime. The wheat crop was below normal, and wheat was hoarded partly in the hopes of realising higher and higher prices as the shortage increased, and partly from fear. In certain areas there was hardship, and minor bread riots occurred. British assistance was given in distributing supplies, and arrangements have now been made for large quantities to be available throughout the winter.

10. A certain amount of political unrest was inevitable. The necessity for safeguarding the interests of France, whose special position we had recognised, on the one hand, and the need for setting up a friendly and stable government on the other were not easy to reconcile. There was much disappointment that Great Britain had not taken over Syria and the Lebanon herself. French administration under the mandate had never succeeded in reconciling the Nationalist opposition, or in attracting popular support. The Free French promises of independence were not believed, and there was general fear that the old regime would be perpetuated. Added to this was a desire to play off the British against the Free French.

Late in September there was trouble among the tribes of the Euphrates and of the Syrian Desert, who had always chafed under French political control. Administrative shortcomings and mistakes on the French side and failure by the local Free French authorities to keep the British military commander of the district informed of their intentions led to tribal outbreaks in the Abu Kemal district. There were several clashes between the Arabs and Free French troops resulting in casualties to both sides. Finally it became necessary for British troops to intervene, but eventually an agreement was reached to cease hostilities and to refer the dispute to arbitration by a joint Anglo-French Commission.

The military security of this vital area was discussed during October both in London with General de Gaulle and in the Middle East with General Catroux. General de Gaulle agreed in principle to the authority necessary to safeguard it being delegated in certain circumstances to the British Command, and General Catroux gave me an undertaking to proclaim Etat de Siège immediately, if troubles begin in any area and threaten to spread, and in the the event of threatened enemy attack.

11. Pursuing the policy previously approved I had already decided that as soon as the Syrian campaign was successfully concluded, every effort should be concentrated on intensive preparations for driving the enemy out of North Africa. Consequently the North must be defended with a minimum of troops. Apart from the Free French forces, which for political reasons have been disposed in detachments all over Syria by their High Command, I have so far been unable to allot more than five divisions at any one time to the defence of Syria and Palestine since the end of the campaign.

The 1st Australian Corps and the skeleton Headquarters of the 10th Corps have already carried out detailed reconnaissances of the defensive areas. Work on the defences has begun and is being pushed on as fast as the number of troops and the amount of civilian labour available will permit.

## CYPRUS.

12. The Defence Committee considered it essential to deny the enemy the use of Cyprus as a base for naval and air operations against our sea communications in the Eastern Mediterranean and our land communications in Egypt, Palestine and Syria.

Hitherto the defence of the island had been considered only on the basis of attack from the West. But now it was necessary to provide against a possible attack by an enemy established in Turkey. In these changed circumstances, General Wavell had determined to increase the garrison of Cyprus, and I decided to adhere to his plan by reinforcing the troops there as soon as possible by one division. The Minister for Defence and the Chiefs of Staff approved this plan accepting the principle that measures to ensure the retention of Cyprus being part of the consolidation of our position in the North, must come before the offensive in the Western Desert.

Accordingly on the 12th July I decided to send to Cyprus the 50th Division (Major-General W.H. Ramsden), just arriving from England, and also the 3rd Hussars (less one Squadron) to replace the 7th Australian Divisional Cavalry Regiment as a mobile armoured reserve. The move of these troops and 90 days reserves of supplies and munitions was completed by the 29th August thanks to the efficient arrangements made by the Royal Navy.

Work on the construction of the defences began at once and is now approaching completion. At the end of October the 5th Indian Division relieved the 50th Division in order to release a British Division for service in the Caucasus. This relief took place without incident between the 2nd and the 8th November, again owing to the efforts of the Royal Navy.

I wish to record my appreciation of the sound judgment and energy shown by Major-General Ramsden in his direction of the preparation of these defences and of the excellent work done by the 50th Division in their construction. I would also like to add my appreciation of the unfailing help and co-operation of the Governor of Cyprus, H.E. Sir William Battershill, K.C.M.G., and of the acting Governor, Captain J.V.W. Shaw, both of whom did everything in their power to assist the work.

## IRAN.

13. While the work of consolidation in Syria was still in its initial stages, it was becoming increasingly evident that it would be necessary to eliminate German influence in Iran.

For some time past nationalist feeling in that country had been rising against Great Britain and Russia and by the end of 1939 there was a well organised German community of about three thousand, almost every one of whom could be relied upon to give as much of his attention to the designs of the Fatherland as to the technical work on which he was ostensibly engaged.

The expulsion of the Germans had been the subject of an exchange of views between London and Moscow, and between the War Office, Commander-in-Chief, India, and myself for some time, when on the 24th July, I received a cable from the Chiefs of Staff informing me that there was general agreement that the Germans must be expelled as soon as possible. If joint British and Russian diplomatic pressure were unavailing, both Powers were intending to take joint military action to enforce their demands.

The enterprise entailed the loan of troops from the Middle East as well as the release of the 10th Indian Division from North-eastern Syria. On the 29th July I arrived in England and had the opportunity of discussing, among other matters, the measure of support the Middle East could afford. I was reluctant to spare more troops than absolutely necessary because of the heavy demands for garrison duties and because it would upset the re-organisation and re-equipment essential to the early resumption of the offensive in the Western Desert. But the success of the operation was of the greatest importance to the common defence of India and the Middle East.

The scale of assistance required from the Middle East grew, in the first place because it was feared that trouble might develop in Iraq and then because it was believed that the Iranians were likely to offer considerable resistance. First I despatched the 9th Armoured Brigade (late 4th Cavalry Brigade) still organised on a truck basis only. The 5th Indian Division (less the 29th Indian Infantry Brigade Group and one field regiment) followed.

Fears of serious resistance however proved groundless, and the 5th Indian Divisional Column had only reached a point about 50 miles within Iraqi territory when the Iranians gave in. The march of the column continued, however, as the Division was needed in Iraq until another arrived from India.

At dawn on the 25th August Russian troops entered Iran from the north and, occupying Tabriz, advanced along the south-western shore of the Caspian, while our troops entered from Iraq in the Ahwaz-Abadan area and in two columns from Khaniqin. The 9th Armoured Brigade formed part of the northern column which rapidly overcame opposition in the Paitak Pass and reached Shahbad on the morning of the 27th August. The Persians offered little real opposition either to the British or the Russian advance, and on the 28th August the Shah ordered all resistance to cease.

On the 8th October the 9th Armoured Brigade returned from Teheran, and on the 18th October the last elements of the 5th Indian Division also reached the Middle East.

## TURKEY.

14. Turkey's reactions to German threats had always been of the greatest moment to ourselves, and now that we had a common frontier her attitude was of even greater consequence. The end of the Syrian campaign and the pacification of Iraq were causes of relief to Turkey because our forces were now in direct contact with her southern frontiers. The outbreak of the Russo-German War, however, caused her misgiving since our new ally was her traditional enemy.

It was most important that the Turks should offer the utmost resistance to a German invasion. From a purely strategical point of view the country fell naturally into our defensive system, as in it the enemy's communications would be most vulnerable to attack, and I was anxious to be able to engage the enemy before he emerged from the mountains of Anatolia into the plains of Syria and Iraq. I was therefore glad when at the end of July, the Chief of the Turkish General Staff, on behalf of the President, made a tentative approach, having as its object the renewal of staff talks on the lines of those held in the Spring. Unfortunately this step was abruptly revoked, the Turkish General Staff having reason to believe that their move had become known to the enemy. It was, however, agreed that informal staff contacts should take place through the medium of our service attaches.

Material for these contacts was carefully compiled in Cairo in consultation with the Commander-in-Chief, India. We were prepared to make a firm offer to send British Forces to Turkey in the event of a German attack. But we stressed the importance of being allowed to build up supplies and stores in advance and to reconnoitre and improve maintenance facilities in Anatolia.

During the early part of the conversations the Turks proposed that we should concentrate in north-western Anatolia; but latterly, with the rapid German advance in South Russia and the possibility that the eventual threat might come from the north-east rather than the north-west, the Turkish military authorities were less averse than I had expected from considering Eastern Anatolia as the possible theatre of the German offensive. There was little doubt, however, that the Turkish statesmen and, to a lesser degree, the senior Turkish Generals, were impressed by the rapidity of the German advance in Russia, and uneasy at our association with the Soviet in the occupation of Iran.

Although I believe that the Turks are genuine in their desire to exclude the Germans from their country and to side with us if the situation is favourable, I cannot conceal from myself the possibility of circumstances proving too strong for them, and I am making my plans accordingly.

## CO-OPERATIVE PLANNING WITH INDIA.

15. The problem of frustrating a German thrust through Anatolia or the Caucasus or both can only be solved by the closest co-operation between India and the Middle East. Before General Wavell left the Middle East for India, we discussed the matter, and it was the subject of an exchange of views between the War Office, India and the Middle East. To facilitate liaison an officer from General Headquarters, India, was posted to the Joint Planning Staff, Middle East, during September.

At a conference at Baghdad on the 26th September, attended by the Commander-in-Chief India and myself it was agreed that the Joint Planning Staff should study the problem of defending Persia, Iraq, Palestine and Syria against invasion either through Western Anatolia or the Caucasus or by both routes. A planning party visited those countries and at the beginning of November representatives of the Middle East Planning Staff went to India to discuss the Northern Front. Since then planning has gone forward on the policy agreed to after the joint review of the problem.

## EAST AFRICA.

16. In East Africa operations have been very nearly at a standstill during this period. The brilliant campaigns of Lieutenant General Sir Alan Cunningham and Lieutenant General Sir William Platt during the previous six months had eliminated all but one centre of resistance, that in the Gondar area. Owing to the heavy rains, our troops could not at once attempt the task of reducing this stronghold. During the months of July, August, and September, therefore, operations were confined to harassing raids carried out by our Air Forces.

17. Owing to the complete success of earlier operations, General Wavell had been able to withdraw three divisions which had been operating in this theatre. By the beginning of July the 1st South African and the 4th Indian Divisions had been withdrawn, and the last brigade of the 5th Indian Division had received orders to move. I carried on my predecessor's policy of withdrawing every unit that it was possible to release. Finally, there remained, only the 11th and 12th African Divisions to carry out all the necessary internal security duties in this vast

stretch of territory, as well as to contain the Italian forces in the Gondar area until these could be finally liquidated, and also to enforce the landward blockade of French Somaliland.

18. The administration of the conquered territories presented a large number of problems, which were ably handled by Major-General Sir Philip Mitchell, Chief Political Officer, who on the 27th June had become British Representative in Ethiopia. On the first of August by formal Proclamation I delegated to him the full legislative, judicial, administrative and financial authority which I exercised in Eritrea and Somalia, and an Administrative Instruction of the Secretary of State for War entrusted to him supervisory powers over the Military Governor of British Somaliland. Although it was impossible in international law for me to divest myself of the authority which I held by right of conquest in Somaliland and Eritrea, by the Proclamation I was in fact released from all but ultimate responsibility.

On the many problems involved in organising and directing the administrations in the conquered territories it is unnecessary for me to enlarge. Let it suffice to say that Sir Philip Mitchell lost no time and spared no effort in handling these problems with the energy and discretion they demanded. The achievements of Sir Philip and his assistants were remarkable, especially as officers and police were scarce and communications difficult. Although it was far from complete when I relinquished command of the areas, much progress had been made in the task of pacification.

19. From both political and military standpoints the problem of French Somaliland was pressing and difficult. This territory, which is controlled by a Government committed to collaboration with the enemy, adjoins the Straits of Bab el Mandeb and is therefore a potential base for hostile naval operations against us in the Red Sea and the Indian Ocean. Yet to reduce it by force might well lead to the destruction of the port of Jibuti and the railway to Addis Ababa, making the evacuation of the numerous Italian civilians interned in the Addis Ababa area difficult, if not impossible. The evacuation of these Italians, for some time past the subject of negotiations with the Italian Government, was essential. Their continued presence constituted a menace to internal security in that they might escape; a military liability, in that they must be protected from the possible vengeance of the Ethiopians; and a political stumbling-block in that their protection involved a measure of interference in Ethiopian affairs which filled the Emperor and his subjects with suspicion and resentment.

To continue the blockade was the only solution. At the beginning of July, prospects of an early capitulation seemed good, but dhows from the Yemen and French submarines from Madagascar succeeded in running the blockade; and, in spite of a considerable tightening of the blockade, the colony was still holding out at the time the East African Command took over and was seemingly no nearer capitulation.

20. It had been suggested earlier that the dividing line between Europe and Africa was not the Mediterranean but the Sahara and the Sudd, and that a second Command should be formed to include the Sudan and all territories south of it as far as and including Southern Rhodesia. Apart from economic and political considerations, it was clearly not true from a strategic point of view, so long as there remained in East Africa large enemy forces able to operate on interior lines against Kenya, Egypt and the Sudan. The suggestion was therefore rejected for the time being.

With the defeat and capture of the greater part of the Italian forces in East Africa, the threat to the Middle East was removed, and military and all other considerations made it desirable to remove the Central and East African areas from the Middle East command. The Belgian Congo as a "sphere of interest" had been transferred to the West African Command on 1st July, and the transfer of the remainder of the territories was considered by a Conference which assembled at Nairobi on the 1st August under the presidency of Lieutenant-General Sir Alan Cunningham, G.O.C. East Africa.

Representatives of Air Headquarters East Africa, Middle East, the 203rd Mission, Southern and Northern Rhodesia, West African Command and the Sudan attended. The representative of the Union of South Africa was absent, because the Conference was finally held at very short notice. The recommendations of the Conference, however, were submitted to Field Marshal Smuts for approval.

The Conference recommended that the new Command should come directly under the War Office and comprise Eritrea, Ethiopia, the Somalilands, Kenya, Uganda, Tanganyika, Nyasaland and Northern Rhodesia. It considered that the Commander in the southern territories of Northern Rhodesia and Nyasaland should advise the Southern Rhodesian Governor on defence matters, and co-ordinate plans in which the three territories and the Union of South Africa were concerned; and that in concerted operations he should command not only his own forces, but any forces Southern Rhodesia might contribute. The Conference agreed that Portuguese East Africa, the Katanga Province of the Belgian Congo, and Angola should be included in the Commander's spheres of influence in co-operation with the Union of South Africa. The recommendations of the Conference were accepted with a few modifications.

On the 15th September, 1941, all the territories with the exception of Eritrea passed to the East African Command. Eritrea passed under command on the 11th October, 1941.

21. Before the East African Command was formed I had arranged for the transfer of considerable quantities of captured arms, ammunition and other material. This arrangement was confirmed and the equipment is being brought to the Middle East as quickly as transport facilities permit. Middle East have also retained a lien on Eritrea for the purpose of siting certain base installations and hospitals in a safe area.

## SUDAN.

22. The Sudan was not included in the East African Command for political and strategic reasons. The Anglo-Egyptian condominium in the country made it desirable that the military authority should be exercised by the Commander-in-Chief in Cairo, as also did the importance of the Sudan as a base for operations in the Western Desert from the south and for possible operations in the Chad.

23. On the 4th October, 1941, Lieutenant-General Sir N.M. de la P. Beresford-Peirse assumed command in the Sudan in place of Lieutenant-General Sir William Platt, who became General Officer Commanding-in-Chief, East Africa Command.

## WESTERN DESERT.

24. While the other areas under my command were the scenes of consolidation and reorganisation, the chief theatre of activity was the Western Desert. Here my policy was dictated by two main considerations. Advantage must be taken of the favourable conditions created by the Russian campaign to resume the offensive at the earliest possible moment. Meanwhile it was necessary to remain on the defensive, employing only a minimum of troops. The maximum effort could then be devoted to organising, training and equipping the forces destined for the invasion of Cyrenaica and to completing the vast administrative preparations. This will receive full treatment in a later despatch.

The situation in the Western Desert from mid-June until mid-September corresponded to that envisaged in my General Instruction of the 26th July laying down the principles of defence in areas in which the attackers might be expected to be considerably stronger in armoured force than the defenders. This was undoubtedly the case in the Western Desert, where our armoured forces were appreciably inferior to those of the enemy. Moreover three of the areas essential to this system of defence already existed, namely, Tobruk, Matruh and Bagush; and General Wavell had already given the order to prepare a fourth situated in the defile between the Qattara Depression and the sea at El Alamein.

Accordingly, on the 21st July, I issued an Instruction (Appendix "A") to Lieutenant-General Sir Noel Beresford-Peirse, commanding the Western Desert Forces, informing him of my decision that in the event of an enemy advance his armoured forces were to be brought to battle in the area south of Matruh, whither the Headquarters and Armoured Brigades of the 7th Armoured Division had already been withdrawn. This decision entailed the surrender of our forward landing grounds in the Sidi Barrani area, which would mean that our ability to provide fighter protection to our shipping engaged in maintaining Tobruk would be greatly impaired. As our armoured forces were relatively weak, this risk had to be accepted.

On the 30th July I issued a further Instruction (Appendix "B") to the Commanders of the Western Desert Forces and of the British Troops in Egypt, elaborating my policy for the general defence of Egypt against an enemy advance from the West.

As the armoured units were re-equipped and became more numerous a more offensive policy was gradually adopted. Finally, immediately following an enemy reconnaissance in force on the 14th September, it was possible to move armoured troops, supported by an infantry division, well in advance of Sidi Barrani to cover the preparations for the coming offensive, and to secure the advanced landing grounds of the Royal Air Force against attack.

25. On the 14th September the enemy advanced to test our strength and dispositions above the escarpment. The force consisted of two columns. The northern column was composed of about 100 tanks, and the southern contained chiefly lorried infantry and maintenance vehicles escorted by armoured cars. Our reconnaissance elements and light columns withdrew, inflicting casualties on the enemy. By nightfall the enemy tanks had reached the Rabia area, but during the night they withdrew. By first light on the 17th September our troops had returned to their original positions.

Our columns and aircraft inflicted greater losses on the enemy than they received. Our losses were fifteen casualties, an armoured car, a bomber and six fighters destroyed and several trucks and one fighter damaged; against this the enemy suffered almost a hundred casualties and lost fourteen tanks, fifteen vehicles and twenty-two aircraft. It was fortunate that the test of our strength and intentions came at a time when our policy was about to be completely altered.

26. The enemy also undertook the re-organisation of his forces in North Africa during this period. On the 19th July General Ettore Bastico took over the Supreme Command in Libya from General Garibaldi. It is probable that the appointment of General Bastico, a reported expert on mechanised warfare, was intended as much to show that Italian interests in Libya were at least equal to German interests in Libya as to reorganise the Italian forces and revive their morale.

There is little doubt that General Bastico made progress in the work of reorganisation, although to what extent he was able to raise Italian prestige and morale remained to be seen. The much-battered Trento Division was relieved at Tobruk by the Bologna Division, and the almost extinct Sabarata Division was reorganised and employed on garrison duties. The 21st Corps Headquarters was reconstituted to control the divisions about Tobruk. But the most important measure taken by General Bastico was the organisation of a mobile corps in Cyrenaica. This corps comprises the Trento and Ariete Divisions and also the Trieste Division, which reached Tripoli by the end of August. Although this division probably lost much of its transport in sea transit, it appears to have refurnished itself from an Autocentro which arrived in Tripoli at about the same time. The Ariete Division was reorganised on a basis of three tank battalions with a total of 138 tanks.

During the same period the German forces had also undergone reorganisation. About mid- August the 5th Light (motorised) Division was converted into an armoured division and renumbered [*illegible*]. Units of a German positional division were identified in Libya, three battalions having taken the place of lorried infantry in the line at Tobruk. There was evidence that the Germans were contemplating the despatch of such a division as early as May, and the first units began to arrive in July. The main purpose in sending this division appeared to be the release of the lorried infantry for their proper mobile role. Both the 5th and 8th Tank Regiments were reinforced from June onwards on a new establishment totalling 136 tanks. Finally, Panzer-gruppe Afrika was formed, consisting of the 15th and 21st Panzer Divisions, commanded by General Rommel.

, Throughout the summer the enemy devoted much attention to building defences on the frontier between Sollum and Sidi Omar. The Halfaya position was completed, and Sidi Omar was also fortified and surrounded by minefields. The enemy further attempted to link these two positions and the intervening posts with further minefields. The whole purpose of this position seemed to be to provide a strong pivot from the shelter of which the enemy could manoeuvre south and south-east of Sidi Omar or against British forces attempting to move from the frontier area towards Tobruk.

## TOBRUK.

27. Our freedom from embarrassment in the frontier area for four and a half months is to be ascribed largely to the defenders of Tobruk. Behaving not as a hardly pressed garrison but as a spirited force ready at any moment to launch an attack, they contained an enemy force twice their strength. By keeping the enemy continually in a high state of tension, they held back four Italian divisions and three German battalions from the frontier area from April until November.

The exploits of the garrison, which was commanded from the first days of the siege until 22nd October by Major-General L.J. Morshead, are famous all over the world and are too numerous to be recounted in detail here. In spite of continuous strain, the spirit of the British, Imperial and Allied troops was magnificent throughout. The infantry displayed great stubbornness in defence and dash in attack, while the work of the field and anti-aircraft artillery and of the machine guns, inflicting many casualties on the enemy, was of the highest order. The exploits of the innumerable patrols carried out almost nightly by the cavalry and infantry units of the garrison deserve the highest praise. Not only did these patrols collect most valuable information and numerous prisoners, but they were in large part responsible for making it possible to hold a perimeter thirty miles long with only seven battalions and one cavalry regiment in the front line.

Major-General L.J. Morshead organised the defence with great ability and resourcefulness. He was assisted in his difficult task by his G.S.O.I., Colonel C.E.M. Lloyd, whose industry and cheerfulness were unfailing.

I also wish to commend especially the work of the anti-aircraft defences under Brigadier J.R. Slater. They formed the sole means of defence against air attack, as our air bases were too distant to allow fighter aircraft to operate over this area. They performed their duties with such efficiency that in spite of continual raids serious damage was rarely inflicted by enemy aircraft, of which several were shot down and many damaged.

28. On the 18th July I received from Lieutenant General Sir Thomas Blamey, commanding the Australian Imperial Forces, a letter, written at the instance of the Australian Government, urging me to consider the relief* of the whole garrison as the health of all the troops composing it showed signs of marked deterioration. He represented to me that the relief of the Australian portion of the Garrison was particularly desirable in view of the growing feeling in Australia that the time had come to fulfil the agreement made between their own and the British Government that the Australian troops should be concentrated under one command and serve as one force. He suggested that the lull in operations presented an opportunity which should not be missed. This letter was followed on the 23rd July by a telegram from the War Office repeating a message to the same effect from the Australian Government and urging me to give full and sympathetic consideration to the views of the Australian Government.

I agreed in principle to the relief of the garrison both for the sake of the troops and an order to fulfil the undertaking given to the Australian Government; but I was doubtful whether it would be practicable to relieve the whole garrison. The Commander-in-Chief, Mediterranean, however, believed that he would be able to effect the relief and maintain the fortress by sea at the same time.

29. A complete plan was drawn up by which the Polish Independent Brigade should replace the 18th Australian Infantry Brigade and the 18th Cavalry (Indian Army) during the moonless period in August and the 70th (6th) Division relieve the 9th Australian Division during the two succeeding moonless periods. The first relief was carried out with complete success between the 19th and the

---

*In order that the conditions which necessitated this relief shall be clearly understood, comments of (i) the Commonwealth Government and (ii) General Blarney, are appended below:-

(i) (Commonwealth Government)
"The relief of Australian troops in Tobruk was supported by three successive Australian Governments. It is in agreement with General Blamey's observations which were confirmed by the Inspector General of Medical Services of the Australian Army (Major-General R.M. Downes) who on his return from a visit to the Middle East reported in 1941: 'The first A.I.F. troops transferred from Tobruk had suffered a considerable decline in their physical powers. The men did not think that they were tired but few of them would be able to march eight miles …'"

(ii) (General Blamey)
"I concur with the statements except that I do not think the first portion of paragraph 29 accurately represents the position. It will be noted that on 18th July I had made representations on the great decline in the physical condition of the troops who had been holding Tobruk. This decline continued and two months later when the Chiefs of Staff directed the relief on 15th September the condition of the troops was such that any strong attack by the enemy might have endangered the safety of the fortress. Moreover, an offensive was contemplated and plans included operations by the defenders at a later date, which I was certain that they could not have maintained owing to their loss of strength and physical condition. I opposed General Auchinleck most strongly in his proposals to retain these troops any longer in Tobruk. It took a considerable time for them to recover their strength after their relief."

29th August, releasing the 18th Australian Infantry Brigade to rejoin its Division in Syria, and the 18th Cavalry to join its formation, the 3rd Indian Motor Brigade, in Egypt.

It was then necessary to consider whether further relief of the garrison was desirable or feasible. The Commander-in-Chief, Mediterranean, the Air Officer Commanding-in-Chief and myself were unanimous in recommending that it was undesirable to continue the programme for the following reasons. The relief effected in August had not only proved a great strain on the Royal Navy and the Royal Air Force, but had inevitably limited the latter's offensive action. To continue in the next two moonless periods would again interfere with other important operational tasks and impose a further heavy strain on the two Services. This would be increased by having to continue to maintain the fortress by sea during moonlight periods and thus expose our valuable shipping to unjustifiable risks. It was impossible to defer the last phase until the November moonless period, as this would have clashed with the date provisionally set for the beginning of our new offensive. Furthermore, no alternative formation being available for the purpose, the immediate employment of the 70th Division in Tobruk would prevent Indian units from Iraq being introduced into it in accordance with a policy which will be explained later in this Despatch. Finally the decline in the health of the garrison, which had been advanced as a pressing reason for effecting relief, did not appear to be so great as to warrant its continuation in the face of so many important objections. I submitted these arguments in a cable to London and stated that, subject to the Prime Minister's approval, I would reinforce the garrison at once with an infantry tank battalion instead of continuing the relief.

On the 15th September, however, I received a cable from the Chiefs of Staff informing me that, after careful consideration of the opinion of the Commanders in Chief, the Australian Government felt compelled to request the withdrawal of the 9th Australian Division and the reconcentration of the Australian Imperial Force.

Accordingly the relief of most of the 9th Australian Division by the 70th Division was completed in the next two moonless periods, between the 18th and the 28th September and the 12th and the 26th October. Only the 2/13th Infantry Battalion now remains in Tobruk.

The 4th Battalion of the Royal Tank Regiment was despatched at the same time.

The withdrawal of the Australian Division necessitated a change in command. On the 22nd October, 1941, Major General R. MacK. Scobie, commanding the 70th Division, took over command of the fortress.

30. I wish to acknowledge the services rendered in the siege of Tobruk by the Royal Navy, the Fleet Air Arm and the Royal Air Force. Not only did they enable the relief to be carried out with negligible loss to army personnel, though at great strain and some loss to themselves, but by continuing to maintain the fortress for

eight months in spite of heavy risks and great difficulties they made it possible to renew the offensive which otherwise would have been considerably delayed.

The services of the following officers were particularly noteworthy:-

*Royal Navy.*
Acting Rear Admiral G.H. Creswell, Rear Admiral Alexandria, Captain A.L. Poland, Senior Naval Officer, Inshore Squadron; Captain F.M. Smith, Naval Officer in charge, Tobruk, Acting Commander H.R.M. Nicholl who performed the duties of Naval Officer in charge, Tobruk, during the sickness of Captain Smith, Lieutenant Commander J.W. Best, Naval Officer in charge Mersa Matruh.

*Royal Air Force.*
Wing Commander E.R.E. Black, commanding the Royal Air Force Detachment; Squadron Leader R.D. Williams commanding No. 145 Squadron; Acting Flight Lieutenant C.W. Morle, commanding the Air Ministry Experimental Station; and Pilot Officer W.C. Mackintosh and Pilot Officer H.M. Briscoe, Code and Ciphers Officers.

## EGYPT.

31. In Egypt certain problems vitally affected the security of our base. These arose in part directly out of the war and in part out of the circumstance that Egypt herself is not a belligerent.

Apart from political difficulties, the problem of telephonic communications has been pressing. The Egyptian State Telegraphs and Telephones Departments have always given us excellent service, but the use of the civilian system manned by civilian personnel is prejudicial to security. Holding the view that, so long as the country is not at war, military considerations cannot override civilian requirements, the Departments have consistently refused to hand over any part of the system to British Control. Nor will they allow the infiltration of British Military personnel to handle our own traffic and become used to the system so as to be able to take over in an emergency; such might arise if heavy bombing attacks occurred. The difficulty became particularly acute in connection with the projected offensive in Cyrenaica; but in October I was able to arrange to take over the working of the lines in the forward area.

32. There has also been an agitation for the declaration of Cairo, as well as other Egyptian cities, as an "open city." As the bombing of Alexandria increased, so did the Cairo "open city" movement gain impetus. In mid-September the Egyptian Prime Minister was handed a Memorandum stating that it was entirely out of the question to move British troops and military depots from Cairo: an end should, therefore, be put to the agitation. The recent diminution of enemy air raids on Egyptian towns has automatically put this question into the background; but it is bound to reappear with its attendant dangers to internal security as soon as heavy scale bombing is resumed. Against that day an elaborate air raid precautions

scheme has been prepared, to which His Majesty's Government have given considerable financial assistance.

33. The worst result of the air raids was that they seriously threatened shipping in the Suez Canal and in the Gulf of Suez. Incidentally they also caused a reduction in the amount of Egyptian casual labour; but this was speedily remedied by improving the arrangements for air raid precautions and importing labour from Upper Egypt. The threat to shipping demanded that immediate and effective measures be taken, and they were the more urgent in that air raids coincided with the arrival of important convoys carrying large numbers of men and vehicles. Moreover it was essential to give adequate protection to American ships which had just begun to arrive. I therefore took every possible precaution. Several anti-aircraft batteries were moved from other areas to Suez during moonlight periods, and anti-aircraft crews were placed aboard American ships, while the Royal Navy stationed an anti-aircraft cruiser in Suez Roads. In addition it was decided to provide two defended anchorages in the Gulf of Suez, at Abu Zenima and at Ras Ghemsa, for use in the event of Port Tewfik becoming unuseable.

34. The help given us by the Egyptian Army is an earnest of the friendly intentions of the Government. In addition to finding internal security guards in the Delta and on the land, they found a garrison for Siwa at a time when it was necessary for us to leave as few of our own troops as possible in the Western Desert. The services of the Egyptian Army have been particularly valuable. Providing as they have a complete and efficient observer system as well as searchlight and anti-aircraft units at Cairo, Alexandria and in the Canal area, they have relieved the strain on our resources to a very great extent.

## PART II – ADMINISTRATION.

35. During this period I was chiefly concerned with the problems of administration. The comparatively peaceful conditions prevailing gave me the opportunity of carrying out the large amount of reorganisation and development rendered necessary by the increasing strength of the Middle East Forces.

## GENERAL ORGANISATION.
### *Formation of Eighth and Ninth Armies.*

36. The conclusion of the Balkan and East African Campaigns caused our forces to be concentrated in Egypt, Palestine and Syria, and narrowed the potential theatres of operations. It was therefore certain that in future the strength of the forces engaged in operations could be reckoned, not in Brigades and Divisions as heretofore but in Corps. The existing small headquarters were obviously inadequate to control operations on this scale. I therefore determined that the basic organisation should comprise two Army Headquarters to command all the troops in the two principal theatres of operations, with two Base and Line of Communication Areas directly administered by G.H.Q. relieving the armies of the administration of these areas.

Accordingly on the 26th September the Headquarters of the Eighth Army, commanded by Lieutenant-General Sir Alan Cunningham, assumed command of all troops in the Western Desert forward of Bahig, with the exception of those in Tobruk who came under command on the 30th October. Headquarters, British Troops in Egypt, became in effect a large Base and Lines of Communication Area Command operationally responsible only for the internal security and anti-aircraft defence of the Egyptian base.

In Palestine and Syria operational command was assigned in the same way to the Headquarters of the Ninth Army, commanded by General Sir Henry Maitland Wilson, and Palestine and Transjordan became a Base and Line of Communication Area.

*Appointment of Lieutenant General Administration.*
37. The great increase in the strength of the Middle East Forces since the collapse of France produced a corresponding increase in the volume of routine administrative work, while the promise of further growth of the forces and the prospect of large-scale operations on two fronts presented a large number of problems in administrative planning.

These matters had hitherto been dealt with by my Deputy Quartermaster General, Major General B.O. Hutchison and by my Deputy Adjutant General, Major General N.W. Napier Clavering. I wish to pay the highest tribute to the industry, efficiency and foresight with which they carried out their work, of which the vast amount of reorganisation and development carried out during the period covered by this Despatch and before is the best testimony.

I realised that, well served as they were, the problems confronting them were already too multitudinous, and that in due course the growing number of day-to-day questions must inevitably usurp most of their time. I therefore decided to ask the Chief of the Imperial General Staff to sanction the appointment of a principal administrative staff officer, who should relieve them of part of their burden, and whose functions should include co-ordinating the work of the Quartermaster General's and the Adjutant General's Departments and directing administrative planning.

On the 18th October Lieutenant-General T.S. Riddell Webster assumed the appointment of Lieutenant-General Administration as my principal administrative staff officer.

*Formation of Union Defence Force Administrative Headquarters.*
38. When South African troops first came to Egypt it was intended that they should be treated in the same way as British troops, matters peculiar to South Africa being dealt with by staff officers attached to my General Headquarters and provided with the necessary clerical staff. The differences between South African and British administration, however, were pronounced; and many of the problems arising had a domestic political bearing. In order to overcome these and other lesser difficulties Field Marshal Smuts decided to form a separate administrative headquarters. Accordingly on the 25th September Major-General F.A.

Theron was appointed General Officer Administration, Union Defence Force, Middle East, with executive powers.

## MANPOWER.

39. Of all the administrative problems of the Middle East the shortage of manpower was the most urgent. It arose in a particularly acute form in the British and South African elements of the force.

### British.

40. The supply of British personnel was necessarily limited by the amount of shipping available and the distance they must travel to reach the Middle East. In order to save British manpower every effort has been made to provide substitutes. It is my policy to dilute British formations with Indian units and an exchange of battalions between Iraq and the Middle East has already taken place.

Men from Cyprus, India, Malta, Mauritius, Palestine, the Sudan, East Africa, and the South African Protectorate have entered the Services and are doing valuable work.

These services have also been tapped for the formation of Pioneer Corps units. By the end of October there were 69 such units in the Middle East.

To supplement uniformed labour, civilian labour has been used to the greatest extent practicable. The number employed has risen from 101,000 in July to 144,000 at the beginning of October. Unfortunately local labour was not altogether satisfactory when bombing first occurred. But confidence gradually returned with experience of the slight casualties inflicted when proper precautions are taken. Labourers enlisted from the Sudan and elsewhere showed themselves better able to stand up to bombing.

I have also examined the practicability of using women in the place of men for non-combatant duties. Appreciable numbers of European women are to be found chiefly in South Africa and Palestine. The Union has already sent 250 women to the Middle East and all are engaged in useful work in Egypt and the Sudan. The Government of Palestine and the War Office have agreed in principle to units of the Auxiliary Territorial Service being raised in Palestine.

### South African.

41. The South African contingent felt the manpower problem even more acutely, and the Government of the Union decided to employ in all units as many Non-Europeans as possible for non-combatant work in order to release Europeans for combatant service. This is to be carried out on a very comprehensive scale, the new war establishment of a South African Division being 14,900 Europeans and 10,400 Non-Europeans.

## DEVELOPMENT OF BASES AND COMMUNICATIONS.

42. The growth of the Middle East Forces was naturally reflected in the tonnage to be handled at ports. To deal with the increased volume of traffic and to provide alternative approaches to the Base, as a precaution against enemy action, extensive Transportation and Works developments have been undertaken.

Much constructional work has been undertaken to meet both future operational requirements and the general needs of the growing force. A comprehensive programme for the expansion of base installations is being carried out. Many improvements to communications and harbours have been put in hand, and much new accommodation is being completed.

*Transportation.*

43. The Movements Branch of the Staff and Transportation Services have been brought under one head in the person of my Deputy Quartermaster General, Movement and Transportation, Brigadier R.K. Hewer, and the new organisation is working well.

Seventy-five miles of the extension to the Western Desert Railway have been completed and the line between Suez and Ismailia has been doubled during the period under review. The Transportation Service has also been engaged in constructing some 390 miles of railway line elsewhere in Egypt, Palestine, and Syria as well as a Depot at Kantara East, a swing bridge over the Suez Canal, and two railway bridges in Syria.

*Works Services.*

44. The considerable achievements of the Works Services are in no small measure due to my Director of Works, Major General E.F. Tiokell.

Constructional work has proceeded steadily, though hampered somewhat by a certain shortage of materials on the sites. The rate of delivery of engineer stores has improved, but is still limited not only by the amount of shipping available but also by restricted transportation facilities in Egypt. These could not be adequately supplemented by service transport because it was necessary to meet the deficiencies of operational and maintenance units. The transport problem will be considerably easier when these deficiencies have been made up.

Works Services have taken over responsibility for the construction of all docks and harbour works.

Preliminary work has been put in hand for deep water quays at Suez and Safaga. The lighter wharf programme has been continued and about one mile of additional wharf has been completed since June.

A pipe line carrying a thousand tons of oil a day from Suez to Port Said has been laid. The Desert water pipe line has been completed as far as Matruh and is being extended. A large number of additional filtering plants have been built in the Delta. Well boring has been continued throughout the Middle East and many hundreds of miles of distribution pipe have been laid.

Work on a large number of roads in Egypt, the Western Desert, Syria and Palestine has continued, and much road maintenance has been carried out in Syria, the Sudan, Eritrea and Abyssinia.

Many aerodromes and landing grounds have been constructed in the Western Desert and elsewhere. Work on a large number of others is continuing.

The programme for building hospitals, as originally planned, has been completed, and many camps have been erected in Egypt and Palestine.

Increased local production has done much to supplement shipments from abroad.

### Vehicle Assembly.

45. By far the greater number of wheeled vehicles arriving from overseas come cased and partly dismantled. The work of assembly has been shared by the Royal Army Service Corps and the Royal Army Ordnance Corps with valuable assistance from the South African personnel sent up by the Union for this purpose.

### Middle East Provision Office.

46. This is now established under the Eastern Group Supply system and provision forecasts for the period 1st April to 31st December, 1942, have been forwarded to the Central Provision Office, New Delhi. A plan for co-ordinating and stimulating local production is now being prepared.

## RE-EQUIPMENT AND REORGANISATION

47. Large consignments of war material of every description made it possible to carry out re-equipment on a large scale. Various tables showing this are set out in Appendix "C".

Vehicles of all types came in a steady stream from Great Britain, Canada, Australia, and the Union of South Africa, and in July tanks and trucks began to arrive in increasing volume from the United States of America. Between the 1st July and the 31st October we received in all almost 34,000 trucks and lorries and 2,100 armoured vehicles. Considerable consignments of artillery and small arms were also received. Among these were 600 field guns, 206 anti-tank guns, 160 light and 80 heavy anti-aircraft guns. Shipments of small arms included approximately 3,700 Bren guns, 900 mortars, and 80,000 rifles, and quantities of ammunition and equipment.

Yet, large as they were, these consignments, necessarily limited in quantity by the amount of shipping space available, were insufficient to replace all the wastage which had occurred or to enable reserves of many important items of equipment to be built up.

48. Limitations of shipping space were much more severely felt in connection with personnel, making it necessary to choose between fighting troops and administrative units, and between complete formations or units and drafts. It seemed best to ask for the greater part of the available space to be allotted to fighting formations, as this brought a greater increase in fighting strength than would have resulted from accepting a preponderance of drafts. Against 27,300 men arriving with units we received 17,000 in drafts. However one half of the number arriving in drafts were absorbed by new units which it was found necessary to form in the Middle East.

A serious shortage of personnel and administrative units had to be accepted as the inevitable consequence of this policy. The shortage of personnel extended to every arm of the Service but the rearward services suffered most. In many cases there were insufficient men to make even units in contact with the enemy up to full establishment. At the beginning of July the overall deficit in personnel, the deficit compared to war establishments plus first reinforcements, was 16 per cent.; by the end of October, when the strain on reserves was increased by the number of complete units received, the deficit was slightly larger. Nevertheless, by disposing personnel to the best advantage and by increasing their efforts all arms contrived to fulfil their functions with great efficiency, and I wish to record my appreciation of the manner in which they overcame this serious handicap.

### Armoured Formations.

49. The armoured formations presented the most striking example of the extent to which it was possible to carry out re-equipment and reorganisation. At the beginning of July I could put into the field only two armoured car regiments and the 7th Armoured Division, whose range and mobility was seriously restricted by the fact that one Brigade was equipped with infantry tanks owing to the shortage of cruisers. At the end of October I had at my disposal the 7th Armoured Division, the 22nd Armoured Brigade, the 1st Army Tank Brigade complete, and the 32nd Army Tank Brigade complete except for one battalion. I was also able to reequip a third British armoured car regiment and to complete the equipment of two South African armoured car regiments.

### Infantry Formations.

50. Similar improvements took place in the condition of other formations. The intake of unarmoured vehicles was sufficient to allow me to replace the transport of the 1st South African Division and to complete that of the 4th Indian Division which had seen much hard service in East Africa and was unsuited to desert warfare. It was also possible to fulfil the requirements of the New Zealand Division, whose transport had been lost in Greece. The equipping of the 1st South African Division was particularly remarkable as the whole process of issuing and delivering 1,300 vehicles from the base to the desert occupied only six days. The 7th Armoured Division, the 1st Army Tank Brigade, and the 22nd Armoured Brigade were also brought up to full establishment in these vehicles during the period. In addition the requirements of a number of divisional and non-divisional troops have been completed while the losses in Greece have been largely replaced.

Table B of Appendix "C" shows the holdings of formations in unarmoured vehicles and equipment at the beginning and end of the period.

### Royal Artillery – Field Branch.

51. There was a great improvement in the general state of equipment of the Royal Artillery Field Branch regiments as is shown in Table C of Appendix "C".

In the case of Field Regiments, however, a shortage of personnel precluded our taking full advantage of all the equipment available.

In spite of the very considerable increase in the number of 2-pounder equipments available, the situation was still unsatisfactory in two respects. There were insufficient guns to bring all regiments up to the full establishment of 48 guns;

and in order to equip four of them on the new 64-gun basis, it was necessary to give them 16 eighteen-pounder guns apiece. However, the added weight of these guns may well prove to be an advantage.

More serious was the fact that three Infantry Divisions were without anti-tank regiments. As this weakness could not be tolerated in a terrain offering few natural anti-tank obstacles, it was necessary to convert the 149th Field and the 73rd Medium Regiments into anti-tank artillery, thereby setting highly trained personnel to a less skilled task.

*Royal Artillery – Anti-Aircraft and Coast Artillery Branch.*

52. Arrivals of Anti-Aircraft artillery increased the heavy anti-aircraft fire power by 40 per cent. and the light anti-aircraft by 75 per cent. (Table D of Appendix "C".) 106 captured anti-aircraft guns were retained in use in addition. Coast batteries provided for the defence of additional ports were mainly equipped with captured guns and searchlights.

The release of additional light anti-aircraft equipment and the arrival of fresh units made it possible to put into practice plans for providing divisional light anti-aircraft regiments. This involved re-organising one Australian and two South African regiments as divisional light anti-aircraft regiments on British war establishments. Five divisional light anti-aircraft regiments, all on a 36-gun basis, were provided for the Eighth Army, and the equipping of two Australian divisional light anti-aircraft regiments for the 1st Australian Corps was started.

*Passive Air Defence.*

53. Special attention has been paid to improving the Passive Air Defence organisation, which now embraces all military fire fighting.

*Royal Engineers.*

54. Unit equipment came forward fairly well and most units are now up to scale in the more important items, though there is still a shortage of certain essentials, and very few reserves. American equipment began to arrive, notably mobile compressor units and bridging equipment with special carrying vehicles.

A considerable number of new units were sent out from the United Kingdom. Several South African Engineer units also arrived from East Africa and the Union, forming a very valuable addition to our Engineer resources. There is still a chronic shortage of electrical and mechanical equipment operating units.

*Royal Corps of Signals.*

55. Considerable supplies of signal stores were received and the situation as regards line equipment for forward areas is now satisfactory. Although now more plentiful than they used to be, supplies of permanent line equipment, telephones and switchboards for lines of communications and back areas are still insufficient to provide a satisfactory reserve. Wireless equipment is still short, but at the end of June it was shorter. The services of the R.A.O.C. workshops and two mobile W/T repair sections have been particularly valuable in reconditioning existing wireless equipment.

Deficiencies in signal units have been very serious. In spite of the arrival of two corps signal units, we are still deficient of six complete non-divisional units and fifty-seven miscellaneous sections required to complete existing non-divisional units – a total shortage of 6,000 personnel.

### Royal Army Service Corps.

56. Apart from the lack of units the Royal Army Service Corps experienced a 15 per cent. shortage of personnel for existing units.

The number of vehicles held by the Corps steadily increased, reaching approximately 86 per cent. of authorised strength by the end of October. But it has not yet been possible to form a reserve of vehicles.

Improvements in bulk storage and distribution of motor spirit resulted in a saving in cost of tins of over £12,500 per month, and great economy in material, labour and transport. Further improvements now in hand should greatly increase these savings.

### Medical Services.

57. Like the other services, the Medical Service suffered from shortages in units, stores and transport. Although the Royal Army Medical Corps had been very nearly completely equipped by the end of October transport resources were still inadequate, as the authorised scale of transport is scarcely sufficient to meet the highly mobile conditions obtaining in the Middle East. Practical experience of mobile warfare in Syria and the Western Desert, where the absence of roads and railways necessitates long evacuation by ambulance cars, had shown the need for increasing the proportion of motor ambulance convoys to fighting troops. Motor ambulances arrived slowly, and it is only recently that deliveries began to be adequate.

Most items of medical stores are now being delivered in satisfactory quantities. The percentage of hospital beds fell in arrears, owing to the exclusion from convoys of even the minimum number required. The number of field hygiene sections was, and still is, inadequate to the needs of the force.

In previous campaigns the need for mobile casualty clearing stations had been experienced. Three units were given sufficient transport to move the complete light section together with half the heavy section in one shift.

It has also been found necessary to form mobile surgical teams provided with their own transport, so that major surgery can be performed as far forward as the main dressing stations.

### Royal Army Ordnance Corps.

58. The excellent example of ceaseless hard work set by my Director of Ordnance Services, Brigadier W.O. Richards, has been emulated by the whole Corps. Several measures have been taken to ensure even greater efficiency.

The Royal Army Ordnance Corps lacked a number of essential units, of which only a few arrived between the end of June and the end of October. On the other hand, deficiencies in equipment and vehicles except for reserves have been largely made up, although there is still a serious shortage of machine tools.

Reorganisation of the Corps in accordance with the latest system designed by the War Office is now in progress, but it is not yet sufficiently far advanced to enable me to see whether the system will need to be modified to suit the conditions in the Middle East. Some five thousand additional personnel will be required to complete the reorganisation and it is therefore unlikely to be completed before next August.

The swift movement and lengthy communications characteristic of mechanised warfare made two innovations necessary.

Strict limits have been set to the scale of repairs to be undertaken by second line repair workshops, recourse being had as far as possible to the system of assembly exchanges.

It has also been found necessary to organise a system for the delivery of urgent spare parts and fighting stores. A special unit has been formed to deliver such stores by road and a further scheme has been prepared in conjunction with the Royal Air Force for the delivery of stores by air.

59. It was no easy task to re-equip and reorganise practically the whole of the Middle East Forces within the space of four months. Units had to be restored to their brigades, and brigades to their divisions. Equipment had to be distributed in such a way as to meet operational needs and to permit a maximum of training to be carried out. At the same time Cyprus had to be reinforced, and Tobruk relieved, units withdrawn from Syria and East Africa and the concentration for the offensive begun. The coordination of all these activities placed a great strain on the Staff Duties Branch of the General Staff and of all subordinate Headquarters. The smooth efficiency with which it was all accomplished is largely due to the untiring efforts of my Deputy Director of Staff Duties, Brigadier B. Temple.

## TRAINING.

60. Under the guidance of my Deputy Chief of General Staff, Major General N.M. Ritchie, every aspect of training in theory and practice has received the closest attention.

The lull in operations made it possible to give almost every fighting unit and formation the opportunity of carrying out further training, although the scope of training was necessarily limited by deficiencies in equipment. Incoming units and formations put in a spell of training in desert warfare before being sent to the operational zone, and particular attention has been paid to desert movement of mechanised columns by day and night.

The Combined Training Centre at Kabrit was employed to capacity throughout. One Brigade of the 5th Indian Division and two brigade groups of the New Zealand Division underwent a complete course at the Centre.

### Air Support.

61. An Inter-Service Committee, consisting of representatives of the Army and the Royal Air Force, was formed late in July to study the question of air support

for the Army. Experiments were carried out during August, and a system was finally evolved.

The first two air support controls in the Middle East were formed at Mena on 8th October, the Army component of the first being formed by the Australian Imperial Force, and of the second from British and New Zealand personnel. The air component of both was provided by the Royal Air Force.

### Parachute Detachment.

62. A small parachute detachment known as "L" Detachment, Special Air Service Brigade, was formed at Kabrit during July. It was composed of about 70 volunteers, recruited mainly from the survivors of the Commando Force.

Preliminary training was carried out during August and September, and the first live drops were successfully made on the 4th October.

Captain A.D. Stirling, who commanded the detachment directed all training without expert assistance. Great credit is due to him and to his officers and non-commissioned officers for their initiative in improvising equipment and inventing an entirely new type of training.

### Schools.

63. The Middle East Officers Cadet Training Unit has been reorganised and expanded. The specialist wings have been abolished; and all cadets now follow the same eight weeks' basic course, specialists passing on to officers' wings at the training school of the arm concerned. The annual capacity of the Training unit has been thereby increased from thirteen hundred to two thousand and forty cadets.

Special stress has been laid on anti-aircraft action at the Weapon Training School, moving targets being employed. Experiments have been made with kites and drogues towed by a truck to produce a satisfactory target.

The School of Anti-Aircraft and Coast Defence moved to Haifa and reopened on the 14th September, as air raids had interfered with instruction at Port Said.

A Royal Army Ordnance Corps School of Instruction, having general engineering and ammunition wings, has been opened.

A school has been opened at the Infantry Base Depot for training regimental specialists.

Six Indian Wings have recently been opened at existing schools.

## CAMOUFLAGE AND TACTICAL DECEPTION.

64. The urgent need for general training in the theory, practice and discipline of camouflage has been met by creating small camouflage training units on the scale of one to each division and higher formation. In addition, the formation of a camouflage training and development centre, Royal Engineers, has been authorised.

The 85th Camouflage Company, South African Engineering Corps, joined the Middle East Forces on 22nd August. It was the first and only complete camouflage and deception works unit in the British and Dominion Forces in the Middle East. It is well equipped. It provides mobile detachments for work in forward areas, and a factory and experimental section capable of limited production of deception equipment and of new devices.

The principal technical developments during the period under review have been improved types of lorry hoods for use on tanks, mobile dummy tanks mounted on lorry chassis, collapsible static dummy tanks of improved design, and collapsible dummy guns.

Under the technical direction of the camouflage staffs, defence lines on all commands have been extensively camouflaged. Much work has been done on installations of all kinds. Progress has been made with organised concealment and display in battle. Operations at Tobruk provided the opportunity for carrying out local schemes of deception both in defence and attack, schemes of misdirection, decoy and ambush being employed with promising results.

Two battalions of dummy tanks using static dummies and two battalions using mobile dummies have been provided.

### HEALTH.
65. The general health of the troops has been very good with comparatively low percentage of cases of dysentery and a very low percentage of cases in the typhoid group. The low incidence of Malaria has, in the circumstances, been satisfactory.

### WELFARE AND EDUCATION.
66. Considerable progress has been made in catering for the welfare of the troops but the demand for amenities of all kinds continually outstrips supply. To meet the growing demand for welfare and educational facilities throughout the Army it has become necessary to provide additional Welfare and Education Officers.

### PRISONERS OF WAR.
67. The evacuation of prisoners of war from Egypt and the Sudan has proceeded reasonably satisfactorily, the number of Italian and German prisoners of war in Egypt having been reduced from 58,000 to 27,000 and those in the Sudan from 23,000 to 9,000.

Many schemes for employing prisoners of war have been considered and tried, but the results have on the whole fallen short of expectations. This has been due to several causes, chief among them being the difficulty of finding the number of guards needed and the restrictions imposed by the Geneva Convention.

### CO-OPERATION OF OTHER SERVICES.
68. I have referred to our great indebtedness to the Royal Navy and the Royal Air Force for enabling us to maintain and relieve Tobruk. This was but a small part of their contribution to the preparations of the Army. Both Services were ceaselessly engaged in preventing the enemy from reinforcing and supplying his forces. It was largely due to the conspicuous success which attended their efforts that the enemy was compelled to allow us the respite we so sorely needed. Moreover it is due to their tireless devotion in organising and protecting convoys that we received the reinforcements and vast quantities of stores which enabled us to reorganise and re-equip the armies of the Middle East. To the Royal Navy and

the Royal Air Force and to Admiral Sir Andrew Cunningham and Air Marshal A.W. Tedder in particular we owe a deep debt of gratitude.

## APPRECIATION OF SERVICES.

69. It must be clear that the manifold activities related in this Despatch were not carried on without the loyal co-operation of every Branch of my own Staff and of Commanders and Staffs of subordinate Headquarters.

I wish to place on record my appreciation of the fighting spirit of all combatant units in the Middle East Forces and of the conscientious and efficient work of all ranks employed in base areas, without whose loyal efforts the usefulness of the battle formations would have been impaired.

APPENDIX "A" (see para. 24).
SUBJECT: Policy covering the defence of the Western Desert.

G.H.Q., M.E.F.
21 July, 1941.
Lieut.-General Sir Noel Beresford Peirse, K.B.E., D.S.O., Commanding W.D.F.

I. Intelligence appreciations indicate that the enemy will not be in a position before September 1941 to launch an attack with the Delta as has first main objective. An enemy advance, before that date, with a series of limited objectives is, however, possible.

2. A comparison of relative strengths shows that, while at present the enemy can put into the field an appreciably superior force of armoured fighting vehicles, this situation should have been considerably alleviated early in September.

3. In view of these factors, the Commander-in-Chief has decided that in the event of an enemy advance, his armoured forces will be brought to battle in the area South of Matruh.

4. In order to concentrate the maximum armoured forces for the main battle South of Matruh, no serviceable cruiser or "I" tanks should be located prior to the battle in the "boxes" at Matruh or Bagush. This ruling will be reviewed at a later date, when the total number of tanks available has increased.

5. In order that as much assistance as possible may be rendered by other formations to 7 Armoured Division during this tank battle, you are authorised to proceed with the development of a position to the West and South of Matruh, for occupation by not more than two Infantry Brigades.

6. The question of W.D.F. coming under the command of B.T.E. is receiving further consideration at this H.Q.

7. Acknowledge.

ARTHUR SMITH,
Lieut-General,
Chief of the General Staff.

APPENDIX "B" (see para. 24).
SUBJECT: Policy covering the defence of the Western Desert.

G.H.Q., M.E.F.
30 July, 1941.

G.O.C.-in-C., B.T.E.
G.O.C., W.D.F.

In continuation of Instruction dated 21st July, 1941.

1. In the event of the enemy launching an attack in the Western Desert, the X Corps, units comprising 5 Ind. Division and 2 S.A. Division, under command of G.O.C.-in-C., B.T.E., will:

    (a) Hold the El Alamein position, provided that a small Armoured Force can be made available.

    (b) Hold a sector of the Delta Defences if no Armoured Force is available.

2. Should the enemy advance necessitate the withdrawal of the W.D.F. (less the garrisons of the Matruh, and Bagush Boxes), G.O.C. and units of W.D.F., on passing out of the Western Desert area, will come under the command of B.T.E. for such duties as G.O.C.-in-C., B.T.E., may decide.

3. The boundary between W.D.F. and B.T.E. remains unaltered, i.e. (all including W.D.F.) Daba-Bab el Qaud – Longitude 28° to Qaret Agnes-Sitra-Siwa-Jalo.

4. As a guiding principle, troops of W.D.F. will rally on the El Alamein position, whether the position is held by X Corps or not.

5. G.O.C.-in-C., B.T.E., and G.O.C., W.D.F., will make mutual arrangements to ensure that units are withdrawn in such a way as to fit in best with the B.T.E. Defence Plan. Such arrangements will include movement tables, traffic control and measures for rallying units.

6. The fortresses of Matruh and Bagush will come under command of G.H.Q. when W.D.F. comes under B.T.E., or earlier, should G.O.C., W.D.F., consider such a course desirable.

7. Acknowledge.

ARTHUR SMITH,
Lieut.-General,
Chief of the General Staff.

APPENDIX "C" (see paras. 47–52)
## TABLES SHOWING COMPARATIVE STATES OF EQUIPMENT

### A. *Armoured Vehicles.*

| Formations | 26th June, 1941 | | 23rd October, 1941 | |
|---|---|---|---|---|
| | No. of Units | A.F.V. | No. of Units | A.F.V. |
| 7 Armd. Div. ... ... ... | — | 50% | — | 100% |
| 7 Armd. Bde. ... ... ... | 3 | 50% | 3 | 82% |
| 4 Armd. Bde. ... ... ... | 3 | 30% | 3 | 100% |
| 10 Armd. Div. ... ... ... | — | | — | |
| 8 Armd. Bde. ... ... ... | 3 | | 3 | Training scale |
| 9 Armd. Bde. ... ... ... | 3 | Forming | 3 | Nil |
| 1 Armd. Bde. ... ... ... | 4 | Nil | 1 | Nil |
| 22 Armd. Bde. ... ... ... | Not arrived | | 3 | 100% |
| 1 Army Tank Bde. ... ... | Not arrived | | 3 | 85% |
| 32 Army Tank Bde. ... ... | 1 | 30% | 2 | 67% |
| *Armd. Car Regts.* | | | | |
| 11 Hussars ... ... ... | | 92% | | 67%* |
| K.D.G. ... ... ... | | 40% | | 100% |
| Royals ... ... ... | | 92% | | 100% |
| 4 S. African Armd. Car R. ... ... | | 50% | | 100% |
| 6 S. African Armd. Car R. ... ... | | 50% | | 100% |

\* Remainder available, but being modified.

### B. *Other Equipment.*

| Formations | 1st July, 1941 | | 31st October, 1941 | |
|---|---|---|---|---|
| | M.T. | S.A. and Equipment | M.T. | S.A. and Equipment |
| 7 Armd. Div. ... ... ... | 75% | 70% | 100% | 90% |
| 10 Armd. Div. ... ... ... | — | 20% | 10% | 20% |
| 1 Armd. Bde. ... ... ... | — | 20% | 10% | 20% |
| 22 Armd. Bde. ... ... ... | — | — | 100%. | 100% |
| 1 Army Tank Bde. ... ... | 50% | 90% | 100% | 90% |
| 50 Div. ... ... ... | — | — | 60% | 90% |
| 70 Div. ... ... ... | 100% | 80% | — | 100% |
| 6 Aust. Div. ... ... ... | 10% | 75% | 60% | 80% |
| 7 Aust. Div. ... ... | 100% | 80% | 85% | 80% |
| 9 Aust. Div. ... ... | 30% | 100% | 10% | 50% |
| N.Z. Div. ... ... ... | 30% | 45% | 100% | 90% |
| 1 S. African Div. ... ... | 90%* | 90% | 100% | 90% |
| 2 S. African Div. ... ... | 50%* | 20% | 50% | 70% |
| 4 Ind. Div. ... ... ... | 30% | 90% | 90% | 100% |
| 5 Ind. Div. ... ... ... | 50% | 75% | 75% | 100% |
| 22 Gds. Bde. ... ... ... | 100% | 65% | 100% | 100% |
| 3 Ind. Motor Bde. ... ... | — | 45% | 100% | 100% |
| Polish Bde. Gp. ... ... | 10% | 100% | — | 100% |
| Greek Bde. Gp. ... ... | Training scale | | Training scale | |

\* Non-desertworthy transport.

## C. *Artillery – Field Branch.*

| | 1st July, 1941 | | 4th November, 1941 | | Increase |
|---|---|---|---|---|---|
| | No. of Regts. | State of Equipment | No. of Regts. | State of Equipment | |
| Field Arty. ... ... ... | 35 | 57% | 39 | 91% | 60% |
| A.-Tk. Arty. * ... ... | 10 | 58% | 11 | 76% | 86% |
| Medium Arty. ... ... | 3 | 100% | 5 | 100% | 40% |

* Figures based on establishment of 36 guns for two regts. on both dates, with remainder on 48 gun basis on 1st July and 64 gun basis on 4th November.

## D. *Artillery – Anti-Aircraft.*

| | 4th July, 1941 | | | 31st October, 1941 | | | Increase British |
|---|---|---|---|---|---|---|---|
| | No. of Btys. | State of Equipt. | | No. of Btys. | State of Equipt. | | |
| | | British | Total | | British | Total | |
| Heavy A.A. ... | 31* | 70% | 70% | 34 | 90% | 95%† | 42% |
| Light A.A. ... | 38 | 50% | 69% | 49 | 68% | 83% | 77% |
| Searchlight ... | 8 | 47% | 47% | 7 | 78% | 78% | 44% |
| G/L Sets ... ... | — | 25 sets | — | — | 32 sets | — | 28% |

* Does not include Free French or Egyptian Units.
† Includes captured equipment.

## E. *Services.*

| | 1st July, 1941 | 31st October, 1941 |
|---|---|---|
| | M.T. | M.T. |
| R.A.S.C. ... ... ... ... ... | 54% | 86% |
| R.A.M.C. ... ... ... ... ... | 84% | 96% |
| R.A.O.C. ... ... ... ... ... | * | 100% |

* Figures not available

# 5

# GENERAL AUCHINLECK'S DESPATCH ON OPERATIONS 1 NOVEMBER 1941 TO 15 AUGUST 1942

*The War Office, January,* 1948
OPERATIONS IN THE MIDDLE EAST
FROM 1st NOVEMBER 1941 TO 15th AUGUST 1942.
*The following Despatch was submitted to the Secretary of State for War on 27th January,*
*1943, by GENERAL SIR CLAUDE J.E. AUCHINLECK, G.C.I.E., C.B., C.S.I.,*
*D.S.O., O.B.E., A.D.C., Commander-in-Chief, The Middle East Forces.*

## INTRODUCTION.

Of the numerous problems of the Middle East Command two ranked high above all others: to destroy the enemy in North Africa and to secure the northern flank.

I had always conceived the former to be my prime task, for the presence of strong and well-equipped Axis forces in Cyrenaica was a constant menace to our base in Egypt. I planned to occupy the whole of Libya, Tripolitania as well as Cyrenaica, so as to leave the enemy no foothold whence he might, at some future date, revive the threat to Egypt. Moreover, it was always possible that we might eventually launch an offensive against Italy herself, and as a stepping stone it seemed essential to capture Tripoli. This policy had the full approval of His Majesty's Government.

The other problem, however, I could not for one moment neglect. The danger that Germany might attack Turkey and that Turkey might collapse was always present. Moreover the German invasion of Russia, which progressed at first with alarming rapidity, meant that danger threatened the Northern Front from the Caucasus also.

Swift as their initial advance was, it seemed impossible that the Germans should appear in the Caucasus before the early spring of 1942, and I thought it might be possible to destroy the German and Italian army in North Africa before that should occur. In November, there were sufficient troops already in the Middle East and enough reinforcements promised, to allow me to conduct an offensive in the west and yet be able to turn in time to stave off a possible threat from the north. The scope of the proposed offensive was ambitious, but it could be contemplated without running undue risks elsewhere, provided that the destruction of most of the enemy forces was effected in Eastern Cyrenaica. Above all, it was essential that there should be no delay.

The offensive was a success, but rather slower, more costly, and less complete than I had hoped. Nevertheless, of the enemy forces in Cyrenaica over two-thirds were destroyed.

Even before Cyrenaica had been reconquered, war had broken out with Japan, and His Majesty's Government were obliged to divert to the Far East two divisions and certain air force reinforcements intended for the Middle East. But there was still no necessity to rescind the decision to invade Tripolitania. The successful Russian counter-offensive in the winter of 1941–42 offset the loss of promised reinforcements in point of time, but not as regards the size of the forces which would eventually be required to garrison the whole Command, if the Germans should take the offensive once more and defeat the Russians. We were always handicapped, in our calculations, I may say, by lack of knowledge of Soviet capabilities and intentions. However, so important to the conduct of the war as a whole were the advantages of securing Tripoli, that it was worth taking further risks.

While we were preparing to resume the offensive, two Australian divisions were recalled from Syria and Palestine to the Pacific theatre and several air force squadrons were withdrawn to the Far East.

In January, 1942, the enemy attacked, thus anticipating our proposed invasion of Tripolitania. Though our naval forces and aircraft had drastically restricted the enemy's build-up of supplies in Africa during the latter half of 1941, by the end of the year the situation had changed greatly to our disadvantage. Powerful German naval and air reinforcements now arrived in the Central Mediterranean and for some months we were no longer able to enjoy the former degree of success against enemy convoys. The enemy's improved supply situation in early 1942 enabled him to exploit his advance, which caught us at a critical time when our forward troops were unavoidably weak and our armoured units in the forward area inexperienced. After an unsuccessful attempt to oppose the enemy advance, the Eighth Army withdrew to a defensive position covering Tobruk. This withdrawal naturally made still more difficult the problem of attacking the enemy's convoys, and he was able to bring in supplies in increasing quantities in preparation for a renewed offensive.

I at once began to plan afresh for an offensive in Libya, although to do so it was necessary drastically to revise our arrangements for defending Syria, Iraq and Persia. It soon became evident, however, that our armoured forces would certainly not be strong enough to take the field with any prospects of success for at least another three months. This caused profound concern in London, where it was feared that unless we acted quickly, Malta might be starved into submission. Grave as Malta's position had undoubtedly become, I believed that by launching the offensive prematurely we should risk an even greater calamity, that we might lose Egypt.

His Majesty's Government were at length persuaded that the delay was inevitable. They were warned that even then the attack could be launched, only if no more of our forces were withdrawn to the Far East. Moreover it was imperative that both Malta and the Middle East should be reinforced with aircraft, and heavy bombers in particular, so that we might effectively impede enemy shipping to Libya which our existing naval and air forces were practically unable to do. But, when His Majesty's Government found themselves unable to provide the reinforcements we asked and were obliged to order more of our air forces to be sent to the Far East, the Middle East Defence Committee were compelled to represent to them that the offensive could not now be undertaken before the middle of June. We pointed out the grave dangers to which the northern flank would be exposed in the event of Soviet resistance collapsing and our continuing with the offensive in North Africa. The whole matter was thoroughly reviewed, and His Majesty's Government ruled that the offensive should be launched by the 15th June notwithstanding.

In the middle of May we found that we had not been able to prevent the enemy reinforcing his North African army and it became clear that our offensive would be forestalled. The enemy advance began on the 26th May. The ensuing battle was fought with the object not only of repulsing the enemy, but of launching an immediate counter-offensive. At times during the first few days it seemed that we might succeed, but at length, after three weeks' fighting had cost it heavy losses, the Eighth Army was forced to retire. Syria, Iraq and Persia had to be stripped bare to enable us to stop the enemy at El Alamein. There we seized the initiative once more, but attempts to turn the tables on the enemy failed, because our own troops were no less exhausted than his and because the armoured troops employed were inexperienced. I then began to plan a deliberate offensive, knowing that a large number of tanks and anti-tank guns of greatly improved design, heavy bombers, and fresh divisions were on the way.

By this time the Germans had reached the Caucasus and only Stalingrad, where the defenders were slowly losing ground, stood between the Middle East and the gravest danger. It was then proposed to remove Persia and Iraq from the Middle East Command and to set up a separate command, in order to allow the Commander-in-Chief, Middle East, to conduct an offensive in North Africa without having to take thought for his northern flank. I could not agree that this was any solution to the problems of the Middle East as a whole.

This is the theme of the general narrative of events which forms Part I of this Despatch. The campaigns in Cyrenaica and the Western Desert were only one, although the most important, of the many activities in my command. A continuous narrative of these operations is therefore given separately in Part II, so that they may be described in appropriate detail without overshadowing matters of general policy.

Part III deals with organisation, training and administration. Many of our difficulties are attributable directly to faults or deficiencies in one or other of these. In my previous Despatch I mentioned some of the administrative and constructional enterprises undertaken. The building of railways, ports, roads and pipelines continued. Some of these enterprises gave an immediate return, the benefit of others will be experienced later.

As far as training was concerned, we had much to learn. In November, 1941, a British Army for the first time took the field against the Germans with a superiority in numbers, for the first time we possessed an imposing array of tanks, for the first time the Army enjoyed full air support in a major offensive against the Germans. All commanders and troops had to learn to use these unaccustomed benefits. An adequate system for controlling air support had been devised, liaison was close, and headquarters of land and air forces formed one camp; but many improvements were possible. Our experience with tanks was less happy: there was much that there was no time to learn and much that could be learned only in action. To learn to handle tanks cost us dear, particularly when we found that ours were no match for the German tanks and that our own anti-tank guns were greatly inferior to the German.

On the 1st November, 1941, the area covered by my Command included Syria, Cyprus, Palestine and Trans-Jordan, Egypt, the Sudan, part of Eritrea, and Aden. The spheres of influence of the Command included Turkey and the Balkans, Crete, Libya, part of French Equatorial Africa, and Arabia. Iraq and Persia were transferred to my Command early in January, 1942, the remainder of Eritrea in February, and Malta in March. The responsibilities of the Air Officer Commanding-in-Chief, Middle East, were wider than mine, including, as they did, the control of air forces in Iraq and Persia, in East Africa and, last but not least, Malta, throughout the period. The responsibilities of the Commander-in-Chief, Mediterranean, coincided, geographically, more or less with my own, except that the Red Sea and the Persian Gulf came under the Commander-in-Chief, East Indies.

Consequently, although this Despatch deals with the work of the land forces in the Middle East, every strategical plan concerned all three Services, and had to be approved by the three Commanders-in-Chief, under the general direction of the Minister of State.

## PART I.
### GENERAL NARRATIVE OF EVENTS IN THE MIDDLE EAST.

In my first Despatch on the Middle East I described how, having arranged for the Northern Front to be placed in a state of defence, I concentrated on preparing to take the offensive in Northern Africa. It was primarily to consider this undertaking that I was summoned to London by the Prime Minister in August, 1941. The various problems involved were discussed thoroughly and at length at meetings of the War Cabinet and the Defence Committee, and the records of these meetings show that His Majesty's Government in the United Kingdom considered it essential to take the offensive in North Africa at the earliest possible moment.

In any event the Germans were then advancing rapidly in Russia and it seemed that, provided this progress was maintained, it would not be very long before the road to the Caucasus would be opened to them. They might then be able not only to strike at Persia and Iraq from the north, but to invade Turkey from the north and east as well as from the west. It seemed not at all impossible that this danger would take shape early in 1942. It behoved us, therefore, to rid ourselves of the threat to Egypt from the west, before we might have to turn to meet an attack from the north and north-east.

By the end of October, 1941, our land forces in the Command seemed strong enough and sufficiently well-equipped to warrant making an attack. But to make this possible it was necessary to concentrate practically all the available air forces in the west, thus leaving Syria, Palestine and Cyprus unprotected. It was not necessary to denude these areas of land forces, although the garrison had to be deprived of transport in order to equip the Eighth Army. However, these risks were felt to be justifiable. Winter was approaching and the enemy could not appear south of the Caucasus for some months. The Germans were heavily engaged in Russia, and, even if they could spare aircraft and troops from the Russian front to reinforce Libya, the Royal Navy and the Royal Air Force could be relied on to make this a hazardous undertaking.

### The Offensive in Cyrenaica.

With the approval of His Majesty's Government, I laid my plans and made my preparations not only to defeat the enemy forces in the field, but also to occupy the whole of Libya. This was to be carried out in two stages. In the first stage it was intended that the Eighth Army should trap the enemy forces and destroy them in Eastern Cyrenaica: in the second the Eighth Army was to occupy Tripolitania. The success of the second stage depended upon how far we managed to achieve our aim in the first and to what extent we were able to overcome the difficulty of supplying our forces over such great distances.

When I originally gave orders in September, 1941, for plans to be prepared, I hoped that it might be possible to launch the offensive about the 1st November. I was careful, however, to explain to His Majesty's Government that the date on which it could be launched depended on the arrival of the troops and equipment, especially tanks, required to give that measure of superiority over the enemy I considered necessary to ensure a reasonable chance of success, and without which I did not think it right to try to defeat him.

My original estimate of the armoured forces needed for the conquest of Cyrenaica was three armoured divisions. The offensive had to be launched with one and a half armoured divisions and one brigade of infantry tanks.

For various unavoidable reasons, I had, most reluctantly, to postpone the opening date from the 1st to the 15th November. The chief cause was the tardy arrival of the 22nd Armoured Brigade from the United Kingdom: this formation was expected to reach Egypt between the 13th and 20th September, but its disembarkation was not actually completed until the 14th October. As a result, the brigade was not fully trained when it took the field.

The offensive had to be postponed for a further three days as the 1st South African Division, which was to play an important part in the initial operations, had not had enough time to train for a mobile role owing to the late arrival of the bulk of its vehicles.

We were working to very close margins as regards equipment and training. The same conditions applied to the building up of supplies and the construction of pipelines and railways. The essential preparations were barely complete when the campaign was launched, and the standard of training of many of the troops engaged left much to be desired. This was due to no fault of their own, but solely to lack of time and shortage of equipment.

For some time before the offensive opened, practically the whole of the German and Italian forces in Libya had been concentrated in the north-eastern angle of Cyrenaica, and I had considered striking direct at Bengasi by way of the desert so as to seize their chief supply port and cut the land reinforcement route from Tripoli at one and the same time. Our land and air forces slightly out-numbered the enemy's (disregarding the formidable Axis air strength elsewhere in the Mediterranean) but our margin of superiority was so small that our forces could not safely be divided, and there were considerable maintenance difficulties; so I eventually rejected this idea as impracticable. Instead I decided to envelop the enemy in Eastern Cyrenaica and destroy him there.

The German armoured divisions were the backbone of the enemy's army, and to destroy them was our principal object. The three armoured brigades were concentrated in the 30th Corps and General Norrie was instructed to use them to seek out and destroy the enemy's armour. When the Panzer divisions had been well and truly dealt with, the rest of our forces would carry out their parts in the operation. The 30th Corps and the garrison of Tobruk were then to secure the two ridges of Sidi Rezegh and Ed Duda which command the eastern end of a valley where the Trigh Capuzzo and the Tobruk by-pass road run side by side. They would thereby sever the enemy's communications with the west. At the same time the 13th Corps, whose initial task it was to prevent the enemy garrisons of the frontier positions moving east or south, would advance northwards and cut off these positions from the west. Part of the 13th Corps was then to move west to help the 30th Corps.

On the 17/18th November, following a month's intensive preparatory air effort, the advance began, the 30th Corps (7th Armoured Division, 4th Armoured Brigade, 1st South African Division, Guards Brigade) being directed by General Cunningham wide to the south of Sidi Omar towards Bir el Gubi and Tobruk, while the 13th Corps (New Zealand Division, 4th Indian Division, 1st Army Tank Brigade) watched the front and southern flank of the frontier positions.

All went well for the first three days. The enemy was certainly taken by sur-prise: his forces were actually in process of taking up fresh dispositions for an attack on Tobruk due to take place on the 23rd November. On the 19th what appeared to be the bulk of the German armoured divisions moved south from the coastal area, where they had been lying, and engaged the 4th and 22nd Armoured Brigades a few miles west of Sidi Omar.

Since the Panzer divisions now seemed to be committed to battle and were reported to be losing a considerable number of tanks, General Cunningham allowed the signal to be given for the Tobruk sorties to begin and for the 13th Corps to start operations. On 21st November, however, our difficulties began. The enemy, as was to be expected, reacted at once to the threat to Sidi Rezegh, and his armoured divisions evaded the 4th and 22nd Armoured Brigades. The whole of the enemy armour then combined to drive us from this vital area and to prevent help reaching the Support Group and the 7th Armoured Brigade which were isolated there. Neither of these formations was designed to carry out a prolonged defence and it is greatly to their credit that they managed to do so, unaided, throughout the 21st. The 5th South African Infantry Brigade, which was expected to reach the scene before the development of the enemy attack, failed to do so, partly owing to the opposition of the Ariete Armoured Division and partly because of inexperience in handling the very large number of vehicles with which it took the field.

Next day all three armoured brigades joined in the defence of the area. But our tanks and anti-tank guns were no match for the German, although they were fought with great gallantry: and on the evening of the 22nd November the 30th Corps was compelled to retire, having lost two thirds of its tanks and leaving the garrison of Tobruk with a huge salient to defend.

The enemy rounded off his success in spectacular fashion. In a night attack he surprised and completely disorganised the 4th Armoured Brigade whose hundred tanks represented two-thirds of our remaining armoured strength. On the 23rd he practically annihilated the 5th South African Infantry Brigade, one of the only two infantry brigades General Norrie had under command – there was no transport for any more – and then on the 24th with his armoured divisions he made a powerful counterstroke to the frontier. Before this, it had become quite clear that the first reports had grossly exaggerated enemy tank losses and that he had at least as many tanks as we had and better, and was in a position to recover more from the battlefield which remained in his hands.

This shifting of the balance of strength between the opposing armoured forces produced a most critical situation and led General Cunningham to represent to me that a continuation of our offensive might result in the annihilation of our tank force, and so endanger the safety of Egypt. I visited General Cunningham at his advanced headquarters on the 23rd November and told him to continue to press the offensive against the enemy. He loyally gave effect to these orders; but on my return to Cairo on the 25th, I most reluctantly decided that I must relieve him of his command, as I had come to the conclusion, after long and anxious consideration, that he was unduly influenced by the threat of an enemy counterstroke against his communications. I therefore replaced him on the 26th November by Major-General N.M. Ritchie.

The enemy's counterstroke caused considerable confusion and some loss among headquarters, troops and transport, and enemy tanks penetrated to Halfaya, Sollum and Bardia. The battered 30th Corps could do little, but the

13th Corps proved equal to the occasion, and its stubborn resistance prevented the enemy from doing much serious damage. The enemy suffered heavy losses by air attack during his thrust.

The New Zealand Division (4th and 6th Brigades) had been despatched westwards as soon as the country west of the frontier positions had been occupied. By the 27th November they had recaptured Sidi Rezegh, taken Belhamed on the northern ridge and joined hands with the garrison of Tobruk, who for their part, after holding the salient for five days against numerous counter-attacks, had completed their sortie by taking Ed Duda. By the 28th the whole of this important tactical locality was in our hands.

Finding that the heavy blows sustained by the 30th Corps and his bold counterstroke had not turned us from our purpose, the enemy returned from the frontier to launch violent assaults on our new positions. The Armoured Division had reorganised but was unable either seriously to impede the enemy's return or to intervene effectively when his tanks attacked the New Zealand Division. In spite of the gallantry with which they fought, our armoured troops were worsted in almost every encounter with the enemy tanks, not only because they were comparatively inexperienced, but also because the enemy tanks mounted guns of greater range. Whenever our tanks attempted to take the enemy in the rear, they were confronted by formidable 88 millimetre guns to which we possessed no counterpart.

Like the Support Group a week before, the New Zealand Brigades holding Sidi Rezegh and Belhamed were thin on the ground, the more so as they had incurred heavy casualties in taking the positions. Realising this, General Ritchie ordered the 1st South African Infantry Brigade to join the 13th Corps. This brigade, which was the only one having its own transport and therefore immediately available, suffered, like the 5th South African Infantry Brigade, through no fault of its own, from lack of training and its movements were also hampered by superfluous transport. Consequently it arrived too late to assist the New Zealanders, who in the face of powerful attacks had to retire, first from Sidi Rezegh and then from Belhamed.

The enemy were now again in possession of the vitally important ground at Belhamed and Sidi Rezegh. The troops of the Tobruk garrison were still holding the Ed Duda salient, but their front was enormous relative to their strength and was exposed to attack from north, east, and south. On the frontier, the 13th Corps had captured the Omars, but the enemy garrisons at Bardia and Halfaya were still holding out and were strong in artillery. Of the two brigades of the 1st South African Division one had been practically destroyed. Two-thirds of the New Zealand Division had been cut to pieces, and had had to be withdrawn to refit. The three armoured brigades with which the offensive had been launched had been reduced to one composite formation mustering about a hundred and twenty tanks, all of them inferior to the German tanks of which there were at least half as many. Moreover there were numerous Italian tanks, which had shown themselves to be better than we had believed.

Apart from the 7th Armoured Division (Support Group and composite Armoured Brigade), there remained the 22nd Guards Brigade, which had scarcely been engaged; the 4th Indian Division, one brigade of which had captured the Omars after heavy fighting; the 1st South African Infantry Brigade; the 5th New Zealand Infantry Brigade; and the 2nd South African Division, only partially trained, which was in process of relieving the 4th Indian Division in front of Bardia and Halfaya. There were also the independent armoured car units, the Oases Force committed in the Gialo region, and the Tobruk garrison, which was not, however, capable of more than a limited offensive effort.

But the enemy also had had a severe hammering both on the ground and from the air and was much reduced in strength. It became therefore a question of maintaining the momentum of our attack, and I was determined that it should be maintained. In order to be on the spot, should a decision be required from me, I stayed at General Ritchie's headquarters from the 1st to 11th December and was able to confer with him constantly on the course of the operations. General Ritchie clearly needed fresh troops. I therefore arranged to make the Royal Dragoons from Syria and the 12th Royal Lancers, newly arrived from England, immediately available, and ordered the 1st Armoured Division, which had just arrived from the United Kingdom, and a brigade group of the 50th Division, which had been ordered to Iraq, to join the Eighth Army. I also formed three Indian battalions into the 38th Indian Infantry Brigade to help in the defence of the lines of communication.

General Ritchie still had enough forces to continue, and he had already made up his mind, rightly, that the ridges north and south of El Adem, due south of Tobruk, were the key to the whole position. He therefore instructed the two Corps Commanders to secure them as soon as possible: the 13th Corps was to advance westwards along the northern ridge from the flank of the Tobruk salient and the 30th Corps to capture El Gubi and close on El Adem from the south. The role of the Armoured Division remained unchanged: to neutralise and destroy the enemy's armoured forces.

For various reasons the operation did not materialise. First, a hitch arose over the provision of transport to lift one of the Indian brigades from the frontier – we were working to very fine margins with transport – and the Indian Division was nearly a day late in assembling. Then a preliminary attack against the enemy's southern flank at Bir el Gubi met with strong opposition and failed in its object of clearing the way for the advance. Finally, when the 30th Corps had massed for the operation, the enemy had occupied the general line El Adem – Bir el Gubi in strength, with the greater part of his armoured forces on the southern flank, astride the proposed axis of advance. The enemy having failed meanwhile in a last attempt to reach Bardia, and, having several times attacked the Tobruk salient furiously but in vain, had divined our plan and withdrawn from the east of Tobruk. The Armoured Division succeeded in destroying quite a number of Italian tanks during this time, but the German armour and the greater part of the enemy forces remained inaccessible behind a powerful screen of artillery and anti-tank guns.

Light columns and armoured cars of the 30th Corps were operating well to the northwest of Bir el Gubi, but the Armoured Division was unable either to dislodge the enemy from the southern flank or to turn the position. Seeing that there was no time to lose, General Ritchie took the initiative with the 13th Corps. During the night of the 7th December the 70th Division began to advance along El Adem Ridge, and by the 9th they were well to the west of the Tobruk – El Adem road, having cleared the whole area between the perimeter and the by-pass road. At General Godwin-Austen's request, General Ritchie sent the 5th New Zealand Infantry Brigade from Bardia to reinforce this advance.

On the 8th December the enemy began to withdraw rapidly but in good order towards Gazala, covering his retirement with rearguards strong in anti-tank artillery. The pursuit was closely pressed by motorised columns on the flanks and by the infantry of both Corps in the centre and was accompanied by harassing air action. On the 10th December the Polish Brigade broke out of the western perimeter of Tobruk, and the long investment of the fortress came to an end.

After the withdrawal to Gazala a brief lull followed during which the supply lines were reorganised with Tobruk as a forward base; but by the 12th December our forward troops were increasing their pressure on the new line which the enemy had taken up, running southwards from Gazala. The 13th Corps took command of operations in the forward area, and the headquarters of the 30th Corps went back to direct operations against the enemy garrisons in the frontier positions.

I had at first thought that the enemy's stand at Gazala was only another delaying action to cover further withdrawal. But the resistance offered to our pressure, his heavy counterattacks, of which the 4th Indian Division bore the brunt, and numerous air attacks showed that he hoped to check our advance on this line and was using all his available forces to this end, probably in a last effort to keep his hold on the valuable base and port of Bengasi. General Ritchie placed more troops at General Godwin-Austen's disposal to enable him to increase the frontal pressure and instructed him to send the Armoured Division to turn the enemy's southern flank. The 4th Armoured Brigade moved wide over difficult country and gained a position to the south of Tmimi well in rear of the enemy's positions, but its subsequent movements were much impeded by bad going. On the night of the 16th December the enemy began to withdraw from his Gazala positions and the remnants of his armoured forces managed to slip away in the darkness.

Having destroyed two-thirds of the Axis army we could justly claim a victory; but our advantages henceforth were more apparent than real, for only very light forces could be sent in pursuit of the enemy and even these were much hampered by supply difficulties. Transport resources had been stretched to the limit to sustain the operations in Eastern Cyrenaica, a hundred and twenty miles ahead of railhead: in Western Cyrenaica we were operating at twice to three times that distance from the new forward base at Tobruk. Rough country, waterlogged in many places after the recent heavy rains, increased our supply troubles.

The 13th Corps set out to follow and cut off the defeated enemy. The 4th Indian Division advanced through the Gebel Akhdar and proceeded at a great pace, occupying Derna on 19th December and Barce four days later. The bulk of the German forces, including forty to fifty tanks, withdrew south-westwards across the desert and guarded the coastal road leading south from Bengasi. The 7th Armoured Division followed as fast as it could; but, as the armoured brigade was held up for lack of petrol, General Gott sent mobile columns ahead with orders to make straight for Bengasi. These columns found the going difficult on the southern slopes of the Gebel which were particularly rough and waterlogged; but as they approached, the enemy forces, holding the defiles through the escarpment to cover Bengasi, retired. Our armoured cars entered Bengasi on Christmas Eve and found the town evacuated. By the 26th December all the hill country up to and including Bengasi, with much booty, but unfortunately few prisoners, was in our hands.

The Guards Brigade was sent even wider to to the south towards Antelat and Agedabia. No supply vehicles could be provided, however, until 20th December, and, when the brigade reached Antelat on the 22nd, they found their way to the coast road barred by a force of German tanks at Beda Fomm. The 22nd Armoured Brigade reached Saunnu on the 23rd December, but there they were again immobilised by lack of petrol. That evening the enemy armoured forces retired to Agedabia.

Agedabia was a naturally strong position and difficult to turn, and, after the 22nd Armoured Brigade had had an unsuccessful encounter with enemy tanks on the 28th December and again on the 30th, it became clear that we needed fresh troops if we were to advance further. The tanks of the armoured brigade were mechanically unsound after the long march across the desert, and this was largely responsible for their lack of success in these engagements. The 1st Armoured Division reached Antelat on 6th January, and the next morning patrols reported that the enemy had withdrawn from Agedabia.

While these operations were going on in Eastern Cyrenaica, General Norrie was eliminating the enemy still holding out on the Egyptian frontier. It was of the utmost importance that direct road communication through Sollum should be quickly restored, as the long detour across the desert was most uneconomical in motor transport upon a sufficiency of which depended our ability to maintain an adequate force round Agedabia and Agheila.

On the 2nd January Bardia was captured by the 2nd South African Division, supported by the 1st Army Tank Brigade, after a sustained bombardment from land, sea and air. Sollum was captured on the 11th January, and on the 17th the last remaining garrison at Halfaya surrendered. With that the first stage of the Libyan offensive was successfully concluded.

In sketching the course of the campaign I have not attempted to describe the part played by the Royal Air Force, and even in the fuller narrative of Part II it has not been possible to do justice to their magnificent work. It is no exaggeration to say that but for the unfailing and complete response of the Royal Air Force to all demands and requests made by the Eighth Army, the relief of Tobruk could not have been accomplished. Co-operation between the two Services was excellent from the beginning, and Air Vice-Marshal Coningham and General Ritchie shared a joint headquarters. It need hardly be said that Air Chief Marshal Tedder and I worked in the closest collaboration and most thorough understanding in this, as in every other enterprise in the Middle East.

Co-operation with the Royal Navy and my own relations with Admiral Cunningham, Commander-in-Chief, Mediterranean, were equally harmonious. During the eight long months of siege Tobruk had been kept continuously supplied at very great risk by ships of the Royal Navy, and when the fortress was at length relieved a very large part of the Eighth Army's supplies continued to be brought by sea. Captain G. Grantham, R.N., permanently accredited as naval liaison officer to General Ritchie's Headquarters, provided a valuable link between the Army Commander and Naval Headquarters at Alexandria.

On the 12th January I wrote to the Prime Minister reviewing the recent fighting in Libya and outlining my intentions for the future. Although our plan to draw the enemy tanks into the open by moving on Tobruk was successful, the ensuing battle had not gone as we had hoped. In spite of the slight numerical superiority our armoured brigades failed in the first instance to neutralise or destroy the enemy armour, which was essential to the complete success of the plan. The Italian M 13 tanks, which, as a result of the experiences of the previous campaign, we had been inclined to dismiss as valueless, fought well and had an appreciable effect on the battle. There was little doubt that the presence of German troops had stiffened Italian morale, particularly that of their armoured troops.

Judging by the results of the tank battles round Tobruk and at Agedabia, it was obvious that not only were all our tanks outgunned by the German tanks, but our cruiser tanks were mechanically inferior under battle conditions. Though the American light tanks, as fighting machines, could not compare with our own or German medium tanks, they were mechanically far more reliable than British medium tanks. The inferior armament and mechanical unreliability of our tanks was aggravated by a great shortage of anti-tank weapons compared with the Germans. We were indeed fortunate in having a reserve of over two hundred fast medium tanks with which to replace those rendered unserviceable in battle, whereas it was doubtful if the enemy could produce more than fifty or sixty for this purpose.

It was also obvious that if we were to fight the Germans on the Northern Front in the coming summer under the same adverse conditions so far as equipment was concerned, the standard of leadership and tactical handling of our armoured forces must be improved. I believed that our tank tactics were inferior to those of the Germans because we had failed adequately to co-ordinate the action of tanks, infantry and artillery on the battlefield. The three arms must therefore associate much more closely and continuously in training and in battle, and I proposed to ensure this by making changes in the organisation of our formations.

I urged that we should be allowed to go forward with our plan for the invasion of Tripolitania. With the equivalent of two armoured and four infantry divisions, General Ritchie had inflicted a heavy defeat on an enemy not only nearly equal in number, but possessing undoubted advantages in tanks and artillery. Out of an original enemy total strength of about a hundred thousand men a maximum of thirty-five thousand were now manning the defences at Agheila, while his armoured forces had been reduced from three armoured divisions to the equivalent of about one regiment. On our side a fresh armoured brigade had moved into the forward area. It seemed that we could reasonably undertake the invasion of Tripolitania, when the great difficulties inherent in the maintenance of considerable forces in Western Cyrenaica could be overcome. Every effort was being made to do this, and Bengasi had just begun to function as an advanced supply base, although regular supply by sea had not yet been assured.

If by any chance we should have to break off the offensive on the borders of Cyrenaica, it was essential at all costs to secure a position which could be held indefinitely against an enemy counter-offensive. Such a position had not been secured the year before when Rommel drove General Wavell's forces back to Tobruk and beyond. To find it we must go forward to the line of marshes west of Agheila and also occupy Marada to cover the southern flank.

*Diversion of Forces to the Far East.*

While Cyrenaica was being cleared of the enemy, events in the Far East began to affect the Middle East Command. War broke out with Japan on the 8th December, 1941, and four days later, before the enemy had been driven from Gazala, the Prime Minister informed me that, owing to the Japanese threat to the Malay Peninsula and Burma, certain reinforcements on their way to the Middle East must be diverted. These were the 18th (United Kingdom) Division, four light bomber squadrons, a number of anti-aircraft and anti-tank guns and the 17th Indian Division. It was also proposed to extend the Middle East Command to include Iraq and Persia, so as to ensure local unity of command on the Northern Front. The Commander-in-Chief, India, would in future have to look east.

The Middle East Defence Committee felt bound to point out the serious implications of the diversion of these reinforcements. A minimum of seventeen infantry divisions, apart from armoured formations which there was then no question of diverting, was required to defend our Northern and Western Fronts. Unless further reinforcements were received, no more than twelve infantry divisions would be available. The diversion of air reinforcements and anti-aircraft guns, together with the proposed transfer of six light bomber squadrons already in the Command, might seriously prejudice our ability to support the Libyan offensive. This was the more likely as the German Air Force in Libya was being strengthened. Moreover the security of our own communications in the

Mediterranean and our power of interrupting the enemy's would be gravely affected.

Two days after the Eighth Army had entered Bengasi, the Prime Minister informed me that four squadrons of Hurricane fighters were also to be transferred from the Middle East to Singapore and asked me to spare at least a hundred American light tanks. The situation in the Far East was obviously very grave, and I therefore informed the Chief of the Imperial General Staff that I was prepared to send fifty light tanks, of which twenty-five would be manned, and a hundred and ten American light tanks, for which I would provide a complete armoured brigade headquarters with signal section and workshops and two armoured regiments, all with experience of the recent fighting. I also offered an anti-tank battery, a field battery, and the loan of an Australian Infantry brigade group, provided that it could be replaced or returned by the spring. These troops I thought could be spared without prejudicing the success of our campaign in Tripolitania.

Grave as the Far Eastern situation undoubtedly was, it seemed to the Middle East Defence Committee that the relative importance of the two theatres must be carefully assessed before the Middle East was called on to provide further reinforcements. The defeat of Germany by a land offensive against her territory was our ultimate object. Therefore, to send any forces to the Far East in excess of the minimum required to secure our bases and sea communications would constitute a diversion from our main object.

Moreover if the American effort was to be directed into the right channel from the outset, it should be decided without delay from which theatre the eventual offensive against Germany was to be launched. The Mediterranean, in my opinion, offered good, if not the best strategical prospects. As a preliminary to a grand offensive from the south against the mainland of Europe it was essential to secure Tunisia, and the Committee urged the Minister of Defence and Chiefs of Staff to consider providing the necessary forces, including possibly American, for this operation.

Apart from this, it was essential to hold the bases of the Middle East including Malta; yet, as we pointed out, our naval, land and air forces already fell far short of our minimum requirements for the spring of 1942. So far as the Army was concerned, I estimated that to defend the whole of the Middle East including Persia and Iraq I required five armoured and seventeen infantry divisions. It now appeared that we could count on no more than three and a half armoured and thirteen infantry divisions and were consequently faced with a deficiency of twenty-five per cent. of our minimum requirements. The Royal Air Force, it appeared, would be twenty squadrons short of the eighty-two needed. Our naval forces also needed strengthening. These estimates were based on the assumption that we might have to meet an attack on the Northern Front in the spring, that we should be able to retain our hold on Cyrenaica, and that the enemy would be incapable of resuming the offensive on a large scale in the west.

His Majesty's Government agreed that the defeat of Germany must remain our primary object and that, consequently, no more of our forces should be diverted for the moment than were necessary to hold the Japanese. Nevertheless it was imperative to call upon the Middle East to provide six infantry divisions and one armoured brigade in all out of existing resources and out of expected reinforcements. We were asked to despatch the 6th and 7th Australian Divisions immediately. Our losses and expectations would be made good as soon as possible.

Within a very few days I was warned by the Chiefs of Staff that Malta, a vital bastion of the Middle East, was also in acute danger, and I was ordered to send an anti-aircraft regiment and two squadrons of tanks to repel an expected attack. These were despatched, but only half of them reached the island. The attack, fortunately, failed to materialise.

The Middle East Defence Committee naturally accepted the withdrawal of troops and air forces as inevitable. They did, however, feel it necessary to stress that the situation in Cyrenaica was still delicate and would continue so until we had secured a position in the Agheila marshes. Troop movements to the Far East should not be allowed to interfere with the attainment of that object, otherwise we should be compelled to retire to the frontier. In the event, the withdrawal of troops did not affect the operations which took place in Western Cyrenaica at the end of January.

I did, however, consider that it might be prudent to abandon the project of invading Tripolitania for the time being. Having once secured El Agheila and Marada, I felt confident of holding Cyrenaica and of being in an advantageous position to launch an offensive at some future date. I, therefore, consulted the Prime Minister on this point.

The Prime Minister's reply conveyed a warning that the remaining Australian Division might be required, but at the same time it held out definite prospects that some at least of our losses would be made good as soon as shipping could be provided. The United States Government was fully impressed with the idea that Germany was the chief opponent, and there was no intention of sacrificing any profitable operation against Germany for the sake of an offensive in the Far East, except with the limited object of making Malaya secure. The President was even considering basing an American army on the ports of the Persian Gulf and participating in an operation to secure Tunisia with or without the connivance of the Vichy Government. We were, therefore, to pursue our preparations for carrying the war into Tripolitania.

The promises that our losses would be made good were reassuring, but it seemed practically certain that the Germans would resume their Russian campaign in the spring and might be expected to attack Northern Persia in the middle of May. It was also possible, though much less likely, that they might invade Turkey from the west in which case we should have to be prepared to meet an attack six weeks earlier. Since we had allotted a minimum of troops to the Western Front in estimating our defence requirements, every withdrawal of troops for the Far East was effected at the expense of the Northern Front and it became necessary drastically to revise our plans for the defence of this flank.

The defence of Syria, Iraq and Persia from the north had always been regarded as one problem, with Cyprus as an essential outpost on the western flank. In September, 1941, I had arranged with General Wavell for India and the Middle East to collaborate in planning. On the 5th January, 1942, Iraq and Persia passed under my command, and Lieutenant-General E.P. Quinan's forces became the Tenth Army corresponding to General Sir Henry Maitland Wilson's Ninth Army in Syria.

In estimating the forces required to defend this thousand mile front we had two objects; first to keep the enemy as far as possible from our bases and oilfields in Egypt and at the head of the Persian Gulf, and secondly to be able to support Turkey if she were attacked. Four armoured and fifteen infantry divisions were needed and in December we could count on no more than two and a half armoured and eleven infantry divisions, after allowing only one armoured and two infantry divisions for the Western Front. Moreover there was a serious shortage of anti-aircraft artillery.

After the two Australian divisions had been withdrawn with their full complement of administrative units and after taking into account the prospects of equipment being diverted to the Far East, the situation became much worse.[1] It now seemed that only nine infantry divisions would be available for the Northern Front. Moreover an acute shortage of tanks, armoured cars and motor transport vehicles would prevent us making even these fully mobile. It was obvious that we could not hope to fight the enemy well forward, but must meet him much further back where the ground favoured defence by weak forces.

These decisions were as distasteful to Admiral Cunningham and Air Chief Marshal Tedder as they were to me; but they agreed that in the circumstances there was no alternative, particularly as our air forces were not strong enough to offset the weakness of our armies.

I at once issued new instructions for the defence of the Northern Front. At the same time the Middle East Defence Committee took steps to guard against a possible failure of the French civil administration in Syria in the event of attack, or threat of attack. On 22nd January I discussed the new policy with Generals Wilson and Quinan at Haifa, and, when I returned to Cairo on the 23rd, I found that the enemy had taken the offensive in the Western Desert.

### *The Eighth Army's Withdrawal to Gazala.*

When the enemy went back from Agedabia to the El Agheila positions he was closely followed by our light motorised columns, and planning and preparations began at once for a further offensive to be launched in mid-February.

It was estimated that the enemy losses since the opening of our offensive in November were 36,000 prisoners of war, of which some 10,000 were German, and 24,000 killed and wounded including 11,000 Germans – a total of about 60,000 out of an original strength of about 100,000. Over 200 German and 120 Italian tanks and some 850 aircraft had been captured or destroyed. In addition the enemy had lost two-thirds of his artillery.

Our own losses came to about 18,000 officers and men out of an army of 118,000; and, although our tank losses had been much heavier than the enemy's, we were fortunate in having a fresh armoured brigade in training. Moreover, many of the tanks now out of commission could be repaired, though our recovery and repair organisation would take some time to cope with the volume of work.

The enemy seemed too weak to stage a counter-offensive. But at the same time our own forces in Western Cyrenaica were also weak, as all available transport had to be applied to building up reserves in the forward area without which further advance was impossible. The possibility of the enemy forestalling us was, therefore, by no means ruled out, and plans were made to meet such an eventuality.

We had in Western Cyrenaica the 1st Armoured Division, which had recently relieved the 7th Armoured Division and, being newly arrived from the United Kingdom, was inexperienced in desert fighting. There were also the 201st Guards Motor Brigade and one or two units of the Oases Force. These troops were watching the enemy at El Agheila and reconnoitring for our resumption of the offensive. In addition there were two brigades of the 4th Indian Division round Barce and Bengasi, temporarily immobilised for lack of vehicles.

Should the enemy move forward to upset our preparations for a further advance, the forward troops were to stand on the line Agedabia – El Haseiat until we could launch a counter-attack and drive him back to his original positions.

It seems doubtful whether the enemy, who was certainly weak and in difficulties over his supply problem, launched his counter-stroke with the definite intention of recapturing Cyrenaica. He does not seem to have used more than one hundred tanks throughout and some of these were light tanks. However this may be, he certainly exploited his initial success with great vigour and skill.

Strongly supported by his air force, the enemy took the offensive early on 21st January, moving in three columns, one north of the main road, the others to the south. He pushed back our troops on the northern flank and was consequently able to move rapidly up the main road outstripping our southern columns which were delayed by bad going. The Support Group, getting into difficulties in the soft sand further south, was overtaken by enemy tanks and lost guns and transport.

By evening the enemy was within thirty miles of Agedabia and Lieutenant-General Godwin- Austen, commanding the 13th Corps, realising that the enemy had advanced in force, ordered a withdrawal to the line Agedabia – El Haseiat, giving Major-General Messervy, who was commanding the 1st Armoured Division, discretion to withdraw on Agedabia, Antelat and Msus, should he consider it necessary for the security of his force. The 4th Indian Division (Major-General Tuker) was told to stop any enemy advance on Bengasi along the coastal plain.

On the 22nd the enemy, driving our troops in front of him and using the main road, again outstripped our slower moving columns on the flanks and occupied Agedabia. On the 23rd our armoured troops engaged the enemy round Antelat and Saunnu, but were unable to prevent him occupying these two places the same evening.

The enemy halted on the 24th and plans were made to counter-attack, retake Antelat and Saunnu and keep him to the south of that line. On the 25th, however, the enemy again advanced very rapidly, out-distancing our troops, and took Msus in spite of being engaged all day by the 2nd Armoured and Guards Brigades. The 1st Armoured Division, which had now become very weak, was then ordered to withdraw through Charruba on Mechili, leaving a detachment to guard the flank of the 4th Indian Division as it withdrew from Bengasi and Barce through the Gebel Akhdar.

On the 23rd January I returned to Cairo from Haifa, where I had been conferring with Generals Wilson and Quinan, and on the 25th I flew to Tmimi to join General Ritchie at his Headquarters, where I remained until the 1st February.

General Ritchie then took the 4th Indian Division under his direct control and counter-manded the 13th Corps' orders for a general withdrawal. I approved of this change of plan as I considered it still possible to make an effort to hold Bengasi and counter-attack.

General Ritchie then ordered a counter-attack to be carried out by the 4th Indian and 1st Armoured Division from the north and west against the enemy concentrations round Msus. Preparations for this were in progress when, on the 27th, the enemy resumed his advance, feinting towards Mechili while making his main effort against the 4th Indian Division round Bengasi. His feint was successful in drawing off our armoured force, and the 4th Indian Division, left without tank support, was ordered to withdraw through the Gebel Akhdar towards Derna, its southern flank being protected by the 1st Armoured Division.

Before the troops holding Bengasi could withdraw, the enemy cut the roads to the north, thus isolating them. With great daring, however, they broke through to the south and the majority eventually succeeded in rejoining the Eighth Army.

Closely followed by the enemy, the remainder of the 4th Indian Division withdrew through the hills fighting a series of rearguard actions. On the 4th February, however, they succeeded in reaching the line at Gazala which the rest of the Eighth Army was fortifying.

I had hoped that General Ritchie would be able to stabilise the position on the line Derna – Mechili – Bir Tengeder. But on the 1st February it was found necessary to order the evacuation of Derna and to withdraw further to a line running south from Gazala. This decision was forced on us by the weakness of our armour and by the discovery, after close examination of new evidence that the enemy's supply situation might permit him to advance in the next few days from Msus with at least one armoured division. He might then try to outflank our positions at Mechili and Tengeder from the south, and thus threaten the safety of our troops round Derna and Martuba, which, owing to the configuration of the coast were liable to be cut off. I took the further precaution of ordering defensive positions to be prepared on the Egyptian frontier and at Giarabub.

While these operations were in progress, Lieutenant-General Godwin-Austen asked to be relieved of his command of the 13th Corps, as he felt that General Ritchie had displayed a lack of confidence in him by issuing orders directly to his subordinate commanders. I had no option but to relieve him of his command, and replaced him by Major-General Gott, then commanding the 7th Armoured Division.

During the withdrawal from Agedabia the 1st Armoured Division lost about ninety of its tanks, thirty twenty-five-pounder guns, thirty two-pounder anti-tank guns and twenty-five light Bofors anti-aircraft guns, besides about a fifth of its load-carrying transport. The 4th Indian Division also lost heavily in vehicles. The losses inflicted on the enemy do not appear to have been serious, though the 1st Armoured Division claimed to have destroyed twenty enemy tanks and damaged twenty-five more.

I returned to my General Headquarters on the 1st February disquieted by the failure of the Eighth Army to check the enemy advance. The weakness of our armour was particularly disturbing, and I doubted whether we might not have to withdraw to the frontier positions. When I got back to Cairo, however, I found that the prospects of rebuilding our armoured force reasonably quickly were better than I had supposed, and I decided to try to hold Tobruk, since to possess it would undoubtedly make it very much easier to resume the offensive. I therefore sent General Ritchie preliminary instructions to hold the enemy as far west as possible without risking the destruction or isolation of the Eighth Army west of the Egyptian frontier.

Whatever happened, I was determined not to allow Tobruk to be besieged a second time. The configuration of the coast invited investment, and with my existing resources of infantry and armour I did not consider I could afford to lock up one and a quarter divisions in a fortress. Admiral Cunningham agreed, particularly since the seige had proved very costly in ships, and so did Air Chief Marshal Tedder, who doubted whether he had sufficient aircraft to provide fighter cover. It was still my firm intention, however, to resume the offensive and for that Tobruk would be invaluable as an advanced base. Consequently I instructed General Ritchie to make every effort to hold Tobruk, short of allowing it to become invested.

Having studied further the problem of destroying the enemy and occupying Tripolitania, I reached two principal conclusions, namely that, when we attacked again we must have complete superiority in armour and that our offensive must not lose momentum as a result of inability to maintain powerful forces beyond Bengasi.

In the open desert country of Cyrenaica superiority in armour was in my opinion the essential of any offensive. To achieve this we needed at least half as many tanks again as the enemy, taking into account the relative efficiency of the German tanks and our own. Over and above that we needed a reserve equal to at least twenty-five per cent. of the number deployed with units. Judging from past experience, the reserve should have been double that figure; but I was prepared to take that risk. Estimates of relative strengths, based on information then available and on the assumption that no troops or equipment would have to be diverted to the Northern Front or elsewhere, showed that we might hope to attain the desired position by the 1st May.[2]

Bitter experience showed the truth of my second conclusion. As transport was still short and distances great, we could not hope to maintain powerful forces round Agedabia and El Agheila unless Bengasi could be used as a port. Our first objective must be to take Bengasi, and we must be able to maintain south of the Gebel Akhdar a force strong enough to protect the place against the powerful and resolute enemy forces which might be expected to be still in existence. Our immediate aim, therefore, was to stabilise a front as far west as possible behind which to build up a striking force and accumulate reserves.

The Middle East Defence Committee approved this policy and I confirmed my orders to General Ritchie, amplifying them in due course.[3] While preparing to resume the offensive at the earliest possible date, the Eighth Army was to hold a line covering Tobruk, and also Giarabub to secure the southern flank. As an insurance, defensive positions were to be prepared on the line Sollum – Maddalena. Tobruk was on no account to be allowed to become invested. The possibility of carrying out a limited advance to secure the landing grounds round Derna and Martuba was to be examined, but there was no intention of under-taking it, if it were likely to prejudice the success of the main offensive later.

The Eighth Army was able to carry out the consolidation of the Gazala posi-tion practically undisturbed, as the enemy had halted and deployed in a defensive position on the line Tmimi – Mechili. After a lull necessitated by supply diffi-culties Rommel sent strong columns forward on the 16th February in what was probably an attempt to draw us into an engagement; but General Ritchie refused to be drawn, and the enemy retired leaving the Eighth Army to continue its preparations.

By the 26th February a strong defensive position had been prepared, well-mined and organised in depth over an area thirty-six miles square. A minefield, extending from the coast at Gazala to Bir Hacheim in the south, blocked the coastal road and all the important tracks from east to west. Within the minefield strong defensive localities had been developed from Gazala to Sidi Muftah and at Bir Hacheim. The fortress of Tobruk gave depth to the defence, and positions were being developed at Acroma, El Adem and Bir el Gubi.

This position was held by the 13th Corps (Lieutenant-General Gott) with the equivalent of three infantry divisions, an army tank brigade, and an armoured division. The 30th Corps (Lieutenant-General Norrie), with two infantry divi-sions less a brigade group was engaged in preparing two positions in the frontier area, and a detachment was occupying Giarabub.

The New Zealand railway construction companies and Indian pioneer com-panies had already begun work again after a well-earned rest, and the railway line was nearing Capuzzo.

## Malta and the Libyan Offensive.

Our position in Cyrenaica had just been stabilised, when I received three disturbing pieces of information, none of them entirely unexpected. On the 17th February came a preparatory order from London to send two more divisions to the Far East. On the 18th Admiral Cunningham received a telegram from the Governor of Malta reporting that the supply situation in the island was extremely precarious. And a few days later I learned that an enemy convoy carrying a large number of tanks had reached Tripoli.

Having explained the necessity for asking for the 70th Division and the 9th Australian Division, the Chief of the Imperial General Staff warned me that one of the Indian divisions from Iraq might also have to go back to India. He added that it was realised that these withdrawals might entail abandoning our plan for regaining Cyrenaica, and adopting a defensive policy in Libya, and that the forces left on the Northern Front would hardly be enough even to keep order there.

The 70th Division did, in fact, proceed to India and Ceylon, equipped with its full scale of transport from Middle East resources; but adjustments in other theatres made it possible to allow me to retain the other two divisions, which was fortunate in view of subsequent events on our Western Front.

Quite apart from its effect on our policy in Libya, the withdrawal of two more, or possibly three, divisions from my command would expose my northern flank to extreme danger in the event of an attack. The troops allotted to its defence were already quite inadequate and our bases and our oilfields destined shortly to be the only oilfields left in British hands, would be at the mercy of the invader. The forces which it was now proposed to leave in those regions, all of them politically unstable, were barely sufficient to ensure internal order. Even if the whole of our available forces were moved to that front, they would still have been too few to defend it. Although the danger was not immediate, since the enemy still had long distances to cover and great supply problems to solve, it was nevertheless one which we must be prepared to meet. The Middle East Defence Committee presented these views again to London and urged that four infantry divisions be sent to the Middle East without delay.

Meanwhile I issued revised instructions for the defence of the Northern Front.[4] Since we could no longer hope to stop a hostile advance in strength through Persia and Syria, I intended to impose the maximum delay on the enemy so as to gain time to enable reinforcements to arrive. The Ninth and Tenth Armies would now retire before superior enemy forces and hold them on a rearward line through Dizful, Paitak, the Lesser Zab River, Abu Kemal on the Euphrates, Damascus, Ras Baalbek and Tripoli. They were, however, to fight delaying actions north of this line whenever a favourable opportunity offered.

This meant abandoning extensive defensive positions round Mosul on which much valuable work had been done but, as we could no longer hold Mosul with our reduced forces against a strong attack, there was no alternative but to concentrate all our efforts on strengthening the new positions in Central Iraq and Southern Syria.

The position in Malta was indeed serious. Until November we had held almost complete mastery of the air over the island; but since then the enemy had made increasingly heavy air attacks and by now had attained virtual dominance. It had become practically impossible for the air force based on Malta either to interfere with enemy vessels passing to Libya or to provide air cover for our own ships seeking to replenish it. The Governor of Malta, Lieutenant-General Sir William Dobbie, now reported that even on siege rations, supplies generally would last only until June, while stocks of diesel oil for submarines were sufficient only for two months. Yet it seemed useless to attempt to sail convoys to the island, since out of three ships which left Alexandria on 12th February none arrived.

The Middle East Defence Committee, therefore, asked that the arrival in Malta of fighter reinforcements should be accelerated. The Chiefs of Staff were equally concerned at the situation reported in the Governor's telegrams. They were of the same mind that Malta was vital to operations in Cyrenaica and were prepared to take the most drastic action to sustain it. It was impossible to supply Malta from the west and the only chance of sailing convoys from the east, they considered, was to secure the aerodromes in Cyrenaica. Accordingly I was asked to consider carrying out an offensive in time to enable adequate air support to be given to a substantial convoy in mid-April.

There was no doubt that the possession of aerodromes in Western Cyrenaica would make it possible to provide aerial protection for convoys. But the converse was equally true; unless Malta could interfere with the enemy reinforcement of Libya the task of recapturing Western Cyrenaica would become more and more difficult. The news that an enemy convoy of seven ships, almost certainly bringing many tanks, had reached Tripoli confirmed my fears.

I had already reviewed the whole situation in the light of this information and my report to the Prime Minister actually crossed the telegram from the Chiefs of Staff. A forecast of the relative tank strength of the enemy and ourselves during the next three months showed that we were not likely to have the requisite superiority in armour to allow us to launch an offensive with a reasonable chance of success before the 1st June at the earliest. In attempting an offensive without this margin of superiority, it seemed to me, we should run a grave risk of being defeated in detail and possibly of losing Egypt.

The possibility of launching an offensive in Cyrenaica, I took care to point out, depended on there being no increase in the threat to our Northern Front. A maximum of four infantry divisions would probably suffice for recapturing Western Cyrenaica. Assuming that the total number of infantry divisions in the Middle East would be reduced to eight in consequence of diversions to the Far East, it would be just possible to find these four divisions by accepting a considerable reduction in the garrison of Cyprus, which I was prepared to risk for the time being. Any threat to the Northern Front would entail an immediate reduction of the infantry and the transfer of all the armour.

My immediate intention, therefore, was to continue to build up an armoured striking force in the forward area as quickly as possible. Meanwhile our defensive positions round Gazala and Tobruk were to be strengthened as much as possible and the work of extending the desert railway to El Adem was to be hastened. I meant to seize the first chance of making a limited offensive in order to regain the landing grounds round Derna and Martuba, provided this could be done without prejudicing the chances of success of a subsequent major offensive, or the safety of our base at Tobruk.

My telegram to the Prime Minister evoked a reply from the War Office in which they declared that they were greatly disturbed by my review of the situation. The dominant factor in the Mediterranean and the Middle East at that time, they pointed out, was Malta, whose position would be critical if it did not receive a substantial convoy during May. They queried the correctness of my estimates of relative tank strengths of ourselves and the enemy, and suggested that my review took no account whatever of the air situation, which seemed favourable to us at the moment but likely to deteriorate as time went on. They went on to urge that an attempt to drive the Germans out of Cyrenaica in the next few weeks was imperative not only because the safety of Malta demanded it, but because it held out the only hope of fighting while the enemy was still comparatively weak and short of resources. I was requested to reconsider the matter urgently.

At the same time I was informed by the Chiefs of Staff that it had been decided to place the military garrison of Malta under my command, just as the Naval and Royal Air Force garrisons were under command of the Commander-in-Chief, Mediterranean and the Air Officer Commanding-in-Chief respectively. The change took place on the 11th March. In actual fact it made little practical difference except that henceforward the three Commanders-in-Chief and the Middle East Defence Committee had a unified responsibility for Malta as an integral part of the Middle East theatre. The position of General Dobbie as Commander-in-Chief of Malta was not affected.

The Middle East Defence Committee appreciated to the full the urgency of securing Western Cyrenaica both to enable Malta to hold out and for broader reasons. From the point of view of the Royal Navy and the Royal Air Force there was nothing to gain and everything to lose by delaying the offensive. But all were agreed that it must primarily be a land battle and that it would be most dangerous to start before the Army, and our armoured forces in particular, were ready. On present showing it seemed that we should not have achieved the requisite superiority in armour until even later than we had at first supposed. It was not merely a matter of issuing tanks to units: estimates depended on many imponderable factors. If, for instance, the Axis failed to reinforce Tripoli, we might be able to start earlier.

A limited offensive to secure Derna was considered, but it appeared that nothing short of recapturing Bengasi and the whole of the Gebel Akhdar would make it possible to sail substantial convoys to Malta. To be able to use the Derna landing grounds, however, would be of some slight assistance in protecting convoys, and much more in preparing the way for a major offensive later. We, therefore, proposed to undertake the operation, but only when a suitable opportunity arose.

A much broader issue than the retention of Malta was raised by the War Office telegram however it was a question of whether or not, in an effort to save Malta, we were to risk the whole Middle East. As regards risks in other parts of the Command, owing to the recent and projected withdrawals of land and air forces, if all the land forces in the Middle East were concentrated in the Northern Front, they would still be insufficient to make that front secure against the anticipated enemy scale of attack. A premature offensive in the next few weeks might result in the piecemeal destruction of the new armoured force we were trying to create. Egypt would then be placed in even more imminent peril.

For the present, therefore, the Middle East Defence Committee believed that we must rely on continuing to run convoys to Malta under existing conditions in the hope of getting a proportion of the ships through, and on using every possible shift and device to pass in supplies. Accordingly it was decided to make another attempt during the moonless period in the middle of March. On the 8th March I issued instructions[5] to General Ritchie to create a diversion with not less than the equivalent of a brigade group to draw off enemy air attack during the daylight passage of the convoy, and on the 20th and 21st the Eighth Army and the Long Range Desert Group raided the landing grounds round Derna and Bengasi. The convoy, however, did not escape notice by enemy reconnaissance aircraft, and only part succeeded in reaching the island; and then the surviving ships were heavily bombed while they were being unloaded.

The divergence of views between London and Cairo as to the ability of the Eighth Army to mount an offensive appeared to be too great to be settled by correspondence, and the Prime Minister requested me to come to England for consultation. Reluctantly and after most anxious consideration I decided that at that time it was impossible for me to leave my command even for ten days or a fortnight and still remain responsible for it. To the Chief of the General Staff who pressed me to go, as there were many large questions of strategy to be discussed, I was compelled to make the same reply. In a telegram from the Eighth Army Headquarters, where I was at that time, I pointed out that large questions of planning and reorganisation needed my personal attention and made it impossible to hand over to anyone else. I suggested instead that a general meeting in Cairo or Baghdad with General Wavell and Air-Marshal Peirse from India would be of great value. At length it was arranged that Sir Stafford Cripps should stop in Cairo on his way to India and explain the views of the War Cabinet. General Nye, Vice-Chief of the Imperial General Staff, was to accompany Sir Stafford.

The visit of a member of the War Cabinet and of the Vice-Chief of the Imperial General Staff was most valuable in that they became acquainted with the problems of the Middle East to an extent which was impossible by telegraphic communication. When the three Commanders-in-Chief had explained the situation to him, Sir Stafford Cripps summarised the results of his investigations in a telegram to the Prime Minister, of which the following were the salient points.

At that time our strength both in tanks and in the air was altogether too low to offer even reasonable prospects of an offensive being successful. In about a month's time our air forces, now weakened by heavy diversions to the Far East, should again have been built up to a strength sufficient to allow them to undertake and sustain intensive operations. Our armoured forces would take longer to prepare, however, because the American "General Grant" tanks, with which new units were now being equipped, had to be modified before they could be used in the desert and because the crews had to receive special training. By the middle of May we should have an effective, trained armoured force of 450 medium tanks with sufficient reserves, and 150 infantry tanks in addition.

For the rest, the date of the offensive depended upon the tank strength which the enemy could attain, which in turn depended upon our ability to interfere with his communications. Apart from one Liberator there were no aircraft either in Malta or the rest of the Middle East capable of reaching Tripoli, nor were Baltimores yet available to bomb Bengasi by day. Sir Stafford urged that heavy bombers and more light bombers should be provided: some of the heavy bombers which were then attacking Germany might profitably be sent to the Middle East.

Mid-May, Sir Stafford suggested, should be accepted as a target date for beginning the offensive: to launch it earlier would be taking an unwarrantable risk. Even this date was conditional upon certain essential requirements being fulfilled: that the "Spitfires" remaining in Gibraltar should be sent to reinforce Malta; that long-range heavy bombers should be despatched at once; that every effort should be made to hasten the delivery of light bombers from the United States; that fitters should be sent by air to help prepare the reserve of tanks which was vital to the offensive; and finally that demands on the Middle East to send aircraft to India or elsewhere should cease.

I had explained that we might have to withdraw aircraft from Libya in the event of Turkey or Cyprus being attacked or of the Germans penetrating the Caucasus, and that, in consequence, we might lose air superiority in the west and be forced to abandon the offensive with serious results. Sir Stafford Cripps alluded to this possibility, but considered that this was a risk we should have to take unless we were to give up all hope of an offensive until the autumn.

General Nye brought with him a questionnaire from the Prime Minister and Chiefs of Staff designed to secure information on all points about which they were in doubt. These questions, twenty in number, affected all three Commanders-in-Chief and the answers were naturally based almost entirely on information supplied by the Joint Staffs, though the responsibility remained with General Nye.

In his telegram General Nye explained that no offensive operations were justified before the 15th May, and then only if our own tanks outnumbered the enemy's by the requisite amount. The only ways in which the date could be advanced were by interrupting enemy shipping to Libya or by increasing the output of our own tank workshops. Even then training was a limiting factor. The Middle East Defence Committee thought it well to stress the point made by General Nye that 15th May was only a tentative date dependent upon the rate at which the enemy could build up his tank strength. They added that any favourable opportunity before or after this date would be taken.

An exchange of telegrams in early April showed that our difficulties and problems had been admirably presented in London. The Chiefs of Staff and the Middle East Defence Committee were now substantially in accord on questions affecting Libya, Malta and the Northern Front. In replying to the Chiefs of Staff review, though, we felt bound to emphasise our great need of heavy bombers and anti-aircraft artillery.

In the Far East, however, matters had gone from bad to worse. Superior Japanese naval forces had established themselves in the Indian Ocean, and our ability to hold Ceylon and Eastern India, it appeared, depended almost entirely on the strength of the air force we could build up. In consequence, the Chiefs of Staff could now hold out no hopes of sending even a squadron of Liberator aircraft to the Middle East for several months and felt obliged to draw further on our existing naval and air forces. Moreover they said that they could not risk sailing a convoy to Malta from the west during May.

This latest withdrawal of aircraft did not affect the date on which the offensive could begin in Libya, but it was bound to affect very seriously our ability to sustain the air effort once battle was joined, since we should lack reinforcement, aircraft and crews. This made it all the more imperative that we should receive heavy bombers so that we might impede enemy reinforcements to the utmost.

The position of Malta was now extremely disturbing. The acting Minister of State, Sir Walter Monckton, had recently visited the island to investigate labour problems and reported that the position was very grave indeed. The decision not to sail a convoy from the west during May, therefore, moved the Governor to a strong protest. The island's chances of survival, he declared, were materially reduced because it was not possible to carry on without food or ammunition. We could not count on more than half of the ships sailing in the May convoy from the east reaching Malta and it was imperative not to rely on this alone. Moreover we could not afford to repeat the experience of the previous convoy, when out of a total of 30,000 tons of stores despatched to Malta only about 5,000 were received: aerial protection must cover not only the arrival of ships, but the period of preparation and unloading. General Dobbie ended by saying that drastic action was needed: more Spitfire aircraft were required in addition to those already allotted, and the air force must be regularly reinforced.

Relief, it now seemed, must be deferred until June when it was hoped that a strong escort for convoys from the east could be provided and that our Libyan offensive would have begun. There was no certainty that either of these conditions would be fulfilled, so that the Middle East Defence Committee repeated their request that a convoy should also sail from the west. Meanwhile we were obliged to instruct the Governor to impose even more stringent rationing and to hope that the island would be able to continue its gallant resistance.

The steady deterioration of the situation in the Indian Ocean gravely affected our plans in the Middle East, and we begged the Chiefs of Staff to acquaint us more fully with developments in that theatre. On the 23rd April we received a long and detailed appreciation of the situation. In discussing possible Japanese plans, an attempt to invade Ceylon was not ruled out, although it seemed more likely that the Japanese would try to exploit their success in Malaya and Burma by advancing into India from the north-east. For the time being we were in no position to offer effective resistance by sea, land, or air to any offensive. Should the Japanese press boldly westward without pause for consolidation, the Indian Empire would be in grave danger. In that event the security of the Middle East and its essential supply line would be threatened. The Middle East and India were therefore interdependent.

So gloomy was the picture thus painted that I felt it demanded a complete reconsideration of our plans. In a paper prepared for the Middle East Defence Committee, I pointed out our present weakness owing to lack of reserves; that we should run great danger, if we were to embark on an offensive in Libya without reserves, sufficient to enable us to carry it through to the Agheila marshes; and that the risk was the greater, seeing there was always the possibility that our supply lines through the Indian Ocean might at any time be cut. I was reluctantly forced to the conclusion that, although the fate of Malta might be sealed, in the circumstances depicted by the Chiefs of Staff, we could not afford to take the offensive in Libya. We should rather concentrate on strengthening our defences in the Middle East and spare all we could to reinforce India in the hope of checking the Japanese advance before it should be too late.

My colleagues on the Middle East Defence Committee were inclined to believe that the Chiefs of Staff review presented the situation in its worst aspect. We were all agreed, however, as to what we could do in the Middle East to save Malta or spare to help India, and decided to inform the Chiefs of Staff accordingly.

We explained that, in view of the serious threat to India disclosed in their appreciation, we felt bound to give the Chiefs of Staff full information about our ability to help India and to mount an offensive in Libya, so that they might decide whether we should continue to prepare for the offensive. Although we could spare no air forces, I believed I could send an armoured brigade group, a motor brigade group and two infantry divisions, all seasoned troops and well equipped, assuming that we stood on the defensive in Libya. This was possible, since it now seemed that no new danger would arise before August or even later, and that, even when our forces in Cyrenaica had been reduced, the enemy were unlikely to muster sufficient strength for a serious attack for about three months. In the latter assumption, as events proved, we were wrong; but the comparative strengths of our own and the enemy forces in Libya at that time and the general tactical situation on that front seemed to warrant this conclusion.

The Prime Minister replied at once, saying that the situation had improved in the last fortnight, and that, although the next two months would no doubt be critical in the Pacific and Indian Oceans, there were no special grounds for assuming that an invasion of India was then imminent or certain. Having described the various measures that were being taken to strengthen our position in the Indian Ocean, he concluded by saying that the greatest help we in the Middle East could give would be to engage and defeat the enemy on our Western Front.

The date by which we could be ready to launch the offensive, unfortunately, had now receded. The rate of increase in our own tank strength had fallen very little short of the estimates given to Sir Stafford Cripps three weeks earlier; but, owing to our inability to interfere effectively with his shipping, the number of tanks the enemy was likely to possess by the middle of May now approached the highest figure we had mentioned. Moreover a new Italian armoured division had been brought over, although it was not yet up to strength. We therefore informed the Chiefs of Staff that, provided that this new armoured division did not materialise, we should now be ready in mid-June. If the division did appear, we should have to postpone the offensive until August. We also explained that success would depend on our retaining supremacy in the air.

I was then informed by the Prime Minister that it had been decided that an offensive must be launched as early as possible, preferably during May, in order to save Malta. We thought it necessary, however, to point out that, in the event of our armoured forces being destroyed as a result of launching an offensive prematurely, we should not be able to hold our prepared positions on the Egyptian frontier for lack of armour, but should be compelled to retire to El Alamein. The peril in which Egypt would then stand would probably have worse results than if Malta were to succumb. The War Cabinet were prepared to accept this risk, being determined that Malta should not be allowed to fall without a battle being fought by my army for its retention. I was instructed to launch the offensive in time to provide a distraction to help the passage of a convoy to Malta in the dark period in June.

### The Northern Front.

It was fortunate that the Russian winter campaign had so thoroughly dislocated Axis plans that the much-heralded spring offensive had to be postponed until early summer. Had the Germans been able to renew their offensive when the snows melted, starting from the line they had gained during the autumn, their advanced guard would in all probability have appeared south of the Caucasus at the very moment when we were considering how we might oppose their gathering strength in Libya. I have described how in January and February Japanese successes in the Indian Ocean made it necessary to withdraw several divisions from the Middle East, and how I was obliged to instruct the Ninth and Tenth Armies to retire in the event of an enemy advance. Developments in Libya during the months that followed caused the troops allotted to the defence of the Northern Front to be still further reduced.

With the approval of the other Commanders-in-Chief, I decided in March temporarily to reduce the garrison of Cyprus, in order to compensate for our losses and to find troops for Libya. It had been estimated that one infantry division with a proportionate amount of armour and artillery and six additional infantry battalions were required to defend the island. My policy was to keep in the island all the equipment, transport, ammunition and stores required for this garrison, but to reduce the infantry and artillery personnel to about one third. It was expected that we should have about three weeks warning of attack, and it should be possible with the help of the Royal Navy to bring the garrison quickly to its full strength.

At about this time the 4th Indian Division relieved the 5th Indian Division in the island, and Major-General Tuker finally reorganised its defences. The basic principle of the defence was that the air forces on the island should be kept in full operation. It was not considered possible to prevent the enemy getting a foothold at some point on the coastline, and the main effort of the defence was therefore to be concentrated on protecting the landing grounds in the central plain. For the same reason all important depots and installations were sited inland wherever feasible. As large a proportion of the garrison as possible was to be made mobile so that it might operate against enemy landings. Instructions laying down these principles were issued on the 1st July.[6]

The reduced strength of the Cyprus garrison caused some uneasiness in London lest the enemy should undertake a combined operation, now that our own naval and air forces in the Eastern Mediterranean were so much reduced. After examining the problem again, the Commanders-in-Chief were able to re-assure the Chiefs of Staff, as it was thought that an attempt at invasion was unlikely unless the enemy had the use of landing grounds in Southern Anatolia.

During April the mounting strength of the German and Italian forces in Cyrenaica had compelled me once more to review the policy for the defence of Syria and Iraq, and on the 29th April I issued revised instructions for dealing with an attack through Anatolia.[7]

By now it had become evident that our original estimate of the forces required to defend the western frontier of Egypt against an enemy attack in strength would have to be considerably increased. This meant that many of the troops allotted to the defence of the Northern Front would not be available, should need arise, and that, therefore, we must contemplate having to withdraw even further to the south. In Iraq and Persia I hoped to be able to hold the same positions as under our previous plan, but on the left, in order to meet the possibility of having to abandon the Lebanon fortresses, I gave orders for fresh positions to be fortified in Northern Palestine and along the Jordan. It was still my object to keep our bases and ports and the oilfields of southwestern Persia secure, but this seemed to be becoming more and more difficult to achieve, if the expected enemy offensive should take shape.

The question of giving aid to the Turks, in the event of their being attacked by the Axis Powers, had been periodically under review ever since the previous December. At that time the Middle East Defence Committee had advised His Majesty's Government in the United Kingdom that, as the existing communications in Turkey were poor and vulnerable, it would be unwise to suggest to the Turks that we should be able to assist them with considerable land forces should they be attacked in the spring of 1942. The Committee recommended instead that we should rather stress the help we might be able to afford them in the air, and also urged that every effort should be made to send the Turks all the small arms, engineering stores, motor vehicles, and raw material for their munition factories that could be spared. The Turks, on their part, though obviously anxious to accept our aid and to see our cause successful, were extremely careful to avoid any overt action which might cause Germany to question their neutrality, and this made it most difficult to make really effective preparations to assist them.

In April, the Commanders-in-Chief recommended to the Chiefs of Staff that Turkey should be included in the sphere of action of the Minister of State in Cairo, in order to enable our relations with her to be co-ordinated by one authority on the spot, particularly in regard to assistance in the event of an Axis attack. This recommendation, however, did not meet with the approval of the Foreign Office in view of the complicated and delicate nature of the relations between Turkey, Great Britain and the Soviet.

In spite of these difficulties we pressed forward steadily with our schemes for assisting Turkey, and a considerable amount of useful preparatory work was done, in the way of improving ports, roads and railways, and aerodromes. We were also able to introduce unostentatiously a large quantity of warlike stores into Anatolia. In all these activities we were greatly aided by the tactful and untiring efforts of Major-General A. Arnold, Military Attaché at Ankara.

On the 19th May I issued instructions governing the action to be taken in the event of enemy attack through the Caucasus.[8] It was fairly safe to assume that the enemy would be unable to invade Turkey at the same time, and that the Ninth Army could therefore be left with just sufficient troops for guard duties. In north-western Persia the country is mountainous, and therefore unfavourable to the employment of armoured forces. Briefly, my intention was to stop the enemy as far forward as we could by moving light forces rapidly to the River Araxes and covering for as long as possible the landing grounds in northern Persia. The Tenth Army was in any event to prevent the enemy establishing himself south of the general line Pahlevi – Kasvin – Hamadan – Senna – Rowanduz Gorge.

The Persian railway was to be extended from its existing terminus at Khorramshahr to the Shatt-el-Arab opposite Basra, so that the Tenth Army operating in Persia might draw on the main Iraq bases at Basra and Shaiba. Various other improvements in communications were also ordered.

During May we pointed out to the Chiefs of Staff that we could not plan and prepare to fight the enemy in Northern Persia, as we must do if we were to keep

Field Marshal Archibald Wavell (centre), the Viceroy and Commander-in-Chief of the Indian Army is pictured with Field Marshal Sir Claude Auchinleck (right), and Field Marshal Bernard Montgomery, Chief of Imperial General Staff. This photograph was taken on 17 June 1946, in the Viceregal Gardens, New Delhi.

A unit of the Somaliland Camel Corps on patrol along the Somaliland-Abyssinian border in the summer of 1940. Soon after British forces returned to the Protectorate in 1941, the Somaliland Camel Corps was reformed and spent the following months rounding up stray Italians and dealing with groups of local bandits. At the beginning of the East African Campaign in the Second World War, the SCC numbered some 1,475 men. (HMP)

A bomb can be seen bursting at Rutba Fort on 9 May 1941. An isolated outpost in the west of Iraq, the fort had been seized at the beginning of May by the Iraqi Desert Police. It was feared that, following the German intervention, it might be used as a base to seize a nearby oil pipeline. As a result, on 9th May four Bristol Blenheims from 84 Squadron attacked Rutba. (*Courtesy of the Australian War Memorial*)

A Junkers Ju 90 military transport – as used by *Sonderkommando Junck* during the German intervention in Iraq. Along with the Junkers Ju 52s, those Ju 90s deployed for operations in Iraq in May 1941 were ordered to be released at the earliest opportunity, their presence required for Operation *Mercury* – the German invasion of Crete. (*Courtesy of Deutsches Bundesarchiv*)

In total, Habbaniya War Cemetery in Iraq contains 292 burials. A memorial within the cemetery commemorates an additional 106 soldiers and RAF Levies who died while serving in Iraq during the Second World War and were buried in remote and un-maintainable graves. (*Courtesy of the Australian War Memorial*)

Following the Allied victory in the Anglo-Iraqi War in 1941, Allied forces launched an invasion of Vichy French-held Syria. After the successful Battle of Palmyra (1 July 1941), Allied troops found this wreck of a Heinkel He 111, a relic of *Sonderkommando Junck*, on Palmyra airfield. With its *Luftwaffe* markings on the tail fin crudely covered over, the replacement Iraqi Air Force insignia (a detail of which is on the right) on the fuselage can clearly be seen. (*ww2images*)

German *Fallschirmjäger* emplaning at the start of Operation *Merkur* (Mercury) – the code-name for the Axis invasion of Crete in 1941. The large-scale German airdrops involved the entire 7 Flieger-Division supported by the 5th Mountain Division. (*Courtesy of Chris Goss*)

A German parachute drop underway over Crete, 20 May 1941. One unidentified German soldier gave this account of his jump that day: 'My parachute had scarcely opened when bullets began spitting past me from all directions. It had felt so splendid just before to jump in sunlight over such a wonderful countryside, but my feeling suddenly changed. All I could do was pull my head in and cover my face with my arms.' (*HMP*)

A pair of gunners at one of the many British anti-aircraft positions surrounding Suda Bay, Crete, in May 1941. The soldier on the left, Gunner E.F. Telling, was subsequently taken prisoner and went on to spend the rest of the war in captivity. (*HMP*)

Two British tank officers are pictured reading an Italian newspaper on 28 January 1941. According to the original caption, the mascot held by one of the men is a puppy found during the capture of Sidi Barrani, one of the first Italian bases to fall in the fighting in North Africa. (*NARA*)

A British patrol is on the lookout for enemy movements over a valley in the Western Desert, on the Egyptian side of the Egypt-Libya border, in February of 1942. (*NARA*)

A Junkers Ju 87 Stuka dive bomber attacking a British supply depot near Tobruk, Libya, during October 1941. (*NARA*)

Two soldiers pictured at work producing a military newspaper or information sheet during the Siege of Tobruk.
(*US Library of Congress*)

Standing amongst the rubble, a soldier looks through holes made by Axis bombs into a church in Tobruk, 1941.
(*US Library of Congress*)

Disaster off Tobruk. A picture showing the Grimsby-class sloop HMS *Grimsby*, on the left, and the merchant ship SS *Helka*, on the right, sinking following the attack by Junkers Ju 87 Stukas, from both the *Luftwaffe* and the *Regia Aeronautica Italiana*, on Sunday, 25 May 1941. (*HMP*)

It was not just from the attentions of Axis dive-bombers that ships supplying Tobruk were at risk. This is the 3,359 GRT Dutch tanker MV *Adinda* pictured on fire in the harbour there during February 1941. *Adinda* had sailed from Alexandria with a cargo of aviation fuel, low grade petrol and lubrication oil. Whilst manoeuvring to a safe anchorage she struck a magnetic mine which exploded under the starboard bow. Seventeen Chinese crewmen who were in the fo'c'sle were killed. (*HMP*)

his air forces at a sufficient distance from our bases and oil installations at the head of the Gulf, unless we had full facilities to explore and prepare the ground. These facilities the Russians, who controlled this zone, would not give us. Moreover, we had no information of their plans for the defence of the Caucasus. We asked that arrangements be made without delay for us to co-operate with the Russians; but this seemed impossible, owing, apparently, to the Russian High Command's insistence on centralisation and great secrecy. We therefore acted ourselves, and on my instructions General Quinan sent reconnaissance parties into Northern Persia to procure at least some of the essential information. These parties established good relations with the Russians and did their work with little friction.

The preparation of defences and communications in Iraq and Syria went on steadily throughout May, and I was concerned to use as much local and hired labour as I could procure, in addition to all available organised labour units, in order to give the few fighting troops the fullest opportunity for training.

At the end of May the Germans launched their expected offensive in Russia and from that moment the danger, against which we were still so ill-prepared, steadily grew more imminent. Simultaneously Rommel launched an attack in Cyrenaica.

### Rommel's Counter-offensive.

The continual reinforcement of the German and Italian army in Libya, which in the absence of heavy bombers and strong naval forces in the Mediterranean we had been unable to prevent, and which had caused our own offensive to be deferred, had progressed so far by the middle of May that it was evident the enemy thought himself strong enough to take the offensive. I was reasonably confident that the Eighth Army was prepared to withstand assault. Although General Ritchie, in close consultation with myself, had been maturing his plans for an early resumption of the offensive, precautions for meeting an enemy attack had not been neglected; and during March, April and early May the defensive system within the quadrilateral formed by Gazala, Tobruk, Bir el Gubi and Bir Hacheim had been steadily developed and strengthened. As the days went by it became more and more certain that our offensive would be forestalled. Accordingly General Ritchie and his two Corps Commanders put the finishing touches to their arrangements for meeting the attack and for passing at once to the offensive, when it had been repulsed.

In planning to launch our own offensive in mid-June, the fact that we should have only a small margin of superiority over the enemy by land and in the air had occasioned me some anxiety. I was disposed therefore to regard the prospect of fighting the first action on our own prepared ground as likely to counterbalance this disadvantage. To enable General Ritchie to form a reserve of infantry, I arranged to send reinforcements to the Eighth Army, including the 10th Indian Division which I brought across from Iraq. I regretted that I had no more armoured formations which were ready for battle, to send him. Numerically the Eighth Army was superior in tank strength to the enemy; but in quality our tanks were on the whole still inferior to his, notwithstanding the inclusion in our armoured brigades of a number of new American medium tanks. On the other hand, the Eighth Army was now getting a quantity of the new six-pounder anti-tank guns which would neutralise to some extent the marked advantage in this type of weapon the Germans had hitherto enjoyed. It was unfortunate that the troops had not more time to become accustomed to their use.

The enemy appeared to have two courses open to him: one to pass armoured forces round the south of Bir Hacheim and then to strike northwards, and the other to concentrate all his armour and most of his artillery in an attempt to break through our centre. In either event his objective would be Tobruk; and in either event our reaction would be the same, namely, to use our armour to counter-attack the enemy and destroy him east of our minefield belt.[9] For this purpose our armoured forces, comprising the 1st and 7th Armoured Divisions, three armoured brigades altogether, under General Nome, the Commander of the 30th Corps, were to be held centrally, ready to act in either direction.

As it turned out, the enemy chose to make his main thrust by the southern route and, having concentrated his armoured formations round Segnali, moved them during the night of the 26th May to the east of Bir Hacheim. Early on the 27th he struck rapidly northwards towards Acroma and El Adem. Meanwhile he made an abortive attack on Bir Hacheim and a half-hearted demonstration against our positions between Gazala and Alem Hamza. Though somewhat scattered, the 30th Corps met the enemy's northward thrust, and heavy but indecisive fighting continued all day and resulted in the enemy being held south of a line through Knightsbridge and El Adem.

We learned later from captured documents that the enemy planned to take Tobruk by the 30th May, after destroying our armoured forces and attacking our troops holding the Gazala defences from the rear as well as from the front. The success of this plan depended upon reducing Bir Hacheim or breaching our minefield further north and then inflicting upon our armour a decisive blow. In all of these objects the enemy was thwarted. On the 28th May the enemy moved against Acroma but withdrew, and on the 29th his main armoured force moved southward, heavily engaged by our armoured formations, but again without decisive result.

Belatedly the enemy was able to clear ways through the minefield in the centre of our position, thus greatly easing the supply and repair of his armoured forces lying to the east. He then settled down to achieving by deliberate methods what he had failed to accomplish by lightning attack, and devoted his efforts to forming a bridgehead, strong in anti-tank artillery, to cover the gaps he had made in our minefields. To do this he withdrew some distance to the west, being vigorously attacked by our tanks, artillery and aircraft in the process.

Though his plan went awry, the enemy had succeeded in breaching our front and creating a dangerous salient in our main position. It was essential to rectify this situation and General Ritchie accordingly had made plans for delivering a powerful counterstroke as soon as possible. The armoured formations of the

Eighth Army had sustained heavy losses; and General Ritchie considered that this precluded his launching a counter-offensive from some other sector and proceeded to make plans for a direct assault on the enemy salient.

The attack was intended originally to have taken place on the night of the 31st May; but, for various reasons, it was postponed till the night of the 4th June. Meanwhile, the enemy had attacked and destroyed the 150th Infantry Brigade, holding the important defended locality of Sidi Muftah. He had also been able to strengthen considerably his forces in the salient, which it was General Ritchie's object to eliminate so that we could close the gaps in our minefield.

The Eighth Army's counter-attack had some initial success and recovered some important ground from the enemy, but it was then brought to a standstill by enemy counter-attacks with tanks, strongly supported by artillery. Our own armoured forces, which should have exploited the initial success of the infantry, met strong opposition from anti-tank guns and failed to make their presence felt. Finally, the enemy succeeded in overwhelming our forward infantry and, more serious still, in destroying four regiments of field artillery which had been moved up to support the advance of our tanks.

This unsuccessful counter-stroke was probably the turning point of the whole battle, which hitherto had not been wholly unfavourable to us. Nevertheless, the Eighth Army still seemed to have more tanks than the enemy and we were better off than he was so far as tank reserves were concerned. Our tank recovery organisation also was functioning with great efficiency. Time was needed, however, to reorganise our armoured formations which had suffered heavily, and our powers of recuperation in this respect seemed less than those of the enemy.

An attempt to advance from the northern half of our position towards Temrad met strong opposition and failed. General Ritchie, meanwhile, intensified his efforts to interfere with the enemy supply lines to the west of our minefields and attacked them from the north as well as from the south with satisfactory results. Our air forces had been working in the closest co-operation with the Eighth Army from the beginning of the battle, and continued to make very heavy attacks against the enemy forces in the salient and on his transport passing backwards and forwards through the gaps in the minefields.

Having defeated our counter-attack, the enemy moved his armour forward to threaten Knightsbridge, the key to the northern half of our positions. At the same time he increased his pressure on Bir Hacheim and subjected it to heavy dive-bombing attacks. In spite of strenuous and partially successful efforts made to pass convoys into the stronghold, it became increasingly difficult to supply Bir Hacheim, which was held by the 1st Free French Brigade under General Koenig. General Ritchie also attempted to relieve the pressure on the garrison by taking the investing forces in the rear, but heavy and repeated enemy attacks began to wear down the defence, and on the 10th June General Ritchie found it necessary to order the post to be evacuated. The majority of the garrison withdrew in safety after a heroic defence lasting for nearly a fortnight.

The loss of Bir Hacheim undoubtedly weakened the general position of the Eighth Army, and the enemy quickly took advantage of this to concentrate his forces against El Adem, a most important tactical locality covering Tobruk from the south. Throughout the 12th and 13th June, the opposing armoured forces were heavily engaged round El Adem and Knightsbridge. This action proved to be the culmination of the armoured fighting, which had begun on the 27th May, and was decisive in its results. After it, we could muster only about fifty medium and twenty infantry tanks in the Acroma area while it seems probable that the enemy had twice that number. The enemy, moreover, was left in possession of the battlefield and could recover his damaged tanks and destroy ours. He also gained possession of the escarpment between El Adem and Knightsbridge, a feature of great tactical importance.

The Eighth Army's losses in tanks and field guns forced General Ritchie to revise his plans for the continuation of the battle. The loss of Bir Hacheim left the enemy free to threaten the southern face of the Tobruk defences and the communications of the 13th Corps, which was still holding the front from Gazala to Alem Hamza. General Ritchie consequently decided that he must withdraw these two divisions and, having obtained my agreement, issued orders accordingly on the 14th June.

I was most reluctant to sanction the withdrawal from Gazala. I had always considered it essential to retain this position in order to enable us rapidly to resume our offensive in Cyrenaica, and thus to aid Malta by regaining our forward air bases in the Gebel Akhdar. Moreover, if it were abandoned, the enemy would be free to concentrate all his forces against Tobruk, and the already limited space available to the Eighth Army for manoeuvre would be further greatly reduced. But the weakness of our armoured forces left General Ritchie no alternative. The 1st South African Division was withdrawn along the coast through Tobruk itself and reached the frontier almost intact, but the 50th Division had to withdraw south-eastwards through the enemy and suffered considerably, though it retained its organisation and admirable fighting spirit. The success of these withdrawals was due in great part to the retention of air superiority by the R.A.F.

I now had to decide whether to try to hold Tobruk or not. I had made it quite clear to all concerned that, in the event of the enemy returning to the offensive in Cyrenaica after his defeat in December, 1941, I had no intention of allowing forces under my command to be again besieged in Tobruk.[10] This continued to be my policy throughout the subsequent fighting. But, unless Tobruk was fully stocked and equipped as an advanced base of supply, it was not possible for us to consider seizing the initiative from the enemy and resuming our offensive against Tripolitania, which always remained my object. It was to protect Tobruk, therefore, that I had ordered General Ritchie to stand fast on the Gazala – Bir Hacheim position. The railway had been extended to Belhamed and much effort had been expended in equipping Tobruk as an advanced base, and our preparations for the offensive were practically complete.

When the enemy, by building up his tank strength more quickly than we could, was able to anticipate our intended offensive, I hoped that, having defeated his armoured forces, we might still be able to make an offensive on the lines we had been planning since the enemy was first checked at Gazala in February. The initial course of the battle, which began on the 27th May, gave me no cause to give up hope of turning to the attack when the enemy's strength should have been spent.

The destruction of an infantry brigade group on the 1st June and of two infantry brigades and four regiments of artillery four days later, the withdrawal from Bir Hacheim, and, finally, the heavy losses of tanks we incurred on the 13th June undoubtedly reduced considerably our chances of making an early change to the offensive. But there was no reason to suppose that, for all the vigour he was displaying, the enemy had not also suffered heavily. When we had reduced our commitments by evacuating Gazala, it seemed to me we should have sufficient forces to man Tobruk and the principal tactical localities to the south and south-east of it as well as the frontier positions, all of which had been prepared for defence. By preventing the enemy from establishing himself to the east of Tobruk, which it still seemed possible to do, we should not only deny him landing grounds further to the east than those he had been using, but also gain time to build up a force with which to strike back. A small armoured force was still in being to assist in the task, besides numerous armoured cars and two motor brigades; workshops were turning out repaired tanks at a satisfactory pace, and the New Zealand Division, which I had ordered down from Syria, was due shortly. The losses we had sustained, considerable though they might have been, did not appear so serious as to make it imperative to abandon the fruits of the previous success, and thus leave Malta to surrender and Egypt to be invaded.

Consequently, when I agreed to General Ritchie's withdrawal of the two divisions from Gazala, I ordered him to stop the enemy on a line through Acroma, El Adem, and then southwards, and not to allow Tobruk to be invested. General Ritchie believed he could fight on the western and southern faces of the Tobruk perimeter, El Adem and to the south. But he did not think it essential to hold Acroma, and considered that our defence south of Tobruk must be ensured by a mobile force with a maximum quota of artillery, since isolated strongpoints would be liable to be overwhelmed in detail owing to the weakness of our armoured forces. It might take time to organise the artillery of the 1st South African and 50th Divisions for employment in a mobile role, and in the interval General Ritchie visualised a situation arising in which Tobruk might become temporarily invested. On the 16th June I told him that, although I was determined Tobruk must not be besieged, I accepted the possibility of its becoming temporarily isolated, and left him full liberty to make his dispositions accordingly.

I was glad to have the assurance of the Prime Minister that the instructions I had given to General Ritchie were approved in London. The position seemed to me to be quite different to that which had obtained in 1941, as we now held fortified positions on the frontier, and it did not seem as if the enemy had enough forces both to invest Tobruk and at the same time neutralise our troops to the east of it. I was therefore able to tell the Prime Minister that I hoped to be able to prevent the control of the country between Tobruk and the frontier passing into enemy hands.

In deciding to hold Tobruk, I had not visualised that the Eighth Army would be unable to interfere with the enemy's operations against the fortress, or that the garrison would be required to hold more than the western and southern faces of the perimeter against a serious attack, which its strength and composition should have enabled it to do, always provided that mobile forces were operating on its southern flank.

The Eighth Army had at that time three infantry divisions and an infantry brigade group comparatively fresh, two more of its divisions still had consider-able fighting value, and the New Zealand Division was on its way from Syria. The armoured divisions, however, had lost heavily and could only muster about a hundred tanks in all; but more tanks were on the way, and there were many under repair in the Eighth Army's field workshops. Two of the motor brigade groups were fighting vigorously and the reorganisation of the third was almost complete.

General Ritchie put four infantry brigade groups into Tobruk with their proper complement of artillery and some infantry tanks, and kept the rest of the Eighth Army as a mobile force outside it. Major-General Klopper, the com-mander of the 2nd South African Division, was put in command of the fortress.

The enemy now concentrated his efforts against El Adem, Sidi Rezegh and Belhamed and this area became just as important tactically as it had been in the previous winter. I instructed General Ritchie to strengthen it without delay, but he was unable to do so; and on the 17th June the enemy took Sidi Rezegh, thus beginning the encirclement of Tobruk. The same afternoon our remaining armoured brigade suffered a severe reverse in an encounter with a powerful enemy tank force and was forced to retire on Gambut, having lost all but twenty of its tanks. This entailed the withdrawal of our troops from Belhamed which enabled the enemy to complete the isolation of Tobruk. On the 18th June, the enemy pushed forward to Gambut and thus denied us the use of forward landing grounds in that neighbourhood, a most serious matter since it then became practically impossible for fighter aircraft to operate in support of the Tobruk garrison.

Early on the 20th, having cleared the arena, the enemy turned on Tobruk. The attack, which was directed against the eastern face of the perimeter and supported by a heavy concentration of artillery and dive-bombers, rapidly penetrated the defences. Exact and reliable accounts of the fighting are still unobtainable. Gallant but isolated counter-attacks were made by our troops. The infantry tanks which formed the principal reserve of the fortress appeared to have been defeated in detail at an early stage of the battle. Thereafter the enemy tanks pressed on deep into the fortress, overwhelming the best part of the artillery and infantry of two brigades, and reached the harbour the same evening.

On hearing that the attack was taking place, General Ritchie ordered General Norrie to relieve the pressure on Tobruk with the 7th Armoured Division, and the 7th Motor Brigade reached an area some 20 miles south of the perimeter that evening. By that time the whole of the eastern part of the fortress was in enemy hands, and General Klopper asked General Ritchie's permission to break out. Permission was accorded, but an hour later General Klopper said that it would be impossible as the greater part of his transport had been cut off in the harbour area. Early on the 21st June, General Klopper reported that all his transport had been captured, and that organised resistance was breaking down. Orders to destroy arms and equipment were circulated to the garrison. In spite of this, however, a number of troops fought on gallantly for a considerable time, and some broke out and rejoined the Eighth Army.

The precipitate and wholly unexpected collapse of Tobruk denied us the respite we so much needed to re-create our armoured force. Owing to our inferiority in armour, we could not hope to hold the frontier positions for long against the full weight of the enemy's attack. There seemed to be no alternative but to fall back on Matruh where there was a position already partially prepared for defence. The best we could hope to do was to impose the maximum delay on the enemy to give us time to strengthen the Matruh defences and build up a sufficiently powerful tank force with which to meet him.

The consequences of withdrawing to Matruh were undoubtedly grave. The Delta, with its ports and base installations, would be exposed to heavier aerial attack. It would become impossible for us to run a convoy to Malta from the east on the one hand, and on the other the enemy would find it easier to supply his forces in North Africa. Moreover, internal trouble might break out in Egypt and the proximity of the enemy to our main bases would make it hard to release forces for our Northern Front, where the danger was daily drawing nearer. Yet, if these consequences were not accepted, even worse might befall. The Middle East Defence Committee approved my proposal to withdraw to Matruh and informed the Defence Committee in London accordingly.

The War Cabinet approved our proposals generally but urged that a more determined stand should be made on the frontier, assuring us that every effort would be made to divert to the Middle East material then on the sea. Nevertheless the Middle East Defence Committee were obliged to reply that to stand on the frontier without the requisite armoured force would be to risk piecemeal destruction. We could only reiterate our intention of imposing the maximum delay on the enemy and of preparing to give battle round Matruh.

The enemy rapidly reorganised his army after the fall of Tobruk and pressed on towards the frontier. By the 23rd his forward troops were in touch with ours in front of Sollum, and he was obviously preparing to advance in strength to the south of Sidi Omar. But his forward troops were successfully held back for the time being by our mobile columns. The withdrawal of our infantry from the frontier positions, covered by our motorised forces, began on the 22nd June and proceeded without interruption from the enemy.

On the 24th June I telegraphed to the Prime Minister, giving him my view of the situation and explaining my future plans. I assured him that it was my firm intention to resume the offensive, immediately our armoured forces were strong enough to make this possible with a reasonable chance of success, and that plans for reorganising our forces to make them better fitted for their task were well advanced. At the same time, I informed him that I did not think it safe further to denude the Ninth and Tenth Armies of troops, as in the whole of this huge area there remained only two and one-third infantry divisions, besides some allied contingents not yet fully trained or equipped.

The enemy began his advance into Egypt on the 24th, striking north-east from Sheferzen towards Halfaya and eastward from Maddalena. He moved very rapidly and our rearguards fell back before him, until by evening they were level with Sidi Barrani. On the 25th he continued his advance in the face of damaging air attacks and his main bodies came within forty miles of Matruh.

Meanwhile, our depleted infantry divisions, under the 10th Corps Head-quarters (Lieutenant-General Holmes) which had recently come from Syria, were taking up positions round Matruh and hastily extending the minefields. The 13th Corps (Lieutenant-General Gott), which had the 1st Armoured Division and was being reinforced by the New Zealand Division, was watching the southern flank. Lieutenant-General Norrie with his 30th Corps Headquarters was organ-ising the defence of the El Alamein position, and had under his command the 1st South African Division and such other troops as could be collected.

I decided on the 25th June that the position of the Eighth Army was so critical and the danger to Egypt so great, that I must assume command myself. I took this step with great reluctance as I knew well that one man could not carry out the duties of Commander-in-Chief and Commander of the Eighth Army with full efficiency. Moreover I had grave doubts as to the wisdom of changing com-manders at so critical a time.

I appointed my Chief of the General Staff, Lieutenant-General T.W. Corbett, to be my deputy at General Headquarters in Cairo, and instructed him to deal with all matters, except those of the highest strategical or political import which he might feel impelled to refer to me. He carried out this task with great wisdom and efficiency.

I then flew to the advanced headquarters of the Eighth Army at Bagush and took over the direct command from General Ritchie the same evening.

### The Battle for Egypt.

When it was found impossible to hold the frontier positions without risking envelopment by the enemy, I had intended that the Eighth Army should stand and fight on the Matruh position, which was partially prepared and mined. General Ritchie had given instructions for this and the Eighth Army was pre-paring to carry them out when I took over command.

The enemy, however, had continued to press rapidly forward with what remained of his original striking force, and I realised that we were so weak in tanks and field artillery, two of the essentials for success in desert warfare, that it was very doubtful whether we could hope to hold the Matruh position, any more than we could the positions on the frontier. With his superiority in tanks, it seemed that the enemy might either envelop our open southern flank or pierce our centre, which we could hold only lightly. In either event, he was likely to isolate part of our forces and defeat them in detail, and this I was determined to avoid. I was convinced that it was necessary above all to hold together the much depleted Eighth Army and to keep it as a mobile force, retaining its freedom of action. I decided, therefore, that I could not risk its being pinned down at Matruh.

The loss of Matruh would be a further shock to Egyptian morale, and Axis propaganda would certainly hail it as another triumph. The disadvantages seemed small, however, compared with the danger of being defeated piecemeal. At that time, with the exception of the 9th Australian Division which I had summoned from Syria, there were no formations outside the Eighth Army which could have stood between Alexandria and Cairo and the enemy. Although a further retreat would bring the enemy to the very threshold of the Delta, El Alamein offered by far the strongest position in the Western Desert as both its flanks rested on impassable obstacles. Moreover, by drawing the enemy forward, we were lengthening his supply lines and shortening our own – no small advantage since the Eighth Army sorely needed an opportunity to re-equip and reorganise. I, therefore, cancelled the orders to stand at Matruh and gave instructions for the Eighth Army to withdraw on El Alamein, delaying the enemy as much as possible in its retirement.

On the 27th June, before these orders could take full effect, the enemy breached our minefields south of Matruh and, reaching the coast road, partially surrounded the 10th Corps which was holding Matruh and Bagush. During the next two days these troops managed to break through the enemy and reachel El Alamein, though they lost heavily in the process and had to be withdrawn to the Delta to reorganise and refit. Meanwhile, the 13th Corps on the southern flank fought desperately and with some success to stem the enemy's advance. The enemy lost no time in following up our withdrawal from Matruh and on the 1st July launched an attack against the 1st South African Division, which was holding the El Alamein fortifications on our extreme northern flank. This attack was beaten off, but on the same day further to the south the enemy managed to overrun one of our defended localities and thus weaken our centre.

We were still very short of tanks and weak in artillery. The Eighth Army was depleted and disorganised after five weeks of desperate fighting ending in a rapid retreat closely pressed by the enemy. I realised that it might not be able to hold the enemy if he made a determined attack on our partially prepared and thinly held positions in spite of the advantage we retained in the air; I took the precaution, therefore, of making the necessary arrangements for a further withdrawal, should this be necessary in the last resort.

It was my fixed intention to wrest the initiative from the enemy at the earliest possible moment; and in spite of our lack of men and equipment I was convinced that the best way to do this was to attack the enemy without delay and give him no rest. I accordingly ordered the 13th Corps, which formed my left wing, to swing forward round the enemy's right flank, which at that time did not extend far to the south, and attack northwards with all the strength it could muster. I had to hold what tanks I had in the centre, ready to counter-attack, should the enemy try to break through and seize the vital Ruweisat Ridge, the key to our position. Consequently I could spare no more than light tanks and armoured cars to support the 13th Corps. Nevertheless their attack, which started on the 2nd July, went forward with vigour and dash and caused the enemy to form a defensive flank, extending some distance to the west, to save himself being cut off from El Daba. He also had to reinforce his Italian troops in the south by German units from the north, which relieved the pressure on our centre and right. Owing to the relative weakness of our armour, I was unable to maintain the momentum of the attack and carry it to a decisive conclusion. On the other hand the operation achieved considerable results. We had at last recovered the tactical initiative and thrown the enemy on to the defensive. The situation in the south then gradually stabilised, until the enemy gained a secure flank by extending his line to the Qattara Depression.

While the Eighth Army, strongly supported by the R.A.F., was carrying on a fierce struggle at El Alamein, continuous and intensive preparations were made to continue the fight in the Delta, in case the battle were to go against us. Defensive positions covering the approaches to Alexandria from the west were constructed, and large tracts of country to the south of the city were flooded. A fortified area was organised between the Wadi Natrun and the edge of the Delta, to provide a pivot of manoeuvre for the Eighth Army which was to be kept mobile to oppose any enemy forces which might move against Alexandria or Cairo. Strong defences were erected round Mena and the Pyramids to cover the immediate approaches to Cairo from the desert. All the fighting men who could be mobilised were pressed into service and organised into improvised units, columns and commandos. The improvement of rearward communications was hurried on: boat bridges were built over the Nile, and existing bridges, railways and roads were safeguarded. Preparations were made to move General Headquarters from Cairo, if necessary, and to carry on the direction of the campaign from a field headquarters.

I was prepared, in the last resort, to continue the fight even if we had to abandon Northern Egypt altogether, by withdrawing southwards along the Nile with part of my forces while the remainder blocked the enemy's advance across the Suez Canal towards Palestine and Syria. Our bases on the Red Sea and our communications down the Nile Valley would have made this possible and plans were laid accordingly.[11]

I myself was fully occupied in directing the operations of the Eighth Army and the burden of planning and co-ordinating these complicated measures fell on my Chief of the General Staff, Lieutenant-General Corbett. He was ably seconded in his task by the Commanders charged with the execution of the work, Lieutenant-General Holmes, commanding the Delta Force and Lieutenant-General Stone, General Officer Commanding the British Troops in Egypt. The speed and thoroughness with which the work was done reflected the greatest credit on these officers.

The 9th Australian Division began to arrive behind El Alamein on the 4th July, and pursuing my policy of wresting the initiative from the enemy and of seizing important tactical points so as to prepare the ground for a decisive attack later, I launched this division on the 10th July against the Tel el Eisa mounds west of El Alamein. The attack was supported by tanks and a strong artillery and was carried out with skill and determination. The mounds were secured and remained in our possession, as a valuable bastion constituting a permanent threat to the enemy positions to the south of it.

Once again the enemy was obliged to weaken his centre to reinforce his flank, and to detach German troops to stiffen the Italians entrusted with the defence of this sector. From the series of determined, but unsuccessful counter-attacks launched against the Australians holding the position, it was evident that the enemy was deeply concerned at the loss of Tel el Eisa.

Although we had arrested the German advance on the Delta and had begun to lay the foundations for a further offensive, developments on the Northern Front made it necessary to consider afresh the general strategy of the Middle East. In order to fight in Cyrenaica at all, we had to concentrate all our armoured forces and practically the whole of our air forces on that front. The losses suffered by the Eighth Army in June had compelled me to withdraw most of the remaining troops from our Northern Front. The Ninth and Tenth armies had thus been denuded of troops and transport, and were not even in a position to impose any serious delay on the enemy should he attack. The final outcome of the battle of El Alamein was still in the balance, and it seemed very doubtful whether we should be able to spare troops from the west to reinforce the north.

The necessity might very well arise in the near future. For, while the battles for Egypt were in progress, the German armies had been advancing swiftly in Southern Russia. By the middle of July the German vanguards had reached the foothills of the Caucasus, and it seemed that only the fact of Stalingrad holding out and threatening their flank would prevent them from pushing into Persia.

Very shortly we might have to take a decision whether to continue to concentrate all our efforts on defending Egypt from the west or to divert the greater part of our resources to protect the Persian oil-fields against attack from the north. It was obvious that with the resources available, we could not do both simultaneously. The Middle East Defence Committee therefore represented the situation to the Defence Committee in London and asked for guidance.

The Prime Minister could hold out no hope of providing the reinforcements we required before the end of October. He added, however, that there was no need to assume that the enemy could invade Persia in force before that date. The only way to ensure that sufficient strength could be gathered to secure the

Northern Front in time, he said, was by inflicting a decisive defeat on the enemy in the west. We therefore continued to concentrate all our efforts on achieving this object and left the Northern Front to fend for itself for the time being. Early in August we received from the Chiefs of Staff a comprehensive review of the situation in Russia from which it appeared that no attack in force through the Caucasus was likely to occur before the spring of 1943, although in the event of the collapse of Russian resistance, light enemy forces might penetrate into Persia early in the coming November.

Having assured myself that it was fully realised in England that in the event of the Russian front breaking, we should be unable to reinforce Persia either in time or in sufficient force, I continued to concentrate all our resources in an attempt to defeat the enemy in the west. The capture of the Tel el Eisa salient on the 10th July had caused the enemy to extend his line and to disperse his strength still more and I determined to try to break through his centre and strike at his communications. Accordingly on the 21st July, taking advantage of the arrival of the 23rd Armoured Brigade which had lately come from England, I ordered an attack along the Ruweisat Ridge and to the south of it, against the enemy positions in that sector. The attack started well and breached the enemy's forward defences, enabling our tanks to pass through. Thereafter the attack lost momentum, partly, it seems, owing to loss of control and direction amongst the leading troops, inexperienced in desert fighting, but also because of the lack of reserves with which to sustain it. Nevertheless, the enemy was thrown into some disorder and suffered considerable loss, and we gained valuable ground.

I then decided to try to break through the enemy's positions to the south of the Tel el Eisa salient. To do so I had to withdraw troops from my southern flank, leaving it very weak, in order to strengthen the 30th Corps in the north with infantry and armoured formations. The main object was the same as before, to make a breach through which the armour could pass to disrupt and destroy the enemy in rear. Once again the infantry broke through, but the enemy had greatly extended and strengthened his minefields, and delay occurred in clearing a passage for the tanks. In consequence, the infantry were left unsupported and had to give way in the face of heavy enemy counterattacks. With stronger and more numerous reserves the attack might have succeeded, but these were not available.

For a month now the Eighth Army had been launching repeated attacks and it was evident that it could undertake no more until it had been thoroughly reorganised and greatly reinforced. The enemy had so strengthened his position that it was beyond the power of the Eighth Army in its existing state to evict him either by manoeuvre or direct attack. The Eighth Army was also strongly posted and well disposed for a defensive battle. The enemy was obviously trying to build up his army sufficiently to renew his efforts to seize the Delta, but was unlikely to be able to make the attempt before the end of August.

By mid-September the Eighth Army might expect to be reinforced by two armoured and two infantry divisions, and might then be able to make a frontal attack against what was likely to be a highly organised defensive position. Our immediate task was to reorganise and rearrange our forces, so as to provide an adequate reserve in the hands of the Army Commander, and to train the new divisions intensively for the offensive which I hoped might begin at the end of September. I informed the Chief of the Imperial General Staff of these conclusions.[12] Meanwhile, in case the enemy should attack first, I gave orders for the El Alamein position to be strengthened and developed in great depth.

During July, the Eighth Army took over 7,000 prisoners; and, though it had lost in battle some 700 officers and 12,000 men during that period, by supreme efforts it had stopped the enemy's drive on Egypt and laid firm foundations on which to build our future counterstroke.

*Conclusion.*

On the 6th August I flew to Cairo from my advanced headquarters with the Eighth Army and met the Prime Minister, Mr. Churchill, and the Chief of the Imperial General Staff, General Sir Alan Brooke, who had just arrived by air from England, and discussed the situation with them. Later the Prime Minister held a conference, at which Field Marshal Smuts, the Minister of State, General Sir Archibald Wavell and the three Commanders in Chief were among those present. The next day I accompanied the Prime Minister on a visit to the Eighth Army. After a short tour of the 30th Corps area the Prime Minister came to my advanced headquarters, where I explained to him the tactical situation in detail and my future plans, after which he met General Gott and other officers of the 13th Corps and then went back to Cairo. General Gott was killed the next day when the aircraft in which he was flying to Cairo on a few days leave was shot down. His death at an early age was a great loss to the Army, as he was an officer of much promise, whom I had already marked down as a possible Army Commander.

On the 8th August, Colonel Jacob brought to Eighth Army Headquarters a letter from the Prime Minister from which I learned that the War Cabinet had decided that the moment had come to make a change in the Middle East Command and that I was to be relieved by General Sir Harold Alexander.

The Prime Minister went on to say that it was proposed to form Iraq and Persia into a new Command, independent of the Middle East Command. He offered me this new Command and hoped I would accept it.

For some time previously, I had been closely examining the possibility of freeing General Quinan from the heavy administrative and political responsibilities he was discharging as commander of the Tenth Army. Since his appointment to command the forces sent to Iraq from India early in 1941, he had carried out these responsibilities with ability and thoroughness, but I considered it essential to free him from them so that he could concentrate on the strategical problem of the defence of Persia.

After prolonged and thorough examination of the administrative considerations involved, which were not easy to reconcile with the simpler needs of a sound system of operational control, we reached a solution which, though possibly not ideal, was workable in practice.

My Lieutenant-General in charge of Administration, General Riddell-Webster, was of the greatest help to me in solving this problem to which he gave much time and thought.

The new system, consisted in the formation of a base area in Southern Iraq and South-western Persia under a commander directly responsible to General Head-quarters in Cairo; the appointment of an Inspector-General of Communications for Persia and Iraq, working directly under my Lieutenant-General in charge of Administration; and the transfer of Mosul and Northern Iraq from the Tenth to the Ninth Army. The transfer of Northern Iraq I considered essential in order to ensure unity of control of all land and air forces along the whole length of the Anatolian frontier, the defence of which was one problem to be handled by a single commander. Moreover, General Quinan would thus be freed from all responsibility for the defence of Iraq from the north and could devote his whole attention to the protection of Northern Persia. These changes also facilitated co-operation between the various army and air force commanders, which had previously been somewhat complicated, as the boundaries of their several Commands did not coincide.

This transfer of responsibility, which I looked on as highly important and necessary, was put into effect shortly before I gave up my command but was never fully tested, as soon afterwards Iraq and Persia and the Tenth Army were divorced from the Middle East Command and given a Commander-in-Chief of their own. It seems likely, however, that the changes described smoothed the way for the formation of the new command.

I handed over my direct command of the Eighth Army temporarily to General Ramsden and went to Cairo the next day and did not return to the Desert. The same day I had an interview with the Prime Minister and told him that I thought it would be difficult for me to accept his offer of the new command, but that I would like to have time to examine thoroughly the probable strategical and administrative effects of the proposal. After careful consideration, I concluded that the arrangement was likely to break down in the event of a serious threat from the north and that, therefore, I could not accept the responsibility of putting it into practice. I informed the Minister of State and the Chief of the Imperial General Staff accordingly.[13]

Before I was aware of the decision to relieve me of my command I had arranged with the Chief of the Imperial General Staff that Lieutenant-General B.L. Montgomery should come out from England to take over the Eighth Army as its permanent commander, as it was obviously impossible for me to continue indefinitely in the dual role of Commander-in-Chief and Army Commander. General Montgomery arrived, before I handed over to General Alexander and I explained the situation to him and my plans for the future.

In accordance with the Prime Minister's instructions, I handed over my command to General Alexander on the 15th August.

\*    \*    \*

I wish to take this opportunity of recording my gratitude and appreciation of the unfailing help and ready co-operation I received throughout my tenure of command of the Middle East Forces from my colleagues in chief command, Admiral Sir Andrew Cunningham, Admiral Sir Henry Pridham Whippell and Admiral Sir Henry Harwood, who successively held the post of Commander-in-Chief, Mediterranean; and Air Chief Marshal Sir Arthur Tedder with whom I worked in the closest possible accord throughout the whole period.

I am deeply indebted also to the Ministers of State who by their assumption of great political and economic responsibilities made it possible for me to devote much more attention to strategical matters than I could otherwise have done. These were successively Captain Oliver Lyttelton, Sir Walter Monckton and Mr. Richard Casey.

My Army Commanders and I owe much to the consistent support and wise counsel of Sir Harold MacMichael, High Commissioner for Palestine and Trans-Jordan, Sir Kinahan Cornwallis, His Majesty's Ambassador in Baghdad, and Sir Reader Bullard, His Majesty's Minister in Teheran. I wish to acknowledge also the great help and encouragement I received from the visits of Field Marshal Smuts to my command. His profound knowledge of the world in general and of war in particular made his comments and advice on matters of higher strategy of great value.

In my first Despatch, I alluded to the great help I had received from the Egyptian Government and the Egyptian Army. This support was continued in full measure throughout the period under review and was greatly enhanced by the calm and generally courageous behaviour of the civil population of the country during the prolonged struggle at El Alamein, when the enemy was at their gates. The absence of panic and disorder made the task of those charged with organising the ultimate defence of the Delta immeasurably lighter than it might otherwise have been. To His Excellency Nahas Pasha, Prime Minister of Egypt, and to his predecessor, His Excellency Hussain Sirry Pasha, I gratefully acknowledge my indebtedness.

## PART II.
### THE CAMPAIGNS IN CYRENAICA AND THE WESTERN DESERT.
### THE INVASION OF CYRENAICA.

On the 2nd September, 1941, after consulting the Commander-in-Chief, Mediterranean, and the Air Officer Commanding-in-Chief, I told Lieutenant-General Sir Alan Cunningham, commander designate of the Eighth Army, in a personal letter that I intended to drive the enemy out of North Africa.[14]

The offensive was to be carried out in two phases, the first being the capture of Cyrenaica and the second the capture of Tripolitania. The immediate object was to destroy the enemy's armoured forces.

At that time two courses seemed possible. We might base our main striking force on Giarabub and advance through Gialo to cut the enemy's line of supply from Tripoli, leaving sufficient forces to contain him in front and prevent his trying to turn the tables on us by advancing on Alexandria, in the hope that he would then be caught between two fires and forced to fight at a disadvantage. Or we might make a direct attack towards Tobruk with our main force, while feinting from the centre and south to distract the enemy's attention and cause him to disperse his strength. I instructed General Cunningham to prepare detailed plans for both courses by the 1st October.

The plan must be flexible, since the enemy might modify his dispositions when he saw our preparations or received information about the growing strength of our forces in the Desert. For this reason and to deceive the enemy as to the direction of our main blow, the original deployment must be on a wide front and our depots of supplies in the forward area disposed to allow of this.

The forces available for the offensive were two corps headquarters, one armoured division, an armoured brigade group, four infantry divisions, two infantry brigades and an army tank brigade. There was also the Tobruk garrison consisting of four infantry brigade groups, a mixed armoured force of about a hundred tanks, and a considerable amount of artillery – anti-aircraft, field and medium.

The campaign would require the closest possible co-operation between the three services. The land and air forces would depend on the Royal Navy not only for direct support, but to a large extent for maintenance. Arrangements would be made to land a brigade group behind the enemy lines, if General Cunningham so wished, but the success or failure of the general plan was not to depend on whether this operation was feasible or not.

Maintenance and mobility would be vital factors, and I directed that formations must be made fully mobile and trained to operate on a strictly limited allowance of baggage, food and water.

I estimated that the forces could be trained and concentrated, and the maintenance arrangements completed by the beginning of November. I asked General Cunningham to make every effort to avoid having to postpone the operation, and to begin building up forward magazines of supplies and munitions as soon as the necessary protection could be provided.

As usual, time was the ruling factor. We were unlikely to be strong enough by the spring of 1942 to conduct an offensive in the west and at the same time hold off a determined attack from the north which, according to information then available, was likely eventually to present the more serious threat to our bases in the Middle East and Iraq. Should our offensive be delayed for some unforeseen reason, we might have to stop short and resist attack from the north before achieving our ultimate object of seizing Tripolitania.

I explained my views in an Instruction issued on the 17th October to the Commanders of the Eighth and Ninth Armies and of the British Troops in Egypt.[15] Every possible step which could be taken must be taken at once and every possible need which could be foreseen must be foreseen at once, so as to ensure the complete success of the offensive. General Cunningham must be given all the forces and resources he needed and must retain them as long as he required them.

On the 29th September General Cunningham gave me his appreciation and plan.[16] Of the two courses General Cunningham preferred that of an attack from the centre along the coast. He explained the reasons for his choice in his appreciation and again at a meeting of the three Commanders-in-Chief.

To capture Bengasi by an advance based on Giarabub and Gialo would not, it seemed, necessarily ensure the immediate surrender of the enemy forces in Eastern Cyrenaica, as they had built up enough reserves there to allow them to subsist for some time. Our lines of communication would be very long and vulnerable. Moreover, we should be compelled to split our air forces and, still more important as their range was limited, our armoured forces. As we seemed likely to have slightly fewer aircraft and to be not greatly superior to the enemy in armour, it was essential to concentrate our forces. We were bent on destroying the enemy's armoured forces as early as possible, and it seemed that the best way of bringing them to battle under conditions most favourable to ourselves from all points of view, was to direct our own armoured formations towards Tobruk.

In the earliest stages of my planning, I had hoped to be able to leave a sufficiently strong armoured force to contain the enemy in the Tobruk area, moving straight with the remainder on Bengasi. This depended on my having at my disposal at least two armoured divisions. The requisite forces were not available, and this plan would, I think, have been impossible in any event owing to maintenance difficulties.

The other plan was examined and analysed many times during the months preceding the launching of the offensive and was considered by all those primarily responsible, including myself, to be the best. The Commander-in-Chief, Mediterranean, the Air Officer Commanding-in-Chief and I agreed that the main attack should be directed not on Bengasi, but towards Tobruk, and that this would be the most likely way of making the enemy give battle on ground of our choosing. At a conference on the 3rd October we gave our approval to the land and air plans which differed only in detail from the final plans to be described later.

*Outline Plan.*

The plan which General Cunningham submitted went no further than the destruction of the enemy's armour and the relief of Tobruk. Subsequent plans for capturing Bengasi depended on the success of the first part of the operation. If any enemy tanks should escape, our further course of action would depend on their strength and movements.

Briefly, the original conception was that our armoured forces should open the offensive by moving directly on Tobruk, followed by a completely motorised division. The two Panzer Divisions, believed to be lying between Bardia and Tobruk, would then be drawn out and compelled to accept battle away from their supporting fortresses and infantry formations.

We counted on being able to oppose between 450 and 500 cruiser and American tanks to the enemy's 250. This latter figure did not include the 138 tanks of the Italian Ariete Division, which, although it lay to the south of Tobruk on the flank of our proposed line of advance, was believed to be not very for-midable. This estimate of its value, based on the experience of General Wavell's campaign of the previous winter, proved to be somewhat erroneous.

The idea was that by moving wide we should force the enemy to come out and fight on ground not of his choosing and away from his minefields and prepared defences round Sidi Omar and Capuzzo. We hoped that our numerical superi-ority in tanks would enable us to destroy his two Panzer divisions and open the way for the motorised divisions to force a passage to Tobruk. Meanwhile the 13th Corps comprising two infantry divisions with all the available infantry tanks, were to contain the enemy in the frontier area. But they were not to expose themselves to attack by enemy tanks by moving forward into the no-man's land between Tobruk and Bardia until this risk had been removed by the victory of our armoured forces.[17]

### *Administrative Arrangements.*

Two great constructional enterprises were undertaken in order to solve the two principal difficulties confronting the army in mounting an offensive in Cyrenaica. In previous operations the railhead and main water-point had been at Matruh, some hundred and thirty miles from the frontier. This was nearly twice the usually accepted distance between railhead and the front, and the frontier was only the starting line, the proposed battlefield being about seventy-five miles further on.

General Wavell, who had himself suffered from this grave disadvantage, had taken steps to remedy it as soon as the necessary resources were available, and had given orders in June for work to begin at once on the extension of the railway above the escarpment towards Capuzzo. Remarkable progress was made and by the end of October a new railhead was opened at Bir Misheifa, seventy-five miles west of Matruh. The new line brought an immense saving in transport, having a carrying capacity which was equal to that of 2,700 lorries.

Water supply in bulk, presented another serious problem. The water sources along the coast forward of Matruh had either been destroyed or left undeveloped, lest they should fall into enemy hands. Almost all the water needed had therefore to be brought from Alexandria to Matruh, and in the absence of a pipeline it had to be brought by sea and rail. From Matruh it was taken by motor transport to the forward area. Water was thus taking up much transport needed for stores.

To supply the large quantities of water now required, I ordered a pipeline to be laid between Alexandria and the forward area. I also gave instructions for the water sources at Fuka and Buq Buq to be developed. The orders for the con-struction of the pipeline and the development of the water source at Fuka were given on the 6th September, and on the 11th November the new water-point was opened sixty-five miles west of Matruh. A strict water ration of three-quarters of a gallon a day per man and vehicle had to be imposed in order to leave enough water to fill the new pipelines and storage tanks. In the space of two months, in spite of many difficulties, one hundred and forty-five miles of pipe had been laid and filled, and ten large reservoirs and seven new pumping stations had been built. Adequate supplies of water were then available without in any way interfering with the transport of supplies.

Large reserves of ammunition, fuel and supplies were required, since the capacity of the railway fell short of the estimated daily requirements of the force by about one-third. As transport was extremely limited and as rival demands were heavy, an early start had to be made on building up these reserves.

On the 8th August I had instructed Lieutenant-General Sir Noel Beresford-Peirse, then commanding the Western Desert Forces, to prepare plans so that work could begin as soon as the necessary resources and protection could be provided. The plan was to provide for dumping on a wide front in order to give the attacking forces complete freedom of movement. Work was to begin first at Giarabub, as the large reserves which would be needed if it were to serve as the base for the main attacking force would take a considerable time to establish.

Orders for the occupation of Giarabub had already been issued, and on the 8th August a detachment of the 7th Indian Infantry Brigade took possession of the Oases. The strength of the garrison of Siwa and Giarabub was increased during the month until it finally consisted of the 7th Indian Infantry Brigade Group and the 6th South African Armoured Car Regiment less one squadron. Covered by this force, the establishment of reserves began in the first week of September; a month later eighty-five per cent. of the total requirements had been placed in position and camouflaged.

Meanwhile the forces necessary to cover the placing of reserves in the northern area moved into position. In the middle of September the 11th Indian Infantry Brigade arrived in the coastal area, and the Headquarters of the 4th Indian Division assumed control of the forward zone, releasing the 7th Support Group to rejoin the 7th Armoured Division. On the 18th September the 7th Armoured Brigade moved forward, followed on the 4th October by the Headquarters of the 7th Armoured Division.

At midnight on 26th September, command of the forces in the Western Desert, except those in Tobruk, passed to the Headquarters of the Eighth Army. The Headquarters of the Western Desert Forces, of which Lieutenant-General A.R. Godwin-Austen had taken command in place of Lieutenant-General Beresford-Peirse, became the headquarters of the 13th Corps.

On the 4th October, as soon as it had been decided to direct the main thrust towards Tobruk, we started to establish further reserves in accordance with the approved maintenance plan. The limiting factor was the small amount of motor transport available in relation to the strength of the force[18] and the distances it was proposed to cover in the advance.

During the preparatory period in particular great demands were placed on transport resources. Material for the new railway and pipeline, water to fill the pipe and reservoirs, supplies for the troops covering the preparations and those in training behind, all had to be transported. Great quantities of petrol had to be moved not only for the operation but for the convoys bringing up reserves, which at one time required 180,000 gallons a day. Weak and ill-constructed petrol containers led to great waste of petrol and, consequently, to a most uneconomical use of transport. Everything possible was done to remedy this weakness, but it is probable that on long desert journeys the loss of petrol between base and consumer came to as much as thirty per cent. Even with the most careful handling the loss between base and forward, base was between five and fifteen per cent. The need of a more efficient container after the German pattern was only too apparent.[19]

All these rival demands severely limited the amount of reserves which could be built up, and consequently the size of the force which could be maintained forward of these reserves once the advance had begun.

Nearly thirty thousand tons of munitions, fuel and supplies were stored in the forward area between the beginning of September and the middle of November. Even so these reserves were only sufficient to cover the difference between the daily rates of delivery and consumption for a week at most; when they were exhausted, the size of the force must be reduced, or an alternative source of supply opened up. Consequently, unless contact were established with Tobruk and part of the force supplied from there, the full weight of our attack could only be sustained for a week. Again the reserves held in Tobruk were not large and could maintain additional forces for a short time only, unless the port could be freely used, which would be possible only when all danger of land attack and sustained attack from the air had been removed.

In the advance beyond Tobruk maintenance would again be the governing factor. Plans for bringing the ports of Tobruk, Derna, and Bengasi into operation at the earliest possible moment were carefully worked out. But, owing to limited transport resources, the size of the forces for the subsequent advance and their radius of action would be severely restricted. For that reason it was all-important that the enemy's main forces should be destroyed before they could withdraw beyond our reach.

*Camouflage and Deception.*
It was of supreme importance to mislead the enemy as to our intention and no effort was spared to achieve this.

*Reconnaissance.*
For many weeks before the operation every part of Libya in which enemy troops were quartered was thoroughly reconnoitred. It cannot be said that any one type of reconnaissance provided more valuable results than any other, but the sum of their efforts produced most accurate information about the enemy. It will be seen that we were acquainted with almost every important detail of the enemy's dispositions, his order of battle and defensive arrangements.

The Royal Air Force covered the whole of the enemy's lines of communication from Tripoli and Bengasi up to the forward area. In addition a thorough photographic survey was made of all the important areas between Gazala and the Egyptian frontier. The interpreters of the Army Air Photo-Interpretation unit attached to the Eighth Army showed great skill in plotting enemy defences and depots of supplies from these photographs. Practically the whole of the enemy's dispositions round Tobruk were pin-pointed from air photographs interpreted by officers of this unit, and the plan for the Tobruk sortie was based largely on this information. The Long Range Desert Group were also engaged in important reconnaissances. Operating over an area approximately five hundred miles from north to south and six hundred miles from east to west behind the enemy lines, desert patrols secured much useful topographical information, enabling existing inaccurate maps to be revised. Small parties lay up for long periods three hundred miles behind the enemy's advanced troops, observing the coastal road and taking a complete census of traffic passing between Tripoli and Bengasi. Both in Cyrenaica and Tripolitania enemy convoys were attacked, and the prisoners taken imparted valuable information.

The armoured car regiments in the frontier zone were also busy supplying information about the enemy's activities. It was particularly important that we should know the extent to which the enemy used the area south of the Trigh el Abd and west of the frontier. Penetrating up to fifty miles beyond the wire, patrols brought back the heartening knowledge that the area was not closely watched and that we might expect to obtain a high degree of surprise.

### Bombardment of Enemy Supply Lines.

A description of the valuable preparatory work carried out by the Royal Navy and the Royal Air Force does not come within the scope of this Despatch, though there can be no doubt that its effect on the subsequent land operations was little short of decisive. For many weeks, while the Army was engaged in making its own preparations, the supply lines of the enemy were subjected to constant heavy attack by sea and air. Many ships carrying reinforcements in men and vehicles were sunk, and many thousands of tons of stores and fuel destroyed.

### Enemy Dispositions.

In mid-November the greater part of the enemy forces in North Africa were concentrated in Eastern Cyrenaica, leaving in Tripolitania only the regular garrison troops and the weak Sabrata Division, which was serving as a drafting formation. The main forces consisted of three armoured, two motorised, and five infantry divisions. These were organised as follows:-

*Panzer Gruppe, Afrika* (General Rommel).
    *Afrika Korps-*
        15th Panzer Division.
        21st Panzer Division.
        90th Light Division. (Afrika Division).
    *Mobile Corps-*
        Ariete Division (armoured).
        Trieste Division (motorised).
        Trento Division.

*21st Corps-*
  Bologna Division.
  Pavia Division.
  Brescia Division.
*Frontier Group-*
  Savona Division.
  Elements of other divisions, German and Italian.

The 21st Corps, stiffened by three German infantry battalions, was investing Tobruk and the Trento Division had lately joined it. The frontier defences at Halfaya, Sollum and Capuzzo, constructed during the summer, were manned by German infantry battalions and those round Sidi Omar by the Savona Division. Bardia, where General Schmitt had his headquarters, was occupied by a mixed garrison of Italians and Germans.

Between these two main infantry groups were the armoured and mobile forces. The 21st Panzer Division lay astride the Trigh Capuzzo some 12 miles south of Gambut, where General Rommel's headquarters were. The 15th Panzer Division and the Afrika Division, an infantry division specially formed for service overseas, were concentrated round El Adem, Ed Duda and Sidi Rezegh. The Ariete and Trieste Divisions had recently moved to Bir el Gubi and Bir Hacheim respectively.

### Date of the Offensive.

I knew before we launched an offensive that preparations pointing to an attack on Tobruk were in train, but I did not know the date of the proposed assault. I did, however, seriously consider postponing my offensive until Rommel struck at Tobruk, with the idea of catching the enemy facing the wrong way and at a disadvantage. However, the urgent need for opening our offensive at the earliest moment and the possibility that Rommel might not be ready for his attack for many weeks made me give up this idea, though with some reluctance. We know now beyond any doubt that Rommel intended to attack Tobruk from the east on the 23rd November and we have all his plans for this operation.

For various reasons our offensive had already had to be postponed. After dumping had been finished, it was not possible to rely on the transport echelons being reorganised before the 11th November in readiness for the advance. Nor was it possible to complete the training of the 22nd Armoured Brigade, which disembarked early in October, and that of the Armoured Corps Headquarters before that date. At the Commanders'-in-Chief Conference held on the 3rd October, therefore, 11th November was fixed as the date for the offensive to begin. Unavoidable delays arose, however, in providing the full quota of transport for the 1st South African Division, and Major-General Brink found it impossible to complete its training by that date. The opening of the offensive was finally deferred until 18th November.

By the evening of the 17th November the formations of the Eighth Army had concentrated behind the frontier and were ready to advance.

*British Forces.*

The principal forces taking part in the offensive were:-

13*th Corps* – Lieutenant-General A.R. Godwin-Austen.
  New Zealand Division. – Major-General B. Freyberg.
  4th Indian Division. – Major-General F.W. Messervy.
  1st Army Tank Brigade. – Brigadier H.R.B. Watkins.
30*th Corps*. – Lieutenant-General C.W.M. Norrie.
  7th Armoured Division. – Major-General W.H.E. Gott.
  4th Armoured Brigade Group. – Brigadier A.H. Gatehouse.
  1st South African Division (two brigades). – Major-General G.E. Brink.
  22nd Guards (Motor) Brigade. – Brigadier J.C.O. Marriott.
*Tobruk Garrison*. – Major-General R. MacK. Scobie.
  70th Division. – Major-General Scobie.
  32nd Army Tank Brigade. – Brigadier A.C. Willison.
  Polish Carpathian Infantry Brigade Group. – Major-General S. Kopanski.
*Oases Force*. – Brigadier D.W. Reid.
  (6th South African Armoured Car Regiment and a battalion group from 29th Indian Infantry Brigade.)
*In reserve* –
  2nd South African Division (two brigades). – Major-General I.P. de Villiers.

## The Plan.
### 30th Corps.

The main attack was to be delivered by the 30th Corps whose primary role was to seek out and destroy the enemy, at the same time ensuring that the left flank of the 13th Corps was protected against an attack in force by the enemy armoured formations. As a first step towards bringing the enemy to battle, the bulk of our armoured forces were to move to a central position round Gabr Saleh whence they could strike north-west or north-east according to developments. Every effort was to be made by ground and air reconnaissance to discover the enemy's whereabouts and the extent to which it would be possible to prevent his southward movement by obtaining control of the few crossings of the coastal escarpment, to the north of which the enemy was believed to be lying.

The Army Commander reserved to himself the responsibility for deciding which direction the armoured forces should take, if the 30th Corps were not able to engage the enemy under favourable conditions on the first day. General Cunningham intended to stay close to the headquarters of that Corps until he had sufficient information to make a decision. In the event of a westward move, he foresaw that it might be necessary to leave some of the armour to protect the 13th Corps.

The more immediate plan was for the 7th Armoured Division to take up a central position astride the Trigh el Abd with the 4th Armoured Brigade on the right, the 7th in the centre, and the 22nd on the left. The armoured car regiments were to push well forward to watch the main crossings of the escarpment north of the Trigh Capuzzo. From this central position the Armoured Division might have to move right or left. If the other two brigades were ordered to move left towards Tobruk, the 4th Armoured Brigade was to remain in its battle position so as to be ready to protect the right flank of the Armoured Division, the communications of the 30th Corps and the left flank of the 13th Corps. On the left, should the Ariete Division withdraw, it was not to be pursued, if pursuit involved dispersing our armoured forces and allowing the German Panzer Divisions to concentrate in superior force against us.

The first task of the 1st South African Division was to protect the western and south-western flanks of the communications of the Armoured Division. Subsequently it might have to secure a defensive locality round Bir el Gubi on which the Armoured Division could pivot. The 22nd Guards Brigade was to protect the lines of communication, supply dumps, and landing grounds in the rear.

### Tobruk.

The secondary role of the 30th Corps was to relieve Tobruk, but no operations were to be undertaken to this end until the main enemy armoured forces had either been defeated or prevented from interfering with the relief. General Norrie was to give the signal when he was satisfied that his own forces were or would be in a position to support the sortie from Tobruk. On receipt of this signal, the Tobruk Garrison was to come under command of the 30th Corps and to remain under its command until all enemy resistance in the neighbourhood had ceased.

The basis of the plan for relieving Tobruk was the capture of two ridges to the south-east of it. These two ridges, Ed Duda and Sidi Rezegh, 5,000 yards apart, between them commanded the two main lines of communication of the Axis forces. The Tobruk by-pass road climbs up from the coast, crosses a saddle, and then turns west along the southern slope of Ed Duda Ridge: in the valley between the two ridges runs the Trigh Capuzzo. Provided that the enemy armoured forces were defeated or heavily embroiled, our forces would have only infantry to compete with and mostly Italian infantry at that.

When the armoured battle was over, the 1st South African Division was to secure a position about Sidi Rezegh to cut the Trigh Capuzao and the bypass road and, by threatening the rear of the Axis forces investing Tobruk, to assist the garrison in their sortie.

At the same time General Scobie was to strike southwards to Ed Duda with the 14th and 16th Infantry Brigades and the 32nd Army Tank Brigade. Two feint attacks were to be made in the western and southern sectors by the Polish Carpathian Brigade and the 23rd Infantry Brigade, and the main attack was to take place soon after dawn on the day after the signal was received from the 30th Corps.

After the relief of Tobruk the area was to be cleared of enemy as rapidly as possible. The 70th Division and the 32nd Army Tank Brigade were to work closely with the 1st South African Division in this task. The enemy was then to be pursued with the greatest energy. The size of the pursuing force would depend on the degree of success achieved in the armoured battle, and on the supply situation at the time. In no circumstances was it likely to be less than one armoured brigade and one lorry-borne South African Infantry Brigade. Should the enemy hold Mechili in such strength as to hinder the pursuit, a special force was to mask that place.

### 13th Corps.

The task of the 13th Corps was to pin down and cut off the enemy troops holding the frontier defences, and then to advance westwards to help the 30th Corps to clear the battlefield, leaving the enemy garrisons to be reduced at leisure.

The 11th Indian Infantry Brigade below the Sollum escarpment and the 5th Indian Infantry Brigade above it were to contain the enemy frontally, and to cover our base and railhead by holding a line running south from Buq Buq. Then, on the first day of the offensive, the 7th Indian Infantry Brigade were to secure a position astride the frontier to mask the enemy positions at Sidi Omar.

The 13th Corps were to make no further move until the enemy armoured forces had been properly engaged and orders received from the Army Commander. When the order was given, the New Zealand Division was to advance on a north and south axis to isolate the frontier defences. Such troops as could then be spared from this division were to move westwards, coming under the command of the 30th Corps for operations against Tobruk, if its relief should not have been accomplished already.

If the enemy were to withdraw from his forward positions, the 13th Corps was to make every effort to cut him off and, if this was unsuccessful, to pursue him vigorously.

After the relief of Tobruk, General Godwin-Austen was to be prepared to move a motorised infantry brigade group to Derna.

### Oases Force.

The primary task of the Oases Force was to protect the air forces which were to harass the enemy in the coastal sector south of Bengasi and to cause confusion among advancing or retiring enemy columns. The Oases Force had orders in the first place to protect a landing ground some eighty miles west of Giarabub which was just within striking distance of the coastal road, and in the second to move on to Gialo to protect our air forces and harass the enemy as circumstances permitted.

Brigadier Reid had been instructed to continue with the deception scheme already in train, so as to make the enemy believe that the force was much stronger than it was and induce him to divert or withdraw his armoured forces to meet this threat. The force therefore included a high proportion of guns and armoured cars and was relatively weak in infantry.

One armoured car company of the 7th South African Reconnaissance Battalion (Lieutenant-Colonel P.H. Grobelaar) was to carry out a raid against a target east of Giarabub and south of the line Tobruk – Mechili, and cause the maximum destruction. The target was to be selected so as to produce the greatest possible disruption in the enemy's rear. After completing this operation, Lieutenant-Colonel Grobelaar's force was to operate under the orders of Brigadier Reid.

### Long Range Desert Group.

The Long Range Desert Group (Lieutenant-Colonel G.L. Prendergast) was given the important role of observing enemy movement along the tracks across the desert south of the Gebel Akhdar to the main battle area and along the approaches to Gialo from the north. Without prejudice to its primary role, it was to give all possible assistance to Brigadier Reid and to maintain communication with the South African armoured cars.

As operations progressed, the Long Range Desert Group was to move westwards and perform a similar observation role in Tripolitania.

### Raids.

Raids were to be carried out to cause confusion and alarm in the enemy's rear by the 11th Scottish Commando (Lieutenant-Colonel G.P.T. Keyes) and by "L" Section of the 1st Special Air Service Brigade.

### The Approach March.

The concentration of the Eighth Army took place during the first two weeks of November. Only a bare minimum of troops had been allowed in the forward area in order to keep the daily maintenance needs as low as possible and to enable the maximum amount of reserves to be accumulated. The greater part of the Army had therefore to be brought up during this fortnight, and the movement of vehicles across the desert was almost continuous. Yet captured enemy intelligence papers revealed no knowledge of what was happening. This praiseworthy achievement was due both to the work of the Royal Air Force in preventing enemy aerial reconnaissance, and to the high degree of camouflage, deception and dispersion reached during the concentration.

By the evening of the 17th November all were in place, and during the night the 7th Indian Infantry Brigade took up its position masking Sidi Omar. Soon after dawn on the 18th, the armoured brigades, with an armoured car screen thrown out far in front, crossed the frontier wire fence near Maddalena, and by evening had reached their battle positions astride the Trigh el Abd, except the 22nd Armoured Brigade which had been delayed and halted ten miles south of its destination. The 1st South African Division, to the south, moved in a wider sweep to cover the western flank, while the Guards Brigade followed to guard the landing grounds and field maintenance centres. On the night of 18th–19th November H.M. Ships Naiad and Euryalus bombarded the Halfaya fortifications.

Beyond increased shelling in the frontier area and the capture of two German armoured cars, no incident marked the approach march. Our offensive surprised the enemy. Indeed, I believe that for at least one day, if not for two, he thought we were making a reconnaissance in force.

As the enemy made no move, General Cunningham decided to follow the original plan and to push on towards Tobruk.

### The Battle of Sidi Rezegh – First Phase.

On 19th November, the armoured battle developed in grim earnest. On the left the 22nd Armoured Brigade engaged the Ariete Division in a sharp, but successful encounter. On the right the 4th Armoured Brigade became engaged with German armoured forces near Gabr Bu Meliha, and General Norrie, judging that the greater part of the enemy armour was in that area, moved the 22nd Armoured Brigade across from Bir el Gubi to assist, leaving the 1st South African Division to watch the Ariete Division. In the centre the 6th Royal Tank Regiment shook itself free from the skirmishing in which the 7th Armoured Brigade was engaged, and moved north-west on Sidi Rezegh which they found virtually unguarded. There the Support Group of the 7th Armoured Division and the remainder of the 7th Armoured Brigade joined them next morning.

The course of events to date seemed so satisfactory that General Norrie wished the 70th Division to make its sortie from Tobruk next morning. According to the original plan the 1st South African Division was to support the sortie. The new proposal meant that the Support Group, backed by two armoured regiments was to take Sidi Rezegh and that the 5th South African Infantry Brigade, which was due to arrive an hour and a half before the attack, was to help them to consolidate and to make touch with the 70th Division. There were strong indications of considerable enemy movement westwards, away from the battleground, and it seemed quite possible that the enemy was trying to avoid conflict. At the same time the greater part of the enemy's armoured forces appeared to be engaged with our armoured brigades away to the south near Gabr Saleh. So General Cunningham consented to the proposal.

On the morning of the 21st, however, the whole scene was transformed. The blow at the bottleneck in the enemy's communications had been shrewdly aimed, and Rommel summoned all his armoured forces to deny us the commanding positions we were clearly about to gain. Only half an hour before the Support Group was due to launch its attack, two strong enemy armoured columns were sighted to the south-east heading for Sidi Rezegh. Zero hour for the 70th Division had long passed and there was no going back. Brigadier Davy, who was directing operations, therefore decided to leave only one armoured regiment to support the attack and took the other two to meet the enemy columns.

At eight-thirty the Support Group put in their attack and after a hard struggle captured Sidi Rezegh. Almost simultaneously the two armoured regiments engaged the 15th Panzer Division to the south-east. One regiment claimed fifteen enemy tanks out of thirty-five in one column, but the other suffered heavily in a gallant action with about a hundred enemy tanks.

The survivors of these actions had scarcely returned to the aerodrome and the Support Group had barely secured Sidi Rezegh, when they had to face about to throw off an attack from the south. This, it seems, was the 21st Panzer Division, which had eluded the efforts of the 4th and 22nd Armoured Brigades to check them near Gabr Saleh. After heavy fighting the enemy drew off to refuel.

By mid-day the situation at Sidi Rezegh had become critical. The enemy armoured divisions had in all probability joined forces and were clearly forming up for another attack. The defenders had suffered many casualties and were isolated. The 5th South African Infantry Brigade had not arrived. Brigadier Armstrong had obtained permission for the brigade to halt overnight on the plea that it was not sufficiently trained to move on a moonless night over unknown ground, and next morning had found himself confronted by tanks from the Ariete Division and could make no progress. The 4th and 22nd Armoured Brigades had been summoned to the rescue, but could not be expected for some time.

The expected attack developed in the afternoon. The Support Group and the 7th Armoured Brigade resisted valiantly and at length compelled the enemy to abandon the attack. The inspiring example set by Brigadier Campbell[20] who led several tank charges in person greatly contributed to this result. The Support Group and 7th Armoured Brigade achieved this success practically singlehanded; for the 22nd Armoured Brigade did not intervene until about an hour before dusk, while the 4th Armoured Brigade had been checked by a screen of 88 milli-metre guns some miles to the south-east and never reached the scene.

The Tobruk sortie started at dawn on the 21st and made good progress against stiff opposition. The two feint attacks achieved their object, deceiving the enemy sufficiently to cause him to bring up reserves to the threatened sectors and to distract his attention from the preparations for the main attack. Owing to un-expectedly severe opposition, however, the sortie progressed more slowly and proved more costly in men and tanks than we had anticipated. The junction between the Bologna and Pavia Divisions had been selected as the best point to attack; but, in the interval between the maturing of the plan and its execution, the Afrika Division had been moved into precisely that sector for the projected enemy assault on Tobruk. Owing to the prevalence of trench warfare conditions an elaborate plan had had to be prepared from which it was impossible to depart at short notice.

In the event the delay was of no consequence. For General Norrie considered that, since the 5th South African Infantry Brigade had still not arrived and as the Support Group was hard put to it even to retain its hold on Sidi Rezegh, the 70th Division on Ed Duda would be exposed to needless peril. He therefore postponed the final phase of the operation.

Desultory fighting broke out again on the aerodrome during the morning of the 22nd November, and in the afternoon developed into a pitched battle in which the enemy employed at least a hundred tanks, besides large numbers of anti-tank guns and infantry. On our side, in addition to the wearied Support Group and 7th Armoured Brigade, all three regiments of the 22nd Armoured Brigade and two of the 4th Armoured Brigade were involved. The fog of war literally descended on the battlefield, for the clouds of dust and smoke raised by tanks and bursting shells made accurate shooting impossible, and at times it was difficult to tell friend from foe. At the conclusion of the battle, which raged until after dark, our armoured brigades were finally driven off the aerodrome. At the same time the Support Group, attacked in overwhelming strength, was compelled to abandon Sidi Rezegh which it had defended for three days against great odds and to retire to the southern escarpment, where it leaguered to the north of the armoured brigades.

The 5th South African Infantry Brigade had arrived during the morning and had been ordered to capture Point 178 on the southern escarpment which overlooked the western end of the valley, where the enemy was assembling to attack the aerodrome. Although they strove with determination to gain their objective, they fell short of it and finally received orders to abandon the attempt. The brigade then retired to leaguer to the west of the Support Group. The enemy lost no time in pressing their advantage, striking two crippling blows in swift succession. A surprise night attack chanced on the headquarters of the 4th Armoured Brigade, and most of its wireless links were captured. For the next twenty-four hours that brigade, which, with its hundred tanks, was the only substantial armoured force we had left, ceased to be a fighting entity. The Germans, on the other hand, still had a number of tanks in running order and could recover others from the battlefield. Moreover, the Ariete Division had not been seriously engaged since the 19th November and must have had about eighty tanks. To these the 22nd Armoured Brigade could oppose about forty-five and the 7th Armoured Brigade only ten. Consequently, when the enemy attacked the 5th South African Infantry Brigade with over a hundred tanks and a large force of lorried infantry in the afternoon of the 23rd, the 22nd Armoured Brigade was hopelessly outnumbered. The South Africans resisted gallantly, but the German attack was by all accounts well conceived and brilliantly executed; and the 5th South African Infantry Brigade was practically destroyed.

After these reverses, General Norrie decided to rally the armoured brigades in a central position north of the Trigh el Abd while the 1st South African Infantry Brigade retired to Taieb el Essem to watch the western flank.

### The Advance of the 13th Corps.

On the 21st November, thinking like everybody else that the enemy's armoured forces had been or were being neutralised by ours, General Cunningham gave the order for the 13th Corps to begin operations; and I agreed with this decision.

A detachment of the 7th Indian Infantry Brigade had already occupied the high ground overlooking the Omars from the west, and the New Zealand Division had moved up in readiness for the advance. When the word was given the New Zealand Division moved forward and gained control of the country to the west of the enemy's line of fortresses up to the outskirts of Bardia. Capuzzo, Musaid and Sollum Barracks were occupied with little trouble.

At the same time the 7th Indian Infantry Brigade took Sidi Omar in the rear and captured two of its defended localities. It was not until several days later, however, that the area was finally cleared by the capture of Libyan Omar.

The 6th New Zealand Infantry Brigade moved straight on westwards along the Trigh Capuzzo, capturing the headquarters of the Afrika Korps on the way. On the 23rd November they stormed Point 175 on the ridge only five miles west of Sidi Rezegh. This occurred a few hours before the mishap to the 5th South African Infantry Brigade. Indeed one of the New Zealand battalions, instructed to make contact with the 30th Corps, arrived just east of the South African leaguer when some of the enemy tanks which had overrun it were emerging.

Fortunately the battalion was able to beat them off and returned safely to its brigade when the 30th Corps retired.

Leaving the 5th New Zealand Infantry Brigade to watch the enemy in Bardia and Halfaya, General Freyberg moved westwards with the remainder of the division on the 23rd November. Having captured Gambut aerodrome the same afternoon, they joined the 6th Brigade at Point 175 on the 24th November.

### Change in Command.

It was on the 23rd November that I heard that the optimistic earlier reports of the damage inflicted on the enemy's armoured forces were not borne out by the latest news. In response to an urgent request from General Cunningham I flew to his advanced headquarters near Maddalena, accompanied by Air Chief Marshal Tedder. Further news had come in by the time we arrived, and I learned of the disorganisation of the 4th Armoured Brigade and of the disaster which had overtaken the 5th South African Infantry Brigade.

General Cunningham was perturbed by the general situation which he considered to be critical owing to the small number of tanks in running order he had left. Five days' heavy fighting and constant movement had resulted in many tanks being destroyed or immobilised either by enemy action or on account of mechanical breakdown. Enemy loses, on the other hand, had been over-estimated. The enemy's facilities for tank recovery were far better than our own, and, being left in possession of the principal battlefield, he was able to repair many tanks previously reported as having been destroyed. Our initial numerical superiority had now disappeared, and it seemed as if we could hope to have, at best, only as many tanks as the enemy. This was a serious state of affairs, particularly since the German tanks were superior to ours in fighting qualities, though this was not true of the Italian tanks. Excluding those of infantry pattern which were too slow to take part in battle against enemy armoured forces, we appeared to dispose of about a hundred tanks, of which a large proportion were American light tanks against about the same number of enemy tanks of which about fifty might be German.

General Cunningham felt it was his duty to point out to me that, if he continued to attack the enemy as he had been doing since the 19th November, we might find ourselves for the time being without any serviceable tanks at all. He considered we now had to choose between two courses; continuing the offensive and risking the possibility of being left with no tanks or very few, while the enemy still retained some, possibly more efficient than ours; or abandoning the offensive. The risks attendant on persisting in the offensive were not negligible, since, should this result in the enemy retaining a appreciable superiority in tanks, the safety of Egypt might once more be endangered.

I was in no doubt myself at any time as to the right course, and at once instructed General Cunningham to continue his offensive with the object of recapturing Sidi Rezegh and joining hands with the Tobruk garrison.[21] It looked as if the enemy was hard pressed and stretched to the limit, and this was borne out by his behaviour at this period of the battle: he was thrusting here, there and everywhere in what seemed to me a desperate effort to throw us off our balance, create chaos in our ranks, and so pave the way for regaining the initiative. The enemy, it is true, had temporarily succeeded in seizing the local tactical initiative, but the strategical initiative remained with us: we were attacking, he was defending. This general initiative it was at all costs essential to retain.

General Cunningham received my decision loyally and at once issued his orders to give effect to it. I was, however, somewhat disturbed by what seemed to be excessive anxiety on his part lest the enemy should break through in force to our rear areas, and dislocate our vulnerable supply and repair organisation east of the frontier. His anxiety undoubtedly grew when the enemy swiftly followed up his recent success by a powerful counter-stroke with that very intention, thrusting eastwards on the 24th November with his armoured divisions to the frontier and beyond. I thought, however, that, after discussing the situation with me and hearing that I was determined to continue the offensive, he would feel himself capable of giving effect to my decision whole heartedly. I therefore returned to Cairo on 25th November.

While at the headquarters of the Eighth Army, I had discussed the situation exhaustively with Air Marshal Tedder and found that he too had grave misgivings about the direction of the Eighth Army in the circumstances then obtaining. After returning to Cairo, I again gave the whole question most anxious consideration and concluded that in so critical a situation, I could not retain in the field a commander in whose ability to carry out my intentions I had not complete confidence.

I therefore decided with great reluctance that I must replace General Cunningham. I selected my Deputy Chief of the General Staff, Major-General N.M. Ritchie, as the best officer available on the spot to succeed him, and ordered him to take over command at once with the acting rank of Lieutenant-General. I informed the Minister of State in Cairo and the Chief of the Imperial General Staff in London of my decision and asked for the approval of His Majesty's Government, which was immediately accorded. Throughout this critical time, and indeed at all times, until he went to England in March to take up a command, I received the greatest possible help and support from my Chief of the General Staff, Lieutenant-General Sir Arthur Smith.

### The Enemy's Counterstroke.

When General Ritchie assumed command on the 26th November the force of the enemy's counterstroke was by no means spent. Showing great boldness and vigour, the enemy had driven eastwards on the 24th November with the greater part of his remaining tanks and lorried infantry, causing considerable havoc in our rearward areas amongst transport and headquarters.

The Support Group engaged one enemy column near Gabr Saleh, and the 1st South African Infantry Brigade shelled others passing within range of their leaguer at Taieb el Essem. The 7th Armoured Brigade with only ten tanks kept up a running fight with yet another column containing more than twice that number over a distance of thirty miles. The 4th and 22nd Armoured Brigades had to be posted to guard the flank of the New Zealand Division and were not available to engage the enemy.

The enemy tanks crossed the frontier wire at several points, and by the 25th November parties of the enemy were scattered all over the country east of it. Twice, enemy tanks attacked the 4th Indian Division at Sidi Omar; but thanks to the staunchness and restraint of the artillery and to the skilful dispositions of General Messervy, they were driven off with heavy loss. Nevertheless the enemy captured many prisoners and reached a point nineteen miles east of Sidi Omar and within fifty miles of our railhead. They also created a stir in the advanced headquarters of the Eighth Army near Maddalena by moving southwards along the frontier wire towards it. On the 26th November the enemy tanks turned north into Halfaya. Then, after an unsuccessful attack on Capuzzo and Musaid, they passed through a gap east of Sollum Barracks, which the New Zealanders had previously tried in vain to close, and entered Bardia, where they were joined by other columns from the south-east.

Part of the enemy's armoured forces did not cross the frontier, but remained to the west to do such damage as they could. The Support Group and the Guards Brigade rapidly formed mobile columns and harassed them very effectively.

On the 27th November enemy tanks, based on Bardia, captured the head-quarters of the 5th New Zealand Infantry Brigade at Sidi Azeiz. Then, after two further attacks on Capuzzo, one of which was comparatively successful, the enemy armoured forces disappeared from the frontier area. By this time most of them were already hurrying back to Sidi Rezegh in response to insistent calls for help.

On the whole the enemy thrust inflicted little material damage, and the moral effect was almost negligible as the transport and other units, which were scattered by his lightning advance, soon re-assembled and reorganised themselves. Inasmuch as the New Zealand Division was able to fight through to Tobruk, which they might never have been able to do if the weight of the enemy armour had been thrown into the scale against them, the advantage rested with us. Moreover the enemy spent much of his strength and used up most of his reserves in this desperate counterstroke. But it might have succeeded, had the 4th Indian Division shown less determination and the mobile columns less offensive spirit, or had the Royal Air Force not bombed the enemy's principal concentrations so relentlessly. Nevertheless the attempt came as a rude shock, and it was with relief that I heard on the 27th November that the enemy was on his way back towards Tobruk.

### The Battle of Sidi Rezegh – Second Phase.

The enemy's thrust failed in its main object of wresting from us the initiative; for, while it was in progress, the New Zealand Division and the Tobruk garrison were making fresh gains in the vital area of Sidi Rezegh, fifty miles to the westward. From Point 175 the 4th New Zealand Brigade struck north and took Zafraan without great difficulty at dawn on the 25th November. The same night by a skilfully planned bayonet attack they captured Belhamed. Simultaneously the 6th Brigade advanced along the ridge from Point 175 towards Sidi Rezegh. They met stiffer opposition, but by the morning of the 25th they had drawn level with the 4th Brigade on the ridge itself and on the eastern edge of the landing ground. Then the 6th Brigade made to capture Sidi Rezegh to conform with the 4th Brigade's attack on Belhamed. Although they pressed the attack with great determination and made considerable progress, they failed to dislodge the enemy from the high ground above the mosque at Sidi Rezegh. The following night, despite the heavy losses they had suffered, they reorganised and in a final spirited effort reduced this last enemy strongpoint.

At midday on the 26th November, the Tobruk garrison opened the long-deferred final phase of its sortie. By dusk they had captured Ed Duda in the face of determined resistance. That night saw the first contact between Tobruk and the Eighth Army, when General Freyberg moved his reserve battalion by the south of Belhamed to join the infantry consolidating on Ed Duda.

It remained to clear the enemy still holding out in the valley, who had closed in after the New Zealand battalion had passed through to Ed Duda. This was undertaken on the 28th November. With the help of tanks and armoured cars New Zealand infantry swept the valley taking numerous prisoners and much booty, while the 70th Division dislodged parties of the enemy from the edge of the escarpment between Ed Duda and Belhamed. The corridor now offered a safe passage, and the 13th Corps Headquarters and the administrative echelon of the New Zealand Division were able to move into Tobruk. At the same time a supply convoy from Tobruk reached the division, which by then had run very short of supplies and ammunition. Next day another convoy arrived from the 30th Corps under tank escort.

The enemy reacted immediately to the capture of Ed Duda, Belhamed and Sidi Rezegh, and on the 27th November wireless messages for the enemy armoured divisions to return from the frontier were intercepted. Appreciating that the New Zealand Division, which had gone forward without its third Brigade and which had suffered serious losses, would need help, General Ritchie ordered the 1st South African Infantry Brigade to join the 13th Corps.

The Panzer Divisions began to return immediately and by the afternoon of the 28th, a heavy assault on the positions held by the 13th Corps was clearly impending. The 7th Armoured Division, which had been reorganised and now consisted of the Support Group and the 4th and 22nd Armoured Brigades with a hundred and twenty tanks altogether, attacked the Panzer Divisions several times on their way back; but, far from doing the enemy sufficient damage to deter him from attacking the 13th Corps, they themselves suffered heavy losses which left them powerless to intervene effectively to save the infantry next day. Our armoured brigades could not prevail against an enemy possessing, in all probability, an equal number of tanks, better armoured and mounting better guns.

On the 29th November violent assaults began on both flanks of the corridor. After several heavy, but unsuccessful attacks on Ed Duda, the enemy at length penetrated between Ed Duda and Belhamed, and secured a foothold on the crest of the position. The garrison launched a counter-attack, and by daybreak the whole position was once more in our hands. Meanwhile the enemy succeeded in making a permanent breach on the southern flank. The New Zealand troops holding Point 175 drove off two attacks in the morning, but eventually fell victims to a ruse, mistaking German tanks for the advanced guard of the South African Brigade. Next day the enemy captured the rest of Sidi Rezegh Ridge. During the afternoon of the 30th November the 6th New Zealand Brigade, reduced to barely one-third of its fighting strength and with only two support tanks left, was assailed by fifty tanks from the west and large numbers of infantry from the south, and after a gallant resistance was overwhelmed. Although reinforcements were received during the night so that they now numbered a hundred and twenty again, our tanks could not go to the assistance of the New Zealanders. The enemy had shielded his eastern flank with anti-tank artillery; and, if our tanks, which had been concentrated into one brigade under Brigadier Gatehouse, had attempted either to penetrate the enemy screen or to outflank it, they would have become too deeply committed to attend to the task which had been assigned to them, that of covering the advance of the 1st South African Infantry Brigade.

Had the 1st South African Infantry Brigade arrived at the time it was expected on the morning of the 29th November, its presence might have turned the scale, and our armour might have been freed to intervene at Sidi Rezegh. But there were several reasons why it was delayed. The 1st South African Division was new to the desert, and its training in desert movement had been cut short. The advance of its 1st Brigade was hampered, therefore, by the large number of vehicles it had to marshal and control. The brigade had frequently to halt, change direction and start again, and the general pace of its movement was slow. It was still some twelve miles south of Point 175 on the 28th November when the 30th Corps Commander halted it on receipt of a message purporting to come from the 13th Corps. Although his communications with the 13th Corps had broken down, General Ritchie well knew that its situation was critical and ordered the brigade to move forward when he heard that it had halted. It broke leaguer at night and moved on. By the evening of the 29th, Point 175 was in sight when Brigadier Pienaar found that his rendezvous was strongly held by the enemy. The wireless set of a South African armoured car which had reached General Freyberg's headquarters broke down at the crucial moment, and

Brigadier Pienaar postponed further advance until daylight when he could see what was happening. By midday on the 30th November wireless touch with the New Zealand Division was restored, and General Norrie, who had stayed with the South Africans, arranged with General Freyberg for them to attack Point 175 from the east. The advance proceeded slowly and there was a long pause when the brigade reached the escarpment east of Point 175. Finally a moonlight attack was staged. But the position was strong and well supported by tanks, so that at dawn on the 1st December the South Africans were still 3,000 yards short of their objective, and spent the whole day attempting to take the position.

Belhamed fell early on the 1st December before a heavy attack launched by enemy tanks and infantry from Sidi Rezegh. The 4th Armoured Brigade rushed from its leaguer some miles south of Point 175, but arrived in time only to cover the retirement of the New Zealand Division to Zafraan.

As the New Zealand Division had had extremely heavy casualties and was now in danger of becoming entirely cut off, General Norrie gave the order for them to withdraw. Having repulsed further attacks on Zafraan during the day, they withdrew during the night with the survivors of the 1st Army Tank Brigade, the partner of their successes, and reached the frontier in the early hours of the 2nd December, exhausted but in good heart. At the same time the 1st South African Infantry Brigade was ordered to abandon the attempt to recapture Point 175. During the night they retired southwards to Taieb el Essem, leaving a rearguard to mask Point 175 until the New Zealanders had passed in safety.

Tobruk was once more isolated, with a greater commitment than before and smaller resources. The length of front to be held had been increased from twenty-seven miles to forty-four. Two New Zealand battalions had been cut off from their division on Ed Duda, but this hardly offset the heavy losses the garrison had suffered. The tank strength was now only twenty runners. It is not to be wondered at that the Corps Commander should have asked leave, if need be, to withdraw to the original perimeter. General Ritchie gave his permission, but pointed out that the garrison would make a valuable contribution to the success of the offensive if they could hold the salient. It reflects high credit on the garrison that the Fortress Commander could decline the idea and that they, far from yielding any ground, were ready within a short time to carry out a further advance.

### *Preparations for Attacking El Adem.*

Judging that the issue of the battle for Tobruk still lay in the balance and wishing to be at hand in case a decision should be required of me as Commander-in-Chief, on the 1st December I flew to join General Ritchie at his advanced headquarters near Maddalena. I remained there for the next ten days, but naturally left the direction of the Eighth Army entirely in General Ritchie's hands.

General Ritchie was already making plans for restoring the momentum of the offensive, undeterred by the loss of the positions which the New Zealand Division so gallantly won and defended, or by the renewed isolation of Tobruk.

On the day I arrived he visited by air the headquarters of the 13th Corps in Tobruk, and also the headquarters of the 30th Corps to concert his plans. It was his firm conviction – and I agreed with him – that the enemy was hard pressed and would be defeated if we continued to give him no rest.

The Eighth Army itself had sustained heavy blows and was in need of reinforcement. I had already given instructions for an armoured car regiment from Syria and the 150th Infantry Brigade from Cyprus to move to the Western Desert, and I formed three hitherto unbrigaded Indian battalions into the 38th Indian Infantry Brigade and sent it forward to guard the Eighth Army's rearward communications. The convoy bringing the 1st Armoured Division from the United Kingdom had just arrived, and I arranged for the divisional armoured car regiment to join the Eighth Army at once. The remainder of the division was to move forward by regiments and undergo intensive training just east of the frontier under command of the Eighth Army.

By regrouping his forces General Ritchie was able to release fresh troops. He had already drawn the 11th Indian Infantry Brigade into reserve near Maddalena and furnished it with transport, and he now arranged for the 2nd South African Division to relieve the other two brigades of the 4th Indian Division.

The new organisation of the Eighth Army was as follows:-

30*th Corps.* (Lieutenant-General Norrie.)
   7th Armoured Division.
   4th Armoured Brigade.
   7th Support Group.
   4th Indian Division.
   1st South African Infantry Brigade Group.
   Five armoured car regiments.
13*th Corps.* (Lieutenant-General Godwin-Austin.)
   70th Division.
   32nd Army Tank Brigade.
   Polish Carpathian Brigade Group.
   Polish Carpathian Cavalry.
   18th and 19th New Zealand Infantry Battalions.
   2/13th Australian Infantry Battalion.
   11th Czechoslovak Battalion.
2*nd South African Division.* (Major-General de Villiers.)
   3rd South African Infantry Brigade Group.
   6th South African Infantry Brigade Group.
   5th New Zealand Infantry Brigade Group (attached).
   1st Army Tank Brigade (attached).
*Rear Area.*
   New Zealand Division
      (4th and 6th Brigades).
   38th Indian Infantry Brigade.

5th South African Infantry Brigade.

*Matruh Fortress.*

2nd South African Infantry Brigade Group.

4th South African Infantry Brigade Group.

Plans for continuing the offensive now centred on El Adem, an area which very much resembles that of Sidi Rezegh, in that the main communications between east and west pass through a valley under observation from ridges to north and south. If we could continue to deny the enemy access to Bardia and to his supply dumps west of it, and at the same time sever his communications again by securing El Adem, his tanks would be forced to leave the valley between Sidi Rezegh and Belhamed, where they were protected by a screen of formidable anti-tank guns, and fight in the open. Both corps were to take part in the operation. The 13th Corps was to push forward from Ed Duda along the El Adem ridge as far as the Tobruk - El Adem road, while the infantry of the 30th Corps, having captured the strong point at Bir el Gubi, were to move northwards and secure first the southern ridge, and then the western end of El Adem ridge. Meanwhile the Armoured Division was to stand off to the east ready to engage the enemy tanks when they emerged.

It was inevitable that there should be a short delay on account of the reorganisation which was necessary. The 11th Indian Infantry Brigade and the 1st South African Infantry Brigade were ready, and it was hoped that it might not even be necessary to wait for the whole of the Indian Division to arrive; but General Norrie feared that the operation might miscarry if it were mounted in haste, and the resistance subsequently encountered at Bir el Gubi proved that he was right. Meantime armoured cars were to raid the Acroma area, where one such raid had already proved successful and had drawn much attention from the enemy air forces.

### The Enemy Again Thrusts Eastwards.

While the Eighth Army was getting ready to attack El Adem, the enemy made a final thrust towards the frontier. On the 3rd December two strong fighting patrols set out for Bardia, one taking the coast road, and the other the Trigh Capuzzo. The 5th New Zealand Infantry Brigade opposed the one north-east of Gambut and a detachment of the 5th Indian Infantry Brigade engaged the other near Sidi Azeiz. Both patrols were completely routed and suffered heavy losses. The next day a third and more powerful column, containing about fifty tanks, left the main leaguer at Sidi Rezegh and set off down the Trigh Capuzzo. It was bombed by our aircraft and attacked by the Support Group; and, on encountering troops of the 2nd South African Division, which had just arrived, the column turned back without making any further effort to reach Bardia.

These raids may have been a final effort on the part of the enemy to obtain supplies from Bardia and, perhaps, to rescue some of the troops besieged there. They may also have been intended to provide cover for a heavy assault on the Tobruk salient which was launched at dawn on the 4th December. Troop reliefs had just taken place in the salient preparatory to the attack on El Adem, when heavy shelling broke out heralding a day of attack and counter-attack. Every side of the salient was attacked. The garrison held the enemy off throughout the morning, but in the afternoon heavy anti-tank guns were brought up within close range and smashed a number of the 32nd Army Tank Brigade's few remaining tanks. The enemy made deep inroads into the salient and, although our troops counter-attacked to some purpose, they could not recapture all the posts lost. They were preparing to continue their efforts by night, when it was discovered that the enemy had withdrawn.

Under cover of this fighting, the Bologna Division began a disorderly evacuation of the eastern sector of the siege lines, and the retreat went on through the night. The Germans attached to the division and some of the Italian officers seized what vehicles there were, leaving most of the rank and file to walk; many of them preferred to give themselves up. The next day the Afrika Korps and the Italian Mobile Corps, which had concentrated round Sidi Rezegh, began to withdraw. Well covered by artillery sited on the southern escarpment, they fell back in good order to the new line running from El Adem to Bir el Gubi which General Rommel had decided to occupy.

*The End of the Siege of Tobruk.*

The Eighth Army embarked on the second stage of the offensive at dawn on the 4th December. Reconnaissance had shown Bir el Gubi to be more strongly held than we had first supposed, and, in order to avoid the risk of the timing of the main operation being upset General Norrie decided to capture it by a separate preliminary operation. The defence of Bir el Gubi turned out to be surprisingly stubborn. The enemy were well entrenched, strongly supported by field and anti-tank guns and some tanks, and the Italian garrison was full of determination. The 11th Indian Infantry Brigade fought courageously, but at the end of two days they had been driven off the few positions they had been able to capture. Having lost nearly a third of their strength, they were ordered to withdraw. They had great difficulty in disengaging, but eventually managed to retire through the Guards Brigade, which had taken up a position to the south-west.

While the 11th Indian Infantry Brigade were trying to reduce Bir el Gubi, a light column from the 1st South African Brigade carried out a particularly valuable raid in rear of the enemy. They located a large enemy dump of supplies about fifteen miles north-west of Bir el Gubi and destroyed fifty thousand gallons of petrol and ten thousand gallons of diesel oil.

It was the general belief that the enemy was playing for time and intended to withdraw further, and General Ritchie was anxious for the attack on El Adem to begin as soon as possible. The numerous moves taking place in the frontier area called for a nice adjustment of transport, and difficulties had arisen over the provision of vehicles to lift the 7th Indian Infantry Brigade. But by the 5th December the 4th Indian Infantry Division was assembling, and General Norrie intended to start the operation on the evening of the 6th December. During the morning of the 6th, however, General Norrie heard that the two German Panzer Divisions were lying on the rising ground north-west of Bir el Gubi, astride the Indian Division's intended line of advance.

The time was clearly not yet ripe for the infantry brigades to move forward, and General Norrie ordered them to take up positions to the south of Bir el Gubi, while the Armoured Brigade sought out the enemy's armoured forces. These were very elusive: apart from two brief appearances in the morning when small parties of enemy tanks were engaged north-east and south-east of Bir el Gubi, they were seen no more until the afternoon, when they appeared to be forming up to attack the Guards Brigade west of Bir el Gubi. The artillery of the Guards Brigade opened fire, and after a short while the enemy moved away. It was discovered later that General Neumann-Silkow, commander of the 15th Panzer Division, was mortally wounded by a shell which may explain why the attack never developed. It is more likely that the enemy intercepted a wireless call to the Armoured Brigade, and had orders not to allow themselves to be dragged into an engagement with a force of tanks now manifestly superior in numbers.

The Support Group had for some days been ranging the country from Bir el Gubi almost to Sidi Azeiz, and every day had brought its toll of enemy vehicles. On the 6th December the Support Group achieved a notable success against an enemy rearguard consisting of five hundred vehicles and twenty-five light tanks east of Sidi Rezegh. All the tanks were destroyed, as well as a battery of medium guns and many of the vehicles. Thereafter the Support Group rejoined the 7th Armoured Division.

The Armoured Brigade spent the 7th December attacking enemy tanks protecting Bir el Gubi and proved unable to outflank or dislodge them, though it claimed to have done them much damage. Although the enemy was hitting out with great vigour, General Ritchie was positive that he was doing so only to cover the preparation of new positions in rear and decided to wait no longer. He therefore ordered the 13th Corps to proceed with their part in the operation against El Adem. Some two hours after dark on the 7th December the 23rd Infantry Brigade began their advance along Ed Duda ridge. By daybreak they had captured an enemy position on the ridge within 2,000 yards of the Tobruk - El Adem road and by evening the whole of the enemy fortifications south-east of Tobruk had been cleared.

The advance of the 13th Corps came not a moment too soon, for on the 8th December the enemy began a rapid but orderly withdrawal to Gazala. As soon as reports of the withdrawal were received, the Armoured Brigade was directed to advance on Knightsbridge in the hope that this would bring them round or against the enemy's western flank. In fact it brought them against the centre of the position the enemy rearguard had taken up astride Genadel ridge. The customary powerful screen of anti-tank guns was produced, and the enemy tanks took cover and fired from hull-down positions when engaged. Repeated attempts to turn the position on either flank were unsuccessful, and when evening came the enemy were still holding the ridge. The early hours of the 9th December brought indications that the withdrawal was continuing. The Armoured Brigade proceeded along the same axis, and came up against a rearguard position running north-east from Bir Harmat covering Knightsbridge. They engaged, this time with more success, twice forcing the enemy to give ground. In the evening they attacked and halted a party of twenty enemy tanks trying to break back and inter-fere with our infantry who by then had occupied El Adem. During the night the enemy retired once more, but the Armoured Brigade could not give chase as the supply system of the 30th Corps had been stretched to the limit.

Although the progress of our armour was first retarded by the enemy rear-guards and finally brought to a standstill by lack of petrol, the momentum of the advance was kept up by columns of the Support Group and the 4th Indian Division. The former were themselves temporarily held up by a strong enemy position at Hagfet en Nezha, until the 30th Corps ordered the 1st South African Infantry Brigade to relieve them. The Support Group then moved round by way of Acroma and on the 10th December was in contact with the outposts of the enemy's new line running southwards from Gazala. The 7th Indian Infantry Brigade struck northwards and made contact with the 23rd Infantry Brigade at El Adem on the evening of the 9th. The 5th Indian Infantry Brigade drew level fifteen miles further west, while on the western flank the Indian divisional motor-ised cavalry, reinforced by infantry, engaged the left flank of the enemy rearguard resting on Bir Harmat, and secured Hagaig er Raml.

The 13th Corps, working westwards round the perimeter of Tobruk, con-tinued to roll up the enemy by the same method of making an outflanking move-ment along the ridge and then clearing the positions in the intervening low ground. On the 10th December both corps carried out a concerted movement against Acroma. The Polish Brigade broke out before dawn along the Derna road; the Polish Cavalry then passed through and, after a successful engagement with enemy rearguards, turned southwards. The 16th Infantry Brigade approached from the south-east and entered Acroma to find it had already been occupied by the 7th Indian Infantry Brigade. The 5th Indian Infantry Brigade came up into line further west, securing the western end of Acroma ridge and all but a small part of another eminence five miles to the west. Thus the eight months siege of Tobruk came to an end.

During the period of the siege, the task of maintaining supplies to the garrison was carried out entirely by the Royal Navy and the Merchant Navy. Between them they transported 72 tanks, 92 guns and 34,000 tons of stores, replaced 32,667 men of the garrison by 34,113 fresh troops and withdrew 7,516 wounded and 7,097 prisoners of war. The cost to the Navy amounted to 25 ships sunk and 9 seriously damaged, and to the Merchant Navy of 5 ships sunk and 4 seri-ously damaged, a total casualty list of 43 ships.

Some of the units forming the garrison of the fortress and the greater part of the administrative and base personnel had been through the whole siege, which began early in April. The remainder, comprising the 70th Division, the Polish Carpathian Brigade Group and Cavalry and a heavy tank battalion had taken over the defence of the fortress in the late summer. The new garrison under Major-General Scobie was most active in harassing the besiegers by ceaseless patrolling and numerous minor enterprises. The part they played in the Eighth Army's offensive has already been described, and there is no doubt that the task allotted to them proved much more exacting than had been anticipated. Their unyielding determination to hold the salient they had created, in the face of the heaviest and most determined attacks, contributed greatly to General Ritchie's eventual victory.

### The Enemy's Stand at Gazala.

The enemy's withdrawal from the neighbourhood of Tobruk marked the beginning of a third stage in the offensive. Had the Eighth Army been able to launch the attack on El Adem, it was anticipated that future operations would fall into two distinct phases, a short period of attack followed by the clearing of the Tobruk area, and then pursuit. But the enemy's orderly retirement, which the 13th Corps, though well placed, was unable to disrupt owing to lack of reserves, allowed him to extricate the Italian divisions besieging the western face of the fortress without serious casualties, and to develop and occupy a line running south from Gazala in some strength. Defeating the enemy now resolved itself into a matter not of clearing the country round Tobruk and then pursuing the remnants of a shattered army, but of dislodging a beaten but still organised force from an entrenched position resolutely held, and of preventing its escape.

So far, the maintenance of the Army had presented some hard problems, but it had been possible to solve them; henceforward, it became increasingly difficult and began seriously to limit the size of the force that could be kept in contact with the enemy. For the moment there was a short check in the pursuit, as the 30th Corps had outrun its supplies. But the plans had been well laid, and the order had gone out for the first convoy taking stores for the development of the port to sail to Tobruk as soon as the 70th and New Zealand Divisions joined hands at Ed Duda. Work on the port had begun, and there were reserves sufficient to tide the Eighth Army over the period until regular supply by sea could be instituted. There was therefore a minimum of delay in changing the supply base from desert railhead to Tobruk, and our main forces were able to take up the pursuit, twenty-four hours after they had called a halt.

General Ritchie had decided to entrust the conduct of the pursuit to the headquarters of the 13th Corps and to send the headquarters of the 30th Corps back to direct operations on the frontier. The chief reasons for this decision were that one headquarters would suffice to control the operations of the limited forces which could be maintained forward; and that the 13th Corps, being already in Tobruk whence the advance was to be supplied, was conveniently placed to assume control at once. Accordingly on the 12th December General Norrie moved back to the frontier, with orders to eliminate the isolated enemy garrisons with the least delay, so that direct road and, eventually, rail comunication might be established. This was a matter of considerable importance as it was known that supplies by sea would have to be supplemented from railhead, and the long detour by the desert was absorbing much transport urgently needed for the subsequent stages of the advance. The 1st South African Infantry Brigade was to follow as soon as the 13th Corps could spare it.

Shortly after midday on the 11th the 13th Corps began its advance. The 5th New Zealand Infantry Brigade, which General Ritchie had ordered to join the 13th Corps, moved astride the coastal escarpment, its left flank protected by the 32nd Army Tank Brigade, and masked Gazala where the enemy had developed strong positions. The 4th Indian Division was directed south of Gazala on Tmimi and Bir Halegh el Eleba. The principal task of the 7th Armoured Division (4th Armoured Brigade and 7th Support Group) was to protect the left flank of the Indian Division, but it was also to send columns and armoured cars to raid the enemy communications near Tmimi and to patrol towards Mechili. The movements of the 4th Armoured Brigade continued to be restricted by supply difficulties until the morning of the 13th December. The 22nd Guards Motor Brigade was placed under command of the Armoured Division and held in reserve near Knightsbridge. The 70th Division was left in Tobruk to round up scattered parties of the enemy lurking in the deep coastal *wadis*.

The New Zealand Brigade and the Indian Division came up against the enemy positions on the evening of the 11th December, and by the 12th it was clear that the enemy was firmly established on a defensive line running southwest from Gazala to the Trigh el Abd. A strong well-prepared position straddling the escarpment to the east of the Gazala inlet was occupied in strength by Italians, and another prepared position on the ridge at Alem Hamza was also held by Italians. From Alem Hamza the line ran due south and then turned west along the Trigh el Abd; this sector was not so well prepared or so strongly manned, but the superior fighting qualities of the German defenders and the superiority of German heavy anti-tank guns made it formidable. What remained of the German and Italian armoured formations were held in rear.

The 13th Corps began to attack this line on the 13th December. In the north the 5th New Zealand Infantry Brigade, which had already captured an important locality on the coast overlooking Gazala, could make no progress. In the centre the 5th Indian Infantry Brigade attempted to capture the Alem Hamza position and was repulsed, but later one battalion occupied a position to the south-west without opposition. The 7th Indian Infantry Brigade were forming up to attack further south when they were themselves attacked by tanks. After a sharp encounter the enemy was beaten off with heavy loss, but no new ground was captured.

Meanwhile the Support Group, reinforced by an armoured regiment, succeeded in making the enemy fall back on the southern flank, although the armoured regiment lost one-third of its tanks in an action fought to the rear of the enemy positions.

Realising that practically all that remained of the German and Italian formations were facing the Eighth Army at Gazala, General Ritchie instructed General

Godwin-Austen to use his armoured brigade with the utmost boldness to strike a decisive blow. Accordingly the 4th Armoured Brigade, covered by the Support Group, was ordered to move wide round the enemy's southern flank. The 5th New Zealand Infantry Brigade and the Polish Brigade Group, which General Godwin-Austen had already drawn into reserve, were then to capture the Gazala position, while the 4th Indian Division, assisted by the 32nd Army Tank Brigade, attacked Alem Hamza.

The combined attack in the north started late, but went well. Only makeshift transport could be provided for the Polish Brigade which was late on the starting line as a result. But when the attack did begin, it was executed with great spirit and between them the New Zealanders and Poles captured half the position and took many prisoners. The Indian Division was by no means so fortunate. The 5th Brigade continued to be held up in its frontal attack on Alem Hamza, so the 7th Brigade was ordered to work round to the west of the enemy locality. It had begun to move forward when a battalion of the 5th Brigade, which had occupied a position to the south-west of Alem Hamza two days before and was somewhat isolated there, was heavily attacked and finally overrun. Although only a hundred of the infantry and one battery of the supporting field regiment survived, the defenders offered a sturdy resistance, for the German regiment which had carried out the assault was heard to report that it was unable to exploit its success.

Extremely bad going over the last twenty-five miles of its sixty-mile march retarded the 4th Armoured Brigade which reached its objective four hours late. But it is doubtful whether the brigade would have assisted the progress of the 4th Indian Division, even if it had arrived punctually, since it was not until after daybreak on the 16th that the enemy seems to have become aware of its presence. Decisive results were hoped for from the action of the 4th Armoured Brigade on the 16th December, but these hopes were frustrated by the extreme roughness of the country it had to traverse. As its supply vehicles could scarcely move in the soft sand, the brigade had to go south to replenish, and this operation was not completed until about midday. Brigadier Gatehouse then took his brigade further east than his original objective, towards Sidi Breghisc and Bir Temrad where enemy concentrations were reported to be lying. Although they were still hampered by bad going, our tanks caused considerable damage and much confusion among the enemy in the heavy fighting which followed.

The 4th Indian Division had to reorganise before it could resume its attack and consequently made no progress on the 16th December. The New Zealanders and the Poles, on the other hand, continued to exploit their success taking numerous prisoners.

Rommel now decided not to risk destruction by staying and ordered a further retreat. The withdrawal began, apparently, at about midday on the 16th December and was continued throughout the night. Fearing this development, General Ritchie had already ordered a column of the Support Group to be sent to hold the cross roads at Carmusa which would make it difficult, if not impossible, for the enemy to hold Derna. This column left in the early hours of the 17th December and occupied Carmusa at about midday on the 18th. A far more substantial success might have been scored, however, if we had been able to cut the main road further east. The 7th Armoured Division seemed to be in a position to do this with armoured cars, mobile columns and even the 4th Armoured Brigade, all of which were operating to the west of Gazala. But the difficult country to the south, which made the movement of supply columns slow and on occasion impossible, prevented it. The Eighth Army now devoted all its energies to carrying out a relentless pursuit.

### *The pursuit to Agedabia.*

The enemy divided in his retreat, the remnants of the armoured divisions and the Italian Mobile Corps going by the desert through Mechili and Msus, and the Italian 21st Corps in a very shattered state, by the main roads through the Gebel Akhdar. The troops of the 13th Corps were likewise divided, the 4th Indian Division being sent by the Gebel Akhdar and the 7th Armoured Division by the desert.

The 4th Indian Division set out at once on the morning of the 17th December. The 7th Infantry Brigade on the southern flank travelled at great speed, and within twenty-four hours reached Carmusa where one of its battalions relieved the Support Group column which had been sent on ahead. Another battalion captured Martuba landing ground, and the third the aerodrome at Derna, where a number of aircraft were destroyed and much transport and many prisoners taken. The 5th Infantry Brigade, originally directed to advance on Martuba by a more northerly route, traversed very rough country all the way and fell behind considerably. As the country round Derna appeared to be falling into our hands without great trouble, the objective of the 5th Brigade was altered, and it was instructed to secure the cross-roads at Giovanni Berta and at Lamluda, so as to cut off any enemy remaining in the Derna region. By making a wide turning movement over country the enemy had believed impassable, the 5th Brigade reached Lamluda on the 19th December and took many prisoners there. Giovanni Berta proved more difficult to capture as the enemy had left a detachment to cover it, but by the evening of the 20th that place, too, was in our hands. Derna was occupied on the 19th December, and by the 21st the 4th Indian Division had overrun the whole of the country east of Appollonia, Cirene, and El Faidia. After offering some resistance, Barce was taken during the afternoon of the 23rd. Bengasi itself was taken by a detachment from the 7th Armoured Division. By December 26th all organised resistance in the Gebel Akhdar had ceased, and the 4th Indian Division became responsible for restoring law and order in the hill country up to Bengasi.

The 7th Indian Infantry Brigade then moved forward to take over the region round Barce and Bengasi with instructions to defend it against attack from the south. The 11th Infantry Brigade having been left behind in Tobruk to make good its losses, only the 5th Infantry Brigade remained to occupy the area betwen Barce and Martuba. The Indian Division then had to give up all but a bare minimum of its transport in order to provide as much as possible for the desert sector, where supply difficulties were already becoming acute. The greater part of its divisional artillery had also to be taken in order to reinforce the rest of the 13th Corps round Agedabia.

The 7th Armoured Division gave chase across the desert and moved with a speed which was remarkable considering the difficulties they encountered. The 17th December had to be spent round Gazala while transport and supplies were assembled for the advance, but the armoured brigade improved the occasion by harrying the enemy's departure. On the 18th the Support Group moved swiftly to Mechili and engaged enemy concentrations to the west of that place. By nightfall practically all the enemy had dispersed westwards. The 4th Armoured Brigade followed and swung south in an attempt to cut off the enemy's retreat. A broad expanse of waterlogged country forced them to make a wide detour which took them over extremely broken ground; their advance was greatly slowed down and they arrived to find the last of the enemy vanishing.

The Armoured Division's supply difficulties now became acute and, until a field maintenance centre had been established, General Gott could employ only the Support Group and two armoured car regiments. He therefore sent one armoured car regiment towards Msus to keep contact with the enemy and another towards Charruba to watch the tracks leading out of the Gebel Akhdar. The Support Group he ordered to advance on Bengasi to repeat the successful manoeuvre of the previous winter by cutting off the retreat of the 21st Italian Corps. Brigadier Renton was ordered to send a column ahead to press on with all speed, and to follow with the main body as soon as it had replenished. The 4th Armoured Brigade had to be withheld at Mechili until sufficient petrol was forthcoming.

While the armoured brigade was at Mechili the headquarters of the 22nd Armoured Brigade, which had been reorganised, took over from that of the 4th Armoured Brigade. The individual regiments had already been relieved, in the course of operations, as and when regiments of the original 22nd Armoured Brigade were re-equipped, for the most part with damaged tanks which had been repaired.

The landing grounds at Mechili were reported safe during the afternoon of the 19th December, and next morning squadrons which had followed close behind our forward troops began to use them. The speed with which aircraft began to operate from landing grounds immediately in rear of our foremost troops helped to compensate for our inability to send large land forces in pursuit of the enemy.

Our hopes of reaching Bengasi in time were soon dashed. The recent rains had been unusually heavy and many parts of the southern slopes of the Gebel Akhdar, which the Support Group had to traverse, were under water. Their own progress was greatly retarded, and that of their supply echelons was rendered even more difficult, with the result that in a short while they were held up for lack of petrol. On the 21st December, therefore, General Gott decided to abandon the attempt and ordered the Support Group to advance on Antelat instead, leaving only a small column to press on to Bengasi.

The maintenance difficulties which the 13th Corps encountered did not come as a surprise. It had been appreciated when the operation was being planned that the difficulties of supply would increase enormously in Western Cyrenaica, and it was for that reason that I had been so anxious to destroy the enemy as far east as possible. Now we had to accept the fact that the size of the forces employed in pursuit would be very much restricted, until the port of Bengasi could be developed and brought into use. Meanwhile we should have to resort to every shift and device to overcome the handicap.

The Oases Force under Brigadier Reid had captured Gialo on the 24th November and squadrons of aircraft based on the landing ground in the Oasis had been attacking enemy supply lines and communications ever since. The Oases Force had fulfilled its mission admirably, but it was not of a size to meet the enemy forces which were now fleeing from the Gebel Akhdar and across the desert. Realising the inability of the weak Oases Force even to impede the enemy's retreat, General Ritchie had sent the Guards Brigade Group with supporting air squadrons straight to Antelat. He had hoped to be able to despatch them some time before the enemy broke at Gazala; but the acute shortage of supply vehicles and the unexpectedly strong resistance encountered at Gazala had compelled him to postpone their departure until the 20th December.

When the Guards Brigade reached Antelat on the 22nd December, they found a hostile force including thirty tanks lying around Beda Fomm, covering the Axis withdrawal down the coastal road. One of its battalions, which occupied Antelat, was driven out again on the 23rd by a strong detachment of this force. By that time the Support Group had reached this neighbourhood and had been sent north-westwards to interfere with whatever the enemy had in hand at Carcura, off which seven ships were lying. When the news reached him that the Guards Brigade had been attacked at Antelat, General Gott ordered the Support Group to turn about and move at once to their assistance. At the sight of both brigades assembled to attack him the enemy withdrew from Antelat towards Agedabia. The pursuit of this force would have been an excellent task for the armoured regiment which had arrived during the morning, but after a brief engagement with enemy tanks it had no fuel left with which to give chase.

While the 13th Corps was struggling to overcome its maintenance troubles, the enemy completed the evacuation of Bengasi. Our armoured cars, ordered to reconnoitre up to the coastal road south of Bengasi on the 22nd December, had found the passes down the escarpment at Sidi Brahim, Sceleidima and to the south held by enemy detachments. But on the 24th a squadron of armoured cars, entering Bengasi by the road from El Abiar, found the town evacuated and the harbour empty.

An enemy flankguard remained round Beda Fomm and to the west of Antelat during the next two days. Columns from the Guards Brigade made several attempts to dislodge them, but the enemy was strong in artillery and the brigade could make little headway. Meanwhile the Support Group finished clearing the coastal area further north. On the 26th December the last of the enemy, harassed as they went by columns from the Guards Brigade, retired to Agedabia.

### Operations round Agedabia.

For the next ten days the 13th Corps was held up at Agedabia, where the enemy had left a considerable force to cover his preparation of positions in the marshes round El Agheila. The country round Agedabia is well suited to defence, and the enemy exploited its natural advantages with admirable skill. The strip of land between the main road and the coast is swampy, and soft sand dunes make the few dry patches practically impassable for vehicles. The ground to the east and south is also covered with soft sand and is bounded by the Wadi Faregh, which, runs in a south-westerly direction from Giof el Matar to the Ageheila marshes and is a formidable natural barrier. Apart from a wide outflanking movement to the south-east of the Wadi Faregh, which it was far beyond the capacity of the 13th Corps to undertake, there were only two courses open to us: either to make a frontal attack on the main enemy position astride the road just north of Agedabia village, or to attempt an outflanking movement over the difficult country to the south.

General Godwin-Austen tried a combination of both. The 22nd Armoured Brigade, for which it at last became possible to provide fuel, was ordered to work round to the south towards Chor es Sufan, while the Guards Brigade made its way through the sand dunes to attack Agedabia from the west. The Guards Brigade's attack, made on the 26th December, failed owing to misdirection, and the following day the 22nd Armoured Brigade was heavily engaged by the remnants of the enemy's armoured divisions which had been lying to the south-east. The long march across the desert from Gazala had been too much for many of the tanks with which the brigade had been fitted out: out of a hundred and thirty tanks, sixty had fallen by the way, and in the battle eight more were lost out of a total of fourteen as a result of mechanical breakdown. Although the brigade failed in its object of getting round behind the main position and was forced to retire to El Haseiat, it inflicted considerable damage on the enemy, destroying twenty of his tanks and damaging twenty more. A further action on the 30th December, in which the 22nd Armoured Brigade again lost a number of tanks, drove General Godwin-Austen to the conclusion that the brigade was not fit for further operations. Accordingly he gave instructions for the 7th Support Group to relieve it, and had to content himself with harassing the enemy until fresh troops arrived.

It was evident that the troops in the forward zone were too weak for their task, and that they must be reinforced if the destruction of the enemy was to be completed. General Ritchie had issued orders for the 1st Armoured Division to move forward and intended that it should be used for the advance into Tripolitania when the time came. On the 3rd January the 13th Corps issued orders for the 4th Indian Division also to move forward, as soon as the administrative position permitted.

Our prospects of pushing the enemy back further depended entirely on our overcoming the difficulties of supply. There is no denying that the administrative position in Western Cyrenaica at the opening of the New Year was far from satisfactory. Transport resources were stretched to the limit to meet daily maintenance needs, and there were practically no reserves west of Tobruk. No substantial enemy stores had been found to supplement our own deficiencies. Moreover the troops had been on the reduced battle ration for many weeks, and it had become necessary to increase the rations to field service scale and to provide some canteen stores. The demand for engineer stores for the forward troops was also continually on the increase.

Until the port of Bengasi could be brought into use, little improvement could be looked for. Derna was opened as a port on the 6th January and thereafter the supply of troops in the eastern part of the Gebel Akhdar was assured. A day later the first convoy arrived at Bengasi, but bad weather and the lack of lighters made unloading a slow business. Owing to the rough seas, lighters could not be sailed round the coast and as a result Bengasi was never brought into full operation. The Eighth Army was, therefore, forced to rely on land transport during the whole time it was operating in Western Cyrenaica.

*The reduction of Bardia and Halfaya.*

While the 13th Corps was pressing the pursuit of the main body of the defeated Axis forces and clearing the rest of Cyrenaica, the 30th Corps under General Norrie proceeded with the reduction of the enemy strongholds at Bardia and round Halfaya. By the middle of December, the 2nd South African Division with a brigade of the 1st South African Division under its command, was in touch with the enemy's forward defences, and communication by land between Halfaya and Bardia had been severed, as had the pipeline which brought water from Bardia to Sollum and Halfaya. The enemy still maintained communication by sea between the two strongholds, however, and sent supplies by launch from Bardia to Halfaya.

General Ritchie had instructed the 30th Corps to restore direct land communication with Tobruk by the main road through Sollum and Bardia as soon as possible, but had, with my full approval, stipulated that the task was to be carried out with the minimum of casualties. This was important in view of the difficulty of providing reinforcements to replace wastage in the infantry of the Union Defence Forces, which were to carry out the attack. The 1st Army Tank Brigade and a strong force of field and medium artillery were allotted to the 30th Corps, which was supported also by a bomber wing of the Royal Air Force.

The defences of Bardia, which was to be reduced first, were much as they had been when General Wavell took the place from the Italians in December, 1940. They consisted of a number of self-contained and mutually supporting defensive localities, covered by machine-gun and anti-tank gun posts, which in their turn were protected by barbed wire entanglements, anti-tank minefields and an efficient concrete anti-tank ditch. There were other defended localities and machine-gun posts in the interior of the fortress to give depth to the defence. The garrison was believed to number about 4,500, of whom 1,500 might be Germans, with a few tanks and some twenty field guns. Actually, at its fall, Bardia yielded nearly 8,000 prisoners, including 2,000 Germans, and about thirty-five guns. Owing to the length of the perimeter to be defended, the garrison could not provide any appreciable reserve.

On the 31st December, attacking from the south, the 3rd South African Infantry Brigade and a regiment of the 1st Army Tank Brigade broke through the enemy's defences to the east of the main road from Sollum, and penetrated deep into the fortress. The enemy counter-attacked, but, generally, we retained the ground taken. On the night of the 1st January the assault was resumed, again to the east of the main road. The enemy resisted stubbornly and inflicted a number of casualties on our tanks which led the attack. This bold night attack convinced General Schmitt commanding the garrison, however, of the futility of further resistance and early on the 2nd January the garrison surrendered unconditionally.

Our casualties in this successful operation were slight and did not exceed 450 all told, of which the majority belonged to the 2nd South African Division. In addition to prisoners and material captured from the enemy, the fall of Bardia released over 1,100 of our own men, who had been kept in the fortress as prisoners of war, in conditions of great privation. Much enemy ammunition fell into our hands.

Preparations were at once put in hand for the reduction of Halfaya, and it was hoped that the fall of Bardia would intensify the lack of food and water from which the place was already suffering, if prisoners' stories were to be believed. On the 11th January the Transvaal Scottish attacked Sollum and completed its capture early the next day, with nearly 350 prisoners. On the 13th the South Africans finally denied to the enemy access to his last source of water supply, and his surrender became inevitable. Plans were made for the final attack, in which the 1st Free French Brigade Group were to take the main part; but early on the 17th January General de Giorgis, the commander of the garrison, surrendered unconditionally. Some 5,500 prisoners were taken, of whom 2,000 were Germans. Few serviceable weapons fell into our hands and no stores of any value. The prisoners were exhausted from lack of nourishment.

### The Enemy retires to El Agheila.

In Western Cyrenaica early January was a period of acute administrative difficulty. The expenditure of artillery ammunition, except by troops actually attacked by the enemy, was limited to twenty-five rounds a gun a day, in order to allow reserves to be accumulated for the projected assault on the enemy holding Agedabia, which was to be launched when the 1st Armoured Division arrived. The move of this division had been delayed owing to the lack of transport to bring forward petrol, but it eventually reached Antelat on the 6th January. On the morning of the 7th our patrols reported that Agedabia had been evacuated.

Columns of the 22nd Guards Brigade followed up, but were delayed by the minefields round Agedabia and by bad going; and it was not until the evening of the 8th January that they came up against the enemy in strong positions sixteen miles further south. The enemy withdrew from these positions two days later, and on the 11th January the Guards Brigade were in contact with the forward positions of the enemy's final line running southwards from Marsa Brega.

The country round El Agheila offers one of the most easily defensible positions in Libya. A broad belt of salt pans, sand dunes and innumerable small cliffs stretches southwards for fifty miles, its southern flank resting on the Libyan Sand Sea, a vast expanse of shifting sand. Apart from the main road from Bengasi to Tripoli only a few tracks cross this inhospitable country, so that the thirty-five thousand enemy now left out of the original hundred thousand sufficed to hold it. Accordingly Rommel set his infantry to guard the approaches at Marsa Brega, Bir el Ginn, Bir es Suera, Bir el Cleibat and Marada, and withdrew his armoured force to re-equip.

I was as anxious to secure this area as Rommel was to hold it. Apart from the need to traverse it to invade Tripolitania, which was my ultimate intention, I considered it essential to control this region in order to hold Cyrenaica. Otherwise, I feared, we should have to retire to the frontier, if the enemy were, at some later date, again to become strong enough to launch an offensive in force.[22]

Before we could approach the task of throwing the enemy out of El Agheila, however, we were obliged to wait for reserves to be accumulated and the administrative situation to improve, so that we might concentrate sufficient troops for this difficult undertaking. Until that time came, which I judged would be about the middle of February, we must content ourselves with leaving only light forces to watch the enemy. It seemed highly unlikely that he would be in a position to attack us before then, but the Eighth Army and the 13th Corps issued instructions against this contingency. On the 21st January the improbable occurred, and without warning the Axis forces began to advance.

## CONSOLIDATION AT GAZALA.
### *Dispositions and Plans of the Opposing Forces.*

Prior to the 21st January, the enemy appeared to have three weak Italian divisions of the 21st Corps, Pavia, Sabrata and Brescia, in Agheila itself and to the east of it. The Trieste, Ariete and Trento Divisions seemed to be round Maaten Giofer about twenty miles to the south, watching the gap between the Wadi el Faregh and the marshes to the west, through which runs the track from Agheila to Marada. At Marada itself were thought to be some of the German 90th Light Division, the Burckhardt battle group and some Italian troops. The bulk of the 90th Light Division was probably in the dangerous sector immediately south of Marsa el Brega on the coast, while the two Panzer Divisions were believed to be between the minefields which covered the 90th Light Division's positions and the north bank of the Wadi el Faregh. Elements of the 90th Light Division were also thought to be watching the coast west of El Agheila towards Ras el Aali.

About the middle of January the enemy's strength was estimated at some 17,000 German and 18,000 Italian troops with about seventy medium tanks altogether, of which twenty-five were German. Another twenty German medium tanks might be available at short notice.

It was not thought possible for Rommel to receive any new German formations for some time, though the arrival of a fresh Italian armoured division with some hundred and forty tanks might be expected within a month or so. Even the arrival of these reinforcements, would probably not enable the enemy to take the offensive, as his supply problem appeared to be acute. He was expected to stand on the Agheila – Marada line until forced to withdraw from it by our pressure, or because of difficulties of supply.

On the 21st January our forward troops were under Major-General Messervy, commanding the 1st Armoured Division. On the right was the 201st Guards Motor Brigade, organised in four columns, each consisting of a company of infantry, a field battery and some anti-tank and light anti-aircraft guns, watching a front running south for some fifteen miles from the coast near Marsa el Brega; the third battalion of the brigade was in reserve at Agedabia. To the south was the Support Group of the 1st Armoured Division also organised in four mobile columns and a reserve, and responsible for the front from the left of the Guards Brigade to Maaten Burruei, south of the Wadi Faregh, an extent of some twenty-five to thirty miles. In reserve, twelve miles north of Saunnu, was the 2nd Armoured Brigade, whose training was still unfinished, with three regiments of field artillery and some anti-tank and light anti-aircraft artillery. The residue of the original Oases Force, now a battalion and one field battery, was in the desert some forty miles east of Agedabia and about to return to the Delta to refit after two strenuous months of unbroken operations.

The 1st Armoured Division Support Group had only just relieved that of the 7th Armoured Division and was inexperienced in desert driving. Moreover many of its vehicles were not thoroughly desertworthy, chiefly owing to weakness in the transmission and lack of spare parts. Tyres, too, were unreliable and liable to burst after a short life. These weaknesses were accentuated by the nature of the ground in this region: north of Antelat and Saunnu the going is good, but it becomes progressively worse towards the south, where it is probably as bad as anywhere in the desert. In consequence, in many places tracked vehicles could outpace wheeled.

General Messervy realised that the enemy might stage a local counter-attack and that his advanced troops were weak and widely dispersed. He had asked General Godwin-Austen that the 4th Indian Division might come forward to consolidate a position about Agedabia and El Haseiat and that the 2nd Armoured Brigade might be moved near to Giof el Matar, where it would be better placed to support the forward troops. Unfortunately these moves, though sanctioned, could not be carried out because of difficulties of supply caused by shortage of transport vehicles. Even as it was, the forward troops were on short rations, as the maximum number of vehicles had to be used for building up reserves to enable our offensive to be resumed. Moreover, it had been found necessary to withdraw all the armoured car regiments, with the exception of one squadron, to enable their vehicles to be repaired and refitted, because of the damage they were sustaining owing to the rough ground.

In the event of an enemy counter-attack, General Messervy's plan was for the forward troops to withdraw if necessary, fighting a delaying action, to the line Agedabia – El Haseiat which was to be held to the last. The 2nd Armoured Brigade were to be brought forward to counter-attack the enemy's right flank and rear.

It is doubtful whether the enemy's original plan went further than a reconnaissance in force to ascertain our dispositions and impede our preparations for a renewal of our offensive. He does not appear to have used more than about eighty or ninety tanks throughout the operations and his troops seemed to have started the advance with only three days rations in hand. As usual, however, he rapidly and skilfully made the most of his initial success, being greatly helped by the remarkable elasticity of his supply organisation.

*The Enemy Attacks.*

The first warning of impending attack was given early in the morning of the 21st January by heavy shelling of our advanced troops. The enemy advanced in three columns. The left column, which included about thirty German tanks, moved up the main road; the centre and southern columns, the latter containing about thirty-five German tanks, moved to the south of the road and along the north bank of the Wadi Faregh. Initially things went well for us, but the Support Group to the south then ran into sand dunes and was overtaken by enemy light tanks which caught some of its infantry and artillery hampered by the difficult going. To the north the Guards Brigade were not in difficulty, and General Messervy told both his subordinate commanders to continue in their delaying role, but cancelled his orders to hold the Agedabia – El Haseiat line to the last, as the reserves of supplies which this line was intended to cover had not yet been placed in position. Enemy dive-bombers and fighter aircraft attacked our troops heavily and persistently throughout the day. Unfortunately our forward landing grounds were marshy after the recent heavy rains, and this hindered our aircraft giving our troops during the initial thrust the full protection and support which they previously and subsequently received.

On the 22nd January, the 2nd Armoured Brigade was ordered to move forward in support of our left flank. Meanwhile, however, the enemy's left column had managed to pass through the Guards Brigade and moved swiftly up the main road to Agedabia, where it was engaged by our tanks. General Messervy ordered the Guards Brigade to destroy this party and to block the main road north-west of Agedabia, as well as the track leading to Antelat. But our columns appeared to be incapable of rapid movement in the rough ground off the main road, along which the enemy moved with great speed, easily outstripping our troops struggling in the bad going to the east. The 13th Corps then ordered the 1st Armoured

Division to interpose itself between the enemy and Msus and the 4th Indian Division, which had been reinforced by a battalion of heavy tanks, to oppose any attempt to advance on Bengasi.

On the morning of the 23rd January enemy tanks were reported to be moving about round Saunnu and Antelat, although Saunnu itself was not yet occupied. Two regiments of the 2nd Armoured Brigade were ordered to clear this area on their way northwards to cover Msus. Each regiment became engaged in a separate action with bodies of enemy tanks about fifty strong and each with its attached artillery suffered heavily. The third regiment reached its appointed position north of Antelat without incident, but when the whole brigade was finally assembled it numbered only eighty tanks altogether. By the evening the enemy were in occupation of Antelat and Saunnu.

The enemy halted on the 24th and the 13th Corps prepared to stabilise the position on a line through Beda Fomm, Antelat and Saunnu. General Godwin-Austen, however, gave orders that, if the enemy again advanced in force and could not be held, the 1st Armoured Division should fall back through Msus north-eastwards to Mechili, informing the 4th Indian Division which would thereupon retire through the Gebel Akhdar. The next stand was to be made on the line Derna – Mechili.

The enemy advanced again on the 25th January. Two columns, one moving north-east along the track from Antelat and the other to the east of the Abd el Hafid bog, converged on Msus. The enemy moved very fast, especially the eastern arm of the pincer, and his tanks outdistanced our guns and transport. The 2nd Armoured Brigade became heavily engaged with the enemy's western column, but successfully extricated itself, though the next day it could muster only thirty or forty tanks. Many parties of our troops were surrounded, and it was feared that the whole of the Guards Brigade might be cut off. They drew out, however, and rejoined the division at Charruba towards which the withdrawal was now directed, the original line of retirement having been found impracticable for movement. The 4th Indian Division was informed of the withdrawal shortly after midday and proposed to evacuate all administrative troops from Bengasi by dawn next day.

### Plans for a Counter-Attack.
I returned to Cairo on the 23rd January from Haifa where I had been concerting plans for the defence of the Northern Front, and on the 25th I flew to the Eighth Army's headquarters at Tmimi. I remained there until the 1st February. General Ritchie had already told the 13th Corps to consider how they might make a counter-attack, but the retirement was by then in progress and Msus was in the hands of the enemy.

After talking the matter over, General Ritchie and I agreed that Rommel had almost certainly intended in the first place to make only a limited advance and was now skilfully exploiting an entirely unexpected success. There was time even now to arrest his advance and repel him. General Ritchie then took the 4th Indian

Division under his direct command and countermanded the orders of the 13th Corps for a general withdrawal in the early hours of 26th January. After ways and means of taking the offensive had been considered, it was decided that the 7th Indian Infantry Brigade from the west and the 1st Armoured Division with the 11th Indian Infantry Brigade from the north should converge on Msus where the main body of the enemy lay. It was reported that the 2nd Armoured Brigade would not be ready to undertake the operation until late on the 28th or early on the 29th. Until then the 7th Indian Infantry Brigade was to delay the enemy advance with mobile columns.

Meanwhile General Ritchie continued to take precautionary measures for holding the Derna – Mechili line. The Polish Brigade Group moved south from Derna and occupied Mechili, where it was reinforced later by the Free French Brigade Group, and the 150th Infantry Brigade Group was ordered to secure Bir Tengeder.

### *The Loss of Bengasi.*

On the 27th January, however, the enemy began to advance again sending a large column towards Sceleidima on the escarpment south-east of Bengasi. He kept his main tank force at Msus and shortly after despatched what appeared to be, and probably was, a strong column north-eastwards in the direction of Mechili. This led us to believe that the enemy had decided to strike directly at our rear, and the 1st Armoured Brigade was ordered to take this column in the flank, as soon as it was ready. So strong did this force appear that it was not until late the next day that it was seen that it was a demonstration to cover an attack on Bengasi. The Guards Brigade did actually engage twenty enemy tanks nearly forty miles north-east of Msus on the 28th.

On the 28th January it became clear that the enemy's next objective was Bengasi. The 7th Indian Infantry Brigade was on its way to attack the force above the escarpment, which had now turned north and was heading for El Abiar, when two columns, each said to contain a considerable number of enemy tanks, were observed moving northwards along the coast towards Solluch. The 7th Indian Infantry Brigade was obliged to turn and deal with these columns and to abandon the attempt to attack the force moving on El Abiar, which captured Regima about noon. General Tuker then obtained permission to evacuate Bengasi, as the 1st Armoured Division was already committed in the opposite direction and would not be able to intervene.

Administrative units and other troops left Bengasi in safety; but when the turn of the 7th Indian Infantry Brigade came, it was found that enemy armoured cars and motorised troops had moved across country and blocked the road out of Bengasi at Coefia. An effort was made to clear the block, but the situation became very confused in the darkness, and the attempt failed. Being out of touch with the divisional headquarters the commander, Brigadier H.R. Briggs, made the bold decision to break out to the south. After a most difficult and strenuous march which took them through enemy occupied country between Antelat and Msus, the greater part of the brigade with much of its artillery rejoined the Eighth Army at Mechili and Tengeder.

### The Retreat through the Gebel Akhdar.

After the fall of Bengasi, General Ritchie had hoped to stabilise the position eventually on a line running from Lamluda, a few miles west of Derna, through Mechili to Bir Tengeder. And, in order to give as much time as possible to prepare that line and to assemble a force with which to strike back at the enemy, he ordered the 4th Indian Division to fall back slowly, occupying two intermediate delaying positions. At first it was thought that it would be necessary to withdraw at once to the line of D'Annunzio and Maraua, but a line further west through Barce and Charruba was eventually selected as being easier to defend. The 4th Indian Division was told to hold that line until midday on 30th January. Having carried out the demolitions ordered, the division fell back without incident to the second delaying position at D'Annunzio and Maraua.

The southern flank of this line at Hagfet Gelfaf was to be held by the 1st Armoured Division. But General Messervy reported that the strength of the 2nd Armoured Brigade was now so low that it could not oppose more than twenty-five German tanks with any hope of success. It fortunately was not put to the test, since the enemy kept his main forces round Msus while pressing the pursuit of the 4th Indian Division. But the weakness of our armour made it necessary to retire rather more swiftly than had been intended, and, having obtained General Ritchie's permission, General Tuker withdrew to Gaf Tartaga and Slonta during the night of the 31st January.

The 4th Indian Division then reverted to the command of the 13th Corps. General Godwin-Austen was preparing to stand on the line Lamluda – Mechili – Bir Tengeder, but intended, in the event of an enemy attack in force, to retire to a line running southwards from Gazala, and, if need be, to a line running south from Acroma. He had ordered the 1st South African Division to prepare defensive positions immediately south of Gazala.

On the 1st February the enemy columns, which until then had only felt their way, made contact with the 11th Indian Infantry Brigade at Slonta. General Tuker had previously obtained permission to withdraw further to Cirene and El Faidia, and the 4th Indian Division retired to that line without delay. At El Faidia the 11th Indian Infantry Brigade was once more heavily attacked by lorried infantry and suffered a number of casualties, but held its ground. The 4th Indian Division completed its withdrawal to the Derna line during the same night.

There was every sign that the enemy was intending to follow our retirement through the Gebel in considerable force, and a fresh assessment of the enemy's supply situation revealed that it was much better than we had supposed and that he might shortly be able to send an armoured division to attack us at Mechili. As our own armoured forces had been so reduced, it was decided not to invite disaster by attempting to stand on a line which would require more troops and armour man we possessed to hold it against attack on the scale that now seemed probable. It would be better to place more distance between the enemy and ourselves and to secure a line which was shorter and easier to defend. Accordingly orders were given for Derna to be evacuated and the installations there to be demolished, and for a general deliberate withdrawal to the line of Gazala and Bir Hacheim. Derna, Mechili and Bir Tengeder were, however, to be held as outposts from which mobile columns were to operate.

The enemy pressed on along both roads through the Gebel on the 2nd February, but our offensive patrols held him up whilst the main body of the Indian Division completed the occupation of the Derna line. Later in the day, however, our troops were forced off their positions in the centre of the line and a detachment at Carmusa was overrun by a force of tanks and lorried infantry using captured transport. As the enemy were penetrating between the 4th Division and our troops round Mechili, General Godwin-Austen gave permission to General Tuker to withdraw on Tmimi and El Ezzeiat at his discretion, while Free French mobile columns struck at the enemy forces moving south from Carmusa. Shortly after, since the pressure on the 4th Indian Division was increasing, General Godwin-Austen gave orders for the withdrawal to be accelerated and to continue by daylight on the 3rd February. The 4th Indian Division having fought several rearguard actions during the day reached Acroma that night.

Except for sending patrols forward, the enemy pressed the withdrawal no further and made no move across the desert from Msus. By the 4th February all our forces had fallen back to the Gazala line.

During the withdrawal the 1st Armoured Division lost over one hundred tanks out of an original total of about one hundred and fifty, thirty field guns, thirty two-pounder anti-tank guns and twenty-five Bofors light anti-aircraft guns. The enemy's losses do not appear to have been heavy, but about thirty of his tanks were probably destroyed. The number of tanks the enemy employed in these operations is difficult to determine, as reports of his tank strength varied greatly, but it is probable that he did not employ more than one hundred, some of them certainly light tanks. The number of tanks employed forward of Msus and Bengasi was considerably less than in the initial stages, owing no doubt to difficulties of supply.

When the withdrawal of the Eighth Army came to an end, the Gazala – Bir Hacheim line was not held in great strength. The 1st South African Infantry Brigade held positions round Gazala and to the south of it, and was about to be reinforced by the Polish Brigade Group on its left above the escarpment. The Free French Brigade Group held Alem Hamza. Bir Hacheim was occupied by the 150th Brigade Group and the Guards Brigade. The 1st Armoured Division was watching the gap between Alem Hamza and Bir Hacheim with orders to counter-attack any enemy who might penetrate the position. The 4th Indian Division was given orders to prepare defences on a line through Eluet et Tamar and Er Rigel and thence southwards, to give depth to the Gazala position.

Having regard to the weakness of our armour, I was doubtful, when I returned to Cairo on the 1st February, whether the Eighth Army would be able to hold this line. If the enemy came forward again, it might well be necessary to withdraw to the frontier where I had given orders for positions to be prepared. But I found on my return that our own prospects of re-equipping the Army with tanks were better than I had supposed and that the enemy's supply situation might not permit him to advance further. On the 2nd February, therefore, I ordered General Ritchie[23] to stand at Gazala so as to preserve Tobruk as a forward supply base for the renewal of our offensive.

### *Fortification and Re-organisation.*

As soon as I had decided that Tobruk was to be held and the enemy stopped on the Gazala – Bir Hacheim line, General Ritchie began to plan and construct a series of strong defensive positions in the triangle lying between Gazala, Tobruk and Bir Hacheim. The Gazala line itself consisted of a series of strongpoints extending from about Gazala to Alem Hamza; a detached strongpoint some twenty miles south of the coast near Sidi Muftah; and a second detached strongpoint at Bir Hacheim. The positions in the north were mutually supporting and well covered by minefields. They were so sited as to bar the direct approach to Tobruk by the coast road and also by the tracks leading east from Bir Temrad towards Acroma along the top of the coastal escarpment, which is a marked feature of the terrain in that neighbourhood. The strongpoint near Sidi Muftah blocked the approaches from Segnali by the Trigh Capuzzo and Trigh el Abd towards El Adem and Bir el Gubi. The purpose of the Bir Hacheim strongpoint was to force the enemy to move wide to the south, should he try to outflank the position, and to canalise his advance should he break through the position to the north, as well as to block the direct approach to Bir el Gubi from Tengeder.

The whole front of over forty miles from the coast west of the Gazala inlet to Bir Hacheim was eventually covered by minefields, and most of the defensive positions were mined on their flanks and rear as well as in front. From Bir Hacheim northwards to beyond the Trigh el Abd the main minefield was duplicated, and the "V" thus formed was blocked in the north by another minefield across its mouth. Depth was given to the position in the north by the Tobruk defences, still in reasonably good order and, as time went on, by the construction of strongpoints and minefields around Acroma, El Adem, at El Mrassas below the escarpment, and, later, at Knightsbridge. The defensive positions on the frontier, which I had already ordered to be prepared, gave added depth to the Gazala line and should prevent its isolation by the enemy. They comprised two main defended areas; one round Sollum and Halfaya, and the other round Hamra some twenty miles to the north-east of Maddalena. Subsidiary strongpoints were to be established covering the defiles through the escarpment running southeast from Sollum.

Several of the formations with the Eighth Army needed to reorganise and refit after their strenuous experiences. Their relief could only be effected gradually as fresh troops became available, but eventually the 5th Indian Division relieved the 4th Indian Division, which meanwhile had been employed in preparing the frontier positions. The Polish Brigade Group and the 5th New Zealand Infantry

Brigade were withdrawn and replaced by the remainder of the 50th (United Kingdom) Division, which I was able to bring back from Iraq. The 1st and 2nd South African Divisions had been reorganised after playing their part in the offensive and on the 12th February, General Ritchie reported that they were certainly fit to hold defensive positions and after another six weeks good training would be ready to undertake offensive operations.

As for armoured forces, General Ritchie already had the 1st Armoured Division. The 7th Armoured Division, which had been training hard in the Delta after being reorganised and re-equipped with American medium(General Grant) tanks, moved up later to join the Eighth Army and continue their training in the desert. In addition, two brigades of heavy infantry tanks eventually reached the forward area.

Detailed plans were made to meet an enemy attack in force, and reconnaissances were carried out and exercises held to test and improve them. The infantry and artillery were to hold fast in their prepared positions, while the armoured divisions were to counter-attack the enemy and destroy him, making the fullest possible use of the support afforded them by our defensive positions and minefields. This plan was to apply equally whether the enemy tried to turn the position from the south or to break through the centre. The armoured formations were to be held centrally in reserve ready to meet either eventuality.

### Planning for a Fresh Offensive.

The months of February, March and April were chiefly taken up with intensive planning and preparation, not only to make the Gazala line a secure base from which to launch a fresh offensive, but also for the offensive itself. Ways and means of undertaking this offensive were constantly being studied by General Ritchie and myself and by our senior staff officers.[24] After discussing the various schemes in detail, we came to the conclusion that we must at all costs prevent the enemy escaping into Tripolitania. Therefore he must be induced to attack us on to ground favourable to us instead of our attacking his prepared positions in the area round Derna, Tmimi, Bir Temrad and Mechili. I decided that the Eighth Army should advance on Bengasi which was the most important and vulnerable link in his communications.

The advance was to be made well to the south of the enemy's established positions, so as to force him to fight at a distance from his forward reserves of supplies. It was to be carried out by stages; strongpoints were to be established as each stage was reached, and held by artillery and infantry so as to form pivots of manoeuvre for the armoured forces. South of this line of strongpoints, forward maintenance centres were to be formed, out of reach of the enemy's armoured divisions. This process was to continue until either the enemy attacked us or we were in a position to cut his communications.

It was estimated that the infantry required for this operation, including those needed to hold the Gazala positions while the advance was taking place, were one motor brigade group, four infantry divisions and two infantry brigade groups.

The infantry were available, but the whole project turned on the relative strengths in armour. Our experience taught us that we should require a 3 : 2 superiority in tanks at the start of the operation as well as a fifty per cent. reserve. The date on which the offensive could be launched therefore depended upon how soon we could attain that superiority. In the event, the rate at which the enemy was able to bring new tanks over to Libya exceeded our calculations, chiefly owing to our lack of means with which to interfere with his shipping. In consequence the enemy was ready to launch his offensive before we had accumulated sufficient armour to undertake our own.

The administrative arrangements involved were extensive and highly complicated, but they were carried out with great rapidity and thoroughness owing to the energy displayed by Brigadier C.H. Miller, Deputy Adjutant and Quartermaster-General of the Eighth Army. Three forward bases were established, one at Tobruk, another at Belhamed which was to be the new railhead, and a third at Giarabub. The Capuzzo railhead opened on the 13th March and the stocking of the forward bases for the offensive began at once. Within a week the railhead was handling 2,000 tons daily. As many as 3,400 tons were unloaded in a single day; this was a remarkable feat and reflects much credit on the East African Labour Group working under Lieutenant-Colonel P. Matthews. On the 3rd April work began on the extension of the railway to Belhamed. Road construction was tackled with much energy, and in particular the roads up the escarpment at Sollum and through the Halfaya Pass were greatly improved.

The provision of adequate water was, as always, a difficulty, although the unusually heavy rains which had filled the desert *birs* eased the problem somewhat. The general water ration was three quarters of a gallon a day a head and for each vehicle while stationary, and one and a quarter gallons when on the move. To maintain even this scanty ration it was necessary to draw on the reserves of water stored at Tobruk which could be replenished only by sea. Only a limited number of tank vessels was available, and some of them were sunk by the enemy. The sources at Buq Buq and Bardia were developed and linked, and reservoirs were constructed to supply the defensive positions on the frontier. Shortage of materials, however, prevented us from undertaking the extension of the pipeline from Mischeifa. The old Italian bulk oil storage tanks in Tobruk were repaired and connected by pipeline to a wreck in the harbour whence petrol could be pumped direct from tankers. A canning plant was erected at Tobruk. The rations issued to the Eighth Army were on the full field service scale and of excellent quality, while canteen stores were also available.

The arrangements for the recovery, repair and delivery of tanks and armoured cars were completely reorganised. A tank delivery regiment, a corps tank delivery squadron and brigade tank delivery troops were created and manned. Many more tank transporters arrived during these three months and the system generally was greatly improved and worked smoothly and efficiently in the subsequent fighting.

The original date set for the completion of these preparations was the 15th May; but this was altered later to the 1st June, when it was estimated the Belhamed base and railhead would be ready. The general administrative arrangements, however, to sustain our own offensive or to meet an enemy attack were completed by the 15th May. The Belhamed railhead was opened eleven days later, but was only used for delivering tanks. By the 15th May it was evident that the enemy would in all probability anticipate our offensive and arrangements to cope with a possible withdrawal to the frontier were put in hand as a precautionary measure.

### Preliminary Operations.

While both the enemy and ourselves were occupied with preparing for the coming conflict, the Eighth Army was by no means inactive, although there were no major engagements to record.

At first after the position had been stabilised at Gazala, the enemy kept his distance, holding back his main forces in the neighbourhood of Martuba and Msus, covered by outposts on the general line of Tmimi, Bir Temrad and Mechili. Our mobile columns were most active during this period and harassed the enemy unremittingly, causing him inconvenience and loss. Then, as his supply position became easier, Rommel gradually concentrated his troops forward, using Italian formations to cover his front and keeping the German divisions in rear.

At the beginning of March I gave instructions for the Eighth Army to create a diversion while a convoy sailed to Malta from the east.[25] General Ritchie arranged for widespread raids to be made deep into the enemy's lines. On the night of 20th March the Long Range Desert Group carried out raids on the landing grounds at Barce, Benina and Bengasi. Meanwhile parties from the 1st South African and 50th Divisions sabotaged enemy material on the landing grounds at Tmimi and Martuba. The next day the 13th Corps sent three columns each from these same divisions to threaten the Tmimi and Martuba landing grounds, while the 1st Armoured Division covered their left flank. At the same time a column from the 1st Free French Brigade moved against an enemy position further south at Bir Hamarin. These operations were successful in diverting a considerable part of the enemy's air forces during the passage of the convoy; some loss was inflicted on the enemy and he was caused to evacuate his forward landing grounds for the time being.

Thereafter the enemy steadily closed up on our positions, occupying and fortifying Segnali, Bir Temrad, Sidi Breghisc and other points. On the 12th April General Ritchie carried out an operation against the Segnali area in connection with his plans for the offensive. The object of this operation was to deceive the enemy and to test his reactions to an advance in force in this direction. Another operation, but further to the south, was carried out early in May with the same object.

### Expectation of Enemy Attack.

By the 10th May it was clear that an enemy attack was impending and it seemed almost certain that our own offensive would be anticipated. I considered that this might very well provide the opportunity we had been seeking. The chief disadvantage in our plan for an offensive, namely that we might have to weaken unduly the forces holding the Gazala position before we succeeded in inducing the enemy's armour to attack us, might well be eliminated. Provided we could throw back his initial thrust with heavy loss, we might be able to turn at once to the offensive with the odds heavily in our favour.

A document which contained the enemy's plan for his projected assault on Tobruk in November, 1941, had been captured, and it revealed that Rommel considered the capture of Tobruk to be an essential preliminary to an advance on Egypt. Now that our supply bases were sited in and about Tobruk, it seemed certain his first blow would be aimed at Tobruk. General Ritchie informed his two Corps Commanders accordingly and made all preparations to meet the expected attack and to turn it to our advantage.

Two courses seemed to be open to the enemy. He might try to smash his way through the minefields by the direct route to Tobruk astride the Trigh Capuzzo, or attempt to turn the whole of our position by directing his main effort to the south of Bir Hacheim and then northwards towards Tobruk and El Adem. There was a third possibility that he might try to break through the northern sector of our position with the object of opening the coast road at once and easing his supply problem, but it was thought most unlikely that he would adopt this course.

### The Enemy Plan of Attack.

Documents captured by our troops at an early stage of the ensuing battle disclosed the complete enemy plan of attack.

The Afrika Korps and 90th Light Division Battle Group were to concentrate north of Segnali on the evening of 26th May. On the 27th May, after a night advance, the Ariete Armoured Division was to capture Bir Hacheim, while the Trieste Motorised Division was to make a gap in the minefield south of the Sidi Muftah strongpoint, where it was crossed by the Trigh el Abd. Simultaneously the Afrika Korps was to form up south of Bir Hacheim with 21st Panzer Division (less one battalion of tanks) on the left, 15th Panzer Division in the centre and the 90th Light Division Battle Group on the right. These formations were then to advance northwards and, after destroying our armoured forces, were to reach Acroma and El Adem before nightfall. Motorised columns were to seize Sidi Rezegh and Ed Duda. On 28th May, the three armoured divisions were to attack our positions between Gazala and Alem Hamza from the east, while four Italian infantry divisions, stiffened by two regiments of the 90th Light Division and one tank battalion of the 21st Panzer Division, were to attack the same positions from the west.

Tobruk was to be captured during the two subsequent days.

### Our Dispositions to Meet Attack.

General Ritchie's final dispositions to meet the enemy's attack were as follows:-

13*th Corps*. Lieutenant-General W.H.E. Gott.
50th Division. Major-General W.H.C. Ramsden.
1st South African Division. Major-General D.H. Pienaar.

2nd South African Division. Major-General D. Klopper.
1st Army Tank Brigade. Brigadier H.R.B. Watkins.
9th Indian Infantry Brigade. Brigadier B.C. Fletcher.

The 1st South African Division was holding the front from the coast west of the Gazala inlet to Alem Hamza, astride the Via Balbia and the approaches to Tobruk south of the coastal escarpment. The 151st and 69th Infantry Brigades of the 50th Division were prolonging the line eastwards from the Alem Hamza salient to the point where it again turned southwards. The 150th Infantry Brigade was holding the detached strongpoint of Sidi Muftah. The 1st Army Tank Brigade (heavy tanks) was divided between these two infantry divisions in a supporting task.

The 2nd South African Division occupied the western part of the Tobruk defences and small strongpoints below the escarpment towards Gazala. The 9th Indian Infantry Brigade held the eastern half of the Tobruk perimeter.

*30th Corps.* Lieutenant-General C.W.M. Norrie.
    1st Armoured Division. Major-General H. Lumsden.
      2nd Armoured Brigade. Brigadier R. Briggs.
      22nd Armoured Brigade. Brigadier W.G. Carr.
      201st Guards (Motor) Brigade. Brigadier J.C.O. Marriott.
    7th Armoured Division. Major-General F.W. Messervy.
      4th Armoured Brigade. Brigadier G.W. Richards.
      7th Motor Brigade. Brigadier J.M.L. Renton.
    3rd Indian Motor Brigade Group. Brigadier A.E. Filose.
    29th Indian Infantry Brigade Group. Brigadier D. Reid.
    1st Free French Brigade Group. Brigadier-General J.P.F. Koenig.

The Free French Brigade Group was holding the detached strongpoint at Bir Hacheim. The 3rd Indian Motor Brigade arrived just before the 26th May and was set to prepare a defensive locality a few miles east of Bir Hacheim. The 29th Indian Infantry Brigade of the 5th Indian Division had moved to a defensive area at Bir el Gubi a few days before the battle began. The 1st Armoured Division was disposed round Knightsbridge and the 7th Armoured Division lay to the south of it with the 7th Motor Brigade holding a defensive locality between the 3rd Indian Motor Brigade and Bir el Gubi.

Advanced headquarters of the Eighth Army with the headquarters of the Air Officer Commanding Western Desert, Air Vice Marshal Coningham, were near Gambut, guarded by the 10th Infantry Brigade of the 5th Indian Division (Major-General H.R. Briggs).

Two brigades of the 5th Indian Division, the 10th and 29th, had been occupying the frontier positions at the beginning of May, but General Ritchie did not like having to immobilise this division which formed his principal reserve of infantry. Therefore, as soon as I received information that an attack was imminent, I arranged for fresh infantry formations to join him. I gave orders for the 11th Indian Infantry Brigade from Cyprus and the 2nd Free French Brigade to take over on the frontier, so as to release the 10th and 29th Indian Infantry Brigades to go to Gambut and Bir el Gubi respectively. On the arrival of the 10th Indian Division (Major- General T.W. Rees), which I had already ordered to move from Iraq, the 11th Indian Infantry Brigade was to be withdrawn and the 2nd Free French Brigade freed for other employment. But very soon after the battle started, I placed these two brigades also at General Ritchie's entire disposal, so that he should be free to concentrate the 5th Indian Division. I also arranged to bring over from Syria the Guides Cavalry, who were equipped with carriers and armoured cars.

I was satisfied that the Eighth Army had enough infantry to deal with any situation likely to arise – more would probably have been an encumbrance. But I wished it could have had more field artillery as there was no reserve of guns at the disposal of the two Corps Commanders, or of General Ritchie himself, with which to reinforce divisions whose fire-power might need strengthening during crises in the battle. Throughout the period of my command, the Middle East Forces suffered from a chronic shortage of field artillery. It was only at the end of my time that we had enough personnel and equipment to give divisions their full complement of this supremely important arm.

On the other hand, the Eighth Army was at last receiving anti-tank guns comparable to the enemy's 88 millimetre dual-purpose weapons which had proved so effective against our tanks during the fighting of the past winter. It was hard indeed that these six-pounder guns should have arrived so recently that the motorised brigades, to whom they were issued first, should not have had enough time to become really familiar with them. The ordinary infantry brigades which took over the two-pounder guns thus released likewise had little chance to train with them before the battle started.

As regards armour, the three brigades deployed with the 30th Corps were fully trained and equipped, although the 2nd Armoured Brigade had only just completed its training. For our proposed offensive, I had intended to place the 1st Armoured Brigade also at General Ritchie's disposal so that the two armoured divisions should each have two armoured brigades. The 1st Armoured Brigade however had only recently received its tanks and its training was far from complete. Nevertheless, I decided to send it forward to complete its training in the Eighth Army area so that it might be available if need should arise. I also arranged to send forward the 32nd Army Tank Brigade with its two regiments of infantry tanks; this brigade began to arrive as the battle opened and was placed under the command of the 13th Corps.

It is not easy to make a true comparison of the enemy's armoured strength and our own. Numerically, the Eighth Army undoubtedly had a considerable superiority, but our infantry tanks were too slow to be put into battle against the enemy's medium tanks, and in spite of the fact that we had a considerable number of American General Grant medium tanks in the line, our tanks were still generally inferior in gunpower and reliability to those of the enemy. Moreover, the General Grant tank though greatly superior to any that had hitherto been available to us, was not free from faults. Chief among these were the very limited arc of traverse of its principal weapon, the 75 millimetre gun, and the low position of this gun in the tank itself which entailed exposing the whole turret when in action. On the other hand, we had a much larger reserve of tanks to draw on than the enemy.

Whether the enemy should try to break our centre or to pass to the south of Bir Hacheim, was not to affect the broad outline of General Ritchie's plan to defeat his attack. In either event, the enemy was to be met by our armoured forces east of our minefields. If the enemy took the southern line, the minefield belt was to be kept intact. If he succeeded in penetrating it, the breach was to be closed at once. The intention in either case was to force the enemy to depend on the long and exposed southern route for his supplies, and having thus placed him at a disadvantage, to defeat him in the triangle formed by Gazala, Tobruk and Bir Hacheim.

I naturally kept in very close touch with General Ritchie so that I might be fully in his mind.[26] I was well satisfied with his dispositions generally. But I stressed two points in particular: that the armoured divisions should be fought as divisions and not split up, and that, having defeated the enemy, the Eighth Army should lose no time in passing to the counter-offensive for which plans had been in preparation for so long.

## THE RETREAT FROM CYRENAICA.
### *Initial Failure of the Enemy Attack.*

The first reports of enemy movement came from the 7th Armoured Division during the afternoon of the 26th May. In the evening an enemy force was reported to be moving southeast from Segnali, and the columns of the 7th Motor Brigade retired to their defensive position between Bir Hacheim and Bir el Gubi and prepared to meet the attack.

The enemy leaguered for the night some fifteen miles south-east of Bir Hacheim and advanced again at sunrise, Panzer Divisions on the left, 90th Light Division battle group on the right. The latter swept over the 7th Motor Brigade, captured the headquarters of the 7th Armoured Division and inflicted a number of casualties on the 4th Armoured Brigade which engaged it. The 7th Motor Brigade rallied at Bir el Gubi, some two hundred of its personnel who had been taken prisoner escaped, and the brigade was ready to fight again next day. The headquarters of the 7th Armoured Division also was soon functioning again. At the same time the 3rd Indian Motor Brigade met the full force of the Panzer Divisions. The brigade had only just begun to dig in, but it gave a brilliant account of itself before being overrun. The survivors rallied at Bir Hacheim and were sent, with eight hundred others who were later released by the Free French, to Buq Buq to reform.

The Panzer Divisions resumed their advance and, despite the opposition of the 22nd Armoured Brigade, the Guards Brigade and the 1st Army Tank Brigade, succeeded in reaching Knightsbridge. There they were again attacked by the 1st Armoured Division but without conclusive results.

The Ariete Division's attack on Bir Hacheim was soon repulsed. The Trieste Division failed to breach our minefield. Demonstrations against our northern positions deceived no one and cost the enemy twenty tanks.

What appeared at first to be the most dangerous threat developed on the east, where the 90th Light Division drove back the 4th Armoured Brigade and reached the area south of El Adem. General Ritchie was concerned for the safety of Tobruk and the forward bases and ordered the 7th Support Group to occupy the ridge south of Sidi Rezegh, until the 21st Indian Infantry Brigade should arrive. Next day the 4th Armoured Brigade put an end to this threat by driving the 90th Light Division well away to the south, and on the 29th May the 29th Indian Infantry Brigade came up from Bir el Gubi to take over the El Adem locality permanently.

On the 28th May, having made a demonstration towards Acroma, the German tanks dispersed into small parties. The Ariete Division, on its way north to join the rest of the enemy armour, likewise broke up when attacked by the 2nd Armoured Brigade and a battalion of heavy tanks. General Ritchie decided to keep his armour within close inter-supporting distance, so that it should be ready either to deal separately with the small bodies into which the enemy now appeared to be splitting, or to deliver a heavy blow should the enemy again appear in strength.

Having failed to get to the rear of our Gazala positions and consequently to open the coastal road, the enemy had to rely for supplies on using the long and exposed route round Bir Hacheim. He was therefore obliged to act on the defensive, until he could either capture Bir Hacheim or force a passage through our minefield. Being now in need of supplies, the enemy striking force made a general move southwards to meet a maintenance convoy which had been sent to them round Bir Hacheim. While the Royal Air Force played havoc with the supply column, both armoured brigades of the 1st Armoured Division and the 1st Army Tank Brigade hurled themselves on the enemy armour, which fought desperately. The issue of the armoured battle at times lay in the balance and, to weight the scale, at about midday the 4th Armoured Brigade was sent in from the south-east to take the enemy in the flank; but at this moment the wind rose and a sandstorm brought the action to a standstill.

Although his original lightning attack had failed, the enemy nevertheless gained a solid advantage; for, while this battle was in progress, the Trieste Division at last succeeded in clearing paths through the minefield where it is crossed by the Trigh Capuzzo and the Trigh el Abd. The 150th Brigade and the Free French engaged the numerous enemy vehicles passing through with all the fire they could bring to bear, but they were unable to obstruct the gaps completely.

Rommel now concentrated on making his bridgehead secure. On the 30th May his main body was still lying on the scene of the previous day's fighting and gave battle when the armoured brigades and the army tank brigade converged on it again at daybreak; but at about midday there were clear indications that the enemy was shifting westwards. Our armour then strove to interpose itself between the enemy and the paths through the minefield; but he covered his retirement in characteristic fashion with a powerful anti-tank screen which our armour could neither penetrate nor outflank. This screen was established in a wide arc on the high ground astride the Trigh Capuzzo with its southern flank resting on the eastern arm of our own minefield, so that the armoured brigades, which had been operating round Bir Harmat, had to fetch a very wide compass to the north to outflank it. The 1st Army Tank Brigade had been operating further north and was therefore better placed to outflank the enemy, but lacked the speed and mobility with which to cover the eighteen or twenty miles to the northern gap. The whole of our armour was thus powerless to close on the gaps. The multitude of vehicles traversing the minefield was subjected to heavy artillery fire and intense aerial attack, but many succeeded in getting through.

*The Eighth Army's Counter-Attack.*

The enemy's intentions were by no means clear at this juncture; but there was no doubt that the time had come for the Eighth Army to counter-attack. The knowledge that the enemy's first plan had gone awry, the destruction of many of his tanks and finally the press of vehicles on the tracks through the minefield pointed to the conclusion that a general withdrawal was in progress. Although this conclusion was incorrect, for it turned out that the enemy was not routed but reorganising, it did not signify, since this was indeed the opportunity for counter-attack.

Plans for seizing the opportunity when it should occur had naturally been made before battle was joined, based on the correct assumption that the first battle would take place astride the Trigh Capuzzo and to the east of our minefields. Having brought the enemy's first onslaught to a standstill, the Eighth Army was to proceed according to its own plan, sending tanks round Bir Hacheim to take the enemy on his southern flank where he was most sensitive.

On the 30th May General Ritchie decided the time had come to put his plan into operation. But he did not think he could safely let his tanks go far afield leaving the bulk of the enemy's armour unwatched, until some definite move on our part had caused the enemy to look to his rear. The 1st South African and 50th Divisions with all the heavy tanks were to attack and secure Tmimi and Afrag. The 5th Indian Division would then pass through and penetrate into the Gebel Akhdar, while our armoured divisions moved towards Mechili, operating against the enemy's southern flank or attacking his armour as opportunity offered.

I had urged General Ritchie to lose no time in developing his counter-attack, and he proposed to begin the operation on the night of the 31st May. But both Corps Commanders asked for twenty-four hours' respite so that they might assemble and prepare their forces. In the course of the day, however, two important facts were discovered which changed the whole complexion of affairs: it became clear that the enemy had no intention of withdrawing, and furthermore that the greater part of his striking force was still lying astride our minefield with a considerable number of tanks in its midst. We could muster about two hundred and twenty medium tanks, and the enemy almost certainly no fewer. Consequently General Ritchie decided that it was necessary first to reduce the main body of the enemy, since they might threaten Tobruk and the Army's rear while the projected offensive was in progress.

Since our medium tank force was at best equal in number to the enemy's and since our tanks themselves were outmatched by his, it seemed that we should have to employ all the infantry tanks as well; and, without tank support, a breakthrough in the north, where the enemy were strongly entrenched, could not be contemplated. All might have been well, had General Ritchie been able to use the 1st Armoured Brigade, with its hundred and fifty tanks, for counter-attack. But that formation had only recently been reformed and equipped with tanks and was just arriving in Libya when the battle started, and consequently had had no training as a brigade. I therefore gave General Ritchie permission to use its units, tanks and personnel to replace casualties in the other three armoured brigades.

As regards tank casualties generally in this battle, our recovery organisation and our arrangements for destroying enemy tanks which had been knocked out were now as efficient as the German. The new organisation worked admirably and displayed none of the shortcomings previously experienced. Moreover, we had many more recovery vehicles than before. Recovery crews worked by night protected by armoured cars, while sapper teams destroyed derelict enemy tanks. Very few of our own tanks other than utter wrecks were left on the battlefield and many enemy tanks were destroyed. Nevertheless on the 1st June our effective strength in tanks relative to the enemy's was such that we must employ them all to reduce the enemy's striking force before passing to our own counter-offensive.

The 150th Brigade at Sidi Muftah was situated already well within the enemy concentrations, and General Ritchie determined to establish two more brigade group positions within the enemy anti-tank screen, so as to provide our artillery with positions from which they could shell enemy concentrations, and our armour with a passage through which to pass to take the enemy in the rear. This operation was to start on the night of the 1st June as a preliminary to a general counter-offensive. Meanwhile the Free French were ordered to capture Segnali, which they found unoccupied.

The situation deteriorated, however, before the operation could begin. Heavy attacks on the 150th Infantry Brigade began early in the afternoon of the 31st May. The 1st Armoured Division and the 1st Army Tank Brigade hastened to its assistance, but the brigade was overpowered before midday on the 1st June after a very gallant resistance. With it went a considerable part of the 1st Army Tank Brigade.

Serious as it was, General Ritchie did not consider that the loss of the position held by the 150th Brigade was so vital as to make it necessary to countermand the whole operation. The 69th Infantry Brigade was to attack from the north with the ridge Sghifet es Sidra as its objective, and the 10th Indian Infantry Brigade from the east from about Bir Harmat. The operation failed completely: the 69th Infantry Brigade was held up short of its objective and the 10th Indian Infantry Brigade could not launch its attack at all, as a raging sandstorm made it impossible to carry out the essential reconnaissances.

I viewed the destruction of the 150th Brigade and the gradual consolidation of the enemy's salient with considerable misgiving. It seemed to me that, if the enemy were to be allowed to continue to occupy a deep wedge in the centre of our minefield, the whole Gazala line and Bir Hacheim in particular would become untenable. Moreover there were unconfirmed reports that the enemy was moving an increasingly large number of tanks into the salient. We appeared to be rapidly losing the initiative we had gained by bringing his first attack to a standstill. I agreed with General Ritchie that he ought neither to split his armoured forces and risk their being defeated in detail, nor order them to try to battle their way through the anti-tank screen to the east of the enemy concentrations. Therefore some other solution must be found.

I suggested two possible solutions.[27] The best course, it seemed, would be to launch a counteroffensive directed towards Bir Temrad so as to threaten the enemy's bases, and at the same time to continue to attack his supply lines from the south. The great majority of the enemy tanks appeared to be lying to the east of the minefield; we were consequently unlikely to encounter many in the northern sector. The Eighth Army, on the other hand, had two battalions of infantry tanks belonging to the 32nd Army Tank Brigade practically intact and sufficient artillery to make success fairly certain. In putting forward this suggestion I expressed concern at what appeared to be the undue dispersion of the 5th Indian Division – 9th Brigade at Tobruk, 10th Brigade at Bir Harmat, 29th Brigade at El Adem. One infantry division at least, I considered, should be held in reserve to provide a strong striking force.

As an alternative to striking westwards, we might profit by the fact that the Alem Hamza position flanked the enemy's supply route. A powerful blow southwards against the Italian divisions protecting it, whose morale was almost certain to be indifferent, might do the enemy much damage.

Having examined these proposals and a third suggestion General Ritchie decided that he could not carry them out.[28] It had been his intention to launch a counterstroke in the north, but he believed that our armoured brigades might still be too weak to contain the enemy while it was in progress. This was due to the fact that tank crews were not being assembled as fast as replacements of tanks were being delivered – a fault which was being set right at once. Since the enemy might thus be able to advance on Tobruk or to take the Gazala positions in the rear, General Ritchie had been compelled to discard this idea. Moreover he feared it would be almost impossible to concentrate the 5th Indian Division behind the northern positions without interruption. The idea of striking southwards from Alem Hamza had also been considered. A third course, that of sending the 5th Indian Division in a wide turning movement round Hacheim towards Afrag had also been rejected for the same reason, that the relative weakness of our armour would make it too great a risk.

General Ritchie finally decided that the only practicable course was to use infantry to make a direct assault on the enemy salient. This was to take the form of a pincer movement, the 69th Infantry Brigade attacking from the north, the 9th and 10th Indian Infantry Brigades from the east. The northern arm was to have a limited objective. The main thrust was to be made by the eastern arm: by seizing the ground round Got el Scerab the Indian brigades were to open a corridor through which the 22nd Armoured Brigade could pass behind the enemy and close the gaps. After this operation had been successfully carried out, the Eighth Army was to take the offensive, striking first in the northern sector.

The 13th Corps attack in the north was a straightforward operation in which the 69th Brigade, supported by the 32nd Army Tank Brigade, was to capture Sghifet es Sidra. Had it been launched in this strength on the 1st June, as General Ritchie had intended, instead of three days later, very probably it would have succeeded. As it was, by the night of the 4th June the enemy had had time to fortify the ridge strongly and could afford to support the garrison with tanks. The 32nd Army Tank Brigade was attacked on its right flank by enemy tanks, and having run on an uncharted enemy minefield and so lost fifty tanks out of its original seventy, could give the infantry no support when they in their turn were attacked by tanks. Consequently, the 69th Infantry Brigade was pinned down short of its objective.

How far the failure of the 69th Brigade to capture Sghifet es Sidra and to support the 30th Corps attack with flanking fire was responsible for the difficulties which the 30th Corps encountered, it is difficult to say; but there is no doubt that the enemy would have been considerably hampered, if the ridge had been taken. The first phase of the 30th Corps operation was entirely successful; the 10th Indian Infantry Brigade captured Aslagh ridge and four regiments of field artillery moved up in readiness to support the 22nd Armoured Brigade which was to pass through followed by the 9th Indian Infantry Brigade, and secure Sidi Muftah. It was then that plans began to go amiss. The 22nd Armoured Brigade came up against a second anti-tank screen covering Sidi Muftah and wheeled north. Having, apparently, been informed that it had no responsibility for the infantry, the 22nd Armoured Brigade did not intervene when the right flank of the 10th Indian Infantry Brigade was attacked and driven back, or when a battalion of the 9th Indian Infantry Brigade, which had pushed forward, was also in difficulties. The latter attack fortunately was not pressed home, so that the battalion managed to withdraw having lost a company. The enemy then engaged the 22nd Armoured Brigade and inflicted on them considerable casualties.

After desultory fighting which lasted all day, a strong detachment of the enemy worked round the southern flank of the newly won position on Dahar el Aslagh, overcame the single battalion of the 21st Indian Infantry Brigade thrown out as a protection to the southern flank, and overran the tactical headquarters of the 5th Indian Division and the headquarters of the 10th Indian Infantry Brigade. The infantry of the 9th Indian Infantry Brigade were withdrawn during the night, and the infantry of the 10th Brigade with the motor battalion of the 22nd Armoured Brigade and the four field regiments were left to defend the ridge.

Although communication with these troops had broken down entirely as a result of the loss of the headquarters, the commanders of the 1st and 7th Armoured Divisions appear to have realised fully their serious plight and to have devised plans for a counter-attack to aid them. General Messervy found that the 22nd Armoured Brigade which had reached its leaguer just before dawn was in no condition to take part. The 4th Armoured Brigade whose losses had been made good by a partially trained regiment from the 1st Armoured Brigade, made very slow progress in consequence, and some misundertaking arose over the orders to the 2nd Armoured Brigade which put in an attack too far to the north and found its progress blocked by an impassable escarpment. Owing to the large number of wireless sets destroyed, communications generally were very bad indeed. The counter-attack therefore came too late to prevent the enemy overwhelming the infantry and artillery holding Dahar el Aslagh, of whom scattered elements only escaped.

### *The Attacks on Bir Hacheim.*

The failure of the Eighth Army's counter-attack on the 5th June was probably the turning point of the battle. Until then our chances of putting the enemy to flight and even of destroying him had seemed good. But even after the attack had failed, it did not at once become necessary to evacuate the Gazala line or to abandon all hope of eventually making a counter-offensive. Our tank force was believed to be still equal in number to the enemy's and our prospects of obtaining reinforcements as good as if not better than his. But before we could take the offensive again we needed time to reorganise, and the enemy's powers of rapid recuperation seemed greater than our own.

The enemy made a swift riposte. Moving the bulk of his armour north-eastwards towards Knightsbridge, where it directly menaced Tobruk, he set to work to reduce Bir Hacheim.

General Ritchie was intent on taking counter-offensive action against the main body of the enemy, but to intensify our attacks on his supply line seemed the only course for the moment. He had again considered launching a counter-stroke from the northern sector, but the 1st South African Division, which had attempted to carry out a limited advance in that area on the night of the 4th June, reported that it was strongly held and would need a strong and carefully staged attack to break through it. A column of the 151st Brigade which penetrated to Sidi Breghise brought back confirmation of this. General Ritchie therefore decided that he could no longer spare the 7th Motor Brigade to support the Free French and ordered it to Metifel to operate against the enemy's supply line from the south, as the 50th Division was doing from the north.

The problem of supplying Bir Hacheim was becoming increasingly difficult, because the 90th Light Division had been methodically surrounding the position with a series of entrenched posts and the eastern face had now been completely masked. Realising that the withdrawal of the 7th Motor Brigade might make it necessary to give up Bir Hacheim altogether, General Ritchie issued warning orders for the Free French to withdraw.

On the 6th June an armoured battle began round Knightsbridge in which both Panzer Divisions and all three of our armoured brigades were involved. Nevertheless neither side gained an advantage, and the tank fighting died down for some days. But the presence of the greater part of the enemy armour round Knightsbridge continued to offer a threat to Tobruk which could at no time be disregarded.

Meanwhile the enemy's assaults on Bir Hacheim were renewed. Beginning on the 6th June, the attacks continued and grew in intensity. The Free French resisted valiantly, but on the evening of the 8th June, General Koenig was obliged to report that the situation had become serious. It seemed likely that the stronghold would fall unless the garrison was given support from outside. Moreover the supply situation was becoming critical. General Ritchie was anxious to retain possession of it since, if it were lost, we should have to form a new and extended front facing southwards behind which we might be hemmed in and deprived of our power of manoeuvre. The threat to our rear would be increased, and, while it would be more necessary than ever to attack the enemy's supply lines, to do so from the south would become correspondingly more difficult. I agreed that we must hold the enemy frontally and do everything in our power to deprive him of supplies. Orders were therefore issued for an armoured regimental group from the 4th Armoured Brigade with two columns each from the 7th Motor Brigade and the 29th Indian Infantry Brigade to attack the 90th Light Division in the rear next day. At the same time a convoy was to be passed in, and arrangements were made for aircraft to drop supplies. It was intended that the armoured regimental group should eventually join the forces operating round Mteifel.

On the 8th June, an enemy attack on Bir Hacheim for the first time made some progress, one of our positions being overrun. Next morning the garrison was subjected to intense dive-bombing and shelling. Attacks from the north continued all day, but in the evening the Free French drove the enemy back once more. On the 10th June General Ritchie decided to order the Free French to evacuate Bir Hacheim. Enemy pressure continued from the south and the attacks of the armoured regimental group had not succeeded in relieving it. It was clear, too, that the resistance of the garrison was being worn down. Having been again subjected to heavy bombing from the air, and having again held off a strong enemy attack, the 1st Free French Brigade withdrew during the night escorted by the 7th Armoured Division. Next morning it was reported that at least two thousand men had been safely withdrawn and that many others were coming in.

### The Defeat of our Armour.

The enemy's reaction to the evacuation of Bir Hacheim was immediate and determined. By midnight on the 11th June, the 90th Light Division had moved up to an area some nine miles south of El Adem where it leaguered. The 15th Panzer Division, having been engaged with inconclusive results by the 2nd and 4th Armoured Brigades, leaguered to the left of the 90th Light Division, with the Trieste Division echeloned in rear, guarding the left flank.

The 29th Indian Infantry Brigade was holding a defensive locality on the ridge south of El Adem, with a detachment thrown out on the northern escarpment where the by-pass road crosses it. The 2nd and 4th Armoured Brigades lay immediately to the west of the locality with orders to destroy the enemy armour. Columns of the 7th Motor Brigade and the 11th Indian Infantry Brigade under the 7th Armoured Division were in the south, ready to attack the enemy's southern and eastern flanks. The 22nd Armoured Brigade remained at Knightsbridge watching the 21st Panzer and Ariete Divisions which had not moved from their positions west of Bir Harmat. All three armoured brigades were under command of the 1st Armoured Division.

The enemy's next move made it seem as if the orders of the 27th May had been issued again. While the 15th Panzer Division protected its western flank, the 90th Light Division attacked the 29th Indian Infantry Brigade at El Adem. This attack was successfully repulsed, but the enemy occupied the landing ground to the north. The 15th Panzer Division then swung north-west to meet the 2nd and 4th Armoured Brigades, whose attempts to get to grips in the morning had been frustrated by a characteristic enemy anti-tank screen. The ensuing armoured battle lasted until nightfall, by which time the 2nd and 4th Armoured Brigades had been forced back some four miles north of the Batruna ridge. The 90th Light Division took advantage of this to establish a series of defended posts on the ridge.

On the 13th June, after a quiet morning, the 15th Panzer Division returned to the attack, engaging the 2nd and 4th Armoured Brigades. Soon the 21st Panzer Division was thrown in from the west, and the 22nd Armoured Brigade also joined in the battle which took place in the area of Maabus es Rigel and Hagiag er Raml. When evening came, the enemy had gained possession of both these ridges and was consolidating, thus extending the line of posts he had secured on the Batruna ridge.

This battle was the culmination of the armoured fighting which had been going on intermittently since the 27th May. At its conclusion our armour in the Acroma area was reduced to thirty cruiser and twenty infantry tanks, while the enemy was believed to possess at least twice this number. Moreover the Eighth Army had lost the inestimable advantage of being able to recover its damaged tanks from the battlefield.

*Withdrawal from Gazala and Investment of Tobruk.*
The loss of so considerable a part of our armour called for a complete revision of our plans. The security of the twenty-four mile long southern flank of our position between Gazala and Tobruk depended on a strong armoured backing which no longer existed. It would be only a matter of time before the enemy cut the

supply lines of the two forward divisions, and their reserves would last them at best a week. In that short time it would be impossible to restore our armoured strength sufficiently to turn the tables on the enemy. Having obtained my permission, General Ritchie therefore gave orders on the 14th June for the 1st South African and 50th Divisions to be withdrawn from the Gazala – Alem Hamza position into reserve. The 201st Guards Brigade, which had been garrisoning Knightsbridge and whose position had become dangerously exposed, had already been ordered to retire to Acroma the previous night.

The Gazala – Alem Hamza position gave us a tactical advantage I was loth to abandon. Straddling the coastal road, it denied the enemy easy access to his supplies and made reinforcement slower. Besides being of great value so long as we remained on the defensive, it was likely to prove still more valuable when the balance of armour should have turned in our favour and we were able to take the offensive once more. But there seemed to be no alternative but to evacuate it.

The 1st South African Division started to withdraw from Gazala at dusk on the 14th June by the road through Tobruk. This was made possible by the stubborn resistance offered by the garrisons of Acroma and its satellite localities, vigorously supported by what remained of our armour. The enemy began to drive northwards at midday, and in the course of seven hours of furious fighting these troops repulsed enemy tanks three times as numerous as our own, with the loss of only one position. Thus the 1st South African Division was able to reach the frontier practically intact. The 50th Division, which helped to cover the withdrawal of the South Africans, was less fortunate, being obliged to withdraw south-eastwards across the desert through country infested by the enemy. Nevertheless by midnight on the 15th June a large proportion of this division, which had lost the whole of the 150th Infantry Brigade with a regiment of artillery a fortnight earlier, also reached the frontier.

Although we had no choice but to give up our bastion at Gazala, I was determined that the Eighth Army should not yield more ground than was absolutely necessary. I therefore ordered General Ritchie not to allow Tobruk to become besieged but to hold a line through Acroma and El Adem and thence southwards. I believed that in spite of his heavy losses he still had enough troops to hold this reduced front of which the key positions were already prepared and occupied. The enemy himself must surely have sustained heavy losses and was known to be short of ammunition. Moreover we were still superior to him in the air, as we had been throughout. General Ritchie had reached the same conclusions as to the respective capabilities of the enemy and ourselves. In a telegram which crossed mine conveying orders to hold that line, he stated that he hoped to be able to stand on the western perimeter of Tobruk, at El Adem and Belhamed and to keep a mobile force in being to the south.

I had always been determined that Tobruk should not again be besieged, but the circumstances now obtaining were rather different to those I had previously envisaged. Although there was no denying that it had sustained serious losses and although it had been obliged to fall back from the Gazala line in consequence of the heavy defeat of the armoured divisions, the Eighth Army was by no means beaten. Out of the original five infantry divisions and two infantry brigade groups, there remained three divisions and a brigade group practically intact. The 1st and 2nd South African Divisions and the 11th Indian Infantry Brigade, had hardly been seriously engaged and the 10th Indian Division had lost one field regiment and a battalion of infantry. Of the other two divisions, the 50th Division still had two brigade groups and the 5th Indian Division one; and a large part of the Free French Brigade Group had survived the attacks on Bir Hacheim and was being reorganised. Moreover, in order to make up for our losses I had arranged for the New Zealand Division to move down from Syria. Of the original three motor brigades,, the 201st Guards and 7th Motor Brigades were fighting vigorously and the 3rd Indian Motor Brigade was being reorganised. The armoured car regiments had naturally suffered casualties, but were still taking their full part in the battle.

The most serious losses had occurred among the armoured brigades. The 1st Armoured Division and the 32nd Army Tank Brigade which were now fighting round Acroma, had been reduced to about thirty and twenty-four tanks respectively. The 4th Armoured Brigade had managed to retain about sixty tanks. On the other hand there were about a hundred and fifty tanks of various types undergoing repair in the Eighth Army's workshops, and the 10th Armoured Division was on its way to the front. The training of that division was not complete, but would not take very long; and, when it was ready for battle, its ninety tanks might well give us the superiority in armour we required.

The Eighth Army was, I considered, still strong enough to provide an adequate garrison for Tobruk and to maintain a mobile field force to the east and south capable of preventing the fortress being permanently beseiged. I was prepared to accept temporary isolation, provided the Eighth Army were able to maintain adequate pressure from the south and east. Meanwhile a new striking force was to be built up in the neighbourhood of the frontier. On the 16th June I telegraphed to General Ritchie that I was prepared to accept temporary investment and authorised him to organise the garrison as he thought best.

By this time the process of encirclement had begun. On the 15th June the enemy left Acroma in peace for the time being and turned his attention to El Adem; at the same time he pushed strong patrols forward to Belhamed and Sidi Rezegh. The 90th Light Division, supported by tanks, attacked El Adem three times. But the 29th Indian Infantry Brigade, with the help of columns from the 7th Motor Brigade from the south and from the 11th Indian Infantry Brigade from the north, repulsed all three attacks. Our air forces also gave effective and unstinted assistance.

The enemy then split his armour. The 15th Panzer Division attacked Acroma again on the 16th June; but the garrison helped by the remnants of the 1st Armoured Division, held firm. At the same time a strong detachment of the 21st Panzer Division slipped past El Adem and formed up to attack one battalion of the 20th Indian Infantry Brigade which was defending Sidi Rezegh, but was dispersed by bombing and artillery fire. Then the main body of the 21st Panzer Division passed down the valley to Sidi Rezegh under cover of a feint made towards El Adem by the 90th Light Division. Columns from Tobruk and from the 4th Armoured Brigade attacked them as they passed, but were not powerful enough to arrest their advance.

I considered it essential to hold El Adem in order to prevent Tobruk becoming permanently isolated, and I ordered General Ritchie to reinforce it without delay. This proved impossible, however, and the 29th Indian Infantry Brigade, except for a detached battalion of infantry and a battery of artillery which fought their way into Tobruk, was withdrawn during the night of the 16th June. On the 17th June our defended locality at Sidi Rezegh was captured.

Tobruk was thus gradually becoming surrounded. But as the remainder of the 20th Indian Infantry Brigade was holding out at Belhamed, and as the 2nd Free French and 21st Indian Infantry Brigades were occupying the high ground overlooking Gambut, the Bardia road was still open. On the afternoon of the 17th June, however, the Eighth Army suffered a further reverse which put an end to our hopes of preventing Tobruk from becoming completely surrounded. After an engagement south of Sidi Rezegh with an enemy force numbering nearly a hundred and twenty tanks, the 4th Armoured Brigade was driven back almost to Gambut, having lost all but twenty of its tanks.

Before this engagement the Eighth Army had about five hundred tanks altogether. But three hundred and eight of these were under repair in workshops and a further forty in course of delivery. Of the remainder, forty-eight heavy tanks were in Tobruk and twenty-three more on the frontier. Apart from a squadron operating with the 7th Motor Brigade, the 4th Armoured Brigade with sixty tanks, had been the only striking force capable of supporting the infantry brigades covering the coastal road, so that, when it was defeated the 20th Indian Infantry Brigade had to be withdrawn from Belhamed.

On the 18th June the enemy made as if to continue his thrust eastwards. He advanced no further than Gambut, however, where he cut off a battalion of the 20th Indian Infantry Brigade, which had been acting as rearguard. It was appreciated that the enemy would be unable to make a serious attempt to invade Egypt so long as Tobruk held out, but the occupation of Gambut was a serious matter, since it was now practically impossible to operate fighter aircraft in support of the garrison of the fortress.

A general movement westwards of the enemy was reported on the 19th June, and on the 20th the attack on Tobruk began.

### The Fall of Tobruk.

On the 15th June, General Gott appointed Major-General Klopper, commanding the 2nd South African Division, to command the fortress and placed the following forces at his disposal:-

Headquarters of the 2nd South African Division-
    4th South African Infantry Brigade.

6th South African Infantry Brigade.

H.Q. 201 Guards Brigade with

  2 Coldstream Guards,

  1 Sherwood Foresters, and elements of 1 Worcesters.

11th Indian Infantry Brigade.

32nd Army Tank Brigade.

4th Anti-Aircraft Brigade (Less 18 guns).

83rd Sub-Area Headquarters.

General Klopper was told to defend Tobruk at all costs and to be prepared to hold it for some time. He was also vigorously to oppose the enemy outside the defences of the fortress. On the 16th June, he was given further instructions concerning his future action in certain circumstances. He was to prepare a plan for co-operating with mobile columns to the south to keep his landward communications open, or to withdraw the garrison if need be. If Belhamed fell, the garrison was to provide a force of all arms to recapture it in conjunction with an attack to be made by the 30th Corps.

General Gott remained for two days in Tobruk to help to organise the defence. He also left a senior administrative staff officer to help General Klopper's staff. General Klopper had been in command of the 2nd South African Division since the 15th May, and during this time had had his headquarters in Tobruk. During the earlier fighting he was responsible for the defence of the fortress and of the coastal area between Tobruk and the rear of the Gazala position. It was well realised, however, that the task was a difficult one, but it was hoped that the experience of the commanders of the 4th Anti-Aircraft Artillery Brigade, the 32nd Army Tank Brigade and of the 83rd Sub-Area, all of whom, with their formations, had been in Tobruk during the siege would help to lighten it.

Prior to the evacuation of the Gazala positions, General Klopper had naturally concentrated his attention on the defence of the western and south-western faces of the perimeter.

Three infantry brigades were disposed on the perimeter, which consisted of a series of mutually supporting posts, each mined and wired. The 6th and 4th South African Infantry Brigades occupied the western and southern sectors respectively, while the 11th Indian Infantry Brigade held the eastern sector. The field artillery was allotted in approximately equal proportions to the infantry brigades, and the anti-tank guns were also distributed between the sectors, being sited mostly in positions close to the perimeter. The fortress reserve consisted of the 32nd Army Tank Brigade and the 201st Guards Brigade. The 4th Royal Tank Regiment was located near the junction of the Bardia and El Adem roads, called King's Cross, while the 7th Royal Tank Regiment were situated near Pilastrino with one squadron north of the Derna road. The 201st Guards Brigade was deployed in the defences of the inner perimeter between the El Adem road and Pilastrino.

The attack opened at about six-thirty in the morning of the 20th June with a heavy artillery bombardment and dive-bombing attacks on the centre of the

11th Indian Infantry Brigade. Within an hour the posts on the perimeter in that sector had been overrun. An immediate counter-attack was made by carriers of the Mahratta Light Infantry, but was brought to a standstill by anti-tank gunfire. Then the enemy, covered by smoke screens, began to penetrate gaps in the mine-fields on the right of the brigade sector, and to advance deliberately on a narrow front towards King's Cross.

At about eight-thirty the Coldstream Guards were warned to move to the west of King's Cross to attack in conjunction with the 4th Royal Tank Regiment. But, when they arrived, it was discovered that both squadrons of that regiment had already been committed to a counter-attack. Meanwhile the 7th Royal Tank Regiment had also been ordered to move to the threatened area. But it seems that they, too, had gone into action along the road towards El Adem. By one o'clock, apparently all our tanks were out of action.

The enemy tanks continued to advance, destroying our field artillery in their defensive positions gun by gun. At about two o'clock King's Cross was taken, and the enemy overran the rearmost artillery position in the eastern sector. At the same time the headquarters of the 11th Indian Infantry Brigade ceased to function. The German thrust then divided. One portion continued along the top of the escarpment, causing the Coldstream Guards a number of casualties and over-running the Sherwood Foresters and, with them, the headquarters of the 201st Guards Brigade. The other column of German tanks proceeded down the road to the town. The harbour came under fire at five o'clock in the afternoon and by six o'clock was cut off from the rest of the fortress.

About noon this day General Ritchie ordered the 30th Corps to use the 7th Armoured Division to advance on Tobruk. The Division reached an area some 20 miles south of the perimeter just before dark. About an hour later General Klopper reported by wireless to General Ritchie's B.G.S. telling him what had befallen and asking to be allowed to fight his way out. He was autho-rised to do so and was told that an endeavour would be made to hold open a gap between El Adem and Knightsbridge. About an hour later General Klopper again communicated with the Eighth Army to say that as the greater part of his trans-port had been cut off in the harbour area, it was impossible to get it to the troops on the perimeter, who had practically no vehicles.

During the night, the headquarters of the Army were intermittently in touch with General Klopper, and early on the 21st June learned from him that all water and petrol had been destroyed. He also informed the Eighth Army that the whole of his transport had been captured and on that account he had been unable to break out. An order was circulated to all units in the garrison that a capitulation had taken place and that all vehicles, equipment and arms were to be destroyed.

Certain detachments, which were in possession of transport, then elected to break out and some succeeded in rejoining the Eighth Army. Other British, Indian, and South African units continued to fight on throughout the 21st and there is evidence that more than one unit was still fighting on the 22nd June.

*The Retreat from Cyrenaica.*

When he knew that Tobruk was about to fall, General Ritchie telegraphed to enquire whether he should continue to try to hold the frontier positions or withdraw to Matruh. He had been relying on Tobruk to contain part of the enemy's armour and to impose at least some delay on his advance; not only would the enemy now be free to employ all his forces in the advance, but the stocks and transport he had captured would greatly simplify his supply problem. The defence of the frontier depended entirely on the backing of an adequate armoured force, which was no longer available; and General Ritchie wished to retire to Matruh, in order to gain time to recruit his armoured strength.

There were serious strategical disadvantages in abandoning the frontier and I did so with the greatest reluctance. The argument that an armoured reserve was essential to the successful defence of the frontier positions, applied with equal force to the Matruh position, which, owing to the configuration of the coast, could easily be isolated by a movement past its southern flank. The matter, however, was one of general policy which could only be decided in consultation with the other two Commanders-in-Chief. In the meanwhile, since General Ritchie alone was in a position to know whether the immediate situation made it imperative to withdraw, I was obliged to leave him to take the decision. But I warned him that I did not consider Matruh to be more easily defensible.

In order to gain time to build up an armoured force, which he believed could be done very rapidly; General Ritchie decided to fall back on Matruh. His decision was subsequently endorsed by the Middle East Defence Committee, and he was instructed to prepare to fight a decisive action round Matruh and to delay the enemy as far west as possible with a covering force. General Ritchie told the 13th Corps to delay the enemy, and sent back the headquarters of the 30th Corps to organise the Matruh position for defence, until Lieutenant-General W.G. Holmes and the 10th Corps Headquarters should arrive from Syria. The headquarters of the 30th Corps were then to go back and control the completion and occupation of the El Alamein position a hundred and twenty miles further east.

The 13th Corps was organised into two elements: a striking force and a holding force. The former was to operate under the headquarters of the 7th Armoured Division, the command of which Major-General J.M.L. Renton had taken over from Major-General Messervy. It comprised the 4th and 22nd Armoured Brigade Groups, with seventy and twenty-two tanks respectively; the 7th Motor Brigade Group, of four battalions; and the 3rd Indian Motor Brigade Group, which had been reorganised, but was below strength. The holding force consisted of the 50th Division, the 10th Indian Division and the 1st South African Division.

There were few troops immediately available to occupy Matruh. The troops allotted to its defence in the first place were the New Zealand Division, which was just arriving from Syria; the 5th Indian Division with one brigade group only; and the 151st Infantry Brigade of the 50th Division when it should be released by the 13th Corps.

The enemy spent the two days following the capture of Tobruk in reorganising for a further advance. But he lost little time, and, whereas on the 22nd June only light forces appeared on the northern flank of the frontier positions and occupied Bardia, on the 23rd his divisions were manifestly gathering for a thrust round the south of Sidi Omar. The 7th Armoured Division, however, succeeded in preventing all but a very few from passing the frontier wire up to the evening of the 23rd June.

General Ritchie had authorised the retirement to begin the previous night. The 10th Indian Division and the 151st Infantry Brigade began to thin out from Sollum on the 22nd June, and the same evening the 2nd South African Brigade also began to retire from the eastern end of the escarpment. On the 23rd June, fearing that they might be cut off, General Ritchie gave General Gott permission to withdraw the remainder of the 10th Indian Division from Sollum and the 3rd South African Brigade from the western end of the escarpment. As there was then no longer any danger of the holding force being cut off, the 4th Armoured Brigade was given the order to retire to the southern flank of the Matruh position, where it came under the command of the 1st Armoured Division. The 22nd Armoured Brigade had already been withdrawn, so that by the 23rd June the columns of the two motor brigades above the escarpment, and of the 69th Infantry Brigade below it, were the only troops remaining in contact with the enemy.

Meanwhile changes had been made in the arrangements for fighting a decisive battle round Matruh. On the 22nd June it was decided that the New Zealand Division was more suitable for a mobile role than the 10th Indian Division, and orders were issued for it to pass to the command of the 13th Corps as soon as the 10th Indian Division arrived from the frontier. There was a great shortage of field artillery, and, as a disproportionate amount of infantry were likely to prove an encumbrance, instructions were given for the infantry divisions, or what remained of them, to be organised into battle groups. These battle groups had as their foundation the maximum number of field guns that could be provided for each, and only just as many infantry as were needed to protect them. The idea was that in this way the defence could be kept mobile, the battle groups being moved rapidly to that part of the front where the danger was greatest. Moreover, these groups, being comparatively weak in infantry, were not encumbered with large numbers of vehicles and could therefore be used in the closest co-operation with the armour. I visited Eighth Army Headquarters on the 22nd June and confirmed these arrangements.

The enemy advance began at dawn on the 24th June. Two columns, one consisting of lorried infantry and the other of fifty to sixty tanks, struck north from Sheferzen towards Halfaya, while a third moved on a more easterly axis from Maddalena. Our light columns could do no more than harass the enemy's movement, which progressed with great rapidity. Our forces retired eastwards and by evening were level with Sidi Barrani. On the 25th June the enemy continued to advance very swiftly and by that evening two of his main concentrations had reached points on the railway and on the coastal road some forty miles from Matruh, while a third lay astride the railway twenty miles further west. Our mobile columns, with which there were some forty tanks, were engaging enemy vanguards operating twenty miles in advance of their main bodies.

## THE STAND AT EL ALAMEIN.

I took over direct control of the Eighth Army from General Ritchie at his headquarters near Bagush on the evening of the 25th June. Major-General E.E. Dorman Smith, my Deputy Chief of the General Staff, accompanied me as my principal staff officer; but no change was made in the staff officers or commanders of the Eighth Army.

The 10th Corps had assumed command at Matruh about twenty-four hours earlier and was organising the defence with the 151st Infantry Brigade and with the 10th Indian Division, which had just arrived. The New Zealand Division was being organised into battle groups and concentrating round Minqar Qaim, about twenty-five miles south of Matruh, for use in a mobile role under the 13th Corps. The 1st and 7th Armoured Divisions were also under command of the 13th Corps. The 1st Armoured Division had taken command of the 4th and 2nd Armoured Brigades which were disposed to the south of Minqar Qaim, while the 7th Armoured Division, with the 3rd Indian and the 7th Motor Brigades, was in touch with the enemy west of El Kanayis. The 69th Infantry Brigade of the 50th Division was withdrawing from Sidi Barrani on Matruh in contact with the enemy.

The 30th Corps Headquarters was organising the defence of El Alamein. The 1st South African Division held the important fortifications round El Alamein railway station and astride the main road, and the 2nd Free French Brigade Group lay further to the south. The infantry made surplus by the organisation of battle groups were being sent back from the forward zone to help in preparing the El Alamein position.

### *The Withdrawal from Matruh.*

The Matruh position consisted of a fortified perimeter round the town itself, which had been constructed before my arrival in the Middle East, a more recent covering position to the west of the town, and a newly prepared detached strongpoint about twenty miles to the south on the high ground near Minqar Sidi Hamza el Gharbi. A deep minefield ran south in front of the covering position from the coast to Charing Cross and then turned eastward. Two further minefields ran northwards from the high ground about Minqar Sidi Hamza. Between the two groups of minefields there was a gap of about six miles, which the 29th Indian Infantry Brigade had been ordered to close with all speed.

Given an adequate garrison and sufficient armoured forces, I considered the Matruh position to be perfectly defensible. But there were no longer sufficient troops to watch closely the whole length of the minefields, which in consequence would present little or no obstacle to the enemy, and the southern flank was open like that of the Gazala and frontier positions. The enemy was pushing eastwards very rapidly – there was some fear that he might cut off the retreat of the 69th Infantry Brigade, but this proved groundless – and it seemed hardly likely that we should be organised in time to meet him. Realising our weakness in armour and field artillery and that the divisions which had fought round Tobruk had inevitably been disorganised I reversed the decision to make a final stand at Matruh. Instead I decided to keep the Eighth Army fully mobile and to bring the enemy's advance to a halt in the area between Matruh, El Alamein and the Qattara Depression. In no circumstances was any part of the Eighth Army to be allowed to be shut up in Matruh, even if this involved abandoning the position entirely. The 10th and 13th Corps were to provide the mobile element of the Army and to take every opportunity of defeating the enemy without allowing themselves to be encircled or overwhelmed. The 30th Corps was to occupy the El Alamein position.

On the evening of the 26th June, enemy tanks broke through the recently closed gap in our minefields south of Charing Cross and forced back columns of the 29th Indian Infantry Brigade which were too weak to stop them. The next day these enemy tanks engaged the 1st Armoured Division and the New Zealand Division which used its artillery with great effect against them. Throughout the 27th, the 13th Corps were engaged with the enemy round Sidi Hamza, while the 10th Corps engaged enemy forces which had passed the minefields and were moving north-eastwards. Towards evening General Gott found that the enemy had succeeded in interposing themselves between his own and the 10th Corps, and ordered the 13th Corps to withdraw towards Fuka.

I ordered the 10th Corps to conform; but the 10th Corps were short of vehicles owing to the withdrawal of transport to make the New Zealand Division fully mobile for the part it had to play on the southern flank. Before they could get clear of Matruh and Bagush, the enemy had cut the road about twenty miles east of Matruh. The 50th Division and the 10th Indian Division had therefore to fight their way out. This they succeeded in doing during the night of the 28th June, though much ammunition, and equipment had to be left behind; and when they reached the El Alamein position, these troops had to be withdrawn to the Delta to reorganise and refit.

The 29th Indian Infantry Brigade was ordered by the 13th Corps to hold the passes down the escarpment at Fuka in order to assist the withdrawal of the 10th Corps, but it was overwhelmed just before dark on the 28th June. The 10th Corps, therefore, completed their break-out on the 29th southwards by way of the desert, covered by the 7th Motor Brigade which continued to attack northwards against the flank of the advancing enemy.

The clearing of stores and materials from Matruh and Bagush was reasonably successful and demolitions were effectively carried out. There was however considerable unavoidable congestion on the railway at El Daba, but most of the rolling stock was got away. The success of this arduous work of evacuation was largely due to the efforts of the Deputy Adjutant and Quartermaster-General of the Eighth Army, Brigadier Sir Brian Robertson, who refused to be shaken even by the most disconcerting events.

### The Occupation of El Alamein.

While this regrouping was going on, the enemy continued to press forward along the coast, and, in spite of the vigorous opposition of the 13th Corps, reached Sidi Abd el Rahman, only fifteen miles west of El Alamein on the evening of the 29th June. On the 30th June I ordered our armoured and motor Brigades, which were still operating far to the west and well behind the line reached by the enemy's advanced elements, to withdraw into reserve.

The 13th Corps took over the southern half of the El Alamein – Qattara Depression line, with what was left of the New Zealand and 5th Indian Divisions, while the 30th Corps, with the 50th and 1st South African divisions, concentrated on the defence of the northern sector and especially of the El Alamein fortifications. Not needing a third corps headquarters on the El Alamein position, I sent General Holmes with his 10th Corps Staff back to command Delta Force which was forming in Egypt to defend Alexandria and the western edge of the Delta.

On the morning of the 1st July the enemy unsuccessfully attacked the 1st South African Division which was holding the fortifications round El Alamein itself. At the same time he launched an infantry attack with strong artillery support against the 18th Indian Infantry Brigade Group, holding the Deir el Shein defensive locality. This attack was beaten off. But the brigade had just arrived from Iraq and suffered from inexperience and from the difficulties of having to take up a defensive position at very short notice. When a further attack strongly supported by tanks developed late in the afternoon under cover of a dust-storm, which undoubtedly favoured the attackers, the brigade was eventually overrun, after five hours stalwart resistance. Only one infantry battalion survived the attack, but the stand made by the brigade certainly gained valuable time for the organisation of the El Alamein line generally.

### Regaining the Tactical Initiative.

Except for the semi-permanent fortifications round El Alamein itself, our positions were still weak, disconnected and lacking in depth. Moreover, there was a serious shortage of troops to hold our extended front, and the defence of the all-important Ruweisat Ridge had had to be entrusted to battle groups, weak in infantry, backed by what remained of our armoured troops. Consequently I decided not to attempt to hold the prepared positions round Bab el Qattara in the centre, and at Naqb Abu Dweis in the extreme south on the edge of the Qattara Depression. In the absence of sufficient armoured troops to support them, I was not prepared to risk their garrisons being isolated and eventually destroyed. I was still very anxious lest a sudden and concentrated attack should break through our defences and repeat what had occurred at Matruh. During the fore-noon of 2nd July the enemy appeared to be massing for an attack on the 1st South African Division holding the El Alamein fortress, and I considered it essential to deprive him of the power to deliver a concentrated blow in the north. The best way to do this was to attack him.

I decided, therefore, to regain the tactical initiative by counter-attacking, and ordered the 13th Corps to wheel north with its right flank on our defended locality at Bab el Qattara, and attack the enemy in flank and rear. The 30th Corps meanwhile was to hold its ground in the north and prevent any enemy attempt to advance eastwards. The 13th Corps started its attack on the afternoon of the 2nd July, using the New Zealand Division and what was left of the 5th Indian Division. Close fighting between our infantry and the enemy's took place on the 3rd July, and we took prisoners and guns, besides destroying some enemy tanks. The operations were greatly assisted by the splendid work of our air forces, which carried out over 150 bomber sorties on this day and over 500 fighter sorties.

The New Zealand and 5th Indian Divisions and the 7th Motor Brigade continued their northward thrust on the 4th and 5th of July, occupying El Mreir and approaching our former defensive locality at Deir el Shein. More enemy tanks were destroyed and more prisoners taken. Our air forces continued to support the infantry and to batter enemy concentrations. The enemy, meanwhile, had been hurriedly entrenching his new southern front, and extending it to the westward to prevent his communications with El Daba being cut. He was also reinforcing it with tanks and infantry from his northern wing.

I had no reserves with which to reinforce the 13th Corps and, in face of the rapidly stiffening enemy opposition, their advance came to a standstill. Although the operation did not succeed in rolling up the enemy and destroying him, as at one time I had hoped it might, it succeeded in drawing off enemy troops from the north, which greatly relieved the pressure on our right and centre and gave us time to consolidate these important sectors.

On the 4th July, the 9th Australian Division began to concentrate on the coast in rear of the El Alamein fortress, but I had to ask its commander, Lieutenant-General Morshead, to detach one of his brigades temporarily to provide some infantry to hold the vital Ruweisat Ridge, which was the key to our whole position. This division was incorporated in the 30th Corps, in command of which Major-General Ramsden succeeded Lieutenant-General Norrie on the 7th July. The enemy now began to move tanks and other troops round the left flank of the 13th Corps which had been stretched as far west as Deir el Harra. Our front was now much extended and loosely knit. In order, therefore, to close the gap existing about Deir el Hima between the left of the 30th and the right of the 13th Corps, the New Zealand Division was ordered to take ground to the eastward, their place on the outer flank being taken by the 7th Motor Brigade. The enemy took advantage of this to extend his positions to the south and east and, on the 9th July, he occupied our defensive locality near Deir el Qattara, which had been evacuated in accordance with my policy of avoiding the isolation of troops in detached posts. The enemy continued to exert pressure on this flank and eventually pushed as far east as Qaret el Himeimat, but he consolidated his position in this sector further in rear on a line through Qaret el Khadim and the El Taqa plateau. I had not sufficient troops to hold this southern sector in strength and had to entrust it to the 7th Armoured Division, which organised its defence on a mobile basis suitable to the light armoured and motorised units composing it. This released a brigade of the 5th Indian Division to take over the defence of the Ruweisat Ridge, which enabled the 1st Armoured Division to be withdrawn into reserve.

### The Capture of Tel el Eisa.

Further progress in the south was for the moment impracticable, but I was resolved not to surrender the initiative we had gained and to continue to force the enemy to conform to our movements. I therefore instructed the 30th Corps to capture the Tel el Eisa mounds on the railway west of El Alamein. The attack, which was launched early on the 10th July with skill and dash by the 9th Australian Division, supported by the 1st South African Division and infantry tanks, was successful. The enemy immediately launched heavy counter-attacks with tanks and infantry, well supported by artillery; but in spite of this, the Australians held fast to all the important ground they had gained. During this operation we destroyed a number of German and Italian tanks, captured fifteen guns and took over a thousand prisoners, nearly all Italians. I had hoped to be able to exploit this success to the west and south, but the enemy offered strong resistance and I had no reserves available with which to reinforce the attack.

The Tel el Eisa salient was an important acquisition, since it threatened the enemy positions further south. Fully conscious of this, the enemy transferred German infantry from the centre of his line to stiffen the Italians on the shoulder of the salient and made heavy and repeated counter-attacks against our new positions. Some posts changed hands more than once, but the Australians held fast to all the principal tactical features. We thus retained a firm base from which to attack southwards against the enemy's centre or westwards along the coast.

### Consolidation of the Position.

In order to improve our position against a possible enemy offensive and to set the stage for a further attack on our own part, the Eighth Army maintained its pressure along the whole front.

On the night of the 14th July, the New Zealand Division and 5th Indian Infantry Brigade attacked along the Ruweisat Ridge and south of it and gained considerable ground to the west, including valuable observation posts on the ridge itself overlooking the Deir el Shein Depression and the country to the north. During the action Major-General Lumsden, commanding 1st Armoured Division, was wounded and replaced by Major-General A.H. Gatehouse, commander of the 10th Armoured Division which was still training and equipping in the Delta. About a week later, during the attack of the 22nd July, General Gatehouse himself was wounded and was succeeded in the command of the 1st Armoured Division by Brigadier A.F. Fisher. Although the enemy counter-attacked with tanks on the evening of the 15th and regained some of the lost ground, our tactical position in this very important part of the front was improved by the operation. Moreover, we took some 2,000 prisoners, mostly Italians.

The enemy showed the value he attached to this ground by attacking the 5th Indian Infantry Brigade once more on the following day. But his tanks and lorried infantry were heavily engaged by our 2nd Armoured Brigade and by a powerful concentration of artillery and failed to gain a footing. In order to relieve the pressure on our centre, I ordered both Corps to press the enemy on the northern and southern flanks. Accordingly, on the night of the 16th July, the 9th Australian Division captured the low ridge of El Makh-Khad, eight miles west of El Alamein railway station, with 500 prisoners, thereby enlarging our salient, which throughout this period was the scene of continuous fighting. Further attacks against the 5th Indian Division on the Ruweisat Ridge on the 18th and 19th July were repulsed.

In the south, the 7th Armoured Division with light tanks and motorised units kept up their pressure and, on the 18th July and subsequent days, attacked the enemy positions at Gebel Kalakh and on the Taqa plateau, but were unable to make much headway, being weak in artillery and infantry and without medium tanks. Moreover, the country in this sector was difficult and broken.

### Attack in the Centre.

Having made the enemy extend his front and disperse his reserves to some extent, I thought the time had come to strike hard at the centre of his line with the object of cutting his forces in half. We should thereby have achance to sever his communications and rollup the northern part of his army. With this end in view I told General Gott to attack the enemy positions about Deir el Abyad and El Mreir.

Just before dusk on the 21st July the 161st Indian Infantry Brigade and the 5th and 6th New Zealand Infantry Brigades advanced along the Ruweisat Ridge and to the south of it with the object of opening a way for our armoured forces to break through. The attack was preceded and supported by very heavy artillery fire and aerial bombardment. At the same time supporting and diversionary attacks were made on either flank. In the north the 9th Australian Division attacked north-westwards from Tel el Eisa and southwards towards Tel el Makh-Khad with the object of improving their positions and of exploiting to the south, while the 1st South African Division was directed on Miteiriya. At the same time the 69th Infantry Brigade, temporarily attached to the 7th Armoured Division, attacked enemy positions on the Taqa plateau in the south.

The initial advance in the centre went well, the infantry gaining most of their objectives by dawn on the 22nd, after which they proceeded to clear gaps in the enemy minefields for the passage of our tanks. The enemy, however, counter-attacked and overran the 6th New Zealand Infantry Brigade, capturing many prisoners. On the right a battalion of the 161st Indian Infantry Brigade entered the Deir el Shein defended locality but was counter-attacked and practically destroyed; the rest of the brigade, however, consolidated their gains on the Ruweisat Ridge. The 23rd Armoured Brigade, which had but recently come from England and was equipped with Valentine tanks, then passed through the gaps made by the infantry and made considerable progress towards their objective. Later, however, this attack seems to have lost momentum and cohesion, apparently owing to loss of control due partly to the failure of wireless communications. However that may be, the armoured thrust was defeated with heavy losses in tanks. The attack was renewed in the evening by the 2nd Armoured Brigade which had been held up during the day by enemy minefields.

By the evening of the 22nd, our main attack in the centre had gained valuable ground, but in spite of considerable losses in men and tanks, had failed in its object of breaking through the enemy's positions and splitting his army in half. The enemy, however, had obviously been hard hit. The 9th Australian and 1st South African Divisions in the north took their objectives, but a successful enemy counter-attack forced the Australians to give up some of their gains. The 69th Infantry Brigade won a footing on the Taqa Plateau, but were counter-attacked and pushed back.

The failure of this operation was largely due to the lack of reserves with which to maintain its momentum, and this was a constant limiting factor throughout the El Alamein battle. The enemy continued busily to dig and lay mines along his whole front and it was obvious that he had no intention of withdrawing; rather, he was hoping to build up his strength with a view to resuming his offensive against the Delta.

### Attack in the North.

I was firm in my intention to go on hitting the enemy whenever and wherever I could with the aim of destroying him where he stood. Having failed in the centre, I decided to attack in the north with the aid which the possession of the Tel el Eisa salient would give me. I had to withdraw the 69th Infantry Brigade from the southern flank, which was thus left very weak, but I was ready to risk this in order to strengthen the 30th Corps, whose infantry had been fighting continuously for a long time.

On the night of the 26th July, General Ramsden launched his attack against the enemy's positions to the south of the Tel el Eisa salient with the object of breaching this front and, if conditions permitted, of passing our armoured and motorised formations through the gap to take the enemy in rear and roll up his position from the north. The 9th Australian Division attacking southwards secured Sanyet el Miteiriya by first light, while the 1st South African Division lifted enemy mines to the south of this point, thus enabling the 69th Infantry Brigade to drive westwards with the object of gaining the track running from Miteiriya through Deir el Abyad. The 2nd Armoured Brigade moved during the night from its position south of the Ruweisat Ridge to an assembly area south of the perimeter of the El Alamein fortress, ready to exploit success. The 4th Light Armoured Brigade, comprising light tanks and armoured cars with motorised infantry and artillery, followed the 2nd Armoured Brigade from the 13th Corps front and was given the task of exploiting further, should opportunity offer. The

13th Corps meanwhile carried out vigorous patrolling and feint attacks to deceive the enemy as to the real front of attack and prevent him reinforcing it.

The main attack started well but ended in failure. The Australians captured Miteiriya but were heavily counter-attacked by German infantry and tanks from the south-west, and, though supported by infantry tanks and a strong artillery, were forced back to their original positions. The South Africans experienced great difficulty in clearing gaps in the enemy minefields sufficiently safe and wide to be acceptable to the commander of the 1st Armoured Division. This greatly delayed the advance of the 2nd Armoured Brigade in support of the 69th Infantry Brigade, which had made good progress towards its objective, though it was unable to establish the strong anti-tank screen on its southern flank which was an essential part of the original plan. About noon the enemy counter-attacked strongly from the west and south and cut off the leading battalions of the 69th Brigade, which the 1st Armoured Division then tried to extricate. Perceiving that the situation had become hopelessly confused and out of control, General Ramsden decided, with my approval, to discontinue the operation and rally the 69th Brigade east of the enemy minefields. The brigade had suffered so heavily that it had to be taken out of the line.

The immediate cause of the failure of this operation was the delay in getting the tanks forward to support the 69th Brigade, but the fundamental cause was, as before, the lack of enough fresh well-trained troops to keep up the impetus of the attack and to take full advantage of the large concentration of artillery which had been built up in support.

*Preparations for a Decisive Attack.*

Throughout July the Eighth Army had been continuously attacking and had materially improved its positions, thus paving the way for a major offensive later on. It had effectively prevented any further enemy advance on the Delta, and had taken over 7,000 prisoners, more than a thousand of them German. This effort on the part of troops, most of whom had suffered severe losses in the fighting round Tobruk in June, and had then been seriously disorganised by having to withdraw rapidly for over 300 miles closely pursued by the enemy, speaks well for their morale, discipline and determination.

The Eighth Army casualties in battle during July were about 750 officers and 12,500 men, of whom 4,000 belonged to the New Zealand Division and 3,000 to the 5th Indian Division. The casualties in the action of the 27th July were about 1,300, mostly in the 69th Infantry and 24th Australian Infantry Brigades.

Our attack in the north having failed in spite of the advantage which the possession of the Tel el Eisa salient gave us, I was forced to consider whether the Eighth Army was capable of further effort in view of the growing strength of the enemy positions for defence, and of the continued weakness of our armoured forces. The weakness of the Eighth Army relative to the front which had to be held or closely watched, prevented me from forming a real reserve, in which troops could be rested, re-formed and trained for fresh assaults on the enemy; and there were no more formations in the Delta or further to the east on which I could call. The 44th Division, which had just arrived from the United Kingdom, was training in desert warfare outside Cairo, but could not be expected to be ready before the end of August. The 8th Armoured Division, also fresh from England, was being re-armed with American medium tanks instead of its original Valentines which, mounting only two-pounder guns, were no match for the German tanks. The 10th Armoured Division was still training and equipping and unlikely to be ready for action before mid-September. On the 30th July, therefore, having discussed the situation exhaustively with the two Corps Commanders, Generals Gott and Ramsden, I most reluctantly concluded that no further offensive operations were feasible for the present. We must therefore remain temporarily on the defensive, and recruit our strength for a new and decisive effort, which did not seem possible before the middle of September. Throughout July I devoted all available resources to constructing defences to give depth to the El Alamein position, and these were now almost complete. The keys to the defensive zone, contained in the triangle El Alamein, El Hammam and the Qattara Depression were the three main ridges running east and west. The most northerly followed the coast that in the centre was the well-known Ruweisat ridge and on our left ran the Alam el Haifa ridge. On these ridges, within field artillery range of each other, were built a series of strongpoints designed to deny the essential observation points to the enemy and to preserve them for ourselves. These strongpoints were designed to take garrisons of two battalions and a regiment of twenty-five pounder guns. But the majority of the field artillery, with its necessary escort of motorised infantry, and all the armoured forces were to be kept mobile to attack the enemy with fire wherever he might appear, using the strongpoints as pivots of manoeuvre and for observation. The preparation of these defences called for great energy and skilful organisation and both of these qualities were admirably displayed by Brigadier Kisch, Chief Engineer of the Eighth Army.

The essence of the defensive plan was fluidity and mobility and the maximum use of artillery fire. The defensive zone extended for thirty miles behind our forward positions. If the enemy attempted to pass round it towards Burg el Arab, he was to be delayed by our light armoured troops in front and struck in flank by our armoured force and mobile artillery groups.

The so-called Barrel Track leading from Qaret el Himeimat directly to Cairo gave me some anxiety in case the enemy should try to make a rapid advance by this route. The track itself was so difficult, however, owing to the soft deep sand which it traversed for a great part of its length, that I did not consider an enemy advance by that way possible. There was also a bare chance that the enemy might try to effect a diversion by striking at Cairo from Siwa along the southern edge of the Qattara Depression through the Bahariya Oasis. I therefore posted troops of the Sudan Defence Force to watch this route.

In anticipation of the renewal of our offensive, I ordered General Ramsden commanding the 30th Corps to begin planning intensively for a deliberate attack south of the Tel el Eisa salient with a view to making a rapid advance along the coastal road. I considered this operation offered the greatest chances of success, but at the same time I told General Gott to continue to explore the possibilities of breaking through the enemy defences about Gebel Kalakh and the Taqa Plateau to turn his southern flank.

From the 1st August until I handed over direct command of the Eighth Army to Lieutenant-General B.L. Montgomery, contact with the enemy was confined to patrolling and exchanges of artillery fire. Both sides were deeply engaged in extending their positions and in preparing for further operations.

Throughout this first phase of the battle for Egypt, our air forces could not have done more than they did to help and sustain the Eighth Army in its struggle. Their effort was continuous by day and night and the effect on the enemy was tremendous. I am certain that, had it not been for their devoted and exceptional efforts, we should not have been able to stop the enemy on the El Alamein position, and I wish to record my gratitude and that of the whole of the Eighth Army to Air Chief Marshal Tedder, Air Marshal Coningham and the air forces under their command.

On handing over command I addressed this Order of the Day to the Eighth Army:-

"It has been a great honour to have held direct command of the Eighth Army for nearly two months, and it is with great personal regret that I now leave you on the arrival of your new Army Commander. During these weeks you have stopped the enemy; and, in spite of your heavy losses and the inevitable dis-organisation consequent on a rapid withdrawal from the frontier, you have forced him on the defensive, taken ten thousand prisoners from him and destroyed or captured many of his guns, vehicles and other equipment. You will, I know, join me in acknowledging the great and glorious part our air forces have played in helping us to achieve these results. Without their aid the story would have been very different. I thank you with all my heart for the magnificent way in which you have responded to the heavy calls I have made on you and for your unfailing cheerfulness and tenacity in the worst circum-stances. I know you will continue in the same fine spirit and determination to win under your new Commander. I wish you luck and speedy and complete victory."

## PART III. – ORGANISATION, TRAINING AND ADMINISTRATION.
### *The Organisation of the Army.*
To find the correct organisation for the fighting troops to enable them to defeat the enemy under the peculiar conditions of mechanised war in the Desert was of prime importance. This problem, therefore, was always foremost in my mind.

At the conclusion of the Eighth Army's offensive in Cyrenaica it was plain to me that our existing divisional and brigade organisation did not allow of that very close co-operation on the battlefield between the armoured corps, the artillery and the infantry which was to my mind essential to success. The Germans had reached a very high standard of co-operation between the three arms and I felt that we must try at least to equal and, if possible, surpass them.

There was no doubt, too, that as a result of the recent fighting an impression had been created in the minds of some junior leaders and soldiers, other than those of the Royal Armoured Corps, that our armour had not altogether pulled its weight in the battle. It was very necessary to eradicate any such feeling, and I felt that the best way to do this was to associate the three arms more closely at all times and in all places.

It seemed to me that our pre-war divisional organisation was too rigid and lacking inflexibility to be really adaptable to the conditions of modern quick-moving warfare in the Desert, or even elsewhere, having regard to the fact that great battles are fought and won in flat country, not in mountains.

I decided, therefore, while keeping the divisional framework with its traditions and associations, to reorganise the brigades, armoured, motorised and infantry, into brigade groups each with its own artillery and engineers, so that they could be self-contained and capable, if necessary, of rapid transference from one higher formation to another to meet the temporary needs of a rapidly changing situation. In this way I felt too that the three arms would be forced into closer permanent contact with each other and all officers would have a chance to acquire a broader outlook, which was often conspicuous by its absence as a result of faulty traditions and training.

Secondly, I was sure that our practice of forming large armoured divisions, strong in tank units and relatively weak in infantry, was wrong, because it tended to encourage the idea that the Royal Armoured Corps was an army within an army and also because, to gain the mobility and flexibility we required for victory, we must have more armoured divisions. By diluting armoured divisions with motorised infantry we could not only form twice as many armoured divisions, each with a smaller content of armour it is true, but also restore the proper balance of the three arms and so secure their better co-operation on the battlefield.

I therefore reorganised my armoured divisions, giving to each an armoured brigade group and a motorised infantry brigade group instead of two armoured brigades and a support group. This organisation, which proved its value in the subsequent operations, was later introduced into the army in the United Kingdom.

At the same time I had considered the inclusion in the armoured division of a lorried infantry brigade group, but later discarded this idea as likely to make the formation too cumbersome. But, as a result of the fighting which culminated in the battle of El Alamein, I again considered changing the basic divisional organisation so as to produce a division of increased striking power and mobility in place of the infantry division, which, as often as not, had proved to be a liability rather than an asset in desert fighting, owing to its relative immobility and its vulnerability in open country.

My idea was that the normal or basic division should contain an armoured brigade group and a motorised brigade group, each with its own artillery component, and, in addition, an artillery group comprising two field regiments and a motorised medium machine-gun battalion. Each division would also have allotted to it a lorried infantry brigade. This brigade would not necessarily move with its division at all times, but, being lorry-borne, could be rushed forward when needed, either to carry out a deliberate attack on an entrenched enemy position, or to consolidate ground gained to form a pivot of manoeuvre. The remaining infantry would be retained in their divisional organisations and used for holding defensive positions, protecting forward aerodromes, and guarding vital points on the lines of communication against air and sea-borne attack. They would be specially trained and equipped for these duties and also to serve as replacements for the lorried infantry brigades in the mobile divisions. These ideas were being examined when I handed over my command.

### *The Training of the Army.*

Reorganisation alone obviously would not bring about that closer co-operation on the battlefield and improvement in mutual understanding between the three arms which was so necessary. I therefore ordered a drastic overhaul and reorganisation of our training system. In this I was most ably assisted by Major-General A. Galloway, my Deputy Chief of the General Staff, and by my Director of Military Training, Major-General A.F. Harding who was appointed in January 1942 to this post, which was created at my request.

Briefly the measures taken to improve the system of training and to ensure closer co-operation between the arms were:-

(i) The establishment at Sarafand in Palestine of a higher war course where potential divisional commanders were to receive instruction in modern methods of war.

(ii) Grouping in one area in Palestine all the tactical and weapon training schools, hitherto scattered throughout the Command. In this way it was possible to ensure that a uniform doctrine, which took account of the characteristics of all three arms and was attuned to modern conditions, was taught under a single direction.

The staff school at Haifa continued to progress and expand under the command of Brigadier G.K. Dibb, who carried on the good work of Major-General E.E. Dorman-Smith. During the period under review a strong Royal Air Force wing was added to the school, which officers of the Royal Navy also attended. A proper atmosphere of inter-service co-operation was thereby created and the value of the course was greatly enhanced.

Training in combined operations continued steadily at Kabrit on the Great Bitter Lake, and many formations and units were put through a comprehensive course of instruction. The services of Brigadier M.W.M. Macleod, who directed this branch of training, were outstanding.

*Intelligence and Public Relations.*

In March 1942 Brigadier E.J. Shearer under whose energetic and skilful direction the intelligence service had grown from nothing into a large, complex and most efficient organisation, was replaced as Director of Military Intelligence by Brigadier F.W. de Guingand, who proved an able successor to him. I took this opportunity of removing the responsibility for public relations from the Director of Military Intelligence, as I felt that it was growing so fast in scope and importance that it required an organisation of its own with direct access to myself. I accordingly appointed Colonel A.B. Phillpotts as my Deputy Director of Public Relations, and he filled this post entirely to my satisfaction.

*Allied Forces.*

*The Free French Forces.* – The Free French Forces continued to share in garrisoning Syria and the Lebanon.

The 1st Free French Brigade Group joined the Eighth Army, at the end of January 1942 and fought throughout the battle of Gazala, distinguishing itself by its fine defence of Bir Hacheim. Troops from the Chad helped our offensive in Cyrenaica by attacking and destroying Italian posts in the Fezzan, some 500 miles south of Tripoli; these operations were ably conducted by General Leclerc in most difficult conditions some 2,500 miles in advance of his railhead in Nigeria.

It was necessary to send some French-African units back to Equatorial Africa for disciplinary reasons, but these units were eventually replaced by others brought from East Africa and elsewhere.

From General Catroux, who had no easy task to perform, I received the fullest assistance and I gratefully acknowledge the helpful and co-operative spirit he always displayed. The Free French Forces had their headquarters in Syria, and it fell to General Sir H. Maitland Wilson, commanding the Ninth Army, to initiate and maintain cordial relations with them, a duty he carried out most successfully.

*The Polish Forces.* – In November 1941 the Polish land forces in the Middle East numbered some 7,000 men. The Polish Carpathian Brigade Group, which served under General Kopanski with particular distinction during the siege of Tobruk and in the pursuit of the beaten Axis forces to Gazala was the chief component of these forces. There was also a Polish Officers' Legion and a Base Depot near Alexandria.

The possibility of withdrawing a large number of Poles from Russia to the Middle East was being considered at that time, and General Sikorski, Prime Minister and Commander-in- Chief, visited Cairo in November to discuss with me the future organisation of the Polish Army.

The first evacuation of Polish troops and civilians from Russia through Persia and Iraq began in March 1942. The number involved, 31,000 soldiers and 2,000 civilians, was much larger and the rate of arrival must faster than had been expected. This imposed a serious strain on the administrative and liaison staffs responsible for the reception and transportation of the new arrivals. I decided to concentrate all the Polish troops in Palestine where accommodation and training facilities existed and the climate was good. The civilian refugees were accommodated temporarily near Teheran. In April, the Carpathian Brigade Group was moved from Cyrenaica to Palestine to form the nucleus of the 3rd Carpathian Division. Palestine proved an ideal training ground and by July an Army Corps of two divisions with the proper complement of Corps troops was beginning to take shape, the cadres for a second division being formed. Many units were under strength, however, and there was a serious, though unavoidable, lack of equipment.

During July the Soviet Government announced their intention of evacuating further Polish troops to the Middle East. The Germans had resumed their offensive in Southern Russia some two months earlier, and, in view of the growing danger of an invasion through the Caucasus, I decided to move the Polish Corps to Iraq and to combine it with the new troops from Russia, which were expected to amount to 40,000 men.

General Zajac took command of the Polish forces in the Middle East at the end of November and held the appointment until I relinquished my command. I found him a willing collaborator and a most competent adviser, and I am glad to have had the privilege of serving with him. I also had the great advantage of being able to consult with General Anders on his journeys to and from Russia and wish to record my appreciation of his ready co-operation and sound advice.

*The Royal Greek Forces.* – The organisation and training of the 1st Infantry Brigade Group of the Royal Greek Army in Palestine went on steadily, but progress was slow, due partly to lack of equipment and partly to the lack of suitable officers and instructors. An officer training unit, started in October 1941, was not a success. To deal with the arrival of a considerable number of Greeks from Greece and the Aegean Islands, a depot and training centre was formed in Palestine in the spring. In June a beginning was made with a second brigade group.

After consultation with me, His Majesty the King of the Hellenes visited Palestine in March and, as a result of his visit, a number of changes were made in the commanders and staffs of the contingent, which led to greater efficiency and more rapid progress.

Lieutenant-General Sir Bernard Freyberg, commander of the New Zealand Expeditionary Force, undertook the responsibility of helping the Royal Greek Forces in their training and organisation, and generously placed his own training schools and facilities at their disposal. This assistance was of great value.

In June the 1st Brigade Group joined the Ninth Army in Syria, and in early August it was moved to Egypt where it helped to build the Amiriya defence works.

*The Royal Yugoslav Forces.* – The Royal Yugoslav forces under my command consisted of a Headquarters and one battalion of Royal Yugoslav Guards.

Early in 1942, the Yugoslav Government in England replaced the commander of their forces in the Middle East by an officer who was unacceptable to the great majority of the Yugoslav army and air force officers serving in the Command. After exhaustive but fruitless efforts to find a peaceful solution, I was compelled to place all the Yugoslav forces temporarily under the command of Lieutenant-General R.G.W.H. Stone, General Officer Commanding the British Troops in Egypt, who carried out this duty with great tact and skill. It was also necessary to intern at their own request a number of Yugoslav officers in order to avoid blood-shed, and a number of officers and men temporarily joined our forces during this period of unrest. My Chief of the General Staff, Lieutenant-General Sir Arthur Smith was tireless in his efforts to compose these unfortunate dissensions.

The Royal Yugoslav Guards battalion did useful work in guarding important installations and in preparing defensive positions in the Western Desert. Towards the end of the period under review the battalion was moved to Haifa. As more than half of the personnel were ex-Italian prisoners of Slovene origin who had volunteered to serve against the Axis, it was considered desirable to remove them from the possibility of contact with their former employers.

*The Czechoslovak Forces.* – The Czechoslovak forces under my command consisted of the 11th Infantry Battalion, which was attached to the Polish Carpathian Brigade Group in Tobruk, where it did well. The Czechoslovak Military Mission then agreed to the conversion of the battalion into a light anti-aircraft regiment, and this was satisfactorily accomplished at Haifa.

### Administration.

Lieutenant-General Sir Thomas Riddell-Webster was Lieutenant-General in charge of administration until the 1st July 1942 when he was recalled to London to become Quarter- Master-General to the Forces. He was succeeded by Lieutenant-General Sir Wilfred Lindsell. To both of these officers I owe a great deal as I was able to leave the administration of the Command in their able hands and thus devote myself to the major strategical and political issues.

By June 1942 the ration strength of the Middle East Command had risen to just over one million persons – an increase of more than three hundred thousand on the strength of November 1941. This figure included troops of many nation-alities, labour units, prisoners of war and interned aliens. The increase was due principally to the incorporation of Iraq and Persia in the Middle East Command. The base and lines of communication organisation for this area was already in existence, and the change hardly affected the installations already functioning in the rest of the Command. The transfer of responsibility for maintaining the troops in Persia and Iraq from the India Command to the Middle East, however, was by no means easy, as the line of supply ran up the Persian Gulf and the natural base is India. But thanks to the labours of General Riddell-Webster and General Sir Edward Quinan, commanding the 10th Army, the change was carried out with the minimum of friction and delay.

When the Eighth Army withdrew to the El Alamein line, it was decided to revise the layout of our western base, in order to give a greater measure of security to the principal installations against danger either from the west or from the north. Henceforth the major base installations serving the Eighth and Ninth Armies were to be sited in Palestine south of Acre, and east of the Nile Delta. Fifty per cent. of the reserves were to be held in Egypt, forty per cent. in Palestine and ten per cent. in the Sudan and Eritrea.

*Bases and Communications.* – Vast distances and inadequate means of communication constitute one of the principal strategic problems of the Middle East Command. The improvement of communications progressed steadily throughout the period under review.

When the conquest of Syria was completed in July 1941, and we began to plan the defence of the Northern Front, the chief factor to be taken into account was the absence of rail communication between Syria and Iraq and our bases in Palestine. In August 1941, the construction of a standard gauge railway to link Haifa with Tripoli in Syria was begun. The enterprise entailed the construction of tunnels, one of them over a mile long, and much rock-cutting along the coast between Haifa and Beirut and was carried out with great skill by technical troops from the Union of South Africa and from Australia, aided by pioneer units from South Africa, India and other parts of the British Commonwealth, as well as by local labour. By the middle of August, 1942, the line had been laid between Haifa and Beirut and much work had been done on the northern section. When completed, the new line will provide through railway communication between Egypt and Turkey, as well as with Iraq.

On the other front the Western Desert railway was extended a further hundred and twenty-six miles, and the line reached Belhamed on the 26th May, 1942.

In Egypt a railway line was laid on the east bank of the Suez Canal from Kantara to Suez. A railway bridge across the Canal was opened shortly before the close of the period under review.

At the head of the Persian Gulf I sanctioned the linking of Tanooma, on the Shatt El Arab opposite Basra with Khorramshahr, the terminus of the Persian Railway system. This railway link will facilitate the transfer of stores and munitions between the Iraq base at Shaiba and the Persian bases as the military situation demands.

The construction of a new deep-water port at Safaga on the western shore of the Red Sea and of a railway and a road to connect it with the Nile Valley railway at Qena progressed steadily. The development of a port at Aqaba and of communications thence northward to Maan on the Hedjaz railway continued. Two deep-water berths were developed at Basra, and twelve more half finished at Suez, Safaga and Adabiya Bay. One and a half miles of lighter wharfs were constructed on various sites.

The desert route from Haifa to Baghdad was developed, and staging posts were established along it. Supplies sufficient to enable it to be used at short notice by one division were put in place. In conjunction with the India Command, from whom the suggestion emanated, an overland reinforcement route from Baluchistan through Persia to Iraq was reconnoitred, and stocking of the route begun.

A thousand miles of bitumen roads and an equivalent area of bitumen aerodromes were laid. Two thousand five hundred miles of gravel and desert roads were completed. Some three hundred bridges were strengthened to take tank-transporters. A bridge was thrown over the Euphrates at Raqqa and a lifting bridge over the Suez Canal at Ismailia.

The stocking of bases and the development of base installations went on without intermission. In Syria we began, early in 1942, to establish advanced bases to hold thirty days' supplies for the garrisons of the fortified areas and for the whole of the Ninth Army at full strength. This work was nearly completed by the 15th August 1942. The construction and stocking of the Persia – Iraq base with stores and munitions sufficient for ninety days for three armoured and fifteen infantry divisions continued.

Workshops, base depots, ammunition depots and hospitals erected during these ten months covered an area of twelve million square feet. Ten cold stores were constructed and two ships fitted with cold storage. Four hundred electric generating plants of varying sizes were installed, and sixty miles of high tension and a hundred and fifty miles of low tension cable laid. A hundred and twenty deep-well pumps, fifteen water-filtering plants producing 32,000 tons of water daily, and fifty-two reservoirs each to hold 35,000 tons were constructed. Extensive defensive lines were fortified in Syria, Iraq, Palestine and Egypt. Among the many anti-aircraft gun emplacements prepared was an artificial island in Suez Bay, weighing 30,000 tons, to take a four-gun battery.

A million tons of cement and six million tons of concrete were mixed and eighty million bricks burnt and laid in the construction of defence works and base installations during these ten months.

The successful execution of these great undertakings was due very largely to the skilful planning and energetic direction of my Engineer-in-Chief, Major-General H.B.W. Hughes, and my Director of Works, Major-General E.F. Tickell.

*American Aid.* – Under the auspices of the United States Government, American civil firms began to erect workshops where aircraft, motor vehicles and armoured vehicles will be assembled and repaired. These workshops are being built in several parts of the Command, and some, notably those in Eritrea, are already working. In Persia and Iraq, besides erecting and operating assembly plants, American firms took a large share in the development of ports and communications.

*Preparations in Turkey.* – Much useful work was done to prepare Turkey as a theatre of operations for our land and air forces, in case we should be called on to help repel an Axis invasion. Activities, however, were restricted by the natural desire of the Turkish Government to avoid making preparations obviously hostile to the Axis Powers.

*Supplies and Transport.* – In order to save shipping, a reduction was made in the scales of rations issued to the troops in May, 1942. By this reduction and by using more local produce about a thousand tons a month were saved. The average amount of Royal Army Service Corps supplies imported during the summer of 1942 was 50,000 tons a month, of which 10 per cent. came from the United Kingdom, 30 per cent. from Canada and the United States, and 60 per cent. from India and elsewhere.

The arrangements for storing and delivering petrol were greatly improved during the ten months under review. The leakage which occurs when the standard four-gallon cans are used gave rise to a very serious problem: losses might amount to as much as fifteen per cent. even in normal conditions, and in the desert where the Eighth Army, by far the largest consumer, half of whose maintenance tonnage consists of petrol and lubricants, was operating, losses were often as much as thirty per cent. To arrange bulk storage and delivery was no easy matter in a Command where seventeen million gallons are used monthly. Nevertheless bulk storage capacity was increased by 345 per cent. against an increase of 250 per cent. in the amount packed in cans; and by July 1942 in Egypt, Palestine, and Syria, which were the principal consumer areas, no less than ninety per cent. was being delivered in bulk. This represented a saving of 2,000 tons of imported tinplate a month, of £140,000 on production costs and an incalculable amount in petrol and transport.

Operations in Cyrenaica made extremely heavy demands on transport resources. When the 13th Corps were operating round Agedabia and El Agheila twenty-four general transport companies were required to supply that corps alone. Even when the remainder of the Command had been allotted the very smallest amount of transport possible, the Eighth Army often had less than its operations demanded. The period under review, however, saw a gradual improvement in the situation, so that by the end of August there were altogether seventy-two general transport companies. To find sufficient drivers was a difficult problem and every source of man-power was tapped to provide them. The ten-ton diesel lorry proved its worth in the desert, being much more economical both in fuel and man-power than the commoner three-ton lorry. More of these vehicles would have been welcome.

Horsed transport and pack mule companies were formed for use in Cyria, Cyprus and Eritrea.

Major-General C. le B. Goldney continued to perform the duties of Director of Supplies and Transport throughout the period, and I greatly appreciated his unfailing and steadfast support.

*Local Production.* – In order to effect further savings in shipping space, local production was stimulated still further. Three and a half million anti-tank mines, forty self-propelled 200-ton landing craft and thirty 100-ton lighters were among the numerous articles constructed in the Middle East. Expenditure on account of Ordnance supplies alone rose from £400,000 to £800,000 Egyptian.

*Salvage.* – The salvage organisation, which had developed enormously by November 1941 as a result of intense propaganda and the inculcation throughout the Command of the need for economy, continued to grow and to extend its activities. Seven salvage depots were operating in Egypt, six in Syria and Palestine, five in Eritrea and one at Khartoum. These depots were staffed largely by local civilians, supervised by a few British personnel.

Among the salvage shipped to the United Kingdom, India and elsewhere, were 5,000 tons of scrap steel, 1,000 tons of tyres and rubber, and 380 tons of brass. Over 30,000 tyres, 1,750,000 bottles, mainly for distilled water for motor vehicles, 865 tons of camouflage material, and 32,000 forty-gallon drums were made serviceable and reissued, besides thousands of tons of re-manufactured metals and other materials.

For the operations in Cyrenaica special salvage officers and units were attached to the Eighth Army. Salvage depots were established as the troops went forward; and, although collection could not keep pace with the advance, much material was salved. Amongst the equipment collected and sent back to the base were 164 British and 330 enemy guns, over 15,000 rifles, more than a million petrol tins, 3,000 tons of ammunition and 1,200 tons of scrap metal.

In view of the poor design of our own petrol containers, a special effort was made to salve as many as possible of the very efficient German petrol and water containers. At Bengasi over two million of them were discovered, but only a few could be removed before the enemy made his counterstroke.

*Printing and Stationery.* – The Army Printing and Stationery Service assumed responsibility for supplying the Royal Navy and the Royal Air Force, and also for providing newsprint for military and semi-military purposes. The base depot at Suez was enlarged to handle five hundred tons a month.

The General Headquarters Printing Press was greatly expanded, the number of machines being increased from thirty to sixty-two, while the output was trebled. The importance of an efficient and adequate printing service to the Army cannot be over-estimated.

*Postal Services.* – Under Colonel W.R. Roberts, Deputy Director, the Army Postal Service continued to serve the troops most satisfactorily and to deal efficiently with an ever increasing volume of business in spite of considerable transportation difficulties.

The airgraph service was further developed and the number of letters despatched and received weekly by this system increased from about three hundred thousand in November 1941 to just over one million in August 1942. Articles of all classes posted weekly in British Army Post Offices in the Command during May 1942 averaged a million and three-quarters.

*Ordnance Services.* – A chronic shortage of base ordnance workshop units was experienced, and as a result it was some time before the accumulation of tanks in need of repair could be cleared. Moreover, every tank imported from overseas had to be modified for the desert. Workshop accommodation was increased, nevertheless, chiefly by impressing civilians and civilian firms. This enabled methods of working to be improved, and repairs and overhauls are on a mass producton rather than on an individual basis. Since November 1941 the number of guns and vehicles overhauled in workshops was doubled. Nearly 40,000 vehicles and 5,000 guns were overhauled and 15,000 vehicles and 5,000 guns modified.

The recovery, organisation was improved by every means that could be devised subject always to the shortage of recovery vehicles. In the campaign of November-December 1941 recovery fell far short of the standard achieved by the Germans, partly because there were very few recovery vehicles and partly because the organisation itself was defective. By June 1942 we had received more recovery vehicles and the organisation had been thoroughly revised with the result that recovery from the battlefield of Gazala was at least as good as if not better than the German.

Major-General W.W. Richards continued to inspire and direct the work of the Ordnance Services with energy, foresight and determination and it is largely due to him that they reached so high a standard of efficiency.

*Signals.* – The signal organisation continued to operate with the utmost efficiency throughout the period and the service was further developed. A serious shortage of personnel as well as equipment continued to be experienced; and it was due to the ingenuity and efficiency of Major-General W.R.C. Penney, my Signal Officer-in-Chief, and his staff that operations and administration did not suffer as a result of these shortcomings. To meet the shortage of signal personnel, it was necessary to convert two Yeomanry regiments into signal units. The regiments concerned accepted this decision most loyally, and rapidly became efficient in their new role.

*Medical Services.* – The medical services continued to function with great efficiency under the able and energetic direction of Major-General P.S. Tomlinson; my Director of Medical Services.

Experience in operations in Libya showed that casualty clearing stations should have their own transport and be fully mobile. It was also clear that all mobile medical units should have their own means of wireless communication. Mobile surgical teams were formed and attached to main dressing stations and casualty clearing stations. These teams worked on the battlefield and proved of inestimable value, as did mobile blood transfusion units. A small number of air ambulances was available, and it is essential that more should be provided to enable serious cases to be evacuated rapidly and smoothly.

### Conclusion.

It may be thought that the administrative effort and the number of persons employed in the base areas and on the lines of communication was out of all proportion to the comparatively small forces actually in contact with the enemy. This matter was constantly in my mind and continually under expert examination; and I was able to satisfy myself that in administration there was little waste of manpower or misdirection of energy throughout the whole Command. I consider this reflects the greatest credit on those responsible for organising and controlling the vast administrative machine on whose efficient running our ability to wage the war entirely depended.

War anywhere is primarily a matter of supply and movement and these problems are particularly acute in the Middle East. Placed at the end of very long lines of sea communications the countries of the Middle East are for the most part undeveloped, possess few modern Industrial plants and are singularly poor in land communications of every kind. Moreover the Libyan Desert itself rivals any country in the world in barrenness.

## APPENDICES.
### 1.
*Letter to Lt.-General Sir Alan Cunningham, Commander, Eighth Army.*

*2nd September* 1941.

*Western Desert Offensive Autumn,* 1941.

1. After consultation with Commander-in-Chief, Mediterranean and Air Officer Commanding-in-Chief, Middle East, I have decided to carry out an offensive this autumn with the object of driving the enemy out of North Africa.

2. The offensive will be carried out in two phases:-

> *First phase:* The capture of Cyrenaica.
> *Second phase:* The capture of Tripolitania.

*First phase:*

3. The object of the operations in the first phase is to recapture and hold Cyrenaica. Your immediate objective is the destruction of the enemy's armoured forces, thereby facilitating the holding of Cyrenaica and the subsequent capture of Tripolitania.

4. The attack is to be launched as soon as the necessary forces can be trained and concentrated, and the necessary maintenance arrangements completed. I estimate that this should be possible by the beginning of November, and every effort is to be made to avoid the necessity for a postponement.

5. In order to deceive the enemy as to the direction of our main blow, the original deployment will be on a wide front from the coast to Giarabub. Arrangements are to be made to establish dumps in the forward areas as soon as the necessary protection can be provided.

6. The establishment of dumps in the forward areas, leakage of information as to the strength of our forces, and other factors may cause the enemy to modify his present dispositions, so it is essential to organize the offensive on a flexible basis. In broad outline there are two courses open to us:-

> *Course A:* To base our main striking force on Giarabub and advance *via* Gialo to cut off the enemy's retreat whilst maintaining pressure and advancing as opportunity offers along the coast.

*Course B:* To attack with our main striking force from the coastal sector, south of the escarpment, and to feint from the centre and south.

7. You will prepare detailed plans on each of the above bases and be prepared to submit your recommendations when called for after 1st October, 1941, so that a decision may be made.

*Second phase:*
8. The object of the operations in the second phase is to capture and hold Tripolitania.

9. Alternative plans for these operations will be prepared in outline by G.H.Q.

*General:*
10. This campaign will be a combined operation entailing the closest possible co-operation between all three Services and dependent on the Navy, not only for direct support from H.M. ships when opportunity offers, but, to a very large extent, for the maintenance by sea of the land and air forces. Arrangements will be made to enable you to effect a landing with a brigade group behind the enemy lines, should you so wish, but the success or failure of your general plan must not be made to depend on the feasibility of this operation.

11. Maintenance will be one of the limiting factors of these operations and mobility one of the most important. Formations will be trained to carry out their mobile roles on a very low scale of baggage, food and water.

12. You may assume that the forces available for the first phase of the operations will comprise:-

One Army H.Q. and Signals.
One Armoured Corps H.Q. and Signals.
One Armoured Division.
One Armoured Brigade Group.
One Corps H.Q. and Signals.
Four Infantry Divisions (of which at least two will be fully motorized).
Two Infantry Brigades.
Tobruk Garrison.

Further details will be forwarded to you separately.

13. Acknowledge.

C.J. Auchinleck,
*General.*
*C.-in-C., M.E.F.*

2.

*Appreciation of the Situation by Commander, Eighth Army.*

*In the Field,*
*28th September* 1941.

1. The following short appreciation examines the problem of the recapture of Cyrenaica under the terms of the C.-in-C.'s directive dated 2nd September 1941.[29]

2. *Object:-*
The destruction of the enemy armoured forces.

3. The appreciation is based on information contained in J.P.S.64, which is not therefore reproduced in detail here. The following are the salient factors which have influenced the plan:-

    (i) Dispositions of the enemy, *viz.*, one armoured division in the forward area and one west of Tobruk have been taken as a basis. It is considered that these dispositions are commensurate with our occupation and preparations at Giarabub and, unless the enemy intends to attack either Tobruk or eastwards from his forward area, are quite possibly those which he will adopt in the future. A note is appended on the effect on the plan of other possible action on the part of the enemy.[30]

    (ii) The relative strengths in tanks will be about 6:4 in our favour.

    (iii) The relative air strengths may be about 3:2 in the enemy's favour. This figure, however, takes into account the Italian aircraft.

    (iv) It is understood that the enemy supply situation cannot be interfered with to a much greater degree than at present. It is known that continuous dumping is going on in the area between Tobruk and Sollum. It is estimated under these conditions that the enemy in the forward area will be in a position to carry on land operations for a period of three months and air operations for at least one month by 1st November.

4. It should be our endeavour to bring the enemy armoured forces to battle under conditions where we can concentrate against them a numerical superiority in tanks. Our armoured division will not have this superiority if faced with both the enemy armoured divisions, and one of our armoured brigades is weaker than one enemy armoured division. In order, therefore, to produce a superiority of tanks against the enemy, as long as the enemy divisions are within inter-supporting distance of each other, a similar condition must apply to our armoured division and our remaining armoured brigade.

5. If the enemy do not withdraw from present positions, an attack on Bengasi as visualised in Plan 'A' is not advocated, for the following reasons:-

    (i) The capture of Bengasi would not necessarily cause the enemy to capitulate in view of his supply situation in Eastern Cyrenaica.

(ii) It would divert a portion of our armoured forces from the main object, which is the destruction of the enemy armoured forces, to the rapid accomplishment of which all armoured forces should be directed. It might, moreover, expose a portion of our armoured forces to be attacked by the enemy in greater strength. *(See* para. 4).

(iii) A controlling factor is the enemy air threat from set bases in the north directed to the flank of a force competing with administrative and operational difficulties. The potential of this threatening force far exceeds our available strength, and its present numbers may be increased at will so long as the enemy possesses the coastal aerodromes which are in direct contact with Greece and Crete.

The second factor is the dissipation of force involved. The bombing threat would necessitate despatching a strong fighter force with the column and this would result in fighter weakness in the Bardia area.

Thirdly, the arrival of the column within reach of the coastal area south of Bengasi would find our weakened air forces opposed by a strong enemy operating from established bases. This would imply further strengthening of the southern fighter force at the expense of the northern, and even then there is doubt that it would be in sufficient strength for the task.

(iv) The maintenance of any forces sent to Bengasi over the period (which might last for some time) during which the main tank battle was being staged, would be extremely difficult and very costly in transport.

(v) There is a possibility of moves in the area south of Bengasi being delayed by rain, with consequent dislocation of any plan decided upon. This also affects the enemy, though to a less extent, due to his administrative situation being easier than ours.

6. Our initial plan, therefore, goes no further than the relief of Tobruk, and destroying the armoured forces in Cyrenaica. Subsequent plans for the capture of Bengasi must depend on the success which has attended the above. If, unhappily, any enemy armoured formations escape, the detail of future plans to be adopted will depend on their dispositions and action. If all enemy armour is brought to battle, the conquest of the rest of Cyrenaica should not be difficult or slow. *(See* para. 13).

7. The following, then, are the essentials of a plan to be adopted if the enemy remain in the forward areas:-

(i) The enemy armoured forces are the target.

(ii) They must be hemmed in and not allowed to escape.

(iii) The relief of Tobruk must be incidental to the plan.

*Re.* (i) the enemy will seek to avoid meeting superior armoured forces, but we should be in a position to force him to do so (*see* para. 8). The destruction of his dumps, particularly petrol, must be an essential part of any plan adopted, as by this means he can be rendered impotent.

*Re.* (ii) the enemy lines of withdrawal must be through his dumping areas, except for such forces as he can supply by air. (Information as to the position of dumps, and extent he can carry out air supply, is of vital importance. Intensive air war against dumps is going on now to full extent of resources.) Lines of withdrawal to Tengeder, Mechili and Derna will, therefore, be those to which attention must be paid.

(ii) and (iii) taken together indicate the necessity of an operation by our forces west of Tobruk, to take place simultaneously with any operation in the frontier area, or between it and Tobruk.

8. The enemy armoured forces are in two different localities and, although within inter-supporting distance, an armoured threat to both Tobruk and the Bardia – Sollum area at the same time should place him in a quandary, and might give us the opportunity of interposing ourselves between his two armoured divisions and defeating each in detail.

The relief of Tobruk would mean much more to him than the loss of Bardia – Sollum. If, therefore, a serious threat develops towards Tobruk, it is probable that he would attempt to concentrate his armoured forces against that threat. It will therefore be necessary for us to be strong in armoured units for any attack carried out in the Tobruk area.

9. The defence system Sollum – Capuzzo – Halfaya – Sidi Omar is well constructed and strong in anti-tank defence. Frontal attack should therefore be avoided initially. It should, however, not be difficult or costly to cut this area off from the rear and to sever the Bardia pipeline on which it depends for water. Any attack on the rear of these positions will have to be accompanied or supported by armoured formations in view of the presence of the enemy 21st Armoured Division in that area.

It will be necessary to reduce these defences in due course to open up the direct route, but once they are isolated this problem should be easier.

10. Lines of advance open to us:-

   (i) Along coast.
   (ii) Hamra – Sidi Suleiman.
   (iii) Bir Sheferzen.
   (iv) Fort Maddalena.
   (v) Giarabub.

   (i) Any advance along the coast is under observation from the escarpment, and entails attacking enemy positions at their strongest points.

   (ii) Was used before, was easily outflanked, and leaves the forces at Sidi Omar in a position to act either way, unless other forces are moving wider south.

   (iii) Too close to Sidi Omar for any but a direct attack on Sidi Omar, etc.

   (iv) Advance by Maddalena gives opportunity of enveloping enemy defences. This line is, however, within forty miles of Sidi Omar and, therefore, if used as a line of supply, as long as the enemy mobile forces remain in the forward area, Maddalena must be covered.

(v) 450 miles from Bengasi, 180 miles from west of Tobruk. It offers best opportunity for surprise, and L. of C. not so vulnerable to air.

11. *Broad Plan.*
(i) *Southern Force* – under command Armoured Corps, to advance from south of Maddalena.

7th Armoured Division.
1st S.A. Division.
22nd Guards Brigade.
One extra anti-tank regt.
One medium regt.

*Object-*

(*a*) To destroy enemy armoured formations in region Tobruk.

(*b*) To relieve Tobruk in conjunction with an attack by forces in Tobruk.

(ii) *Centre Force* – initially under command 13th Corps, to advance from Maddalena area.

4th (or 22nd) Armoured Brigade.
One sqn. or more armoured cars.
One field regt.
One bty. anti-tank guns.

This force will operate between the northern and southern forces. Its object will be to find and draw off and, if in a position to do so, attack the enemy armoured formations (at present enemy 21st Armd. Div.) which may try to interfere with the operations of the northern force. If the enemy are met in superior armoured strength, the object of this brigade group would be to draw off the enemy armoured formations in the direction of the southern force, where a concentration of our armoured forces could be brought to bear on him.

(iii) *Northern Force* – 13th Corps.

N.Z. Div.
4th Indian Div.
1st Army Tank Brigade.
One or two army field regts.
Two or three medium regts.

*Objects-*

(*a*) To isolate the enemy forward defences by an advance in rear of them from the south on a north and south axis, and to pin them from the east.

(*b*) to clear the enemy from the area between the forward defences and excl. Tobruk, thereafter joining hands with our forces at Tobruk.

(*c*) In due course to reduce any pockets of the enemy left in the forward area.

12. The above plan would be associated with the formation of a "phantom" force operating from Giarabub towards Bengasi.

Wireless deception to represent the presence at Giarabub of a force equivalent to the southern force shown above will be put in hand. A skeleton force consisting of one or two armoured car regts. supported by a small composite force will advance from that area, and bombers will also be flown down and operated from the southern route.

13. Opportunity will be taken, for exploitation westwards at the earliest possible moment, *i.e.*, as soon as Tobruk and the area east of it are secure, and supply arrangements allow. In the latter connection, it is estimated that a minimum of forty days' supply will be in Tobruk, which should allow of the advance westwards being continued as soon as Eastern Cyrenaica is secure.

A. Cunningham, Lieutenant-General,
Commanding Eighth Army.

3.
*G.H.Q., M.E.F. Operation Instruction No. 103.*

17th October, 1941.

Commander, Ninth Army.
Commander, British Troops in Egypt.

1. Our primary object at present is to clear the enemy out of Libya, and to establish ourselves up to the Tunisian frontier. This object must be achieved before we have to turn and resist an attack from the north, which may eventuate next April.

2. To enable this object to be attained in the time available, every possible step which can be taken, and every possible need which can be foreseen, must be taken and foreseen now.

3. General Cunningham must be given now all the forces and resources he needs, and he must retain these for so long as he requires them.

4. Should the attainment of our object be retarded, for reasons now unforseeable, until such time as it becomes evident that we must turn and prepare to resist attack from the north, then we may have to stop short in our offensive in the west. In this event, General Cunningham will retain the minimum necessary to enable him to establish a defensive front in Cyrenaica or Eastern Tripolitania, and the maximum force which he can release will be withdrawn from his command to reinforce the Northern Front. This step will be necessary in view of the fact that the threat to our bases in the Middle East and Iraq is likely to be more serious from the north than from the west, according to the information at present available to us.

5. We are unlikely to be in sufficient strength by next spring to prosecute an offensive in the west and at the same time hold off a determined attack from the north.

6. Apart from the possible need for withdrawing forces from General Cunningham to reinforce our Northern Front, it may still be necessary to withdraw troops from him in order to keep demands for maintenance within the transport resources available. Every effort is to be made, however, by all concerned to avoid having recourse to this expedient, if it is likely in any way to prejudice the full attainment of his object by General Cunningham.

C.J. Auchinleck, General,
C.-in-C., M.E.F.

4.

*Note on "Crusader" by Commander-in-Chief, M.E.F.*

30th October, 1941.

1. *Object.* – To destroy enemy armoured forces.

2. *Implications of object.* – (*a*) Must do something to bring enemy to battle on ground of our choosing – not of his.

Q. What will make enemy move out to meet us?

A. An obvious move to raise siege of Tobruk.

I*st Deduction.* – Therefore strong forces must be directed on Tobruk.

(*b*) Enemy must be brought to battle east of Tobruk, otherwise he will fight delaying actions and evade destruction.

Q. What must be done to effect this?

A. Surprise in time and direction of main thrust is essential.

2*nd Deduction.* – Long range plans for deception as to intention to attack and date of attack and possible direction of attack must be thorough and continuous.

3*rd Deduction.* – Weight and nature of main concentration must be concealed as long as possible.

4*th Deduction.* – Preliminary movement by feinting columns or detachments must not take place prior to advance of main attacking force.

3. *Our Action.* – (*a*) To move strongest possible armoured and motorised force (30 Corps) towards Tobruk.

(*b*) Break-out to be made by tanks and infantry of Tobruk garrison in conjunction with this move.

(*c*) Vigorous feints and raids by light mobile forces to west and north-west from the line Maddalena – Giarabub.

4. *Enemy reaction.* – Enemy may: (*a*) Keep his two armoured divisions where they are, north of escarpment beween Bardia and Tobruk, hoping later to strike at maintenance service of our 30 Corps and thus paralyse it, while retaining free communication with his own base in above-mentioned area.

5*th Deduction.* – If he does this we should at once secure escarpment, picquet gaps, so as to prevent tank movement; then relieve Tobruk and invest or overrun Bardia – Sollum – Capuzzo with 13 Corps.

(*b*) Keep his armoured force north of escarpment, move west towards Tobruk and then position himself south of it, with a view to taking in flank attempts by us to raise siege. This entails his abandoning forces in Bardia – Sollum – Capuzzo.

> *6th Deduction.* – In this event, we must be ready to push on with all speed with 30 Corps, join hands with Tobruk sally force and pinch his armoured force between the escarpment and Tobruk.

(*c*) Allow our 30 Corps to move on towards Tobruk and thrust with his armoured force through his defences in the area Sidi Omar – Halfaya, and attempt to destroy 13 Corps and our advanced dumps, railhead, etc., south of Sidi Barrani.

> *7th Deduction.* – To guard against this, all possible defensive measures, such as laying minefields, positioning field and anti-tank artillery and holding "I" tanks in readiness must be taken.

(*d*) Abandon Bardia – Sollum, raise siege of Tobruk and withdraw towards Derna, Bengasi and El Agheila without giving battle.

> *8th Deduction.* – In this event, which is possible but not likely, we must be ready to improvise highly mobile columns comprising artillery and motorised units to pursue him at once, and by outflanking his columns and infiltrating between them delay him, and so enable our armoured forces to bring him to battle before he can consolidate in new positions to the westward.

(*e*) Move his armoured force south of escarpment to a suitable area north of Trigh el Abd and west of Capuzzo with object of striking at our 30 Corps in flank and heading it off Tobruk, his eastern flank being protected by his Sidi Omar – Halfaya defences.

> *9th Deduction.* – If the does this, which seems to be his most likely course, we must accept battle and concentrate the strongest possible armoured force against him in this area.
>
> *10th Deduction.* – Any subsidiary movements, which might require the detachment of tanks, other than "I" tanks, for their local protection, against possible attack by enemy armoured forces, must be foregone, in the interests of ensuring the strongest possible concentration of fast armoured units for the decisive battle. This does not forbid the movement of motorised forces mentioned in para. 3(*c*), as these depend on speed for safety, but does preclude the movement of large forces of infantry and artillery round the southern flank of the Sidi Omar – Halfaya – Bardia positions with the idea of isolating the enemy holding these positions; the forward movement of highly mobile motorised forces in this area, however, is not precluded. If the armoured battle ends in a decisive success, these enemy troops can be dealt with at leisure, and the same applies to the enemy investing Tobruk.

5. *Summary.* – (*a*) 30 Corps with all available Cruiser and American tanks to be directed on Tobruk with a view to bringing enemy main armoured formations to battle and destroying them east of Tobruk.

(*b*) Tobruk garrison to sally out and assist main attack by threatening enemy rear and flank and distracting his attention.

(*c*) 13 Corps to hold ground east of Halfaya – Sidi Omar enemy position, ready:-

   (i) to stop any enemy attempt to strike at our advanced base areas, and

   (ii) to move forward at once on successful outcome of armoured battle, against rear of enemy in area Bardia – Sollum – Sidi Omar, and towards Tobruk.

(*d*) Light mobile forces, based on Maddalena and Giarabub to move west and north-west against enemy L. of C. and aerodromes, etc., in area Mechili-Gialo, but not before 30 Corps commences its advance on Tobruk.

(*e*) Full arrangements to be made to pursue enemy with improved mobile columns at once, if he tries to slip away towards Bengasi and El Agheila after an unsuccessful battle.

5.

*Letter to Lieut.-General Sir Alan Cunningham, Commander, Eighth Army.*

Advanced H.Q. Eighth Army, 24th November, 1941.

1. Having discussed the situation with you and learned from you the weak state to which 7 Armoured Division has been reduced by the past five days fighting, I fully realise that to continue our offensive may result in the immobilisation, temporarily at any rate, of all our Cruiser and American M3 tanks.

2. I realise also that should the enemy be left with a superiority of fast moving tanks as a result of our continued offensive, there is a risk that he may try to out-flank our advanced formations in the Sidi Rezegh-Gambut area and cut them off from their bases in Egypt. I realise also that in this event there would remain only very weak forces to oppose an enemy advance into Egypt. On the other hand, it is clear to me that after the fighting of the last few days, it is most improbable that the enemy will be able to stage a major advance for some time to come.

3. There are only two courses open to us:-

   (i) To break off the battle and stand on the defensive either on the line Gamibut-Gabr Saleh or on the frontier. This is a possible solution, as it is unlikely that the enemy would be able to mount a strong offensive against us for many weeks; and it would enable us to retain much of the ground we have gained, including valuable forward landing grounds. On the other hand, it would be counted as an Axis triumph and would entail abandoning for an indefinite time the relief of Tobruk.

   (ii) The second course is to continue to press our offensive with every means in our power.

There is no possible doubt that the second is the right and only course. The risks involved in it must be accepted.

4. You will therefore continue to attack the enemy relentlessly using all your resources even to the last tank. Your main immediate object will be, as always, to

destroy the enemy tank forces. Your ultimate object remains the conquest of Cyrenaica, and then an advance on Tripoli.

5. To achieve the objects set out in para. 4 it seems essential that you should:-

   (i) Recapture the Sidi Rezegh-Ed Duda ridge at the earliest possible moment and join hands with Tobruk garrison. It is to my mind essential that the Tobruk garrison should co-operate to the utmost limit of their resources in this operation.
  (ii) Direct the Oasis Force at the *earliest possible moment* against the coast road to stop all traffic on it and if possible capture Agedabia or Benina, neither of which is strongly held apparently.
 (iii) Use the Long Range Desert Group patrols offensively to the limit of their endurance against every possible objective on the enemy lines of communication from Mechili to Bengasi, Agedabia and beyond to the west. All available armoured cars should be used with the utmost boldness to take part in this offensive. The advantages to be gained by a determined effort against the enemy lines of communication are worth immense risks, which will be taken.

C.J. Auchinleck, General,
C.-in-C., M.E.F.

6.

*G.H.Q., M.E.F. Operation Instruction No. 110.*
*Western Front.*

19th January, 1942.

Lieut.-General W.G. Holmes,
   Commander, British Troops in Egypt.
Lieut-General N.M.R. Ritchie,
   Commander, Eighth Army.

1. My present intention is to continue the offensive in Libya and the objective remains Tripoli.

2. In view, however, of the fluidity of the general strategic situation, we must face the prospect of being unable to continue the Libyan offensive, and of having to pass to the defensive on the Western Front.

3. If this should be forced upon us, it is my intention to stand on the line Agheila – Marada and prevent any enemy advance east of it. General instructions for the defence of this line will be issued separately.

4. If we should be unable to secure this line; or, having secured it, to hold it, I intend to withdraw north-eastwards and eastwards to the general line Sollum – Giarabub, on which the enemy will be stopped.

   During this withdrawal every effort will be made to delay the enemy and thereby to retain the use of forward landing grounds as long as possible.

5. The main axis of withdrawal will be Agheila – Agedabia – Bir Ben Gania – Bir Hacheim – Sidi Omar.

The coast road Bengasi – Derna – Tobruk – Sollum may be used for the clearance of material and stores, but will not be used by fighting formations or units except those located north of the line exclusive Bengasi – Mechili.

6. It is not my intention to try to hold permanently Tobruk or any other locality west of the frontier.

7. The general arrangements for the defence of the line Sollum – Giarabub will be as follows:-

   (a) A defended locality in the area Capuzzo – Sollum – Halfaya, to be held by one infantry division with infantry tanks.
   (b) A defended locality round Maddalena to be held by an infantry division, less a brigade group, with infantry tanks.
   (c) A defended locality at Giarabub to be held by an infantry brigade group.
   (d) A general reserve of one armoured division and an infantry brigade group, to be located in the Bir Abu Misheifa area.

8. The Mersa Matruh defended locality will be maintained and improved for occupation by an infantry division.

9. The Maaten Bagush position and the enemy positions at Bardia will be dismantled, and the material thus salved used for other positions.

10. Work will be continued in accordance with the original plans on the El Alamein position as opportunity offers, until it is completed.

11. Acknowledge.

C.J. Auchinleck, General,
C.-in-C., M.E.F.

7.
*Note on Possible Commitments in the Spring of* 1942.

20th January 1942.

1. In the spring, 1942, we may be faced with the following commitments:-

   (a) The defence of our Western Front.
   (b) The defence of the Northern Front, including Cyprus, and probably also including assistance to Turkey.
   (c) The protection of our bases in the Suez Canal and Persian Gulf areas.

2. On 28th December, we reported our estimated deficiencies on 1st April 1942 to the Minister of Defence and the Chiefs of Staff. As a result of recent diversions the situation has changed again.

3. Our minimum estimated requirements for these purposes, and our estimated resources, assuming that the necessary armoured vehicles and transport are provided, are as follows:-

|  | Minimum Requirements. | Estimated Resources. | Deficiency. |
|---|---|---|---|
| Armoured Divisions | 5 | 3½ | 1½ |
| Infantry Divisions | 17 | 12 | 5 |
| Heavy A.A. Regiments | 34 | 15 | 19 |
| Light A.A. Regiments | 55 | 18 | 37 |

These requirements are based on holding forward on the general line Tabriz – Mosul – Syro – Turkish Frontier to deny the enemy air bases and on the despatch of a force to Western Anatolia to assist Turkey.

4. Apart from this serious shortage of formations and anti-aircraft artillery, there are indications that the delivery of A.F.V.'s and M.T. vehicles will fall far short of requirements. Consequently some of the formations will not be complete in transport and therefore unable to take part in active operations.

5. Excluding forces in Iraq (one armoured brigade group and three infantry divisions), about which details are not yet fully known, the following is an estimate of the position on 1st April 1942:-

(*a*) *Armoured Divisions.*
Two armoured divisions completely equipped and mobile.
(*b*) *Infantry Divisions.*
Two infantry divisions completely equipped and mobile.
Six infantry divisions nearly complete as regards equipment but deficient of transport in varying degrees.

6. From the above it will be seen that we shall be quite unable to carry out operations as envisaged, in paragraph 3.
     Our only course will be to fall back on defences in rear in Persia, Central Iraq and Southern Syria, and to fight a defensive battle, thereby surrendering to the enemy all air bases and landing grounds north of this line, the effect of which will be greatly to increase the scale of enemy air attack on our bases.

7. Progress in re-equipment after 1st April depends mainly on M.T. arrivals which cannot be forecast accurately. The following is an estimate based on the probable rate of arrivals:-

(*a*) *Armoured Divisions.*
A third armoured division should be complete with tanks and transport by mid-May.
(*b*) *Infantry Divisions.*
It is estimated that sufficient transport for an infantry division should be available each month.

8. Therefore by 15th May the position should be as follows:-

(*a*) *Armoured Divisions.*
Three armoured divisions fully mobile.

(*b*) *Infantry Divisions.*
Three infantry divisions completely equipped and mobile.
Five infantry divisions nearly complete as regards equipment but deficient of transport in varying degrees.
(*c*) *Tenth Army (Iraq).*
One armoured brigade group.
Three infantry divisions.
Equipment position not yet fully known.

C.J. Auchinleck, General,
C.-*in*-C., M.E.F.

8.
*Note on the Western Front by the Commander-in-Chief, M. E. F.*
*(For Middle East Defence Committee.)*

4th February, 1942.

1. The recent enemy successes in Cyrenaica make it necessary to reconsider how we are to achieve our object, which was and is to destroy the enemy forces, and particularly the German forces, in Cyrenaica and then to occupy Tripolitania.

2. The campaign in Cyrenaica has shown that generally the German tanks are superior to ours in mechanical reliability and in gun-power, while the modern Italian tank now coming into service is slightly inferior in performance and armament to our Cruiser tank, but is generally superior to the American light tank except in respect of speed.

After consulting those best qualified to give an opinion, I have concluded that we need at least a fifty per cent. numerical superiority in tanks, if we are to have a reasonable chance of beating the enemy armoured forces on ground of his own choosing.

Our inferiority in tank equipment may improve as we are able to employ more American medium tanks, but this remains to be proved in battle.

3. The following is a forecast showing the extent to which the enemy might build up his tank force in Libya and of our own prospective tank resources in this Command.

*Cruiser or Equivalent Tanks.*

| | Enemy – with units. | | | (Ours – with units.) | | Ours. |
|---|---|---|---|---|---|---|
| | German. | Italian. | Total. | Excl. Iraq | Iraq. | Reserve. |
| 1 *February* | 42 | 185 | 227 | 226 | 8 | – |
| 1 *March* | 168 | 276 | 444 | 334} | | 193 |
| 1 *April* | 272 | 276 | 548 | 496} | 252* | 249 |
| 1 *May* | 272 | 276 | 548 | 570} | | 285 |
| 1 *June* | 272 | 276 | 548 | 680} | | 340 |

*\*Date of arrival not known, and reserves for Iraq not included.*

Heavy or infantry tanks are not included in the table as they cannot take part in the main tank battle owing to their low speed and small circuit of action.

4. The table allows for our holding a 50 per cent. reserve of the total number of tanks with units. This may seem a large figure, but the initial stages of the Cyrenaican campaign amply proved that this is not so. Had we not been able to draw on large reserves to replace tanks lost or disabled in battle, we should not have been able to raise the seige of Tobruk. The enemy had a very small reserve of tanks at his disposal, but the greater reliability of his tanks and his better tank recovery equipment made up for this.

It would, however, be possible to take a risk and reduce the ratio of tanks in reserve to those with units to 25 per cent., particularly as the American tanks, with which we shall be equipped increasingly in future, are more reliable mechanically than British tanks, which have formed the major part of our equipment hitherto.

The 252 tanks shown as allotted to the Tenth Army in Iraq should not be counted upon, as they will be delivered at Basra and are needed to equip the Indian Armoured Division now forming in Iraq, though in an emergency it might be possible to draw on them to replace losses in the field.

5. Taking the worst case, which is that the enemy can and will reinforce his armoured forces to the extent shown in the table, and working to a 25 per cent. reserve of tanks for our own units, we may expect to be able to put in the field on 1st March 1942, from 450 to 500 tanks against a possible total of 400 enemy tanks. To give us a 50 per cent. numerical superiority, we should have 600 tanks.

On 1st April we ought to have about 620 tanks against the enemy's 550, still short of our needed margin of superiority.

On 1st May we might count on about 770 tanks compared with 550, which would just give us the superiority we need, but only at the expense of reducing our reserve of tanks still further from 25 per cent. to 11 per cent. Should the enemy bring over no more reinforcements of tanks or stop short at the 400 mark, which he is expected to reach on 1st March, then we should have our required superiority by 1st April, or even by the 1st March if he ceases at once to bring over any more tanks; but this is considered to be unlikely.

6. These calculations depend on concentrating all available tanks and armoured units on the Western Front, leaving none for the Northern Front, except those already allotted to Iraq whose date of arrival is uncertain. There is a risk; but one which can be taken, unless there is a rapid change in the situation on the Russian Front, as it now seems most unlikely that Germany will be able to mount an attack against Syria and Iraq through Anatolia, or against Persia through the Caucasus, before the beginning of August.

7. Provided, therefore, we are not forced by enemy action to fritter away our tank resources in detail in the meanwhile, we should plan now to resume the offensive possibly on 1st March or 1st April and certainly by 1st May, if we are prepared to take a risk on the number of tanks held in reserve.

8. So much for relative strengths. The other factor governing our ability to resume the offensive is maintenance.

When we resume the offensive the enemy may withdraw again to his defended area in southwest Cyrenaica round Agedabia and El Agheila in the hope that, by forcing us to fight at the end of a long and difficult line of communications, he will be able to discount our numerical superiority in tanks. A withdrawal on his part to this area does not necessarily imply that he will voluntarily abandon Bengasi.

9. We know from experience that unless we can make free use of Bengasi as a port of supply, we cannot maintain a force of more than about a hundred tanks and a few battalions of infantry with the necessary artillery in the Agedabia area.

Therefore our first action on resuming the offensive must be to take Bengasi.

It is not enough to take Bengasi; we must be able to maintain forward sufficient forces to hold it, while the necessary reserves of supplies are being built up for the further advance to the southward. This is likely to be the hardest part of the business, as it is likely to entail stationing the bulk, if not the whole, of our armoured force south of the Gebel Akhdar area to guard against any enemy attempt to move north against the garrison of Bengasi, which itself must be strictly limited in size by maintenance considerations. The operation should not be impossible, however, though it will be more difficult than in December last, as we shall not have a beaten and disorganized enemy to deal with as we had then. The implication of this is that the operation is likely to have to be much more deliberate.

10. Our immediate need therefore is to stabilise a front in Libya behind which we can build up a striking force with which to resume the offensive at the earliest possible date.

This front should cover Tobruk and as many as possible of the forward landing grounds in Eastern Cyrenaica. It should not, however, be too far to the west, as during the period which must elapse before we can launch our offensive, we should aim at making it as difficult as possible for the enemy to concentrate strong forces against our covering position and so force us to waste our strength in opposing him. This can best be avoided by making him extend his line of communications to the maximum extent without thereby endangering points vital to ourselves.

11. I propose therefore to confirm the instructions already given to General Ritchie, which are:-

  (i) To hold a line covering Tobruk.
  (ii) To hold Giarabub in order to secure our southern flank against enemy raids based on Siwa.
  (iii) To proceed, as an insurance, with making of defensive areas at Sollum and near Maddalena, in accordance with the policy previously laid down.

And to tell him at once to begin to build up a striking force for the resumption of the offensive at the earliest possible moment.

12. It is vital to the success of this plan that every possible effort should be made from now on by our naval and air forces to deny the use of Bengasi to the enemy for supply purposes.

To do this effectively it is necessary that we should have the use of landing grounds in the area Derna – Martuba and be able to base motor torpedo boats, with which to attack enemy shipping using Bengasi, on the port of Derna.

The possibility of undertaking a limited offensive at an early date to secure Derna must therefore be seriously and urgently considered. It is important, however, that such an operation should not prejudice the chances of success of a main offensive later.

C.J.A.

9.

*G.H.Q., M.E.F. Operation Instruction No. 111.*

Lieutenant-General N.M. Ritchie,
Commander, Eighth Army.                                        11th February 1942.
1. I intend to resume the offensive in Libya as soon as possible with the aim of defeating the enemy forces in the field, occupying Cyrenaica and subsequently Tripolitania.

2. The enemy, however, may try to drive us back from our present positions round Gazala and from Tobruk, before we are ready to launch our offensive.

3. It is essential to retain Tobruk as a supply base for our offensive. Our present positions on the line Gazala – Hacheim will, therefore, continue to be held, and no effort will be spared to make them as strong as possible.

4. If, for any reason, we should be forced at some future date to withdraw from our present forward positions, every effort will still be made to prevent Tobruk being lost to the enemy; but it is not my intention to continue to hold it once the enemy is in a position to invest it effectively.

Should this appear inevitable, the place will be evacuated, and the maximum amount of destruction carried out in it, so as to make it useless to the enemy as a supply base. In this eventuality the enemy's advance will be stopped on the general line Sollum – Maddalena – Giarabub, as laid down in Operation Instruction No. 110.

5. It is extremely desirable to regain for our air forces the use of the landing grounds in the area Derna – Martuba, for the following reasons:-
    (*a*) To enable our air reconnaissance and air striking forces to join up with those from Malta, so as to cover the whole sea area.
    (*b*) To enable them to keep up a more effective offensive again Bengasi, and thus prevent or severely restrict its use by the enemy for supply purposes.
    (*c*) To reduce the degree of support the enemy can give his forward troops.

The possession of Derna would also permit the use of motor torpedo boats against enemy shipping using Bengasi.

6. To get and keep possession of the area Derna – Tmimi – Gazala entails holding firmly up to, and inclusive of, the general line Lamluda – Mechili – Tengeder, and it is not my intention that you should attempt this operation until you are sure:-

(*a*) That it will not endanger the safety of Tobruk.

(*b*) That it will not involve the risk of defeat in detail and so prejudice the chances of our launching a major offensive.

I wish you, however, to study the possibilities of such an operation, and to make all preparations for carrying it out immediately circumstances permit.

7. Meanwhile you will do all you can by the use of offensive mobile columns to prevent the use by the enemy air force of landing grounds in the area Derna – Martuba – Mechili.

8. The Royal Navy and the Royal Air Force are making every effort to deny the use of the ports of Bengasi and Derna to the enemy.

9. Your tasks are, therefore:-

(*a*) To hold the enemy as far west of Tobruk as possible without risking defeat in detail.

(*b*) To organise a striking force with which to resume the offensive, with the object of destroying the enemy forces in the field, and occupying Cyrenaica at the earliest possible date.

(*c*) To study the possibility of regaining the landing grounds in the area Derna – Martuba – Mechili for our air forces at an early date, provided this can be done without prejudice to the tasks defined in (*a*) and (*b*).

(*d*) To prevent to the utmost extent possible, without prejudice to the tasks defined above in (*a*) and (*b*), the use by the enemy air force of the landing grounds in the area Derna – Martuba – Mechili.

(*e*) To avoid your forces being invested in Tobruk in the event of our having to withdraw to the east of that place.

(*f*) To complete the preparation of defensive positions on the general line Sollum – Maddalena – Giarabub at the earliest possible date.

10. To allow you to plan for the future, a list of the troops likely to be available to you is attached to this instruction.

C.J. Auchinleck, General,
C.-in-C., M.E.F.

### APPENDIX "A" TO OPERATION INSTRUCTION No. 111.

*Assumed Order of Battle for planning the offensive.    Available for Battle.*

| | |
|---|---|
| H.Q. 13 Corps. | – |
| H.Q. 30 Corps. | – |
| I Armd. Div. | – |
|   One Armd. Car Regt. | – |

| | |
|---|---|
| 2 Armd. Bde. Gp. | – |
| 201 Gds. Motor Bde. Gp. | – |
| 7 Armd. Div. | |
| One Armd. Car Regt. | End-February. |
| 4 Armd. Bde. Gp. | Early March. |
| 7 Motor Bde. Gp. | Mid-April. |
| 10 Armd. Div. | |
| One Armd. Car Regt. | Late-March. |
| 1 Armd. Bde. Gp. | Mid-April |
| One Motor Bde. Gp. (if ready) | Unable to forecast. |
| 22 Armd. Bde. Gp. | End-March. |
| 8 Armd. Bde. Gp. | Mid-May. |
| 1 Army Tank Bde. | |
| 4 S.A. Armd. Car Regt. | |
| 6 S.A. Armd. Car Regt. | End-April. |
| 3 Ind. Motor Bde. Gp. | Mid-March. |
| 50 Div. | End-February. |
| 1 S.A. Div. | |
| 2 S.A. Div. | |
| Free French Bde. Gp. | |

N.B. – (*a*) An Armd. Bde. Gp. will consist of three Regts.

(*b*) The above dates are based on the arrival of equipment and "A" vehicles, but also depend upon the arrival of transport, which cannot be forecast with any accuracy.

## 10
### *G.H.Q., M.E.F. Operation Instruction No. 112.*

General Sir H.M. Wilson, Commander, Ninth Army.

Lt.-General E.P. Quinan, Commander, Tenth Army.      23rd February, 1942.

1. With a view to providing reinforcements for the East and the Far East, the following formations will be, or may be, moved from the Middle East:-

(*a*) 70 Division – as soon as the move can be arranged, and utilizing ships earmarked for 6 Australian Division.

(*b*) Remainder of 6 Australian Division.

(*c*) 9 Australian Division, as soon as the move can be arranged.

(*d*) Possibly, though not yet decided, one Indian infantry division from Iraq. Moreover,

(*e*) It is unlikely that more than one infantry division will arrive in the Middle East from the United Kingdom before mid-August.

2. If all these formations are withdrawn, the infantry formations remaining in the Middle East will comprise:-

50 Division.

New Zealand Division.

Two South African Divisions.
Four Indian Divisions.
161 Indian Infantry Brigade Group.
Two Free French Brigade Groups.
Polish Brigade Group.
One Greek Brigade Group.

A total of eight infantry divisions and five infantry brigade groups.

3. After providing for:-

   (*a*) The security of the Western Front of Egypt – Three infantry divisions; one infantry brigade group.
   (*b*) The security of Cyprus – One infantry division.

There remain four infantry divisions, and at most four infantry brigade groups, to meet the requirements of Ninth Army, Tenth Army and G.H.Q. Reserve.

4. This force would be inadequate to stop an enemy attack in strength through Persia and Syria, directed on the Persian Gulf and the Suez Canal.

5. Should this eventuality arise, I intend to impose the greatest possible delay on the enemy's advance with the object of gaining time to enable reinforcements to arrive.

6. This delay will be imposed upon the enemy:-

   (*a*) By supporting Turkey if she resists and if the necessary air forces are available, in accordance with our present plans.
   (*b*) By protecting advanced aerodromes from which our air forces can attack the enemy's vulnerable communications through Turkey.
   (*c*) By the thorough demolition of communications and all oil stocks and installations.
   (*d*) By holding delaying positions astride his main lines of advance in country unsuited to armoured fighting vehicles.
   (*e*) By counter-attacking with armoured formations whenever a suitable opportunity can be created.

7. It may be assumed that the following forces will be available:-

*Ninth Army.*

One armoured division of
  One armoured brigade group
  One motor brigade group
Two infantry divisions.

*Tenth Army.*

One armoured division of
  One armoured brigade group
  One motor brigade group
Two infantry divisions.

### Cyprus.

One armoured regiment
One infantry division.

### G.H.G. Reserve.

(For allotment as may be necessary to Eighth, Ninth or Tenth Armies.)
Up to three armoured brigade groups.
One army tank brigade of two battalions.
Two or three infantry brigade groups.

8. Having regard to the probable disparity in strength between the enemy and our own forces, it is essential that our forces should not be irretrievably committed, and that we avoid engagements with the enemy except on ground favourable to ourselves. In the event of an enemy attack, my policy will therefore be:-

(*a*) To protect aerodromes in Northern Syria and Northern Iraq, from which our air forces can attack the enemy's vulnerable communications through Turkey.

(*b*) To effect the demolition of communications and oil installations north of the line Dizful – Paitak – Little Zab River – Ana – Abu Kemal – Damascus – Ras Baalbek – Tripoli, and to withdraw to previously prepared positions on that general line.

(*c*) To delay the enemy as long as possible in front of that line by making bold use of the forces available to attack him in flank and rear.

(*d*) To fight a series of delaying actions on ground of our own choosing, back to positions in Southern Iraq and Southern Palestine, covering the ports on the Persian Gulf and on the Suez Canal.

9. Our plans and preparations must be adjusted without delay to this new situation. On the other hand it is of paramount importance that we avoid disclosing our weakness or our intentions to the enemy, to Turkey, or to the local populations, because by so doing we may encourage the enemy to attack, drive Turkey into submission, and bring about a serious internal security situation.

My policy, therefore, is:-

(*a*) To maintain troop movement in the northern frontier areas on the same scale as in the past.

(*b*) To continue slowly with the construction of those roads in the northern areas on which a start has been made, and with work now actually in progress on defences at Mosul and Qaiara, but not to start any new works in these areas. The object is to avoid giving the impression that we have changed our plans, and at the same time to make available the maximum amount of material and labour for the essential task defined in (*c*) below.

(*c*) To complete defences on the general line Dizful – Little Zab River – Ana – Abu Kemal – Damascus – Ras Baalbek – Tripoli in the following two stages:-

Stage A. – On a scale suitable for a delaying action by the forces given in para. 7.

Stage B. – On a scale suitable for the forces given in Appendix "A", so that prepared positions may be available, if reinforcements arrive in time.

(*d*) To prepare, without delay, bases of supply for mobile striking forces in the neighbourhood of Fatha, Haffa and Qatana, and in the Jebel Druze and Lava Belt. The bases of supply hitherto contemplated at Palmyra and to the north will not be formed for the present, but plans will be completed so that the bases can be made available at short notice, if required.

(*e*) To complete the bridges at Raqqa (because construction cannot now be stopped without disclosing a change in policy) and Haffa and Fatha.

Approaches to the bridges to Deir ez Zor and Meyadine will be completed if not already started, but the bridges will not be built. Similarly, work started on the Khabur bridges should be completed, but no new work initiated.

(*f*) To prepare a defended staging post in the Rutba area – if possible at Al Ga'ara – without delay. A reconnaissance will be carried out immediately, and a report submitted to G.H.Q.

(*g*) To reconnoitre immediately, positions in Southern Iraq and Southern Palestine, in each case for a force of two infantry divisions and attached troops.

10. An immense amount of work remains to be done, and all available resources in the immediate future will be applied to the completion of the defensive arrangements required on the line given in para. 9 (*c*). Reconnaissances of the rearward lines, supply bases and staging posts will be carried out simultaneously, and reports will be submitted to G.H.G. by 10th March 1942.

11. The policy of stocking will be decided when the recommendations of Army Commanders have been received.

12. The success of a withdrawal of this nature will depend very largely upon the state of training of our formations in mobile warfare. In the near future, a proper proportion must be maintained between the conflicting demands for training and for the construction of defences. Local labour will be used to the greatest possible extent, to free formations for the training in manoeuvre which will be so essential to success.

C.J. AUCHINLECK, General,
C.-in-C., M.E.F.

## APPENDIX "A" TO G.H.Q., M.E.F. OPERATION INSTRUCTION No. 112.

Forces to be assumed as available when the defences on the line Dizful – Little Zab River – Ana – Abu Kemal – Damascus – Ras Baalbek – Tripoli, are constructed – (para. 9 (*c*) Stage B, refers.)

*Ninth Army.*

One armoured division of
  One armoured brigade group
  One motor brigade group
One army tank brigade.
Four infantry divisions.
Polish Brigade Group.
Greek Brigade Group.
Free French Forces.

*Tenth Army.*

One armoured division of
  One armoured brigade group
  One motor brigade group
One army tank brigade.
Three infantry divisions.

*G.H.G. Reserve.*

One armoured division of
  One armoured brigade group
  One motor brigade group
One infantry division.

11

*G.H.Q., M.E.F. Operation Instruction No. 116.*

8th March 1942.

Lieutenant-General N.M. Ritchie, Commander, Eighth Army.

1. A convoy will be despatched to Malta during the coming dark period. The supply situation in Malta is serious, owing to the failure of the last convoy to arrive. The Commanders-in-Chief have therefore decided that measures for the protection of the next convoy will be accorded first priority.

2. Full particulars concerning the movement of the convoy will be made known to you by the Naval Liaison Officer attached to your Headquarters. In outline, the movements of the convoy will be as follows:-

(*a*) Leave Alexandria afternoon DI day.

(*b*) Arrive Malta early D4 day.

D1 day may be altered if the weather is unfavourable, but you will receive twenty-four hours notice of the time of departure of the convoy from Alexandria.

3. The Commander-in-Chief directs that you will create a diversion with the object of drawing off enemy air attack from the convoy throughout D2 day.

4. This diversion will be of an appreciable size – not less than the equivalent of one bde gp. The diversionary effect of your operation is not required to continue after the evening of D2.

5. The maximum possible fighter protection is to be afforded to the convoy, therefore your diversionary operation may have to be carried out without any air protection.

6. Your outline plan will be forwarded to reach this Headquarters by 13th March 1942.

12

*Note on the Libyan Offensive* – I.

21st March 1942.

1. *The object.* – Our permanent and overriding object is to secure our bases in Egypt and Iraq against enemy attack.

2. *Factors affecting the achievement of the object.* – Our policy on the Western Front in North Africa has been hitherto: first, to protect our main base area in the Delta, and secondly, to drive the enemy out of North Africa so as to increase the security of the Delta base, to open the Mediterranean sea route, and to provide a base for operations against Sicily and Italy.

3. So long as the enemy is able to send convoys freely to Tripoli and Bengasi, he is in a better position to build up his forces on this front than we are, because the route is much shorter than our reinforcement route round the Cape and from India. The most effective way, therefore, to secure Egypt from attack from the west is to control the Central Mediterranean.

4. To gain control of the Central Mediterranean, we require:-

  (i) To operate strong air forces and light naval forces from Malta. This will not be possible unless we can keep Malta adequately supplied, and provide it with reasonable protection against air attack.
  (ii) To operate strong air forces from bases in Western Cyrenaica.
  (iii) To provide air protection for our fleet operating from Alexandria.

5. If we could establish a high degree of control over the Central Mediterranean, the enemy's strength in North Africa must gradually decline. Both the capture of Tripolitania and, alternatively, the defence of Cyrenaica would then be easier, thus enabling us to release forces for the Northern Front, if required.

   It is obvious that the advantages of capturing Tripolitania would be largely discounted if the enemy could establish himself in Tunisia. The only certain way of preventing this is to occupy that country ourselves.

6. The carrying out of our policy falls, therefore, into three phases:-

  (i) The securing of Cyrenaica.
  (ii) The building up of our striking forces in Cyrenaica and Malta, with a view to gaining control of the Central Mediterranean.
  (iii) The occupation of Tripolitania and, if necessary, of Tunisia.

7. Viewing the war as a whole, we must concede that the enemy will have the initiative during the summer of 1942, and that some reverses are to be expected. This will influence our Operations in North Africa in the following ways:-

(*a*) We must not become involved in operations in Libya which cannot be broken off at short notice. To be in a position to release forces to meet the enemy elsewhere, we must aim at being able to pass quickly to the defensive, and to consolidate our gains without delay.

(*b*) The morale of the public will require sustaining. A successful offensive would be beneficial, but another failure would have a harmful effect.

8. From the foregoing considerations, the phases of offensive operations in Libya can be defined:-

(i) To secure Cyrenaica.

(ii) To gain control of the sea communications in the Central Mediterranean.

(iii) To capture or secure Tripolitania, which may depend on whether operations to secure Tunisia can also be undertaken, either from the east or from the west.

9. *Factors affecting offensive operations in Cyrenaica.* – Experience has shown that it is more difficult to hold than to capture Cyrenaica. Therefore, an essential element in the plan to capture Cyrenaica is the destruction of the enemy forces, and particularly the most effective part of them, the German armoured and infantry formations.

10. The configuration of the coast of the Gulf of Sirte and the defensive possibilities of the El Agheila area are the governing considerations in any plan for the defence of Cyrenaica. A much smaller force is needed to defend Cyrenaica in the Agheila position than in any other, and, since we must be ready to secure Cyrenaica with the minimum force, the capture and consolidation of the Agheila position is essential. This fixes our maintenance needs.

11. The supply situation in Malta is bad and will become worse after May. Moreover, Malta's effort is waning, so that enemy convoys are passing more easily to North Africa; and his situation there is improving accordingly. We should, therefore, strike as soon as we can with a reasonable prospect of success, that is, as soon as we have the needed relative superiority over the enemy and the resources to enable us to sustain the momentum of our attack.

12. The relative numerical strength of our own and the enemy's armoured forces is shown in the Annexure to this paper. In comparing the strength of these forces, the following factors must be borne in mind-

(*a*) The enemy's cruiser tanks are better than ours. The leadership and training of his armoured formations is probably still better than ours. To give a reasonable chance of our offensive succeeding, we should have about 50 per cent. numerical superiority over the German armoured forces, though we can accept equality with the Italians.

(*b*) Our Valentine tanks are too slow to be employed with our cruiser tanks, as they are for this reason at a great disadvantage when operating against enemy cruiser tanks. They are, however, a most valuable asset for counter-attack within defensive positions held by our infantry, or to support our infantry in attacks on enemy defensive positions.

(*c*) Our infantry formations, supported by Valentine tanks, are superior in quality, and at present in quantity also, to enemy infantry formations.

13. An examination of the figures in the Annexure shows that we are severely handicapped by the lack of reliable information, which may result in lost opportunities, or in our attempting the impossible. It is clear, however, that we cannot pass to the offensive now, but that we might be able to attack about 15th May, though 1st June is a more likely date.

14. *Derna – Martuba.* – The maintenance of Malta would be easier if we could operate air forces from landing grounds in the Derna and Martuba area, and the possibility of a limited operation to secure these aerodromes is being carefully and continuously examined.

To secure these landing grounds we must secure Derna and Mechili. The enemy has prepared positions on this line, and we would be playing into his hands if we attacked him on this ground of his own choosing. We would require the same superiority of forces to capture this line as we would to capture Cyrenaica, because the enemy's strength is all deployed forward. There is no reason for limiting the objective of our offensive to the capture of the line Derna – Mechili, unless for administrative reasons it is impossible to advance with adequate forces beyond it. Our losses in this limited operation would almost certainly exceed those of the enemy, and the launching of the main offensive would be likely to be correspondingly delayed. Apart from any considerations of supply, were we to attempt this operation, with inferior armoured forces, we should jeopardise the security of Egypt, because the integrity of our own defensive positions in the Gazala – Tobruk – Bir Hacheim and Sollum – Maddalena areas, strongly entrenched and mined as they are, depends entirely on the availability of a reasonably strong mobile reserve of armoured forces with which to counter-attack the enemy armoured troops, should they succeed in breaking through or passing round the infantry positions. The fronts held in these positions are perforce very extended, and the troops available to hold them are relatively few. Consequently, the various defended localities comprised in them are situated at some distance apart and there is in no sense a continuous line of defence, though the whole may be covered by a more or less continuous minefield. Moreover, if forced to halt on the Derna – Mechili position and then to adopt a strategically defensive attitude on our Western Front, we should be much less favourably placed tactically than in the Gazala or Sollum positions, because of the longer frontage to be held, and the far greater vulnerability of our communications, consequent on the configuration of the coast.

15. *Conclusions.* – It is evident, therefore:-

  (i) That our first objective is to secure Cyrenaica.
  (ii) That in securing Cyrenaica, we must destroy as much as possible of the enemy's army.
  (iii) That to secure Cyrenaica we must be able to maintain sufficient forces in the El Agheila neighbourhood to hold it against heavy enemy attack.
  (iv) That the sooner we can launch an offensive the better.
  (v) That, to give our offensive a reasonable chance of success, we should have a numerical superiority in tanks of 50 per cent. over the Germans, and equality with the Italians,
  (vi) That a limited offensive to secure the landing grounds in the Derna – Martuba area is likely to need the same relative superiority in tanks as an offensive to recover Cyrenaica, and has nothing to recommend it except that it may be possible, from the maintenance point of view, before the latter.

C.J. Auchinleck, General,
C.-in-C., M.E.F.

## ANNEXURE "A".
### *Comparative Armoured Strengths.*

NOTE. – (i) The enemy figures are based on no new formations being sent other than Littorio.

  (ii) It has been assumed that enemy tanks are available for shipment.

  (iii) Shipping will not be a limiting factor.

|  |  | Enemy tanks. |  |  |
|---|---|---|---|---|
| 1st *April*, 1942- | Our tanks. | German. | Italian. | Total. |
| Best case for us | (*a*) 300 | 260 | 90 | 350 |
| Worst case for us | (*a*) 300 | 360 | 140 | 500 |
| 15th *May*, 1942 | (*b*) 450 | 350 | 300 | (*c*) 650 |
| 1st *June*, 1942 | (*b*) 600 | 350 | 300 | (*c*) 650 |

(*a*) Infantry tanks, numbering 150, have been omitted. These 300 are cruiser tanks with approximately 40 per cent. Grants.

(*b*) Infantry tanks, numbering 150, have been omitted.

(*c*) This represents "worst case" for us. It is not possible at this date to state a "best case".

13
*Note on Libyan Offensive* – II.

20th April 1942.

1. *Object.* – The permanent and overriding object is to secure Egypt from attack.

2. *Considerations and deductions.* – The best way to secure Egypt from attack from the west is to remove enemy from Libya.

  *Deduction.* – This entails destruction of his armed forces.

3. If enemy can withdraw before us, keeping his forces, and particularly his armoured forces, in being, he becomes stronger as he gets nearer Tripoli, while we become weaker the farther we get from railhead.

*Deduction.* – Enemy armed forces must be decisively defeated in Cyrenaica and not allowed to withdraw into Tripolitania.

4. Enemy has consolidated his positions in area Derna – Tmimi – Temrad – Mechili.

*Deduction.* – Frontal attack on these positions, even with our present superiority in infantry, likely to be lengthy and costly, and to place our forces in an unfavourable strategic position should we have to stop our offensive before we have got a decision because of threat to our Northern Front.

5. Key to enemy present positions is Mechili, which cannot be safely attacked from east or south until enemy armoured forces have been neutralised or destroyed.

*Deduction.* – We must have sufficient armoured forces to give reasonable chance in early stages of our offensive of hitting enemy armour so hard as to prevent it interfering further with our advance.

6. We are unlikely to have such superiority in armour as to be certain of decisively beating the enemy's armoured forces on ground chosen by him.

*Deduction.* – We must, therefore, induce the enemy armour to attack us on ground favourable to us.

7. To induce the enemy to attack us we must threaten something so valuable to him as to make him move to guard it.

The enemy is most sensitive in his supply system. Vulnerable points in this system are Barce, Bengasi, Agedabia, and El Agheila. Barce, an important road junction, is difficult of access from the south and to attack it would entail a wide turning movement within striking distance of the enemy reserves in the Gebel Akhdar, and out of supporting range of our fighters from their present forward bases. Interception at Agedabia of the enemy's supply route by the coast road from Tripoli would hamper him a lot, but might not make him move if he could still count on using Bengasi. The same applies to El Agheila; but this operation is not possible because of supply difficulties.

A threat to Bengasi directly affects the enemy's ability to remain in Eastern Cyrenaica beyond the limited period during which he is able to live on such reserves of supplies as he may have been able to build up. It is therefore the most likely operation to make him move to attack us on ground of our own choosing.

*Deduction.* – Our threat should be made against Bengasi, and must be sufficiently permanent to prevent the enemy being able to rely on living on his reserves of supplies until it is past.

8. The object being to induce the enemy armour to attack our armour, we must be ready to meet him with the strongest possible armoured force, in conditions most favourable to us.

*Deductions.* – All our available fast medium tanks must be included in the striking force, and be strongly supported by infantry and artillery holding mined and entrenched positions, which will act as pivots of manoeuvre and bases of supply for them.

9. The ground on which we wish the enemy to attack must be chosen to give us the greatest possible advantage over him. It should be so far from his probable starting points as to force him to refuel at least once before he attacks, and to make it hard for him to supply his troops. It should not be so far, however, as to make it too difficult for the enemy to move against us. It should give good going over which our tanks can pass freely and quickly to the counter-attack. If this condition can be combined with areas of broken ground in which our infantry can form strong defensive areas, so much the better.

*Deduction.* – The area round Ben Gania appears to be suitable for our striking force, which would then be close enough (120 miles) to Bengasi to threaten it. This area is just about the limit of enemy tank radius of action from his probable starting point near Mechili, so that he must refuel before giving battle. The going is reasonably good, and there are stretches of broken ground which should make good defensive areas for the infantry.

10. To establish an armoured force near Ben Gania strong infantry forces are necessary to form pivots for the armoured force itself, and to establish strong-points protecting its lines of communication to Tobruk.

*Deduction.* – At least two infantry divisions, which must be fully mobile, will probably be needed for this purpose.

11. To mislead the enemy and to prevent him interfering with the initial seizure and consolidation of ground necessary to give the armoured force security and mobility, a strong force must be available to demonstrate against the enemy positions north of Mechili with the object of pinning him to them.

*Deduction.* – At least one infantry division with heavy tanks is needed for this.

12. To prevent an enemy break-through with armoured forces to Tobruk to upset the supply of our striking force and other forward troops, the Gazala – Tobruk – El Adem defensive system must still be held.

*Deduction.* – An infantry division and a brigade group will probably be needed for this, and also to guard against possible airborne or seaborne raids against our forward bases in the same area.

13. Our present aerodromes and landing grounds are too far back to enable full air support to be given to forces operating in the Ben Gania area and west of it. Without such support, the operations cannot hope to succeed against the strong enemy opposition which must be expected.

*Deduction.* – New forward landing grounds in the general area Bir Hacheim – Meduar Hsan – Ben Gania will be needed. These will require protection by a motor brigade group, or an infantry brigade group, or both.

14. It is essential to hide from the enemy the date and direction of our intended offensive.

*Deduction.* – Deception must be most thorough and continuous, and feints and demonstrations to deceive the enemy as to the objective of any possible offensive by us must be carefully planned and carried out beforehand.

15. *Plan.* – The plan in outline is first to carry out three preliminary deceptive operations; one against Tmimi (already done), one towards Tengeder, and a third against the area Temrad – Tmimi, and then:-

> *Phase A.* – To move one infantry division with heavy tanks against the enemy positions in the area Temrad – Tmimi. This advance must be deliberate and ground secured must be consolidated, the object being to pin the enemy to his ground and distract his attention from Phase B. This feint attack should if possible be preceded by a reconnaissance in force.
>
> *Phase B.* – Concurrent with the latter part of Phase A, to move one infantry division with heavy tanks in support and establish two or three defensive areas, each to be held by a brigade group. The object being to establish strongpoints and pivots of manoeuvre for our armoured forces, should the enemy armour strike south against them.

*Note 1.* – If the enemy armour can be induced to attack us on ground favourable to us during Phase B this will be all to the good. In fact, the closer to our main Gazala position he attacks us the better, provided we are ready to receive him. The location chosen for the striking force near Ben Gania is of no special value as a battleground. The only reason for going there is to threaten Bengasi, and so make the enemy move against us. If he moves before we get there, we may achieve our object, which is to destroy his armour, with a smaller expenditure of effort.

During Phases A and B, therefore, our armoured divisions will be placed so as to be able to engage the enemy armour on ground and in conditions favourable to themselves, should it move against our infantry engaged in these operations.

*Note 2.* – The infantry engaged in Phase A, once Phase B is completed, will either consolidate ground gained and keep up pressure on the enemy to their front, or withdraw to the Gazala position and harass the enemy with mobile columns, as may seem best. It must not become involved to an extent which will entail the intervention of our armoured forces to extricate it.

*Note 3.* – During this phase forward landing grounds should be established.

> *Phase C.* – On completion of Phase B, to move a third infantry division with some heavy tanks to secure an advanced base near Ben Gania from which Bengasi can be threatened.

*Note 4.* – During Phase C, the armoured divisions will be centrally placed so as to be able to engage the enemy armour under favourable conditions, should it move against the new advanced base or against the infantry holding the defensive areas covering the line of supply. Forward landing grounds should be further developed.

*Phase D.* – To build up reserves of supplies in the Ben Gania area to admit of a move by the striking force on Bengasi or against the enemy, in the area Antelat – Saunnu, or if the situation invites it, against Mechili.

*Note 5.* – Provision should be made for the rapid move of a small but powerful raiding force against Bengasi soon after the occupation of the advanced base near Ben Gania. The object being to provoke the enemy to move against the striking force in the advanced base area.

*Note 6.* – Throughout these phases an infantry division and one or more brigade groups will hold the Gazala – Tobruk – Bir Hacheim defences to guard against a break-through by enemy armoured forces aimed at dislocating our system of supply and control.

Giarabub will also be held by a detachment to prevent enemy based on Siwa raiding our communications east of Tobruk and to carry out raids against enemy communications south of Bengasi.

*Note 7.* – Subsequent action must depend on enemy reaction to our opening moves, but this does not imply surrendering the strategical initiative to him. So long as we threaten his lines of communication, the strategical initiative remains with us. On the other hand, we hope the enemy will take the local tactical initiative and attack us on our ground instead of our having to attack him on his. This is the result the plan sets out to achieve, and, as already explained, the earlier in the operation the enemy can be made to do this the better it should be for us.

16. *Forces needed.* – The forces required by this plan are:-
  (*a*) For holding attack on north – One infantry division, one heavy tank bde.
  (*b*) For protection forward line of supply – One infantry division; one battalion heavy tanks.
  (*c*) For holding Gazala – Tobruk – Bir Hacheim area – One infantry division; one infantry bde. group, one battalion heavy tanks.
  (*d*) For holding Giarabub and raiding forward – Some infantry and armoured cars.
  (*e*) For protecting forward landing grounds – One motor brigade group.
  (*f*) For striking force – Two or three armoured divisions; one infantry division.

TOTAL. – Two or three, armoured divisions, depending on strength of enemy armoured forces in forward area; one motor brigade group, four infantry divisions, two infantry brigade groups.

C.J. Auchinleck, General,
C.-in-C., M.E.F.

14
*G.H.Q., M.E.F. Operation Instruction No. 117*[31]. *Northern Front.*

29th April 1942.

General Sir H.M. Wilson, Commander, Ninth Army.
Lieut-General E.P. Quinan, Commander, Tenth Army.
This Instruction covers the action to be taken by Middle East Forces in the event of an enemy attack through Anatolia only. It is considered that, although an attack through Persia from the Caucasus is at least equally probable, it could not be staged so early as the attack through Anatolia. The steps necessary to meet such an attack will, therefore, be dealt with in a subsequent Instruction.

1. *Object.* – The object is to ensure the security of our bases and ports in Egypt, Iraq and Persia and of our oil supplies in South-western Persia and the Persian Gulf.

2. *Forces Available.* – Forces likely to be available in this Command during the next four months, are given in Appendix "A".

3. The following forces are the minimum required to provide for the security of the Western Frontier of Egypt and Cyprus in existing circumstances:-

(a) *Western Frontier of Egypt-*
   One armoured division.
      (One armoured brigade group.)
      (One motor brigade group.)
   One armoured brigade group.
   One army tank brigade.
   Three infantry divisions.
   Two infantry brigade groups.

(b) *Cyprus-*
   One armoured regiment.
   One armoured car regiment.
   Three infantry brigade groups.
   One infantry battalion (general reserve).
   Five infantry battalions (static).

4. The forces at present available for Ninth and Tenth Armies and G.H.Q. Reserve are too weak to prevent an attack through Anatolia, on the maximum scale the enemy can develop, from penetrating Northern Iraq and Syria. These forces are given at Appendix "B".

5. *Intention.* – Should this attack take place, I intend from the start to impose the greatest possible delay on the enemy's advance, so as to gain time for reinforcements to arrive. The enemy will not in any event be allowed to establish himself south of the general line Little Zab River – Ana – Amman – Jericho – Nablus – Haifa.

6. *Method.* – It is essential that, while inflicting the maximum loss and delay on the enemy, our own forces should not be depleted to such an extent that on reaching this line they cannot hold it. The defences on this line will therefore be completed as soon as possible for occupation by the forces given in Appendix "B".

7. Delay will be imposed upon the enemy:-

(*a*) By supporting Turkey if she resists, provided the necessary air and land forces are available.

(*b*) By protecting, for as long as possible, the northern aerodromes so as to allow our air forces to carry out the heaviest possible attacks against the enemy's lines of advance through Anatolia.

(*c*) By thorough demolitions, as laid down in Operation Instruction No. 115 and a Joint Directive by the Commanders-in-Chief to be issued shortly, and by early evacuation of such war materials as would be of value to the enemy if they fell into his hands.

(*d*) By holding positions, in country unsuited to armoured fighting vehicles, astride his main lines of advance.

(*e*) By counter-attacking whenever a suitable opportunity offers.

8. The process of delaying the enemy will start as far forward as possible, depending on the land and air forces available and the attitude of the Turks. The plans made by Armies for initial concentrations will provide for any of the following opening moves, and the opening move will be selected and ordered by the Commanders-in-Chief, according to the conditions prevailing at the time.

*Case A.*

*Hypothesis.*

Turkey resists German aggression. Adequate Army and R.A.F. resources exist for operations in Northern Anatolia, in co-operation with the Turks.

*Opening Move-*

(i) Air striking force, with an Army component from Ninth Army will move into Turkey under separate instructions from G.H.Q., M.E.F. and H.Q., R.A.F., M.E.

(ii) When maintenance facilities permit, Ninth Army (less special force referred to in para, (i)) and Tenth Army will advance into Turkey to general line El Azig (Kharpur) – Malatya – Taurus Mountains, with a view to improving communications, preparing demolitions on main Turkish communications, and subsequently covering withdrawal of special force, if this becomes necessary.

*Case B.*

*Hypothesis.*

Turkey acquiesces in German aggression, or collapses quickly. Probable attitude of Turks, if we enter from the south, unknown.

*Opening Move-*
Ninth and Tenth armies enter Turkey and seize and hold general line Diyarbekir
– Siverek – Gaziantep (Aintab) – Bulanik (Baghche) – Payas, with the object of
demolishing communications and delaying enemy as far forward as possible.

*Case C.*
*Hypothesis-*
    (*a*) The Turks come in openly on the side of the Germans; *or*
    (*b*) The Turks have strengthened their forces on the Syrian frontier with
        evident intent to come in on the German side, and entry of our forces into
        Turkey will obviously be opposed.

*Opening Move-*
Ninth and Tenth Armies carry out demolitions as far forward as possible, and
delay enemy's advance.

9. – (*a*) The Boundary between Ninth and Tenth Armies will be:-

(Ninth Army incl.) Malatya – excl. Karacali Dagh (Karadja Dagh) – incl.
Hasseche (El Haseke) – Garat Motteb – thence Syrian-Iraqi Frontier to Abu
Kemal – Qasr Muhaiwir – thence a line due south to frontier of Saudi Arabia.

(*b*) Until hostilities break out on Northern Front the boundary will be:-

(Ninth Army incl.) the political boundary between Persia and Iraq south to
Abu Kemal – Qasr Muhaiwir – then a line due south to frontier of Saudi
Arabia.

10. It is essential to avoid disclosing our weakness or our intentions to the enemy,
to Turkey, or to the local populations, because by so doing we may encourage the
enemy to attack, drive Turkey into submission, and bring about a serious internal
security situation. My policy, therefore, is:-

    (*a*) To continue the despatch of stores to Turkey in accordance with the pro-
        gramme now in operation.
    (*b*) To maintain garrisons in forward areas, as nearly as possible on the same
        scale as in the past.
    (*c*) To continue slowly with the construction of roads already started in the
        forward areas.
    (*d*) *Tenth Army.* – To complete work on defences already in preparation in
        Mosul area. To prepare positions for occupation by two divisions in area
        Basra – Shaiba to cover base and port installations.
        *Ninth Army.* – To complete work on Southern Syria and Lebanon
        defences for occupation by five divisions.
    (*e*) To prepare, without delay, defended bases of supply to enable mobile
        striking forces to operate from (*a*) Haffa (*b*) Amman.
        The projected base at Palmyra will not be formed at present, but plans
        will be made to form it at short notice, or to destroy the facilities already
        existing there.

(f)  To complete the following bridges:-

Raqqa – (To avoid disclosing a change in policy) (Heaviest loads).
Haffa – Cl. 24.
Fatha – Cl. 40.

Approaches to the bridge at Deir ez Zor will be completed, but the bridge will not be built. Similarly work started on the Khabur bridges will be completed, but no new work started.

(g)  To prepare defended staging posts at Rutba and Tel Ghosain.

11. The policy for garrisoning and stocking the bases of supply and the staging posts is given in Appendix "C" and annexure thereto.[32]

C.J. Auchinleck, General,
*C.-in-C., M.E.F.*

APPENDIX "A" to G.H.Q., M.E.F. OPERATION INSTRUCTION No. 117.
*Forces Likely to be Available in Middle East (referred to in para. 2).*

| *Ready now.* | *Ready 1st June.* | *Ready 1st July.* | *Ready 1st August or later.* | *Possibly due from overseas and ready 1st August or later. (Not to be relied on).* |
|---|---|---|---|---|
| 1 Armd Div. | 3 Ind Motor* | 31 Ind Armd Div.* | 10 Armd Div.* | 8 Armd Div.* |
| 7 Armd Div. | Bde Gp. | 1 Armd Bde Gp.* | 9 Armd Bde Gp.* | Two Ind Divs.* |
| 1 Army Tank Bde. | 2 F. F. Bde Gp.* | | Polish Div.* | 251 Ind Armd Bde.* |
| 22 Armd Bde Gp. | Sudanese Bde Gp.* | | Greek Bde Gp.* | |
| 50 Div. | 32 Army Tank Bde.* | | | |
| 9 Aust. Div.‡ | | | | |
| N.Z. Div.‡ | | | | |
| I S.A. Div.‡ | | | | |
| 2 S.A. Div. | | | | |
| 4 Ind Div.‡ | | | | |
| 5 Ind Div.‡ | | | | |
| 6 Ind Div.‡ | | | | |
| 8 Ind Div.‡ | | | | |
| 10 Ind Div.‡ | | | | |
| I F.F. Bde. | | | | |
| Desert Bde.‡ | | | | |

*Short of certain equipment and transport.
‡Dates of readiness depend on arrival of equipment and transport and priorities of issue.

APPENDIX "B" to G.H.Q., M.E.F. OPERATION INSTRUCTION No. 117.
*Probable Forces available – Ninth and Tenth Armies and G.H.Q. Reserve
(referred to in para. 4).*

*Ninth Army.*

Desert Bde.
N.Z. Div.
9 Aust. Div.
Greek Bde. Gp.

*Tenth Army.*

10 Armd. Div.
3 Indian Motor Bde. Gp.

31 Indian Armd. Div.
6 Indian Div.
8 Indian Div.
10 Indian Div.

*G.H.Q. Reserve.*

7 Armd. Div.
I Armd. Bde. Gp.
32 Army Tank Bde. (Two Bns.).
5 Ind. Div.

15
*G.H.Q., M.E.F. Operation Instruction No. 118.*
*Operations in Persia.*

Commander, Tenth Army.                                    19th May, 1942.

*Introduction.*

1. This instruction covers the action to be taken by Middle East Forces in the event of an enemy attack through Persia from the Caucasus, and assumes no immediate threat to Northern Iraq and Syria from Anatolia.

2. We shall be on the defensive in the Western Desert.

*Object.*

3. My object is to ensure the security of our bases, ports, oil supplies and refineries in Iraq and Persia.

*Forces available.*

4. Forces likely to be available in this Command during the next four months are given in Appendix "A".

5. The following forces are estimated to be the minimum required to provide for the security of other commitments in the circumstances anticipated:-

   (*a*) *Eighth Army.*
        One Armd. Div.
        Two Armd. Bde. Gps.
        One Army Tk. Bde.
        Three Inf. Divs.
        Three Inf. Bde. .Gps.
   (*b*) *Cyprus.*
        One Armd. Regt.
        One Armd. Car Regt.
        One Inf. Div.
        Six Inf. Bns.
   (*c*) *Ninth Army.*
        One Inf. Div.
        One Inf. Bde. Gp.
        Desert Force.

6. The remaining forces available for Tenth Army and for G.H.Q. Reserve are given in Appendix "B".[33]

7. D.I. is the day on which the code word for action under this instruction is issued by G.H.Q., M.E.F.

*Intention.*
8. Should an attack from the Caucasus develop, I intend from the start to stop the enemy as far forward as possible. The enemy will not in any event be allowed to establish himself south of the general line Pahlevi – Kasvin – Hamadan – Senna – Saqqiz – Rowanduz Gorge.

*Method.*
9. It is essential that, while inflicting the maximum loss and delay on the enemy, our own forces should not be depleted to such an extent that on reaching this line they cannot hold it. Defences in this area will therefore be completed as soon as possible (*see* para. 13 (*b*) below).

10. In the event of the Russians asking for help in the defence of the Caucasus and of an air striking force being provided, the maximum light and motorised forces will move as far forward as possible, into the Caucasus, but not north of the main Caucasus range, with a view to:-

(*a*) protecting the air striking force.
(*b*) preparing demolitions for delaying the enemy's advance into Persia.

Subsequent action will be as in para, 11 below.

11. In the event of no such striking force being provided, delay will be imposed on the enemy by:-

(*a*) Moving light forces with the utmost possible speed to the line of the River Araxes, between the Caspian Sea and the Turkish frontier, with a view to ensuring the demolition of all the bridges over the river and to acting as a screen to cover our concentration forward.
(*b*) Covering, as long as possible, the aerodromes in the area Pahlevi – Teheran – Ramadan.
(*c*) By thorough demolitions, as laid down in Operation Instruction No. 115 and in a joint directive dated 27th April, 1942, by the Commanders-in-Chief, and by early evacuation of valuable war materials.
(*d*) By holding positions in country unsuited to A.F.Vs. astride his main lines of advance.
(*e*) By counter-attacking whenever a suitable opportunity presents itself.

12. The boundary between Ninth and Tenth Armies will be (Ninth Army inclusive):- Malatya – excl. Karali Dagh (Karadja Dagh) – incl. Hasseche (El Haseke) – Garat Motteb – thence Syrian-Iraqi Frontier to Abu Kemal – Qasr Muhaiwir – thence a line due south to the frontier to Saudi Arabia.

13. The following action will be taken forthwith:-

(*a*) Preparation and stocking of landing grounds (in consultation with R.A.F. Iraq).

(*b*) Preparation of defences on the general line Pahlevi – Kasvin – Hamadan – Senna – Saqqiz – Rowanduz Gorge to be ready for operations in this area by four inf. divs., two armd. divs. and one motor bde. gp.

(*c*) Selection, preparation and stocking of the staging posts necessary for the movement of formations into Persia.

(*d*) Improvement of routes in Iraq and Persia for the passage of tank transporters.

(*e*) Development of the route to India *via* Kerman for the passage of troops.

14. The construction and stocking of the Persian base for the area Ahwaz – Andimeshk will henceforth have priority over the extension and improvement of the Shaiba base and the advanced base at Musaiyib.

Buildings at Shaiba and Musaiyib on which construction has begun or for which materials are on site will be completed. Otherwise material coming forward will be diverted to the construction of the Persian base to the scale, and with the order of priority as between installations laid down in M.E. letter dated 2nd May, 1942. Stocking will take place as soon as possible to the scale laid down in M.E. letter of 14th May, 1942, without waiting for the construction of covered accommodation except for small ordnance stores and spares. Every possible means of transportation will be made available for the carriage of material to Persian base sites, but the order of priority already laid down for the use of the Persian ports and transportation facilities; namely:-

(*a*) Port construction and transportation material.

(*b*) Aid-to-Russia stores.

(*c*) Essential Persian civil imports.

(*d*) Military stores and base construction material;

will be adhered to. Persian civil imports should be reduced to a minimum.

Though the Persian base is hereby given priority over the Iraq bases, it may well occur that material can be used in Iraq which cannot be used in Persia. Provided therefore no delay is caused to the construction of the Persian Base, extension may be continued in Iraq.

15. As a precaution against delay in the construction, stocking, and organisation of the Persian base it is essential to improve the communications between the Shaiba base and the Persian L. of C.

The Persian Railway at Khorramshahr will therefore be extended to the bank of the Shatt el Arab at Tanuma. This extension should terminate in a lighter wharf opposite the wharves at Margil so that stores can be rapidly transhipped across the Shatt el Arab from the Iraq to the Persian system. The construction of this railway extension and the terminal lighter wharf will be given the highest priority.

16. In order to facilitate transportation of base construction material by the Karun River, landing facilities for stores at Ahwaz will be improved to the maximum possible extent.

In order to save transportation on the link Ahwaz-Andimeshk, it may be advisable to consider the transfer of certain installations now planned for Andimeshk to Ahwaz.

Maximum dispersion may be sacrificed to economy of material and in the interests of rapid construction.

17. An advanced base area will be reconnoitred, for which the Sultanabad area appears most suitable.

As building will have to be reduced to a minimum, it is important to obtain existing buildings as workshops and stores for spares or small stores. If these are not obtainable at Sultanabad, Teheran may have to be considered as an alternative, though it is not so well placed as Sultanabad. A full report will be rendered, after reconnaissance, with your recommendations including a detail of construction required, estimated completion date and proposed reserves to be held there.

C.J. Auchinleck.
*C.-in-C., M.E.F.*

### APPENDIX "A" to G.H.Q., M.E.F. OPERATION INSTRUCTION No. 118.
*Forces likely to be available in Middle East by 1st August or later.*
(Referred to in para. 4.)

| | |
|---|---|
| 1 Armd. Div. | 2 S.A. Div. |
| 7 Armd. Div. | 4 Ind. Div. |
| 10 Armd. Div. | 5 Ind. Div. |
| 31 Ind. Armd. Div. | 6 Ind. Div. |
| 1 Army Tank Bde. | 8 Ind. Div. |
| 32 Army Tank Bde. | 10 Ind. Div. |
| 1 Armd. Bde. Gp. | Polish Div. |
| 9 Armd. Bde. Gp. | 1 F.F. Bde. Gp. |
| 22 Anmd. Bde. Gp. | 2 F.F. Bde. Gp. |
| 3 Ind. Motor Bde. Gp. | 3. F.F. Bde. Gp. |
| 50 Div. | Greek Bde. Gp. |
| 9 Aust. | Div. Sudanese Bde. Gp |
| N.Z. Div. | Desert Bde. |
| 1 S.A. Div. | |

*Possibly due from overseas and ready 1st August or later (Not to be relied on).*
8 Armd. Div.
Two Inf. Divs.
251 Ind. Armd. Bde.

16

*Letter from the Commander-in-Chief, M.E.F., to the Commander, Eighth Army.*

Cairo, 20th May, 1942.

I am sending you this by Corbett, as I feel that you should know how I think the enemy may attack you. I have had my ideas put on the enclosed maps in order to make them clearer.

Corbett is thoroughly in my mind and can explain any doubtful point to you.

Do not think I am trying to dictate to you in any way, but this coming struggle is going to be so vital that I feel that you must have the benefit of our combined consideration here, though I realise we cannot be so conversant with the details of the problem as are you and your staff.

2. As you already know, I feel that there are two main courses open to the enemy:-

   (i) To envelop our southern flank, seizing or masking Bir Hacheim en route, and then driving on Tobruk. This would probably be accompanied by a strong diversion with plenty of artillery, dive-bombers and smoke against your northern flank, aided possibly by landings from small craft in rear of the Gazala inlet, with a view eventually to clearing the coast road to Tobruk.

   (ii) To put in a very heavy attack on a narrow front with tanks, artillery, dive-bombers, smoke and lorried infantry against the centre of the main position, with the object of driving straight on Tobruk. This would probably be helped by a feint against Bir Hacheim in which the Italian tanks might well be used with the aim of drawing off the main body of your armour to the south, and so leaving the way open for the main thrust.

This course would also almost certainly include an attack from the sea round about Gazala for the same object as before.

3. I feel myself that the second course is the one he will adopt, and that it is certainly the most dangerous to us, as if it succeeds it will cut our forces in half and probably result in the destruction of the northern part of them. We must of course be ready to deal with the enemy should he adopt the first course, and in either event, you must of course be most careful not to commit your armoured striking force until you know beyond reasonable doubt where the main body of his armour is thrusting.

4. Now, as to the method I think he is likely to adopt to put the second course into effect. I believe he will try to put the main body of his armour through our front on both sides of the Gadd el Ahmar ridge, which, as you know, runs more or less east and west along the boundary between the 1st S.A. and 50th Divs. This attack will be supported by every kind of weapon, including especially dive-bombers and anti-tank artillery. It will be pushed relentlessly on a narrow front.

As we agreed the other day, it is likely that such an attack will break through in spite of our minefields. Let us assume that it does break through on a comparatively narrow front.

I think that then he will immediately put out defensive flanks, taking full advantage of the main coastal escarpment to the north, and of the escarpment which runs along the Trigh Capuzzo to the south. If he can get his anti-tank and other artillery, protected by infantry, established on these escarpments, he will have established a corridor which may be difficult to cut, especially for your armour, if it is positioned as at present, somewhat far to the south.

Having secured his flank, he will drive in on Tobruk, assisted almost certainly by parachute attacks on the place itself and the troops guarding the entrances, and, possibly, also by landings from the sea which may be supported by naval bombardment. At the same time he may try to open the Gazala defile for the passage of M.T. and troops by landings from assault boats east of it.

As I have already said, this main attack will almost certainly be accompanied by a strong and resolute feint against Bir Hacheim, which will develop into a real attack if it has any initial success.

5. I know that you have taken and are taking numerous measures to meet an eventuality such as I have described; but I must tell you that, speaking from an office chair at a great distance from the battlefield, I wonder whether you should not put your armoured reserve a good deal further to the north, where it can hit the enemy immediately he emerges from his break-through and before he can establish a defensive flank, which all our experience teaches us he will certainly try to do. I suggest that both your armoured divisions complete should be positioned astride the Trigh Capuzzo. It does not look from the map as if this would be too far north to meet the main attack, should it come round the southern flank, instead of against the centre as I anticipate. Your covering troops should give you good warning of any main enveloping movement on your left, even if you do not hear of it before it starts.

As always, the difficulty will be to decide which is the real attack and which the feint.

6. I feel that your reaction to my suggestion that you should put your armour more behind the centre of your position will be that your southern flank will be left bare of any mobile troops to delay and harass the enemy, and also of any armoured units to give immediate support to the Free French. I propose to send you at once the 3rd Indian Motor Bde., which, though not absolutely fully equipped, is fit for battle. I suggest you might like to keep them on your southern flank, and that this will obviate any need to leave either of the motor brigades of the two armoured divisions in this area. I consider it to be of the highest importance that you should not break up the organisation of either of the armoured divisions. They have been trained to fight as divisions, I hope, and fight as divisions they should. Norrie must handle them as a Corps Commander, and thus be able to take advantage of the flexibility which the fact of having two formations gives him. Moreover, you will be getting the 1st Armoured Brigade before long, and it should join the 7 Armd. Div., I feel, thus making both divisions similar.

As regards armoured support for the French, I suggest that if you move your armoured divisions further north you might spare some infantry tanks for them. I am sending you up as soon as possible the 7th Royal Tanks, with one Valentine squadron of 4th Royal Tanks and two Matilda squadrons of its own, to increase your force of infantry tanks.

As to the rest of the infantry tanks, I suggest that, if possible, they should be placed so as to support the infantry in that part of the position which is likely to bear the brunt of the enemy attack. I admit that this may be uneconomical, as tending to immobilise them, but I feel that it is essential to give this infantry all possible support in order to encourage them to hang on. It is of the highest importance that they should hold on whatever happens. I will be glad if you will consider this also.

7. If you can stop the enemy short of Tobruk and then get at him in flank with your armour and in rear with infantry and guns, I feel you may have the chance of scoring a decisive success. I think, therefore, that you should at once lay mine-fields across the corridor between the two escarpments to the west of Acroma and cover these with guns. You will see from the sketch what I mean. I suggest also that you should consider mining the coastal corridor in more depth, so as to stop any break-through by that route, which, though it might not be serious, would be a serious nuisance and divert effort from the main task of destroying *once and for all* the enemy's armour.

8. Finally, I suggest that you should fortify El Gubi and protect it with mines. I am sure you will feel much more comfortable when you have something there threatening any wide turning movement from the south against Tobruk or from the west against Sollum, unlikely as this may seem to be. I know you want to keep 5th Indian Division as compact and uncommitted as possible for use as in a mobile role, should opportunity offer, either under Gott or under yourself. I am absolutely certain that this is right. I am sending you, therefore, at once, the 11th Brigade of 4th Indian Division to replace 29th Infantry Brigade in Capuzzo, in case you still feel you need another brigade there as well as the 2nd Free French Brigade. If you don't, so much the better; as you might then relieve the 9th Infantry Brigade of the 5th Indian Division in Tobruk, and so increase your mobile reserve. You could then use a brigade of the 5th Indian Division for El Gubi, if you feel so inclined.

The 11th Infantry Brigade is not mobile, and I do not want it committed forward of Sollum unless it is absolutely necessary to do so. I am bringing the whole of 10th Indian Division from Iraq, and the leading brigade will be sent up to you as soon as it arrives in relief of 11th Infantry Brigade, which I shall then hope to get back here, as it is part of the garrison allotted to Cyprus.

9. I am also bringing from Syria the Guides Cavalry (armoured cars and wheeled carriers) which I will give you if you want them to replace a battle-worn unit, or for the pursuit which I hope to see you carrying out.

10. I suggest that you must reorganise your system of command for this battle. For a defensive battle I feel you must have your mobile reserve, that is your armoured force, freed from all static commitments and responsibilities. Your Army falls, as I see it, into two parts one whose task it is to hold the fort, which is the Gazala – Tobruk – El Gubi – Bir Hacheim quadrilateral, and the other whose task it is to hit the enemy wherever he may thrust and destroy him. I think Gott should be solely responsible for the first, and Norrie for the second. I would relieve the latter of all responsibility for Bir Hacheim at once.

11. I am sorry to have inflicted such a long letter on you, but as I said before, so much hangs on this battle that I feel nothing must be left undone by anyone to help to win it. As you know I have absolute confidence in you and your troops, and I am sure that if the enemy attacks, you will deal him a blow from which he may find it difficult, if not impossible, to recover. *This is the object.*

17

*Letter from the Commander-in-Chief, M.E.F., to the Commander, Eighth Army.*

Cairo, 3rd June, 1942.

1. You will have had my Signal in answer to your telegram of 3rd June.

2. I am glad you think the situation is still favourable to us and that it is improving daily. All the same I view the destruction of 150th Brigade and the consolidation by the enemy of a broad and deep wedge in the middle of your position with some misgiving. I am sure, however, there are factors known to you which I do not know.

3. I feel myself
   (*a*) that if the enemy is allowed to consolidate himself in his present positions in the area Bir Hacheim – Sidra – Harmat – Mteifel, our Gazala position including Bir Hacheim will become untenable eventually, even if he does not renew his offensive.
   (*b*) that, situated as he is, he is rapidly becoming able to regain the initiative which you have wrested from him in the last week's fighting. This cannot be allowed to happen.

4. I agree with you entirely that you cannot let your armour be defeated in detail and that you cannot risk it against his now strongly defended front north and south of El Harmat. Therefore he must be shifted by other means and quickly before he can begin to act against the exposed southern flank of 50th Division or against Bir Hacheim, or in an attempt to cut your supply line east of El Adem, all of which seem possible courses for him to adopt.

5. I feel that the quickest and easiest way to shift him is by an offensive directed towards Temrad, so as to threaten his bases, coupled with threats from Segnali and the south against his lines of supply.

His tanks cannot be in two places at once, and you still have some infantry tanks with which to support your infantry and protect your artillery of which you should have a good deal now. It is, I think, highly important that you should keep at least one infantry division concentrated and complete in mobile reserve, so that you have at your disposal a really strong weapon with which to strike. I am a little perturbed by the apparent dispersion of 5th Indian Division, but I daresay it is more apparent than real.

6. I repeat that in my opinion you must strike hard and at once if we are to avoid a stalemate, that is unless the enemy is foolish enough to fling himself against your armour. I wish he would but I don't think you can count on this at present.

18

*Letter from the Commander, Eighth Army, to the Commander-in-Chief, M.E.F.*

Main H.Q., Eighth Army,<br>3rd June, 1942.

1. Your special message reached me in the middle of last night. Thank you so much for it. I agree almost entirely with all its contents, but there are one or two points I would like to make.

The two alternatives appear to me to be:-

(*a*) to resume the offensive as early as possible directed on the line Tmimi – Afrag;

(*b*) to deal first with the *Cauldron*.

Of these two alternatives it had been my intention to resume the offensive and leave the armour to mask the *Cauldron*, and I left this H.Q. at 5 a.m. this morning for a conference with the Corps Commanders to get this fixed up. For various reasons, with which I am dealing, replacements in armour are not coming through as quickly as they should. This is due to the crews not being collected together quickly enough; that is most serious. It will be righted to-day; but the net result is that I now feel that our armour may not be able to contain the enemy while the offensive is in progress, and the enemy's armour may therefore be a real danger to me, being able to continue supplies forward and against the rear of the Gazala – Alem Hamza position.

2. I was, as you are, most keen to carry out the offensive with the right shoulder forward, but the enemy in his present position makes it extremely difficult to form up a division behind our present frontage between Gazala and Alem Hamza without fear of its preparations being interrupted. For this reason I had to discard that plan.

3. My next idea was to make a very wide turning movement with the 5 Indian Division south of Hacheim directed on Afrag; but, after the information I have had from the Corps Commanders to-day respecting the strength of our armour, I cannot risk this.

4. It is absolutely essential that we should wrest from the enemy the initiative which he is now starting to exercise, and this must be done at the soonest possible moment. In the circumstances I have decided that I must crush him in the *Cauldron*; and the plan for doing this will be a pincer movement, one arm coming from the north with 69 Infantry Brigade supported by "I" tanks, the other from the east to be carried out by 5 Indian Division supported by 4 R.T.R. and 22 Armoured Brigade for exploitation. This latter will, of course, be the main thrust, the one from the north I would not bring further south than Sidra (3641). Much of the preparatory reconnaissance and work for the main thrust has already been covered by the operations of 10 Infantry Brigade, and I am reassured in my belief of the feasibility of this operation being carried out by night by the fact that Messervy is of opinion that it is quite feasible. I hope by this means to drive a wedge through the enemy's anti-tank defences under cover of darkness and seize the ground in the vicinity of Got el Scerab, and this will enable me to exploit with armour through this corridor into the rear of the enemy and close the gaps behind him. Once it is completed we will return to the offensive generally on the lines of the right shoulder forward.

5. I am going at once into the question of a raiding force to threaten the Martuba and Derna landing grounds, and I am sorry that I had not understood your intention in regard to this matter.

6. The operation I have decided to undertake is the one which can be put into action quickest and will therefore wrest the initiative from the enemy in the shortest possible time.

7. De Guingand takes this letter and can give you more details of my plan.

19

*G.H.Q., M.E.F. Operation Instruction No. 128.*
*Defence of Cyprus.*

Major-General F.I.S. Tuker.                                    1st July, 1942.
1. *Introduction.* – This Operation Instruction supersedes G.H.Q., M.E.F. Operation Instruction No. 114, dated 18th March, 1942 and lays down the policy to be adopted for the defence of Cyprus against attack by airborne and seaborne forces.

2. *Appreciation.* – In order to launch a large scale attack on Cyprus by airborne and seaborne forces, it is necessary for the enemy to be established in Southern. Anatolia. Without this he cannot give fighter cover to his troop carrying aircraft or sea convoys, nor can he give them air support for their landings and subsequent operations. The possibility of an attack will become apparent when the enemy begins an advance into Anatolia.

3. The probable scales of attack are given in Appendix A.[34]
    While the enemy is not established in Southern Anatolia only small scale raids by parachutists or landing parties are to be expected.

4. *Object.* – My object is to secure Cyprus so as to ensure the use of air bases on the island for ourselves and to deny them to the enemy.

5. *Forces available.* – The forces available for the defence of Cyprus against the scales of attack given in Appendix A. are detailed in Appendix B.[35] They will be known as the "Approved Garrison."

6. *Intention* – Should an attack on Cyprus develop, my intention is that the garrison shall meet the enemy with a mobile and aggressive defence based on secure keeps and prepared positions astride the main lines of approach inland from the coast.

*Method-*
7. *Command.* – You will take command of all troops in Cyprus and become Commander 25 Corps. The present Commander 25 Corps and staff will remain in Cyprus at your disposal and his functions will be decided as a result of recommendations to be made by you as soon as possible after receipt of this Instruction. You will submit your recommendations to G.H.Q. for approval, including any possible reduction or adjustment of his staff.

8. Your task is to revise and adjust the defence scheme of the island according to the principles laid down in succeeding paragraphs. In making this plan every consideration will be given to the present layout of R.A.F. and administrative installations. The plan will be submitted to G.H.Q., M.E.F. for approval, and when approved will not be altered without reference to G.H.Q.

9. The highest possible proportion of the "Approved Garrison" must be made available for mobile operations against enemy landings. Mobile columns must, however, be based on secure keeps, which must be held by nucleus garrisons until the tactical situation requires their reinforcement up to the full garrison for which they are designed.

10. The security of aerodromes is important both to ensure their use by our own air forces and to deny them to the enemy. It is not possible to provide from the resources available sufficient troops for adequate protection of all aerodromes now in existence, but in the siting of defended keeps and mobile reserves due consideration will be given to the security of R.A.F. landing grounds. Any landing grounds which are not required by the R.A.F. will be demolished now. Any which are essential to the R.A.F. for operating seawards will be thoroughly mined and kept ready for destruction at shortest notice.

11. The A.M.E.S. stations in Cyprus must be kept in action to enable our air forces to operate with maximum efficiency. They must, therefore, be protected against damage by saboteurs, raiding parties from the sea, and parachutists. Their siting and protection will be reviewed in consultation with the R.A.F.

12. The siting of dumps and installations in places near the coast to which access from the sea is easy will be avoided unless they are given adequate protection, and

their location will be planned to take advantage of the protection afforded by the general layout of the defences of the island.

13. The use of underwater obstacles at beaches favourable for enemy landings will be examined in consultation with the naval authorities, and they will be installed where useful and practicable.

14. *Administration.* – Ammunition and supplies for the "Approved Garrison" for 90 days will be held in the island.

15. Equipment and transport for any units of the "Approved Garrison" which are not yet in Cyprus will be kept in good condition and ready for issue at three days' notice.

16. The garrison will be made up to the approved strength as soon as possible. In order to ensure that incoming units will be ready for operations without delay, you will submit to G.H.Q., M.E.F. on the first of each month a statement in terms of the "Approved Garrison", showing units strengths, unit equipment, units transport, reserves of ammunition, reserves of supplies and petrol (in days), ordnance reserves, medical reserves.

Deficiences will be made good as soon as possible.

17. *Evacuation.* – Should the strategic situation require the evacuation of Cyprus, the existing plan for complete evacuation will be put into effect. It is not my intention to attempt evacuation once battle has been joined in the island.

T.W. Corbett, Lieutenant-General,
for C.-in-C., M.E.F.

20
*G.H.Q., M.E.F., Operation Instruction No. 134.*

22nd July, 1942.
(This Operation Instruction cancels Operation Instructions 123, 129 and 133)

1. *Introduction.* – This Operation Instruction is designed to cover the improbable case where the enemy is strong enough to launch a large scale offensive against Eighth Army before the latter can itself resume the offensive.

2. *Information.* – Our positions at El Alamein are being rapidly strengthened with a view to giving battle in this area should the enemy take the offensive.

3. Defensive positions are being prepared in the Burg el Arab and Wadi Natrun areas and are being prepared and improved on the general line western edge of the Delta from inclusive Alexandria to inclusive Cairo Bridgehead.

4. The Delta is at present garrisoned by-

(a) Delta force in the general area Alexandria and as far south as Kafr Dawud.
(b) B.T.E., which is responsible for the rest of the Delta and has Reesforce and 44 Div. under command.

5. Reinforcements are arriving by sea.

6. *Intention.* – Middle East Forces will secure our bases of supply in the area Suez Canal – Red Sea – Cairo – Alexandria with a view to covering the arrival of reinforcements with which to resume the offensive.

7. *Method.* – On the assumption that the enemy first takes the offensive, Middle East Forces will operate in the first and if necessary, the second and third of the following phases:-

Phase I. – Eighth Army will give battle in the El Alamein area should the enemy take the offensive.

Phase II. – If, however, the enemy's superiority makes it necessary to break off the battle at El Alamein, Eighth Army will detach two divisions to Deltaforce in the Alexandria area and will withdraw to prepared positions in the Wadi Natrun, with a view to striking at the rear and flanks of the enemy as he advances towards Alexandria or Cairo.

B.T.E. and Deltaforce will secure Alexandria and the cultivated area.

Deltaforce will be prepared to strike west and south at enemy advancing on Natrun.

Phase III. – Should a further withdrawal become necessary, B.T.E. and Deltaforce will act as in Phase II. Eighth Army will withdraw to the general line Gebel Abu Rauwash – Gebel el Khashab – Gebel Qattrani, and will be prepared to attack the enemy in the flank, if he moves against Cairo Bridgehead.

8. *Intercommunication.* – Separate instructions will be issued.

## PHASE I.

The battle at El Alamein will be fought in accordance with instructions already issued.

10. *Boundaries:*-
   (*a*) Eighth Army Rear Boundary (inclusive Eighth Army) Burg El Arab – (all exclusive Eighth Army) Bir El Makadriya – El Nubariya Canal to Kafr Dawud (598862).
   (*b*) Boundary between B. T. E. and Deltaforce. (All inclusive Deltaforce) from 520892 – Gebel Mreir – Kafr Dawud – Minuf El Bagur – Benha – Burdein, exclusive T rds. 682869.
   (*c*) Deltaforce Rear Boundary. (All inclusive Deltaforce) Rosetta Mouth – Disuq – Damat – Shoubra Millis – Zifta – Zagazig – exclusive T rds. 682869.
   (*d*) Boundary between Eighth Army and B. T. E. (all inclusive Eighth Army) from Siwa Oasis – Cicely Hill (purple 7514) – El Maghra (purple 8823) – (all exclusive Eighth Army) – Black Paps (4884) – Bir Hooker (5585) – Kafr Dawud (5986).

11. *Internal security.* – B. T. E. and Deltaforce are responsible for internal security within their respective administrative boundaries.

12. *Vulnerable points and special measures.* The following need special attention by B.T.E. and Deltaforce within their respective areas:-

(*a*)　Supply of water to Canal area and Sofaga by the Sweet Water Canal, the defence and repair of which will be secured at all costs.

(*b*)　The Barrage.

(*c*)　Insurance that water level of canals and rivers shall be adequate and that water control points are secured, and arrangements made for rapid repair of controls, dykes, etc.

(*d*)　Headworks of Nubariya Canal

(*e*)　Protection against hostile action by airborne troops and saboteurs.

(*f*)　Preparations to meet a worsening internal situation and possibly a hostile Egyptian Army.

(*g*)　Denial to the enemy of boats on the Nile and westernmost canals. B.T.E. is responsible as far down the Nile as Kafr el Zaiyat and has under command the Nile Flotilla.

(*h*)　Securing all landing grounds for our own use.

(*i*)　Training and equipment of all personnel, however employed, in the art of tank hunting.

(*j*)　Retention of bridgeheads in the Alexandria, the Barrage and Cairo areas as long as possible with a view to subsequent offensive.

(*k*)　Early warning of an enemy approach to the Nile Valley from the Qattara Depression southwards.

(*l*)　Securing all traffic bottlenecks of military importance.

(*m*)　The policy concerning demolition of oil, intercommunication and other installations has been issued separately.

(*n*)　Preparation for the rapid occupation of the various defensive positions should the occasion arise.

13. B. T. E. will reconnoitre and prepare protected observation posts on a battalion basis on the high ground north-west and west of Mena in the following localities:- Gebel Abu Rauwash (6281), Gebel el Ghigiga (6181), Gebel el Hiqaf (620809), Gebel el Khashab (6180). Deltaforce will prepare the Amiriya Defences.

14. *Communications with Gulf of Suez.* – In order to improve the communications between the Western Desert and the Gulf of Suez, the following work will be put in hand forthwith:-

(*a*)　Bridges. Class 30 Military bridges will be provided at (i) Helwan, (ii) El Qubabat (640750) or Wasta.

(*b*)　Roads. The following tracks will be made or improved to take A.F.V.'s and M.T.:-

　　　(i) Maadi – Bir Odeib (745777).
　　　(ii) Helwan – Bir Qena (700772) – Bir Odeib.
　　　(iii) Bir Qena – Pt. 235 (712785) *and, if feasible,*
　　　(iv) Helwan – Bir Gindali (680800).

15. *Command.* – Command during Phase I will remain as at present.

B. T. E. will organise a Tactical H.Q. from Which to conduct operations on a mobile basis.

16. *Nile L. of C. Area.* – In order to be prepared for Phase III, plans will be made for the formation of a Nile L. of C. Area to form a link between Egypt and Sudan. (*See* para. 22 below.)

## PHASE II.

17. – (*a*) In Phase II Eighth Army, less two divisions, will take up positions in the area north and north-east of the Wadi Natrun and form front facing north-west in a position to strike at the flank and rear of an enemy's advance on Cairo or Alexandria.

(*b*) Two divisions will withdraw on Alexandria and come under command Deltaforce.

18. *Thinning out Delta.* – Installations and troops not required for the immediate support of the fighting formations will begin thinning out. Detailed instructions will be issued separately.

19. *G.H.Q.* – During Phase II G.H.Q., less Tactical G.H.Q., will move to Palestine. Instructions for the move will be issued separately.

20. *Command.* – (*a*) If C.-in-C. is exercising command from Tactical H.Q. Eighth Army, Deltaforce will come under command Eighth Army.

(*b*) If C.-in-C. is exercising command from Tactical G.H.Q.; B.T.E. and Deltaforce will remain under G.H.Q.

21. *Delta Garrison.* – All available forces in the Delta will be mobilised. The defences of the Delta will be manned, full use being made of all combatant personnel in the Delta by B.T.E. and Deltaforce within their own areas. These personnel will include all fighting troops arriving in the Delta from Eighth Army, unless they have been specially routed to other commands or formations. Where units are thus appropriated, G.H.Q., M.E.F. will be informed without delay.

22. *Nile L. of C. Area.* – Nile L. of C. Area will be formed under command B.T.E. with H.Q. located at Wasta.

23. *Boundaries.* – (*a*) Boundary between Eighth Army and Nile L. of C. Area (inclusive Nile L. of C. Area) Ras Zafarana – Beni Suef – excluding Fayoum.

(*b*) The southern boundary of Eighth Army (para. 10 (*d*)) will be cancelled and Eighth Army will take over the responsibility for all the desert north of the northern boundary of Nile L. of C. Area. (*Vide* para. 23 (*a*)). The existing rear boundary of Eighth Army (para. 10 (*a*)) will be extended as follows:- from Kafr Dawud – exclusive Raiyah el Beharira (6084) – thence Mudit Drain to 616828 – thence southwards along west edge of cultivation to inclusive Abusir Pyramids to inclusive Hawamdiya (641798) – then exclusive R. Nile.

24. *Traffic Control.* – Steps will be taken now to ensure that adequate arrangements are made for the control of traffic.

A survey of the likely bottlenecks and focal points will be carried out and plans made for the laying on of control posts and the dissemination of information to these posts.

## PHASE III.

25. If Phase III occurs Eighth Army (less the two divisions mentioned in para. 17 (*b*) above), will withdraw to the area Giza – Wasta – Gebel Qatrani and form front facing north and northwest with its right on high ground west of Mena and left towards the Fayoum.

26. *F.D.L.'s Eighth Army.* – F.D.L.'s will be on general line Abu Rauwash (6281) – Gebel el Khashab (6180) thence south-west towards Gebel Qatrani (5777) and will include the protected observation posts being prepared by B.T.E. (*vide* para. 13 above).

27. *Cairo Bridgehead.* – Defences will be held to give depth to the position, but will remain under command B.T.E.

28. *Command.* – Eighth Army, B.T.E. and Deltaforce will be under the direct command of Tactical G.H.Q. from where the C.-in-C. will be controlling the operations. Tactical G.H.Q. will remain at Cairo.

## ADMINISTRATION.

29. *Policy for withdrawal of installations-*

(*a*) In Phase I no units or personnel will be moved so long as their services are needed by the fighting troops.

(*b*) In Phase II installations in the Alexandria Area will be closed down.

(*c*) In Phase III installations in the Cairo Area will be closed down.

Detailed instructions are being issued separately.

30. *Maintenance.* – On withdrawal from El Alamein position, maintenance arrangements will be as follows:-

(*a*) By rail from Canal Area depots *via* Tanta, with railhead in first instance at Damanhur.

An Advance Base will be opened at Tanta under G.H.Q. arrangements on advent of Phase II.

(*b*) Eighth Army. From railheads or base depots in Cairo, supplemented as and when necessary by Nile Valley L. of C.

(Sgd.) T.W. Corbett,
Lieut.-General,
For C.-in-C., M. E. F.

21

*Appreciation of the Situation in the Western Desert.*

El Alamein, 1445 hours,
27th July, 1942.

*Object.*

1. The defence of Egypt by the defeat of the enemy forces in the Western Desert.

*Factors.*

2. *Comparison of Strength* – Table A[36] shows a rough comparison, on a brigade group basis, based on what we now know of the enemy's present strength and his reinforcement schedule. From this it seems that the enemy will hardly be able to secure a decisive superiority over us in the first half of August, provided we fight united, since the Germans would begin any offensive with an inferiority of about three infantry brigade groups and possibly 40 per cent. superiority in armour. The enemy may also be inferior in artillery. It would seem that, though the Axis forces are strong enough for defensive action, they are hardly strong enough to attempt the conquest of the Delta except as a gamble and under very strong air cover. There remains for the Axis to use one German Air Landing Division, but this is taking over I.S. duties in Greece and Crete and seems unlikely to be an asset. It might, however, be used to redress the balance at a decisive moment. Throughout August the anticipated balance of strength hardly justifies a German offensive, unless we make a serious mistake and leave an opening. He may, however, be reinforced in the second part of August, though nothing is known to be scheduled. On the other hand the Axis may make great efforts to strengthen *Panzer Armee* in the shortest time.

3. *Land Forces – Numbers and Morale.* – Broadly speaking, though all our forces have been through hard times, their morale is high. German morale is probably a little lower and Italian morale not more than 50 per cent. In view of the known inefficiency of the Italian forces, any offensive action taken by the Axis forces in August would have to be 80 per cent. German.

4. Material – The Eighth Army has some 60 Grant tanks now and will receive another 60 Grant tanks early in August, but there will be no more coming until September. The deduction is that it is necessary to husband our armour carefully in view of the fact that during August the enemy may build up to between 150 and 200 German tanks.

Eighth Army's deficiencies in transport are mounting. A summary of the present state of equipment of the major formations of Eighth Army is attached as Appendix X.[37] It is also necessary to husband our ammunition resources. These stand at present as shown in Appendix B[38] attached. The enemy has however similar deficiencies and his reinforcing division is notably deficient in anti-tank weapons and transport.

5. *Training.* – None of the formations in Eighth Army is now sufficiently well trained for offensive operations. The Army badly needs either a reinforcement of well trained formations or a quiet period in which to train.

6. *Fighting value with reference to air forces.* – At present we have such air superiority that, while our troops are relatively free from molestation, the enemy is continually attacked by night and day. Our land forces are considerably heartened by this, and a large measure of tactical freedom and security accrues from it. Unless the enemy is strongly reinforced and our air forces are correspondingly reduced, this superiority will assist our offensive or defensive and gravely impede the enemy. Our air superiority is a very considerable, if somewhat indefinable, asset.

7. *Vulnerable Points.* – To us the two vulnerable points are Cairo and Alexandria. Occupation of the Cairo area by the enemy would eventually dry up the Sweet Water Canal besides securing an important area for air and land maintenance. Alexandria is useful as a naval base and port of ingress for supplies. The present position of Eighth Army at El Alamein denies direct access to either place by road and flanks any attempt to by-pass. The defences of Alexandria – Cairo – the Delta proper, east of the Nubariya canal and the Wadi Natrun area will be well forward by 14th August and should be complete, in so far as defences are ever complete, by the end of August. Bottlenecks exposed to air action are the Nile crossings at Cairo and northwards, these are being supplemented by two floating bridges south of Cairo and by improving the routes from these bridges eastwards. All arrangements for demolitions in the Delta are being made. The enemy has few really vulnerable points. There are bottlenecks at Sollum and about Matruh and Bagush, and his long L. of C. is vulnerable to attack by raids from the air or inland or from the sea. But otherwise the enemy is not physically vulnerable, except to direct assault. Morally his Italians are always vulnerable. The soft sand areas of the country east of El Alamein, notably the "Barrel Track" axis, the Wadi Natrun, the sand area to its north, are all added difficulties for the enemy's movement, particularly as they cannot be widely known to him.

8. *Ground.* – The armies are now in close contact over a forty mile front between the sea and the Qattara Depression. Most of the area is open and can be largely controlled by artillery fire.

The front divides into three main sectors:-

*A.* From Tel Eisa to exclusive the Ruweisat Ridge. This area is held by two divisions (five infantry brigade groups). The Tel Eisa salient has considerable offensive value, but is not essential to its defence, unless the Miteiriya Ridge is also held by us. Most of the area is difficult for wheeled movement. It is on our side strongly defended by the fortified locality of El Alamein and the mined positions to the south. This area is well supported by strong prepared localities to a depth of twenty-five miles. The enemy lies in open flat country. His positions lack any well defined features and are covered by extensive minefields. At El Daba he has dumps.

*B.* From inclusive the El Mreir depression to inclusive the Bab el Qattara depression. This area is held by two divisions (four brigade groups) supported by the equivalent of one armoured brigade. We hold the high ground in this area at Pt. 63 on the Ruweisat Ridge. This position is naturally strong and has been fortified to considerable depth. The enemy holds strongly a series of depressions which give good cover. His front has been well mined and has some wire.

In sectors *A* and *B* both the enemy and ourselves have attacked in turn without success.

*C.* From exclusive the fortified locality in the Bab el Qattara depression to inclusive the complete obstacle of the great Qattara Depression. The enemy is well posted on strong ground at Kelat and Taqa in positions which he has prepared for defence. The object of these positions is to protect his southern flank from being turned by our mobile troops. We have no defences in depth opposite this sector, which is lightly covered by mobile troops.

9. *Time and Space.* – Had the enemy the available resources, Italy and Germany are far nearer to El Alamein than is anywhere in the United Nations. The enemy should therefore be able to reinforce quicker than we. On the other hand, apart from distant Bengasi, he has only two serviceable sea ports, Tobruk and, much less useful, Matruh. He may also make use of the railway to a limited extent. He is faced with long road hauls and a sea passage vulnerable to air and submarine attack. This affects the building up of reserves for an offensive. We are nearer our bases. Our limitation is the rate that men and material can reach Egypt from overseas. His limitation is the rate at which it can reach his troops when it arrives. This indicates the necessity of blocking Tobruk and Matruh and attacking his road and rail transport and his shipping.

10. *Political Factors.* – Hardly enter into this appreciation, except inasmuch as pressure may be put on the Axis command to press on to Egypt before their army is ready or has sufficient margin of force. Our danger lies in a politically unstable Egypt in our rear. So far this danger has not developed.

11. *The Russian Front.* – The operations of Eighth Army are linked to the fate of Russia. Should the Axis penetrate the Caucasus, Eighth Army might be reduced to the lowest margin to provide reinforcements for the new front. Moreover a considerable Axis success in Russia would release air and land forces and equipment for the reinforcement of the Western Desert.

12. *Maintenance.* – The enemy is experiencing great difficulty in maintaining his present forces at El Alamein. This condition may improve gradually when more heavy transport vehicles come from Italy. It is not likely to improve so much that he can maintain an appreciably larger force than that envisaged in Appendix A[39]. Our maintenance presents no real difficulties, except that our stocks of 25-pounder shells are not inexhaustible, and we could certainly maintain forces of double the present size of Eighth Army in this area if they existed.

*Courses open to ourselves and the enemy.*

13. *Ourselves. – A.* To continue to attack the enemy in the hope that he will crack before his army is reinforced by fresh troops. The pros and cons of attacking are:-

In the northern and central sectors we have made two attempts to break the enemy's front without success. Failure has been due to lack of trained troops, rigidity of organisation and limited resources in armour and infantry and it seems that the enemy's positions are now too strongly held to be attacked with success with the resources available.

We have also attacked in the southern sector, but weakly and largely as a diversion. Our attack failed, but the enemy though strongly posted is not numerous here, and this front might go if suddenly attacked. If it did go, it offers access for our mobile troops to the enemy's flanks and rear.

The problems of attack on this front are, firstly, how to find the supporting fire without unduly weakening the northern and central sectors. Secondly, how to find the troops. The only formation which might be used is the weak N.Z. Division supported by its own artillery, the artillery of 7th Armoured Division and some of 5th Indian Division's artillery. This would have to be deployed in secret and developed as a complete surprise. Failure would probably make the N.Z. Division unfit for further operations for a considerable time. Having in mind the weakness in numbers and training of this division the chances of success can only be rated as 60 – 40. Failure would seriously deplete our present resources. On the whole this attack hardly seems advisable at present.

*B.* To adopt the tactical defensive until we are strong enough to attack, which, unless the enemy's position deteriorates, will, not be till mid-September at the earliest. The obvious objection is that we give the initiative to the enemy if he is able to use it. It is very doubtful if he will be able to take the initiative till late in August with any hope of success. In fact if he attacks before, provided we have a reserve in hand including up to 100 Grant tanks, we have a good chance of defeating him seriously in the area El Alamein – Hammam. Moreover the critical period for the preparation and manning of the Delta and Cairo defences is now over. There is little danger of the enemy getting any value out of by-passing the Eighth Army on its present ground. There may be a critical period late in August before the new divisions (two of armour, two of infantry) are ready, but this might be tided over by preparing their artillery battle groups in advance of the rest of the divisions and so reinforcing Eighth Army. (This project requires further examination.)

This defensive could also be mitigated by enterprises against Siwa and the southern sector of his front and by seaborne attacks.

14. *Courses open to the enemy.* – The enemy must resume the offensive without delay, but he is unlikely to be able to do so before mid-August and even then no real margin of superiority except in A.F.Vs. is apparent. He will certainly try to attack before the end of August and as Eighth Army defences gain in strength and

depth he will be more than ever tempted to avoid them and seek success in manoeuvre. This may well land him into serious difficulties in the soft desert.

Alternatively, he may have to adopt the strategical defensive because our forces are too strong and too well placed for attack. If he does, he may either stand his ground or withdraw to an intermediate position covering Matruh, which will eventually be to our advantage for he will still be in striking distance when we are again fit to attack. If he goes back to the Egyptian frontier, it is questionable whether he should not be left undisturbed.

15. *Course recommended.* – Seeing that we are hardly fit at present to do any more attacks, our best course is the defensive combined with offensive gestures from time to time, including raiding. The cover plan should be such as would induce the enemy to strike prematurely, *i.e.*, mid-August, say, between 10th and 20th August. Meanwhile the Army front should be strengthened, and so held that at least one formation could come into reserve and train. At the same time the command of Eighth Army should be put on a permanent footing.

16. *Plan recommended.*
*Intention.* – Eighth Army will defeat any attempt of the enemy to pass through or round it.

17. *Method.*
   (*a*) *Forward troops-*
        30 Corps: I South African Division, 9 Australian Division.
        13 Corps: I New Zealand Division, 7 Armoured Division.
   (*b*) *Reserve-*
        5 Indian Division (4 Indian Division eventually): I Armoured Division.
   (*c*) *General line of F.D.Ls.* – El Alamein defences – Pt. 63 (eastern) on Ruweisat Ridge vicinity of Alam Nayal. South of Alam Nayal the flank will be covered by 7 Armoured Division.
   (*d*) *General line of reserve positions.* – For forward bodies, the most western line of the new rearward position.
        Should it be desired to avoid the full effect of an enemy attack in great strength the above F.D.Ls. can become the outpost line and the main front can be withdrawn accordingly.
   (*e*) *Matruh.* – Should be blocked by the Navy without delay.

*Tactical Technique and Future Organisation.*
18. In the light of the course recommended it will be necessary to adjust our tactical technique. This should be based on three facts:-
   *A.* – We have to be prepared to fight a modern defensive battle in the area El Alamein – Hammam. The troops detailed for this must be trained and exercised so as to get the maximum value from the ground and the prepared positions.
   *B.* – Eighth Army may have to meet an enemy's sortie developing into manoeuvre by the southern flank from his firm front on the general line Bab el Qattara – Taqa Plateau. We must therefore organise and train a strong mobile

wing, based on 7th Armoured Division, comprising a divisional artillery, 7th Motor Brigade, 4th Light Armoured Brigade, and possibly extra Crusader units. This mobile wing must be well trained in harassing defensive technique. *C.* – Eventually we will have to renew the offensive and this will probably mean a break-through the enemy positions about El Alamein. The newly-arrived infantry divisions and the armoured divisions must be trained for this and for pursuit.

19. From the point of view of G.H.Q., the organisation of our available forces in August and September might take the following form:-

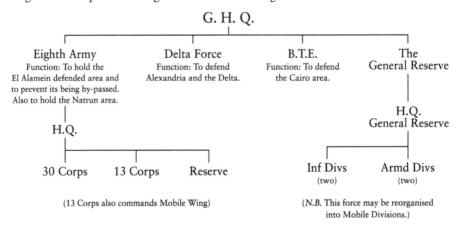

This goes further than the present appreciation, but can hardly be separated from it because, should this idea be adopted, it means that the formations now in Eighth Army will not be relieved and the new formations will be built up and reorganised irrespective of the immediate needs of Eighth Army.

20. *Summary.* – The enemy now holds in sufficient strength for his purpose a front from which he cannot be dislodged by manoeuvre or any attack Eighth Army can at present deliver. We are strongly posted for a defensive battle. The enemy is attempting to build up his strength and renew his attack on Egypt. Eighth Army requires re-equipment and training before it will be fit for offensive operations. During August it is unlikely that either ourselves or the enemy will be strongly reinforced on land; a successful offensive by either side is therefore unlikely. Provided the land and air situation does not change, Eighth Army can be reinforced about mid-September by two armoured divisions and two infantry divisions. This may give us a superiority sufficient to justify a direct attack on what may be by then a strongly organised front. Alternatively, we may develop a threat to the enemy's rear *via* Siwa. The immediate need is to reorganise present forces with Eighth Army and to rearrange the front so as to provide an army reserve. The longer term policy is to train the newly-arrived divisions for the counter-offensive which it is hoped might begin in the latter part of September.

22
*Letter to the Chief of the Imperial General Staff.*

14th August, 1942.

1. I wish to place before you my views on the proposal to separate Iraq and Persia from the present Middle East Command and to constitute them as an independent command under a Commander-in-Chief directly responsible to the Chiefs of Staff.

I am aware that I have not been asked for my opinion, but I consider that in view of my experience as Commander-in-Chief both in India and the Middle East, and because I have made an exhaustive study of the problem of the defence of the area in question, it is my duty to place my views on record. I do this solely in the hope that they may be of some service to the nation, and not because I wish to attempt in any way to contest the decision to divide up my present command.

2. You are aware, I believe, that I have recently approved a reorganisation of the system of command in Iraq and Persia.

The object of this reorganisation is to free Commander Tenth Army and his staff to direct operations in Persia, without, as has hitherto been the case, being distracted by the large administrative responsibilities inseparable from a the control of the bases and lines of communication in Iraq and Southern Persia, and the need for keeping in touch with the complicated political situation in Iraq.

Briefly, the reorganisation consists in the setting up of an L. of C. and base area in Southern Iraq and South-western Persia under an Inspector-General of Communications and a local defence commander, and the transfer of Northern Iraq to the control of the Ninth Army thus ensuring unity of command along the length of the Anatolian frontier, should an enemy threat to Syria and Iraq materialise through Turkey. In this event such unity of control is in my opinion essential, if only to ensure efficient co-operation between the Army and the Air Force, and the most economical use of the available air forces. This reorganisation was decided upon after long and careful examination by qualified staff officers of all three services and has the full approval of the three Commanders-in-Chief.

This reorganisation produces, in my opinion, and I believe in that of the A.O.C.-in-C., a workable system for the conduct of operations in Persia and along the Anatolian frontier, and ensures the maximum of efficiency and the minimum of friction which can be expected in view of the admittedly complicated nature of the problem.

As Commander-in-Chief, Middle East Forces, I was prepared to meet the threat to our Northern Front once this reorganisation had been effected, assuming that the requisite forces were available.

3. Regarding the proposal to set up an independent army command in Iraq-Persia, I feel that the main difficulty is in the provision and control of the air forces which will have to work with the army in this new command. In my opinion it would be impossible to expect the new Commander-in-Chief to accept

the responsibility of the new command unless a definite allotment of air forces is made to it. This allotment must not be susceptible to reduction except with the consent of the Commander-in-Chief, or by order of the Chiefs of Staff. Any arrangement whereby the full control of all air forces on the entire Caspian – Cyrenaican front is vested in a single A.O.C.-in-C. located at Cairo or elsewhere, while the land forces on the same front are divided into two separate commands, each under an independent Commander-in-Chief directly responsible to the Chiefs of Staff in London, must, in my opinion, result in constant friction and consequent inefficiency, and may well be disastrous in times of crisis. It would be impossible, I think, to expect a Commander-in-Chief in Baghdad to be dependent on an A.O.C.-in-C. in Cairo for the provision of the air forces essential to the carrying out of his plans. He would, presumably, have an A.O.C. available as an adviser and local air force commander, but this officer would not be able to give any decision on important matters of policy without the approval of the A.O.C.-in-C. The position of the C.-in-C. would, I submit, be intolerable and is not one which I could myself accept.

I fully realise that any arbitrary division of air forces between the two commands is likely to be uneconomical and to deprive the air of that flexibility which it now possesses under the existing organisation, whereby the C.-in-C. and A.O.C.-in-C., Middle East, have the same territorial responsibilities so far as the Caspian – Cyrenaican front is concerned. This is one of the chief objections I see in the new proposals.

4. At present the Tenth Army in Persia has a full staff and is reasonably well off for signals. The administrative staff of the newly constituted Iraq-Persia L. of C. area and base could, I think, be transformed without great difficulty or delay and be made into the administrative staff of the new G.H.Q., Iraq-Persia. A new General Staff will, however, have to be created from nothing, as no such organisation exists at present. This will entail a great deal of work and the transfer of a mass of information and accumulated knowledge from the present G.H.Q., Middle East, to the new G.H.Q. The new Commander-in-Chief can hardly be expected to rely on any organization in Cairo for information. He must control his own machinery.

I estimate that it will take at least six weeks to two months before the new G.H.Q. can begin to function with adequate efficiency. During this interim period it is inevitable that G.H.Q. Middle East should remain in control of Iraq and Persia otherwise the whole system of operational control is liable to break down. The result of such a breakdown at such a time does not need to be stressed.

5. There are many other important adjustments which must be made in the administrative, training and operational fields before the transfer of responsibility can be effectively completed. These will all take time, as it is physically impossible to conclude them in the course of a few days. I have already had experience of these difficulties in the comparatively recent transfer of this sphere from G.H.Q. India to G.H.Q. Middle East, so I do not speak without knowledge. The

result may well be that the process of changing over will not be completed before active operations start in Northern Persia. This would produce a most unsatisfactory and probably critical situation.

6. As regards the chances of successfully preventing an enemy advance through Persia from the Caucasus towards the head of the Persian Gulf, I agree generally with the General Staff estimate as to the minimum forces required. In my opinion the following are needed:-

One Army H.Q. and Signals.
Two Corps H.Q. and Signals.
Two Armoured Divisions.
Seven Infantry Divisions (including two for internal security duties and L. of C. protection in Iraq and Persia, but excluding any garrison required in the Persian Gulf itself).

It is essential that all these troops shall be fully mobile including the divisions allotted for L. of C. protection and internal security duties. I estimate the minimum requirements in air forces at some twenty-five squadrons which will also need to have a high degree of mobility. This full mobility is of prime importance as without it there is no likelihood whatever of being able to conduct a successful defence of Northern Persia.

It is well known that there is insufficient transport available in the Middle East to give these forces full mobility and at the same time to enable an offensive to be conducted in the Western Desert. Since I have held this command this has always been the case, and, I have several times emphasised it, and given as my considered opinion that it is not a practical proposition to attempt offensive operations in the Western Desert and at the same time carry out major defensive operations in Persia or Iraq. I see no reason whatever to change this opinion now. Apart from the shortage of transport, it is not possible to provide the fighting troops required for the defence of Persia without so weakening the Eighth Army as to make it doubtful whether it could carry out a successful offensive.

7. I fully realise the desirability, even the necessity of driving the enemy further west and so lessening the imminence of the threat to our bases in Egypt, and no one could be more desirous of assuming the offensive in the Western Desert than I. But I am deeply impressed with the general weakness of our position in the Middle East, so strongly emphasised by the Russian collapse north of the Caucasus, and by the immense risks we are running in exposing the head of the Persian Gulf to enemy attack. We cannot be strong everywhere, and I feel that we must husband our resources, such as they are, and try to preserve what is essential to us, hoping that before long the tide may turn and enable us to take the offensive in earnest. I feel myself that only the annihilation of the enemy in the Western Desert is likely materially to affect the course of events in Northern Persia. It is impossible, in my opinion, to set an arbitrary limit to the duration of offensive operations in the Western Desert once these have been embarked upon,

nor is it possible to control the enemy's reactions to such operations. The length of time taken, and the amount of transport required, to transfer troops from Egypt to Iraq and Persia is not always sufficiently taken into account by those who plan operations in this theatre from a distance, but it is a very important factor.

I consider that, by attempting to carry out an offensive in the Western Desert simultaneously with a defensive campaign in Persia with our present resources, we will run a grave risk of failing in both and of being defeated in detail. This is my considered opinion and, though I hope it may prove to be wrong, I feel bound to give it for what it is worth.

8. I have studied the report of the Committee on the implications of setting up an independent command in Iraq – Persia and I consider it makes the best of a bad case. Its conclusions and recommendations make it very obvious that the working of the scheme in practice must depend on compromise in practically every sphere of activity to an excessive degree. It is also clear that the Commander-in-Chief in Iraq – Persia will have to depend on the machinery at the disposal of his colleague in Cairo to an extent which cannot fail to place him in a subordinate position to the latter and so bring about again the situation which I understand the scheme is expressly designed to avoid.

I do not myself think that the scheme is workable in practice, and I feel that there is a grave risk of its breaking down under the stress of active operations. I do not therefore feel able to accept the responsibility of this new Command, and I have informed the Minister of State accordingly.

*Notes*

1. Note on "Possible Commitments in the Spring," 20th Jan. 1942 – Appendix 7.
2. Note on "Future Operations in Libya," 4th Feb. 1942 – Appendix 8.
3. G.H.Q., M.E.F. Operation Instruction No. 111, 11th Feb. 1942 – Appendix 9.
4. G.H.Q., M.E.F. Operation Instruction No. 112, 23rd Feb. 1942 – Appendix 10.
5. G.H.Q., M.E.F. Operation Instruction No. 116, 8th March 1942 – Appendix 11.
6. G.H.Q., M.E.F. Operation Instruction No. 128, 1st July 1942 – Appendix 19.
7. G.H.Q., M.E.F. Operation Instruction No. 117, 29th April 1942 – Appendix 14.
8. G.H.Q., M.E.F. Operation Instruction No. 118, 19th May 1942 – Appendix 15.
9. Letter to Commander, Eighth Army, 20th May 1942 – Appendix 16.
10. See Appendices 6 and 9.
11. G.H.Q., M.E.F. Operation Instruction No. 134, 22nd July 1942 – Appendix 20.
12. Appreciation of Situation in the Western Desert, 27th July 1942 – Appendix 21.
13. Letter to C.I.G.S., 14th August 1942 – Appendix 22.
14. Letter to Lt.-Gen. Sir Alan Cunningham, 2nd September 1941 – Appendix I.
15. G.H.Q., M.E.F. Operation Instruction No. 103, 17th October 1941 – Appendix 3.
16. Appreciation by Lt.-Gen. Sir Alan Cunningham, 28th September 1941 – Appendix 2.
17. My ideas on the general strategy of the offensive are given in a note prepared on the 30th October 1941 – Appendix 4.
18. The forces to be maintained numbered about 118,000 men, and 17,600 vehicles, and some 24 motor general transport companies and seven motor water-tank companies were used for this purpose. Average daily maintenance needs came to about 3,000 tons.

19. The special merits of the German 20 litre petrol can, popularly known as the "Jerrican", were readily apparent, but its production entailed special machinery which was not immediately available. Ultimately, when the necessary plants were set up both in the U.K. and U.S.A., and also in the Middle East, the "Jerrican" pattern can became the standard British Army petrol container.
20. Afterwards Major-General Campbell, V.C.
21. Letter to Lieut.-General Cunningham, 24th November 1941 – Appendix 5.
22. G.H.Q., M.E.F. Operation Instruction No. 110, 19th January 1942 – Appendix 6.
23. G.H.Q., M.E.F. Operation Instruction No. 111, 11th February 1942 – Appendix 9.
24. Note on the Libyan Offensive – I, 21st March 1942 – Appendix 12.
25. G.H.Q., M.E.F, Operation Instruction No. 116, 8th March 1942 – Appendix 11.
26. Letter to Commander, Eighth Army, 20th May 1942 – Appendix 16.
27. Letter to General Ritchie, 3rd June 1942 – Appendix 17.
28. Letter from General Ritchie, 3rd June 1942 – Appendix 18.
29. Appendix 1.
30. Not attached.
31. Supersedes G.H.Q., M.E.F. Operation Instruction No. 112 of 23rd February 1942 – Appendix 10.
32. Not reproduced.
33. Not reproduced.
34. Not reproduced.
35. Not reproduced.
36. Not reproduced.
37. Not reproduced.
38. Not reproduced.
39. Not reproduced.

# Index

## (1) Military and Air Forces

## (2) Index of Persons